Culture and Technology in the New Europe: Civic Discourse in Transformation in Post-Communist Nations

Civic Discourse for the Third Millenium
Michael H. Prosser, Series Editor

Culture and Technology in the New Europe: Civic Discourse in Transformation in Post-Communist Nations

edited by
Laura Lengel
Richmond American International University in London

Ablex Publishing Corporation
Stamford, Connecticut

Copyright © 2000 by Ablex Publishing Corporation

Printed in the United States of America

Library of Congress Cataloging-in-Publication Data

Culture and technology in the new Europe: civic discourse in transformation in post-communist nations / edited by Laura Lengel.
    p. cm. — (Civic discourse for the third millennium)
    Includes bibliographical references and index.
    ISBN 1-56750-466-3 (cloth) — ISBN 1-56750-467-1 (pbk.)
    1. Intercultural communication—Europe, Eastern—Congresses. 2. Internet (Computer network)—Europe, Eastern—Congresses. 3. Trans-border data flow—Europe, Eastern—Congresses. 4. Civil society—Europe, Eastern—Congresses. 5. Social change—Europe, Eastern—Congresses. I. Lengel, Laura. II. Series.

HM1211.C85 2000
303.4′0947—dc21   99-34301
                                                       CIP

Ablex Publishing Corporation
100 Prospect Street
P.O. Box 811
Stamford, CT 06904-0811

To my grandparents—
Frank Lengyel and Elizabeth Bartok Lengyel
Anton Broski and Lillian Zaleski Broski

to my parents—
Francis Lengel and Heliodora Broski Lengel

and to my spouse and our baby daughter—
Daniel Fedak and Daniella Beth Fedak-Lengel

whose Hungarian, Polish, and
Ukrainian heritages I honor

Contents

Part III: Contexts and Practices in the New Europe

Part IV: The New Europe the New Millennium

Foreword

Alfred Hermida
News Editor, BBC News Online, London

T he collapse of the Communist bloc freed Eastern Europe from an overwhelming political ideology that affected every area of life. In many of these countries, the fall of Communism was put down to people power. Since then, we have seen the emergence of what is described as a "New Europe." Eastern Europe has become divided by new fault lines, based around regional alliances, economic interests and perhaps most significantly, ethnic minorities.

The blooming of political freedoms has been mirrored by an explosion in the flow of information, with the Internet as its backbone. True, problems of technology access and usage are prevalent in many parts of the New Europe. It is easy for those outside the region to take access to the technology for granted. But the emergence of the new media technologies has made key differences. It provides easy and immediate access to information, unheard of in the past. If information is power, then the Internet is bringing power to the people.

Whereas people once relied on newspaper, radio, or television to filter and digest the news for them, now they have direct access to primary sources. In an unprecedented exercise in democracy, the report by the U.S. special prosecutor Kenneth Starr on the Clinton affair was available on the Internet just minutes after it was published. Americans and people across the world could read word for word the result of an investigation costing millions of dollars without waiting for the media to report on it. Such a document would have been available in libraries, but only after some time. In any case, how many people would have made the trek to their local library to wade through pages and pages of text?

There has been much talk of the Internet's coming of age. I argue that it is over the Kosovo conflict that the Internet has become a force in its own right. It has provided a platform for governments, opposition, and people in the street to voice their opinion.

The Internet has become the focus for a propaganda battle. While NATO warplanes attacked Serb forces, another war was fought in cyberspace. Organizations from the Yugoslav Government to NATO have made full use of the public access afforded by the Internet. "It is a sign of the times that a conflict of almost medieval atrocity can also be fought in the safety of cyberspace. But this is, of course, a war of words. Rarely have the lives of so many hinged on the interpretation of so few syllables" (*PR Week,* 1999, p. 12).

In the information war, the Internet means it is far more difficult to silence independent or rebel voices. When Serbian troops burned to the ground the Kosovo Information Center in Pristina, Kosovo Albanians set up a website (Kosovo Press, 1999). Likewise, when the authorities closed down the independent radio station B92 in Belgrade, its Internet site continued to publish the latest news in text, audio, and video.

"One of the ways in which the Serb people can get the truth that is blocked by [Yugoslav President] Milosevic is through the Internet," said UK Foreign Minister Robin Cook in a March 1999 briefing.

But the Internet does not take sides. The Serbs also took to cyberspace to present their version of events (Ministry of Information, 1999). And one of the few sources of information from inside Kosovo came from a monk at a 14th-century Serbian Orthodox monastery—Father Sava Janjic at the Visoki Decani monastery.

The war on the ground spread to the Net, with NATO suffering attacks on its computer systems from Serbia and the alliance counterattacking by escalating its propaganda campaign through official websites.

"It seems we are dealing with some hackers in Belgrade who have hacked into our website and caused line saturation by using 'ping' bombardment strategy," said NATO spokesman Jamie Shea on April 1. The Atlantic alliance was also subjected to thousands of e-mails from Yugoslavia, some containing viruses, designed to bring its computer system to a halt.

Nationalist and ideological attacks on official websites are becoming a fact of life in cyberspace. In October 1998, a Serbia-based group known as Black Hand attacked a Kosovo Albanian website and threatened to sabotage NATO's site. There have also been cyberattacks on an Indian army website on Kashmir and even on the website of the president of Belarus, Alyaksandr Lukashenka. "Hacking, previously dominated by teenage computer whizzkids often with no particular axe to grind, now looks set to become a propaganda tool," said BBC Monitoring's Laurence Peter (1998).

The turmoil in Kosovo showed how the Internet can provide a vehicle for ordinary people to express themselves. BBC News Online received thousands of e-mails from across the world during the Kosovo conflict. A large proportion of these came from Eastern Europe, in particular from the ".*yu*" domain name of Yugoslavia. "World, do you know that we are almost day and night in bomb shelters," said one e-mail. Voices from the ground that have previously gone unheard have emerged.

Laura Lengel and the authors who contribute to this volume present an up-to-the-minute awareness of concerns and challenges in East-Central Europe, South-Eastern Europe, and the former Soviet bloc. With the region in a state of constant change, the authors' knowledge and insights are vital to our understanding about post-Communist nations. These changes, and the resulting uncertainty and vulnerability, position media and communication technology, as Thomson (1994) argues, more powerfully and influentially than ever before.

I came to know Laura in 1993 when she was a Fulbright Scholar in the North African state of Tunisia and I was the BBC correspondent for North Africa. During that time, the "information superhighway" was just beginning to be hyped by political, press, and corporate voices in developed countries. Researching in Africa, however, Laura discovered very different attitudes to the "techno hype." Through her work in Tunis with African media practitioners and scholars, and the MacBride Roundtable, an international group of media experts who examine world communication imbalances, she came to understand why those in developing nations reacted with distaste to the utopian visions of the so-called "information superhighway."

Drawing from her research experience above and her family roots in Hungary and Poland, Laura focuses on critical analysis of the utopian visions within and about the New Europe. She and the authors contributing to *Culture and Technology in the New Europe* examine a diverse range of issues, including pirate technology, hate speech online, and independent media in and online support to the former Yugoslavia.

Each chapter addresses questions surrounding the relatively new democratic developments in the region, in politics, education, commerce, and individual and collective dialogue. This focus on democracy, both the positive impact initially after the fall of Communist rule, and the more recent crisis of confidence in democracy, is important to inform those, particularly outside the region, that following the lead of advanced industrial societies is not necessarily the best plan.

The citizens of Eastern Europe and the former Soviet bloc face a double challenge in the shape of new media technologies and vast socioeconomic changes. Emerging from the legacy of state socialism, New

Europeans now have the opportunity to be active participants in the infancy of democracy in the region.

The challenges, concerns, and successes of communication in the New Europe are well documented and analyzed in this volume. The focus on the future in this work is key to the understanding of the transformations in the region, and the wider political, economic, and social developments that may develop in the New Europe in the third millennium.

REFERENCES

Kosovo Press. (1999, February 18). *Agjencia Shtetërore Informative* [Online]. Available: <www.kosovapress.com> [1999, April 17].

Ministry of Information. (1999, April 17). *SerbiaInfo* [Online]. Available: <www.serbia-info.com> [1999, April 17].

Peter, L. (1998, October 25). *War of words on the Internet* [Online]. Available: <http://news.bbc.co.uk/hi/english/world/monitoring/newsid_200000/200708.stm> [1999, March 10].

PR Week Magazine. (1999, April 2). Leader column, London, p. 12.

Thomson, M. (1994). *Forging war: The media in Serbia, Croatia and Bosnia-Hercegovina*. Avon, UK: International Center Against Censorship and Bath Press.

Preface

A s a researcher on culture and technology with a family heritage stemming from Hungary and Poland, I have watched with great interest the growing presence of East Central Europe, South-Eastern Europe, and the former Soviet bloc on the Internet. Firmly planted in the "West" after my ancestors emigrated to the U.S. in the final moments of the 19th century and the first moments of the 20th century, I began development of this book from a position of a researcher on the outside of the New Europe, desirous of the knowledge gained from extensive lived experience in pre- and post-socialist social, economic, and cultural conditions.

A lack of knowledge "from within" can lead researchers to assumptions and simplifications. Lack of lived experience in regions outside the technology-advantaged "West" has left many researchers with broad assumptions about global connectivity and how the Internet affords an opportunity for open and equal dialogue between "West" and "East," "North" and "South." In the "East" and the "South," however, such an open and equal dialogue is a problematic concept, as many lines of communication are anything but open. Access to and negotiation with technology in the "East" and the "South" requires careful examination. While scholars and practitioners are beginning to examine the impact of technology like the Internet in these regions, broad assumptions about user opportunity and access are still made. These assumptions result in an imagined and idealized world where all have equal opportunity to engage in open, democratic, pluralist communication.

The authors in this volume, however, bring no such assumptions to the chapters they have expertly crafted. Their deep immersion in the region results in analyses that can teach those outside the New Europe in intensive ways. It is to the authors that I am indebted. Our collaboration has helped me, not only intellectually, but to personally connect with the homeland of my grandparents and great-grandparents.

The collaboration that makes this book possible stems to other colleagues and organizations who have provided immense effort and encouragement. I am grateful to the Faculty Curriculum and Development Committee at Richmond American International University in London, who provided funding to conduct the field research, an opportunity to interact with others during my conference presentations about culture and technology in the New Europe, and the release time from teaching, all of which were vital to the realization of this work.

I am indebted to the faculty at St. Kliment Orhidski University, Sofia, Bulgaria, particularly Kornelia Merdjanska and Madeline Danova, who afforded me an opportunity to meet their brilliant students and exchange ideas about culture and technology. I thank the students, especially Dessislava Mladenova, Maria Varbeva, and Ilko Batakliev in Sofia, and Dimiter Tsotorkov, Gueorgui Pirinski, and Michael Daley in London, for helping me make connections with the Sofia-based students. I thank Mariana Lenkova for her enthusiasm and her insights on media representation of communities in the Balkans and Miglena Nikolchina, vice president of the Bulgarian Association of University Women, for sharing the excellent work to which the association has been committed.

I am grateful to the BBC headquarters and the United States Information Service American Center Library in Sofia and for affording me the opportunity to engage in an exciting dialogue about media and communication technology with women students and faculty. At the BBC, I had a unique opportunity to watch and discuss the news coverage of the events of 1989 and heard expert responses by the students and faculty regarding media representation of the fall of Communist rule. At the USIS Library, I had the chance to introduce students to the Internet for the first time, and we had an exciting meeting examining the representation of women in the region on the World Wide Web.

I extend my deepest thanks to Inke Arns, Catherine Davidson, John Fraser, Julia Hathaway, Camille O'Reilly, Alison Phipps, and, in particular, Alice Tomić, Sharon Foley, and Ivan Zmertych who offered support, encouragement, and critical readings of the work presented in this volume. I am especially grateful to Michael Prosser, series editor for Ablex's Civic Discourse for the Third Millennium series, who initially took an interest in my work as a fellow Fulbright Scholar, and maintained ongoing encouragement of my research through other publications. I also thank him and K.S. Sitaram for the opportunity to present a plenary lecture on the impact of communication technology on human rights in the New Europe at the "Human Rights and Responsibilities: Communication Strategies among Nations and Peoples" Conference in Rochester, New York, in July 1999. I also thank the Ablex staff, who have been wonderful to work with.

Most importantly, I thank my family and my spouse, Daniel, whose undying confidence in my work has uplifted me more times than I can count. A very special thanks to our baby daughter, Daniella Beth, who kindly allowed me to bring the manuscript to completion just hours before she came into the world.

To all others who have shown friendship and understanding, I am also indebted. Finally, I am most grateful to the authors who contributed to this volume. Their academic and professional expertise, coupled with insights gained from their lived experience in the New Europe, bring this project to life.

Laura Lengel

Introduction:
Culture and Technology in the
New Europe

Laura Lengel

Richmond American International University in London

I n the first decade of the 20th century, my grandfather, Frank
Lengyel, envisioned connecting with a world far beyond his native
Hungary. Born and raised in Gödölö, 20 miles northeast of Budapest, he longed for a life in the "New World." Travelling northwest by
train to Hamburg, he intended to board a ship sailing through the
North Sea and the Atlantic to the United States. Only in his teens, he
was turned away three times. Finally, at age 17, he managed to purchase
a ticket, pass inspection, and start his journey to a new world. Arriving
at Ellis Island in 1914, after weeks in the ship's dark, damp steerage,
Frank entered that new world, one that many in the "Old Country"
believed had streets paved with gold. Upon arrival, the newcomers did
not find the mythic gold streets, but rather hard work and hard lives.

Now, in the first moments of the 21st century, traveling to "new
worlds" is a far less treacherous endeavor than in my grandfather's time.
The lands that were once thousands of miles out of reach and prohibitively costly to visit, are more accessible than in decades past. The myths
are less far fetched. Due to media, telecommunications, and technology,
rather than myths of gold-paved streets there are more realistic images,
to which those even in the far reaches of the globe are exposed. Yet
there are new types of "gold," desirous and often unobtainable to those

in developing nations and regions in political and socioeconomic transition. This "gold" stems from the same 20th-century phenomena, telecommunications and technology, which forged links, making "old" and "new" lands more connected and open to each other. This openness, resulting from the advances in telecommunications, has been termed "Telestroika" by Pekka Tarajanne, secretary general of the International Telecommunications Union (1990, p. 22). This "Telestroika," however, is an openness not enjoyed by all. In many places around the world, it is still a golden commodity that is out of reach, inaccessible for those without economic resources to make a telephone call, much less click a mouse, link to an Internet service provider, and connect with another world.

Connecting with worlds, both within and outside post-socialist nations, is a primary focus of this book. *Culture and Technology in the New Europe* presents the insights of an international group of academic researchers and media practitioners who examine the impact of connecting worlds through technological developments in East-Central Europe, South-Eastern Europe, the Newly Independent States, and the Russian Federation. Drawing from the expertise of authors from and working in the region, the book addresses uses of and concerns about technology that the New Europe faces at the eve of the third millennium and a decade after the fall of Communist rule. The book is distinguished by diverse studies ranging from the problems of "cyber hate" from and about the New Europe; to online activism in war-torn Kosovo, Bosnia, Croatia, and Yugoslavia; to how digital media art articulates the sociocultural and political transition experienced in the region. Finally, *Culture and Technology in the New Europe* looks to the future of media, technology, and communication in the region, particularly the gaps between post-Communist nations and those more technologically advantaged, and how these gaps can be narrowed or eradicated in the third millennium.

CIVIC DISCOURSE AND THE TRANSFORMATION OF THE NEW EUROPE

East Central Europe, South-Eastern Europe, the Newly Independent States, and the Russian Federation have been named the "New Europe" by the media, the commercial sector, and political leaders such as Czech President Vaclav Havel[1] (BBC World Service, 1998; New Europe Group, 1998). Citizens in the New Europe have shared Havel's optimism for the creation of a new, economically and politically strong entity. They have been faced with vast socioeconomic and political changes that are driving them to redefine their roles and identities. Emerging from the legacy of state socialism, citizens in the region have increased opportunities to be active participants in the infancy of democratic practice in the region, and active participants in the civic discourse previously oppressed under Soviet rule.

Civic discourse, or communication between and among communities that focuses on intercultural, gender, race, and ethnic diversity and sensitivity, can be particularly compelling in regions experiencing vast social, political, and economic change. Current research being conducted on civic discourse in Africa (Prosser, forthcoming), international human rights (Over, 1999), Asia (Jia, forthcoming; Kluver & Powers, 1999), and Kosovo and other Yugoslav successor states (Lengel, 1999) indicates that citizens in these regions are struggling in their complex negotiation with the transformations they are experiencing both locally and globally. These transformations, however, occur against a backdrop of relative insecurity. Despite economic instability, political turbulence, and human rights threats, citizens living with the changes in the above regions are actively seeking opportunities to develop a new civil society and a civic discourse once silenced by those in power.

Kluver and Powers, in their book *Civic Discourse, Civil Society, and Chinese Communities* (1999), argue that "civil society is formed discursively, in that it is through discourse that the society 'discovers' itself, and formulates values, character, and, ultimately, its ethos" (p. xi). The contributors to this current book, through diverse methodological and theoretical spectra, investigate how civic discourse is changing and how it will continue to transform the diverse societies of the New Europe as it enters the third millennium. As "civil society is formed discursively," one communicative channel for civic discourse in the New Europe is information and communication technology. Information technology has revolutionized communication practices in the New Europe with its global reach and immediacy, opening up opportunities for civic discourse and collaboration both within communities, and connecting communities worldwide.

The authors contributing to this volume aid the understanding of the intersections of intercultural, international, and cybernetic communication in the New Europe against the face of the current sociocultural, political, and economic challenges within the region. Citizens in the New Europe are using communication technology to express themselves in ways not possible before the fall of Communism, to connect with the diaspora of post-socialist citizens living abroad, and to call out for assistance to others, particularly during the war in Yugoslavia and the refugee crisis in Kosovo. Thus, citizens and nongovernmental organizations use technology to create an equal dialogue, combatting the political and economic changes that have created an "Otherness" in post-Communist nations. As a result of the ideas disseminated through communication technology, those outside the post-Communist New Europe can understand how technology impacts cultural and national identity, provides a space for attacking "Otherness," and allows for an understanding of contemporary issues, community development, and intercultural and international communication in the region.

The authors in this book examine the possible empowering capabilities of communication technology such as computer-mediated communication to engage in a dialogue in and beyond the New Europe. The opportunity for such dialogue, many argue (see, for example, Loader, 1997; Reeve, 1995; Richardson, 1995; Sobchack, 1996; Woods, 1993), provides spaces for communicative power, to have a "voice" that would normally be silent in traditional communicative contexts. However, "empowerment" through the Internet, a term often applied uncritically, needs to be questioned. Certainly, getting "online," in and of itself, provides no more "empowerment" than picking up the telephone. This "virtual empowerment" (Loader, 1997, p. 10) is only empowering if some pro-social benefit emerges from computer-mediated communication. In other words, it is not ownership of communication technology that is so important, but how it is used and by whom. The notion of empowerment through communication generally, and communication technology specifically, is not applied uncritically in this book, however. Just as getting "online" is not empowering in and of itself, surfing the World Wide Web has little social benefit. However, unlike predominantly user-passive services of the Internet like the Web, synchronous communication services such as Internet Relay Chat, Usenet and newsgroups can provide an active space for interactive dialogue. This dialogue affords opportunities to interact without the constraints of race, class, ethnicity, and gender bias. While scholars discuss how computer-mediated communication (CMC) is capable of creating a means for all persons to be equally heard in a global arena, the opportunity to be equally heard is, in fact, unequal. The opportunity to engage in "online" "voice" is granted to merely a select few, excluding both global regions and communities, which have been traditionally marginalized politically, socioculturally, and economically. While the Internet provides a forum for voices outside the dominant powers that typically control international mass communication, the minimum needs to access this technology require maximum expense, including computers, modems, telephone lines, and electricity.

In the post-Communist New Europe, where economic changes have been vast, computers and links exist at a premium, and Internet service can cost more than monthly rent, cybernetic "empowerment" is not an option for many. For those that do have access to technology or are helping others to gain access, as in the case of the ZaMir Transnational Network, the uses of the Internet as well as more traditional media like video and radio in the New Europe are meaningful. For example C3, the Center for Culture & Communication [Kulturális és Kommunikációs Központ/Soros Alapítvány], in Budapest, a forum for debate and innovation regarding communication, culture, and open society, creates opportunities for civic discourse through creative practice (C3, 1998). Others organizations, like the Tajfun Czech youth theater, the Network of East–West Women, and the Friends and Partners initiative, are discussed in this book as exemplars of how online communities are creating civil societies within the New Europe and connecting to others around the world.

THE FIRST INTERNET WAR: THE IMPACT OF TECHNOLOGY ON THE WAR IN THE BALKANS

Perhaps the most compelling uses of communication technology discussed in the following chapters concern those in the Balkan war. It is known as the first Internet War (Collin, 1999), the "first large-scale war fought on the Internet. On the worldwide web you could rub shoulders with the Kosovo Liberation Army [KLA], the Serbian government, Bill Clinton and Tony Blair" (Rogers, 1999, p. 6). Government discourse from all sides has flowed freely on the Net, each with its own take on the crisis.

Beyond the governmental representation on the World Wide Web, the nongovernmental civic discourse has made this "Internet War" unique. While CNN brought the Gulf War into homes around the world with its reporting immediacy, online reports on the crises in the Balkans are very different. These reports have emerged from the grassroots level, from those who have lived the terror of war. Collin (1999) notes, "it is at a deeper and more personal level that the Internet is having its real impact" (p. 19). From chat rooms to listservs to discussion forums, people have engaged in dialogue and debate, in a "sometimes bitter, violent argument" (p. 19). The Internet has "enabled those ordinary people who are bearing the impact of the conflict to talk directly, without mediation, to those whose governments are carrying out the ethnic cleansing on the one side or sending in the bombers on the other" (p. 19).

At this civic level, Internet users have typed as the bombs hit (Collin, 1999). They typed from Kosovo where they have volunteered to be members of humanitarian aid and grassroots organizations such as the Independent Women Journalists in Kosova (see, for example, Ahmeti, 1999). They typed to their friends outside the region to say goodbye.

They received supportive e-mail messages from the outside urging them not to give up hope (Tesanovic, 1999).

Not only have Internet users in the region created a discursive space for aid and support, but they have also turned the Internet into a "virtual battlefield" (Collin, 1999, p. 20). Hacking has become a "propaganda weapon" (Peter, 1998) with organizations from all sides disseminating their views on NASA, governmental, and university sites in the U.S., UK, China, the Balkans, and elsewhere in the New Europe.

The impact of the Internet in this war has been unprecedented. In the Balkans, where Western journalists have been expelled and where, in many cases, telecommunication infrastructures have been literally blown away, the lack of communications links have isolated those who needed to link with others outside the region. Even where infrastructures remained, those independent media and civic organizations that relied on them were subject to shut down by governmental power. Although award winning Independent Radio B92 in Belgrade was banned by the Yugoslav authorities, it has proceeded to broadcast on its website. While the authorities have also attempted to silence the web site, B92 has continued to stay alive by broadcasting from secret locations (Rogers, 1999), and has continued to be a voice from within the crisis. Another, perhaps unlikely, voice from within the crisis is known as Cyber-Monk. Sava Janjic, a 33-year-old Serbian Othodox monk, rose at 1:00 a.m. in the 14th-century Visoki Decani monastery in Kosovo "to take advantage of quiet traffic in cyberspace, prays and then gets online" to "bombard" Western journalists with his reports on the Kosovan refugee crisis (Rogers, 1999, p. 6). U.S.-based analyst Steve Clift says that the Internet is "giving people in the middle of the situation a chance to put their stories across" (cited in Rogers, 1999, p. 6).

There have been, however, many in the first Internet War that had no voice. Collin (1999, p. 19) asks, "But what of the ethnic Albanians fleeing Kosovo—those with no computers and e-mail connections? They are, for the most part, unheard."

RESOURCES AND STRATEGIES FOR COMMUNICATION IN THE NEW EUROPE

There are many in the New Europe who are unheard. Much of the debate into communication technology, primarily the Internet, assumes that access to technology is taken for granted and, under that assumption, scholarship tends to focus on what Nyaki Adeya calls the "'problems' of *being* connected" (original emphasis, 1996, p. 23). Adeya argues for the importance of keeping "sight of the fact that for much of the world's population there are also very real problems in simply connecting up to what already exists" (p. 23). Problems of technology access have been assessed in Africa, Latin America, India, and the Middle East (Fedak, 1998, forthcoming; Gonzalez-Pinto & Roman, 1998; Kapoor, 1998; Kraidy, 1996; Lengel & Fedak, forthcoming). However, little has been done to examine concerns in the New Europe. While an important contribution to knowledge, work examining communication flow and media in the region (Casmir, 1995; Hopkinson, 1996; Paletz, Jakubowicz, & Novosel, 1995) does not address technology and the complexities of intercultural and international communication through "new" media. Conversely, scholarship specifically addressing information and communication technology (see, for example, American Political Science Association, 1994; Anderson et al., 1995; Loader, 1997; Sardar, 1996) largely ignores the New Europe. Thus, this book is crucial in its explication of how post-socialist Europeans are participating in cybernetic civic discourse, despite the problematic socioeconomic and political conditions of the region, which have been widely reported in scholarship (see, for example, Bennahum, 1997; Goldman, 1997; Heitlinger, 1993; Ognianova & Scott, 1997; Paletz, Jakubowicz, & Novosel, 1995; Perlez, 1998).

The following chapters reveal that, in many cases, the New Europe at the beginning of the third millennium is experiencing not a glorious new age, but a period of frequent confusion and occasional defensiveness. This confusion and defensiveness emerges from a history of Soviet technological initiatives, such as the development of computer hardware and software in Bulgaria. Since the fall of Communist rule and because of limited financial resources, many technological initiatives have ceased to exist. Similarly, lack of funds to develop telecommunications infrastructure has created problems. For instance, the Ukraine has only one telephone for every seven or eight citizens, which falls far below the telecommunications access of developed countries (New Europe Group, 1998). More economically advantaged areas in the region, particularly major urban centers such as Prague and Budapest, have telephone lines that reach far more citizens. However, the infrastructural problems in the Ukraine are similar elsewhere in the New Europe, where electricity is inconsistent, telephone lines are poor, and technology generally is primitive. At present, national governments may be too consumed with economic and political survival to address these problems.

These problems are some of the roadblocks to the so-called information superhighway. Despite its often-hyped democratic structure, this superhighway, like traditional transportation systems, contains some "roads" that are quicker and can carry more traffic (Uncapher, 1995). Other "roads" are structured more like one-way alleys or dead-end lanes.

In technology-advantaged regions, the roads are wider, faster, and transport more information. To those on the "outside" of these regions, argues Walter Uncapher, "that far off world of massive data flows seems enwrapped in the mystery of complex network protocols and hardware, probably best left in the hands of the giant firms and governmental agencies" (p. 1). Giant firms and agencies have stepped in to assist the construction and improvement of the New Europe's technological "roads." The World Bank, for instance, has donated monies to put computers in universities in Hungary and elsewhere in the region (Malderez, personal communication, December 16, 1997). Similarly, the Open Society Foundation and NetSat Express, a supplier of Internet access via satellite, is providing new Internet technology throughout East Central Europe (Moffett, 1997). Despite assistance from these organizations and corporate leaders like Hungarian George Soros, the director of the Open Society Foundation, or Andrew Grove, once a Hungarian refugee, now chairman and CEO of Intel, "roads" on the so-called superhighway are in many cases not "super." Soros's funding is a particularly interesting case. Said to earn over $4,000 a minute, Soros reportedly loaned the Russian government one billion dollars in its efforts to privatize telecommunications (Reeves, 1998). Through the Open Society Institutes in New York and Budapest and the Soros Foundation, he has funded technology-focused educational initiatives and nongovernmental organizations throughout the New Europe. Soros is seen as an ambiguous figure, a one-man International Monetary Fund (IMF) saving the region. Many argue that he will gain from funding privatization moves and will solidify a financial dependence on the industrialized world generally and on him specifically. Despite his financial self-interest, however, his commitment to developing opportunities to use communication technology is not insignificant. Mentioned throughout this book, Soros funds have allowed traditionally silenced communities to be heard.

From a technical perspective, the entirety of the New Europe can be heard through communication technology. While it is difficult to measure the number of "wired" nations, as the numbers are changing constantly (Fedak, 1998), the international connectivity table developed by the Internet Society (Landweber, 1997) reports that all of East Central Europe, South-Eastern Europe, the Newly Independent States, and the Russian Federation have some level of connection to the Internet, either through Internet Protocol (IP) links on the open Internet, or through Unix to Unix Copy Protocol (UUCP) with e-mail and Usenet newsgroups, or FidoNet, a store-and-forward e-mailing wide area network (WAN) with gateways to the Internet. Thus, post-Communist nations are connected and the windows of opportunity that exist are promising. World Wide Web sites from the Open Media Research Institute and from news services like Radio Free Europe/Radio Liberty and Peredatsja are emerging from the region, affording opportunities for new voices to be heard globally. Within the region, conflicts may be resolved by the Internet. ACCESS, a nongovernmental organization in Sofia, Bulgaria, promotes national and ethnic relations through the Internet (M. Lenkova, 1997, personal communication, October 24, 1997). Veran Matic, a leading Serbian journalist and editor-in-chief of the independent Serbian radio station B92, announces that "the Internet is today's key to bringing down totalitarian regimes and breaking the state's monopoly on the media" (Borchanin & Moffett, 1997). With the breakdown of state monopolies and increase of privatization (New Europe Group, January 8, 1998), the economy-building capacity of communication technology can, as Dyker argues, "provide one of the most valuable resources currently available to east European economies" (1996, p. 915). Both the political and economic opportunities opened up by communication technology allow activists and entrepreneurs to enact change, a change perhaps only possible after the fall of the old regimes.

In many instances, however, remnants of the old regimes remain. Bureaucratic red tape, coupled with economic need, have led some to seize their own opportunities, including telephone line piracy, Internet account piracy, and the subversive elements of noninstitutional networks in the region. With their entrepreneurial attitude (Perlez, 1998) and keen technological savvy, many youth in the New Europe have resisted the sanctioned route through local telephone authorities and Internet service providers by pirating lines and accounts. Following the sanctioned route requires necessary resources (primarily capital), telecommunications equipment approved by the local authority, and the persistence and patience to navigate through sometimes unwieldy bureaucracies. This sanctioned system excludes (or marginalizes) many potential users in the New Europe. Resourceful individuals and groups in this region, lacking economic means, have found ways around this system and have, through nonsanctioned means and methods, "appropriated" Internet connectivity. These range from smuggled modems, other telecommunications devices and computers, to the pirating, or illegal connection, of telephone lines.

The case of Bulgaria is noteworthy, particularly when considering the history of the nation as the designated "Silicon Valley" of the Soviet regime. Until the 1980s, the Politburo positioned Bulgaria as the center of "socialism's first and only centrally planned home-computer industry" (Bennahum, 1997, p. 228). Because of this designation, Bulgarian students and technology professionals had far more computer access than their counterparts elsewhere in the region. While the Soviet initiatives have ceased, Bulgarians have retained a level of technical brilliance known internationally, if only for their infamous computer viruses that swept the world in the early 1990s. Today, the viruses are no longer produced, however, the nation outputs other items, like 25 million pirate audio CDs (Bennahum, 1997), which are sold on the street in Sofia. Internet accounts are also pirated. In Bulgaria, where monthly service charges of ISPs like Bulnet and Eunet can cost more than monthly rent, the technologically astute connect phones into telecommunications networks illegally, pay a lower fee to black-market "unlimited" service providers and have affordable access. In other instances, e-mail accounts are created on servers through an "insider" employee of the ISP, doing so in what might be construed as "democratization" of the means of communication. Other, more legal initiatives are also developing in Bulgaria. Those who were once the students of the Soviet computer initiatives are now forming their own, in many cases more affordable, ISPs. Such moves, as David Bennahum contends, are "sparking a small renaissance of entrepreneurial activity, showing, by example, that there are economic alternatives to emigration of collusion with criminal enterprises" (p. 266). The end result is that some users who would otherwise be denied access to the sphere of the Internet have equitable access.

EQUITABLE ACCESS/EQUITABLE DISCOURSE?

Equitable access, however, does not necessarily mean equitable discourse. Nor does it mean that access is stable and ongoing. Those who have succeeded in finding ways around bureaucracies and high costs are now suffering the consequences. In Bulgaria, for instance, upward to 90 percent of computer software is pirated. Microsoft, obviously unhappy with their lack of power in the nation, has made an agreement with the Bulgarian government to eradicate piracy. The company has authorized searches of both public offices and private homes. Penalties for offenders include computer confiscation, 5,000,000 leva (U.S. $2,700), or five years in prison (Bloomberg News, 1999). As part of the agreement, Microsoft has offered to cut prices of their software in Bulgaria so that the software costs 60 percent of U.S. prices, a prohibitive cost to the average Bulgarian, whose salary totals $100 (U.S.) per month. This salary level, coupled with the nation's reputation for outstanding proficiency in programming, may be of interest to Microsoft. There is talk that Microsoft wants to start up an outsourcing company in Bulgaria. Many Bulgarians are asking, however, if the company pays 60 percent of the going U.S. rate in wages to the Bulgarian programmers.

There are other concerns beyond affordability of software and hardware. With a lack of national, ethnic, and linguistic diversity online, Stokes and Stokes (1996, p. 5) argue that "networked computers are already reproducing rather traditional disparities in opportunity." Furthermore, the authors note U.S. Internet users still comprise the majority of all activity on "the allegedly world wide Web" (p. 5). Although the lack of diversity is changing, still the vast majority of content on this "allegedly world wide Web" is in English. Perhaps this homogeneity of users explains why New Europeans have been overlooked in research on civic discourse and communication technology. The ability to participate in civic discourse after years of Soviet-imposed silencing and the new roles and identities in post-socialist societies are valuable to explorations of intercultural and international communication. The exploration can begin with the Radio Free Europe/Radio Liberty website, which includes news scripts in Russian and RealAudio live radio broadcasts in languages such as Armenian, Azerbaijani, Belarusian, Bosnian, Croatian, Kazakh, Kyrgyz, Russian, Serbian, Tajik, Tatar-Bashkir, Turkmen, and Uzbek (Radio Free Europe/Radio Liberty, 2000). Similarly, nongovernmental organizations (NGOs) are developing non-English language web material and, when resources are low, ask members to volunteer to translate web sites into other languages, widening readership and, where interactive web sites are concerned, affording more opportunities for open dialogue. These opportunities, scholars and practitioners argue, will create spaces for civic discourse. Reeve (1995) argues, "To attain useful participatory democracy, it is essential that all sections of society have an equal voice" (p. 4). He notes that communication technology "leads to many doors, whether these can be open from the inside or the out remains a question to answer" (p. 1).

DIVERSE EXPLORATIONS OF CULTURE AND TECHNOLOGY IN THE NEW EUROPE

The "many doors" to which technology leads create many questions, both theoretical and practical, for the study of civic discourse in the New Europe. While *Culture and Technology in the New Europe* focuses on information and communication technology, underlying issues of economic struggle, legal reforms, and the development of a participatory democracy are addressed by the contributors to this volume. The authors represent a range of nationalities, from Czech, Bulgarian, Hungarian, Polish, Romanian, Russian, and Slovenian. They have lived, worked, and conducted research in the New Europe, which forms the basis of their understanding of the impact of technological access and advancement on the region and its diverse cultures. These authors have written chapters that progress from a foundation of theoretical, historical, and cultural issues of intercultural and cybernetic discourse in the region, to explore national and international divides and the challenges of civic discourse based on ethnic, gender, and class difference. The authors present civic discourse and communication technology in practice: in political activism, education, and in connecting the diaspora of post-Communist citizens to those inside the region. While it is challenging to present the most up-to-the-minute research on the rapidly challenging nature of events and of technology, the authors provide a snapshot of the developments in the New Europe on the eve of the third millennium.

The first part of the book provides a theoretical foundation to the contemporary concerns in the New Europe. In Chapter 1, "Ferment and Transition in the New Europe: Challenges for Intercultural and International Communication," Priya Kapoor examines how intercultural communication within the region has transformed since the fall of Communist rule and how international communication has connected the New Europe to the world. Anna Lubecka, in Chapter 2, "Contemporary Economic Sociocultural, and Technological Contexts in the New Europe," addresses the vast changes in the post-Communist New Europe. She draws from specific examples in her native Poland to illustrate how the New Europe is defining and redefining its new political and economic status and sociocultural identity, and the impact that technology and globalization play in these processes. Based on her research and teaching experience in Romania, Noemi Marin traces the development of civic discourse through the efforts of the intellectuals in Eastern and Central Europe in Chapter 3. She traces the cultural and sociopolitical contribution of key intellectuals, particularly Havel, Michnik, and Konrad, before and after the fall of Communist rule and examines how their ideas have been disseminated to a technologically saavy, contemporary audience. Marin argues that a technologically equipped New Europe seems to be the cultural response to the former, pre-1989, era of communist propaganda, thus creating democratic dialogue in the new civil society.

Drawing from Jurgen Habermas's important concept of the political public sphere, Jon Mided, in Chapter 4, "The Internet and the Public Sphere: What Kind of Space is Cyberspace?" examines the transformation of the public sphere in the New Europe, a virtual community of support groups and common interest forums, which creates social interaction and links both within and outside the New Europe. He also explores the Internet as public sphere for political activism and mutual assistance online, particularly during the crises in Yugoslavia, Bosnia, and Kosovo. Writing from Hungary, John Horvath, in Chapter 5, examines how, despite the potential of digital technology to encourage international discourse among regions and nations, the New Europe is still considered a "terra incognita" by many. This is in part due to the poverty of liberal democracy at its foundations, for not only is a weakened state of civic discourse nurtured, but a lingering bias, which views the region as a homogeneous whole, is maintained. Accordingly, Horvath presents an overview of the disparate levels of telematic access and digital infrastructure that exist, revealing that this "bloc" attitude, a vestige of the cold war era, is clearly unfounded. He addresses how history and tradition exert a certain amount of influence on the way in which computer-mediated communication is developed within individual countries, in addition to the cybernetic civic discourse that takes place. He concludes by noting that, if present trends continue, congenital feelings of insularity will be reinforced and thus carried over into the third millennium, thereby threatening to increase gaps that already exist between "east" and "west," as well as within the region itself, in terms of communication, economic development, and even minority rights.

The second part of the book addresses the contemporary concerns about media, telecommunications, and technology in the region. Bulgarian born and educated researcher Dina Iordanova, in Chapter 6, "Mediated Concerns: The New Europe in Hypertext," challenges us to examine both optimistic and pessimistic views of communication technology now and how technology impacts the future of the New Europe. Iordanova focuses on the importance of examining both "traditional" and "new" media in the New Europe. She argues that while the New Europe uses the Internet to mediate its concerns, it should not invalidate print- or broadcast-mediated communication in the region. Iordanova explores the specific presence that East Europeans have established for themselves on the World Wide Web in a period of dynamic and sometimes unsettling transitions. She focuses on projects concerned with projecting the specific culture of the region in the global context of the Internet, as well as with the presence of some civic organizations and grassroots activism.

In Chapter 7, "Organized Innocence and War in the New Europe: On Electronic Solitude and Independent Media," Dutch media theorist Geert Lovink addresses independent media in the former Yugoslavia. He examines how the hype of the "digital revolution" and the utopianist visions of global communication are very different from the cultural situation in the New Europe, particularly in the Balkans. Hungarian-based researcher Elliot Glassman, in Chapter 8, discusses another anti-utopianist concern of communication technology in the New Europe. Analyzing "CyberHate," he presents arguments from and against hate groups and advocates of free speech regarding the hate speech disseminated through the Internet either from or directed at the region. In Chapter 9, "Gender and Technology in the New Europe," I examine the cultural position and socioeconomic conditions of post-Communist women generally, while specifically addressing how women and girls have worked to gain respect as technology students and professionals. I present women's voices about the technology gap and electronic spaces for women's dialogue previously silent in the region. I focus on women's activist and nongovernmental organizations that are using the Internet to raise awareness about the ethnic and nationalist tensions in the Balkans and to seek aid for the refugees fleeing Kosovo. The chapter concludes with an assessment of future opportunities for international and intercultural discourse as New European women move into the new century.

In Chapter 10, Bruce McClelland, drawing from his experience as the Director of the Internet Access and Training Program in Russia and his interest in Russian culture, examines the Internet as a space for folklore. The Internet, he argues, is a likely medium for folklore, a discursive and cultural form that frequently crosses the boundary between the private and public domain. McClelland discusses how the Internet has been a space for folkloric protest and other types of civic discourse in Russia, a nation where freedom of expression is not taken for granted.

The third part of the book addresses specific contexts and practices of civic discourse in the New Europe. Marina Gržinić, in Chapter 11, "Video as Civic Discourse in the Former Yugoslavia: Strategies of Visualization and the Aesthetics of Video in the New Europe," addresses how video has been employed as an artistic, political, and cultural tool in her native Slovenia and the former Yugoslavia. Her chapter is the first attempt to write simultaneously about the general history of electronic arts across East Central and South-Eastern Europe, while focusing on the particular history of the media condition in the former Yugoslavia and, more specifically, on Slovenia. Gržinić's work on the underground and alternative movements in the region paints a clear picture of the strategies of visualization and the aesthetics of electronic media in the New Europe.

In Chapter 12, Margot Emery and Benjamin Bates address how the Internet's power of communication can be found in an online community and information resource known as "Friends and Partners." From a chance encounter in a chatroom in 1993 between one Russian and one U.S. citizen, "Friends and Partners" has grown into a wide-ranging Web- and mailing-list service whose aim of creating peace through understanding has brought together thousands of people around the globe. Impacts of the service include aiding the Internet's diffusion in Russia, establishing Russia's first civic networks, and exploring joint U.S.–Russian applications. Emery and Bates examine the motivation, history, and development of "Friends and Partners," and the changing patterns of discourse it supports. The initiative indicates the Internet's potential for international community relations. It also exemplifies the complex interplay of technology and its uses that determine, at the macrosocial level, the Internet's impact and significance in global communication flows.

John Parrish-Sprowl and Eric Paul Engel, in Chapter 13, "The Evolution of Cybernetic Civic Discourse in Post-Communist Poland," contend that it is not surprising that capitalist markets do not hold much respect for tradition. Tradition, however, plays a critical role in Polish cultural identity, leaving the citizens enmeshed in a transformative discourse as they seek to reconcile Polish culture with the discourse of the marketplace. Parrish-Sprowl and Engel argue that nowhere is this more evident than in the growing presence of Polish organizations on the Internet. Their chapter explores these issues through primary research on Polish Internet users. Embedded in these users' stories is the struggle for cultural identity in the midst of the rise in consumerism within the Polish post-Communist transformation.

In Chapter 14, Zdenka Telnarová, Eva Burianová, and I explore the impact of technology on youth in the New Europe. Based on research in the Czech Ostrava region, where Telnarová and Burianová live and teach, the chapter addresses how Czech youth use the Internet to dialogue about East Central European culture and interact in ways far less possible during Communist rule and before access to computer-mediated communication. The research presents the views of Czech youth who participate in computer-mediated civic discourse to feel connected to the world, a connection that is, for many, beyond reach through traditional communicative means. It also, however, focuses on the dangers of this connectedness when Czech youth consume increasingly commercial, "Westernized" World Wide Web content, diminish their own interest in Czech culture, and adopt an apoliticized stance toward the current and future stability of their nation. Many in the Czech Republic fear that their youth are losing their interest in cultural traditions and politics, in favor of a capitalist New Europe.

Amy Herron and Eric Bachman, in Chapter 15, focus on the ZaMir Transnational Network, an electronic community that has been one of the most valuable tools for the peace movement in the Yugoslav successor states. The authors argue that the wars in the Balkans have received much media attention, but little notice has been given to peace efforts like the ZaMir ("for peace") Transnational Network or their impact. Herron and Bachman discuss how this network was created to improve communication between peace-oriented people and groups, humanitarian organizations, nongovernmental organizations, independent media in the former Yugoslavia, and refugees and their families. The chapter also addresses Herron's field research in Croatia on war, peace, and resistance music in the Yugoslav successor states and how this music was disseminated through the Internet. The musical texts that Herron researched and translated are important illustrations of how citizens articulate the turmoil of the war in the Balkans.

The final part of the book looks to New Europe in the third millennium. Drew McDaniel, in Chapter 16, "Socialist Media in the Post-Soviet Era Now and in the Future: Reflections on the Asian Experience," forecasts the probable outcomes of current policies and the future evolution of technology in post-socialist nations, mainly those in the Central Asian region. He provides a survey of the status of media and media policies in socialist nations of Asia. This survey is juxtaposed against the nations of the New Europe formerly allied to the Soviet Union that are covered elsewhere in this book. The contrast between Asia and Europe, the two world regions most influenced by socialist political movements of the 20th century, provides us a somewhat larger framework within which to view the events of the past decade in Europe. McDaniel addresses future challenges in socialist nations, particularly how politicization of mass communication represents a major stumbling block to democratization and national reconciliation.

In Chapter 17, Nicholas Johnson focuses on the future of Georgia's media and telecommunications, examining the current situation for the Internet and wireless communications, and future options and opportunities for technology and media advancement. His vast experience as a U.S. federal communication commissioner and an advisor to the government of Georgia provide us with a keen awareness of the needs and challenges in Georgia as well as in other post-Communist nations.

Bozena Mannova, writing from Prague, and Christina Preston and I, from London, examine how communities both within and outside the New Europe collaborate through technology to develop personal, professional, and educational links around the world in Chapter 18. The work of the international, not-for-profit organization MirandaNet creates links to preserve linguistic and cultural identities of communities in developing nations and regions in transition, such as the Czech Republic. The chapter focuses on the importance of partnerships with government, education, and industry for information and communication technology initiatives to continue and flourish in the third millennium. Finally, in Chapter 19, Anna Lubecka looks to the New Europe in the third millennium. She argues that Europe, traditionally divided between the West and the East, is in a period of unrest, where tendencies toward both unification and regionalization will impact its future. Lubecka asks if Europe will continue to be divided in the Third Millennium or if the dichotomy will disappear, through efforts resulting from collaboration, cultural convergence, and local, regional, and national partnerships.

Through such partnerships, as well as collaboration and cooperation both from within and outside the New Europe, connecting worlds is possible. Collaboration and cooperation are foundations of civic discourse. These foundations have an increased potential to be realized through communication technology. At the same time, media and communication technology can cause divides between advantaged and disadvantages worlds. Technology is simply a tool that can be used for either equal and open dialogue or for one's own cultural, commercial, or political gains over another. The hope is that the New Europe will benefit from these relatively new dialogic channels. Such channels were, in the relatively recent past, either closed or unavailable to those living under Communist rule. Now, a civic discourse in transition is unfolding in the New Europe. We will continue to examine this transition with great interest as the New Europe enters the new millennium.

NOTES

1. The "New Europe" is a term used, not uncritically, throughout this book to address a broad and diverse region, including East-Central Europe, South-Eastern Europe, the Newly Independent States, and the Russian Federation. The diversity and the problematic notion of nationhood within the region are addressed in Arns and Broeckmann (1997) and Žižek (1992).

REFERENCES

Adeya, N. (1996). Beyond borders: The Internet for Africa. *Convergence: The Journal of Research into New Media Technologies, 2*(2), 23–27.

Ahmeti, S. (1999, March 22). *Kosova war chronicle of the week: 15-20 March* [Online]. Available: <http://www.neww.org/kosova/Sevdie's%20Chronicles/032299bko.htm> [1999, April 17].

American Political Science Association. (1994). *A new way of talking politics: Democracy on the Internet.* Washington, DC: Author.

Anderson, R. E., Lundmark, V., Harris, L., & Magnan, S. (1995). Equity in computing. In C. Huff & T. Finholt (Eds.), *Social issues in computing: Putting computing in its place* (pp. 352–385). New York: McGraw-Hill.

Arns, I., & Broeckmann, A. (1997, June 9-15). Small media normality for the east [Online]. *Rewired—The Journal of a Strained Net.* Available: <http://www.rewired.com/97/0609.html> [1999, March 12].

BBC World Service. (1998, September 17). *World: Europe. Havel: USA central in building new Europe* [Online]. Available: <http://news.bbc.co.uk/hi/english/world/europe/newsid%5F173000/173429.stm> [1999, April 28].

Bennahum, D. S. (1997, November). Heart of darkness. *Wired*, *5*(11), 226–277.

Borchanin, N., & Moffett, J. (1997, April 4). *Serbia: Internet plays key role in Belgrade politics* [Online]. Available: http://www.rferl.org/nca/features/1997/04/F.RU.970404192806.html [1999, January 8].

Bloomberg News. (1999, February 23). *Microsoft goes after Bulgarian pirates* [Online]. Available: < http://www.news.com/News/Item/0,4,32775,00.html? tag=st.nw.sr1.dir> [1999, March 12].

C3. (1998). *WHY? Center for Culture & Communication* [Kulturális és Kommunikációs Központ/Soros Alapítvány] [Online]. Available: http://www.c3.hu/c3/txt-c3_why.html [1999, April 10].

Casmir, F. L. (Ed.). (1995). *Communication in Eastern Europe: The role of history, culture and media in contemporary conflicts*. Mahwah, NJ: Lawrence Erlbaum.

Collin, M. (1999, April 19-25). The mouse that roared. *The Big Issue*, *331*, 19–20.

Dyker, D. (1996). The computer and software industries in the East European economies: A bridgehead to the global economy? *Europe-Asia Studies*, *48*, 915–930.

Fedak, D. (forthcoming). The politicization of cyber-power: Government control, technological advancements and the Internet in the Arab world. In M. Prosser & K.S. Sitaram (Eds.), *Communication, technology, and cultural values*. Stamford, CT: Ablex.

Fedak, D. (1998, July). *Africa in the third millennium: Organizing new communication technologies for the future*. Paper presented at the International Communication Association/National Communication Association Conference, Rome.

Goldman, M. F. (1997). *Revolution and change in Central and Eastern Europe: Political, economic, and social changes*. London: M.E. Sharpe.

Gonzalez-Pinto, R., & Roman, M. (1998, November). *Digital citizens down the border: How they see the world now and in the future*. Paper presented at the National Communication Association Convention, New York.

Heitlinger, A. (1993). *Women's equality, demography, and public policies: A comparative perspective*. New York: St. Martin's Press.

Hopkinson, N. (1996). *Strengthening the media in the developing world and Eastern Europe*. London: HMSO.

Jia, W. (forthcoming). *Civic discourse and face in China*. Stamford, CT: Ablex.

Kapoor, P. (1998, July). *The future of the Internet in the Indian and South Asian women's movement*. Paper presented at the International Communication Association/National Communication Association Conference, Rome.

Kluver, R., & Powers, J. (1999). *Civic discourse, civil society, and Chinese communities*. Stamford, CT: Ablex.

Kraidy, M. (1996, November). *Glo/calization, new technologies and Lebanon*. Paper presented at the Speech Communication Association Convention, San Diego, CA.

Landweber, L. (1997, June 15). *International connectivity, version 16* [Online]. Available: lhl@cs.wisc.edu

Lengel, L. (1999, July). *Human rights in the New Europe: Communication technology, activism and agency in war-torn South-Eastern Europe*. Plenary lecture presented at the "Human Rights and Responsibilities: Communication Strategies among Nations and Peoples" Conference, Rochester NY.

Lengel, L., & Fedak, D. (forthcoming). The politicization of cybernetic discourse: Discourse conflict and the Internet in North Africa. In M. Prosser (Ed.), *Discourse and discourse conflict in Africa*. Stamford, CT: Ablex.

Loader, B. D. (Ed.). (1997). *The governance of cyberspace: Politics, technology and global restructuring*. London: Routledge.

Moffett, J. (1997, August 14). *Eastern Eruope: Internet—testing new technology* [Online]. Available: http://www.rferl.org/nca/features/1997/04/F.RU.970404192806.html

New Europe Group (1998a, January 5). *New Europe online, daily release no. 18* [Online]. <ne@new-europe.com> [1998, January 5].

New Europe Group (1998b, January 7). *Ukraine to streamline telecoms sector in 1998 (980107:19)*. *New Europe online, daily release no. 24, full version* [Online]. <ne@new-europe.com> [1998, January 7].

New Europe Group (1998c, January 8). *Bulgaria seals 33 privatisation deals in two days (980108:25)*. *New Europe online, daily release no. 25, full version* [Online]. <ne@new-europe.com> [1998, January 8].

Ognianova, E., & Scott, B. (1997). Milton's paradox: The market-place of ideas in post-Communist Bulgaria. *European Journal of Communication, 12*(3), 369–390.

Over, W. (1999). *Human rights in the international public sphere: Civic discourse for the 21st century*. Stamford, CT: Ablex.

Paletz, D., Jakubowicz, K., & Novosel, P. (1995). *Glasnost and after: Media and change in Central and Eastern Europe*. Creeskill, NJ: Hampton.

Perlez, J. (1998, January 1). Central Europe's new generation: Driven and smart. *New York Times*, Section C, p. 1.

Peter, L. (1998, October 25). *War of words on the Internet*. BBC News Online [Online]. Available: <http://news.bbc.co.uk/hi/english/world/monitoring/newsid_200000/200708.stm> [1999, March 10].

Prosser, M. (Ed.). (forthcoming). *Civic discourse and discourse conflict in Africa*. Stamford, CT: Ablex.

Radio Free Europe/Radio Liberty. (2000, February 11). *Homepage* [Online]. Available: <http:www.rferl.org> [2000, February 12].

Reeve, C. (1995, September 7). *Democracy through the information superhighway*. Paper presented at the "Shouts from the Street: Popular Culture, Creativity and Change" Conference, Manchester Metropolitan University, Manchester, England.

Reeves, P. (1998, March 6). "A good man to know if you're broke." *The Independent*, p. 3.

Richardson, D. (1995, March). *Community electronic networks: Sharing lessons learned in Canada with our African colleagues*. Paper presented at the MacBride Roundtable on Communication: Africa and the Information Highway, Tunis, Tunisia.

Rogers, S. (1999, March 27). Web witnesses put fresh spin on news. *The Guardian*, p. 6.

Sobchack, V. (1996). Democratic franchise and the electronic frontier. In Z. Sardar & J. Ravetz (Eds.), *Cyberfutures: Culture and politics on the information superhighway* (pp. 77–89). London: Pluto.

Tarajanne, P. J. (1990, April). Open framework for telecommunications in the 1990s: Access to networks and markets. *Telecommunications*.

Tesanovic, J. (1999, March 27). Still alive, looking every second at each other for proof. *The Guardian*, p. 1.

Uncapher, W. (1995, May). *A geodesic information infrastructure: Lessons from restructuring the Internet*. Paper presented at the International Communication Association Conference, Albuquerque, NM.

Woods, B. (1993). *Communication technology and the development of people*. London: Routledge.

Žižek, S. (1992). The malaise in liberal democracy. In M. Frankfurt (Ed.), *Heaven sent* (pp. 47–48). Ljubljana: DDU Univerzum.

Part I
Theoretical Foundations

chapter 1

Ferment and Transition in the New Europe: Intercultural Imperatives for a Europe in Transition

Priya Kapoor
Portland State University

C hange such as global conflict, political upheaval, education, employment, and travel are immediate motivators for theorizing culture and communication today. The extended ethnic conflict in Yugoslavia and the economic-political change in the former Soviet Union promise to modify the study of intercultural communication forever in Europe, the United States, and other parts of the modern Western world. However, the dominant theories of intercultural communication in the West continue to stress on issues of business and tourism and extrapolate resultant experiences to understand other vital issues such as race, class, and ethnic strife. So far these dominant theories of intercultural communication have not been able to account for the tremendous complexity regarding changing identity, political and religious affiliation, and nationality. Recent theories inspired by cultural studies have done a better job of articulating multiple identities, shifts in political terrain, and current technological innovation. The study of feminism and popular culture also opened up the field of culture and communication to critical and post-colonial thought and introduced the notion of power, political-economy, hegemony, and dominance. In this chapter, I will review some important aspects of intercultural communication as they first developed in U.S. academe and then were radically reflected by cultural studies scholars and feminist thinkers. I will later outline the role of the academy in supporting difference so as to facilitate a radical cultural understanding of the New Europe during a time of transition.

Thomas Nakayama and Judith Martin have tried to comprehensively evaluate the different theories of intercultural communication using as framework the Burrell and Morgan (1988) typology for assumptions about the nature of social science and society. This model differentiates between objective and subjective research, and the four paradigms—critical humanist, interpretive, critical structuralist, and functionalist. However, scholars (Gudykunst & Nishida, 1989; Martin & Nakayama, 1999) assert that the boundaries of these paradigms are porus and flexible. No one piece of research can establish the purity of one paradigm. The importance of this study is that it ushers an annihilation of boundaries between research studies that claim different traditions of social science research. Second, the Martin and Nakayama (1999) study proposes a dialectical approach to communication that accepts uncertainty and ambiguity as an acceptable trope of intercultural interaction. What follows from this brief overview of current trends in intercultural communication is a thematization of classical thought in the field.

STRANGER

A dominant and influential thought among theorists is that intercultural communication occurs between two parties that are eager to establish sameness of cultural ways, or better still, do business together. If sameness is not established, the powerful group will be able to label the other as stranger. A recent article in the journal *Communication Theory* by Everett Rogers (1999) has outlined the antecedents of the concept of stranger to Georg Simmel, a German theorist, and later traced the concept to its adoption in intercultural communication by William B. Gudykunst and Young Yun Kim (1984). Rogers's article does not analyze the importance of the notion of stranger in human interaction. The concept of stranger is important because dominant theories of intercultural communication still seem to describe and answer the question of what happens when two dissimilar parties meet. Within a limited context, such as while doing business or visiting the hospital, this may be a relevant question, but in a plural, globalized context where nationalities and identities are not neatly defined, this two-party model of communication may be insufficient.

Gudykunst and Kim (1984), in their study of Georg Simmel's work, provide a likely profile of a stranger. A stranger is one who lacks closeness to the host culture in a way that they remain outside of a situation. A stranger is usually from "a different place." There is no call for questioning the assumptions of the host culture that looks upon difference in values strangely. Gudykunst and Kim (1984) are of the belief that

> since we do not have information regarding individual strangers, our initial impression of them must, therefore, be an abstract or categoric one (i.e., a stereotypic one). Strangers are classified on the basis of whatever information we can obtain. If the only information we have is their culture, we base our initial impression on this information. If we have additional information (their race, ethnic group, sex, class, etc.), we use that as well. (p. 21)

This functionalist analysis of stranger puts the outsider in a position of powerlessness about the labels that can be used by the host to describe individual identity. This theory of stranger refuses to put aside the us–them binary opposition, nor does it acknowledge the contemporary critical theories of identity politics as articulated by authors such as bell hooks (1984) and Cornel West (1992).

French feminist writer Julia Kristeva (1991) examines the idea of stranger in Western thought. Kristeva does not simply see the stranger or foreigner as a person who is outside the established system, but rather, "strangely, the foreigner lives within us: he is the hidden face of our identity, the space that wrecks our abode, the time in which understanding and affinity founder" (p. 1). For Kristeva, the entry of a foreigner is time for self-reflection of one's values and closely held assumptions. She questions whether traditional hostilities toward foreigners among Western society can be erased simply by modernity.

> The violence of the problem set by the foreigner today is probably due to the crises undergone by religious and ethical constructs. This is especially so as the absorption of otherness proposed by our societies turns out to be unacceptable by the contemporary individual, jealous of his difference— one that is not only national and ethical but essentially subjective, unsurmountable [sic]. Stemming from the bourgeois revolution, nationalism has become a symptom—romantic at first, then totalitarian—of the nineteenth and twentieth centuries. (p. 2)

This articulation is almost prophetic of the current crises in East Central and South-Eastern Europe, primarily Yugoslavia and Kosovo, since it theorizes the nature and structure of intolerance, of difference and otherness in everyday life, and at the institutional level. Kristeva acknowledges the hegemony of the state that excludes the foreigner or stranger from established legal, judicial, and educational structures. The reasons for exclusion are nonrecognition of national, ethnic, and religious status other than the dominant one. Kristeva, then, becomes an advocate for the acceptance of a transnational status where identity is not stable. Identity, then, becomes a hybrid blend of experience in different locations and situations.

COMMONNESS

In order to escape a dichotomized model of intercultural interaction, Joseph J. Pilotta (1983) proposes a mediating term: commonness. According to Pilotta, intercultural communication is based upon establishing commonness. Pilotta (1983) advocates a "given world common to all" (p. 282). Pilotta is of the view that "having a common world means being able to be in communication with one another. Therefore in all conceivable cultures, there is something that is shared before all differences" (pp. 281–282). Here, the author presents a philosophy of conflict and acceptance that places faith in a human effort at coexistence. Feminists and critical theorists, however, have defined difference as a strategy of establishing identity in a fragmented, dominant culture, though Pilotta does not necessarily refer to that tradition of scholarship. Pilotta goes on to say that "the possibility of viewing the other world from his or her perspective widens our own horizons and is the evaluative criterion for successful intercultural communication. Intercultural communication is possible given the multitude of cultures or *world views* because the multitude of world views are nevertheless views of the same world" (p. 281). This articulation of intercultural communication espouses tolerance and open-mindedness without invoking the binary—same or stranger. This articulation does not limit difference to persons of different nationalities, but presupposes cultural difference as ethnic, political, racial, or gender based.

GLOBAL VILLAGE

Another influential metaphor in intercultural communication is the global village. Marshall McLuhan (McLuhan & Powers, 1989) first coined the term at a time when technological innovation and media growth changed the nature of almost all institutions in society from industry to family relations. At a basic level, global village, a utopian term, suggests an ideal scenario of gaining community through technological access, assuming that all humanity is equal. McLuhan envisions a brave new world where the sheer speed of communication will overshadow personal identity. His co-author and he say, "All persons, whether or not they understand the process of computerized high-speed data transmission, will lose their old private identities. What knowledge there is will be available to all. So in that sense, everybody will be nobody...the more information one has to evaluate, the less one knows. Specialism cannot exist at the speed of light" (p. 129). His notion of identity departs from the cultural studies articulation of identity as evolving, multiple, and politically alive rather than as a static concept about self.

McLuhan and Powers (1989) envision a theory of unity with technology as a medium that defies the skepticism about national unity of modern-day political scientists. McLuhan opines, "the national unity which Canadians sought by the railway 'hardware' now proves to be irrelevant under electronic conditions which yet create an inclusive consciousness" (p. 166). This statement differs from Benedict Anderson's (1991) notion of imagined communities, since Anderson's analysis is based upon a questioning of contemporary nationalism(s), whereas McLuhan and Powers assume a cohesive unity that comes automatically from adopting a national boundary and citzenship. The above quoted sentence from McLuhan and Powers betrays the belief too that technology can order our universe and create a problem-free reality that allows us an escape from the divisiveness of everyday life. McLuhan and Powers here do not display a strong connection between the economic, social, and political structures of everyday life and the world of technology. Despite the obvious assumption of an ideal, unified world, this metaphor that seems to suggest that our world is a village has fired the imagination of many a thinker and writer. Artists, architects, media practitioners, technocrats, and visionaries have used this term as a catch-all phrase to describe the reach and scope of their work. Most advocate the development of a global consciousness where cooperation and compassion are the order of the day.

Global village as an ideal concept has given way to several utopian and futuristic writings envisioning a society bound by a similar purpose, ideology, and ethics. Here, most solutions to human problematics are technologically based. Cook (1990) even proposes reversible vasectomies for all male children in order to control population growth and preserve the environment. Cook imagines a problem-free world with no nuclear weapons, world solidarity, finally resulting in the formation of a world government. What may seem like naivete about difference seems to have served a creative function in visualizing a humanistic role for emerging technologies.

Within the U.S. academy, metaphors such as melting pot, tossed salad, tributary, and tapestry served to consolidate the imagery associated with global village. The message of these metaphors is that assimilation into a dominant culture is desirable and easy. Scholars see a predominance of these metaphors as an effort to erase the rigorous study of difference. It is important to emphasize the importance of context. Most studies of intercultural communication pedagogy are located in the United States. This field's applicability and appropriateness in a situation that is gravely affected by ethnic and economic battle is unmistakable. In such case, context is an appropriate reason for modification and adaptation. Use of intercultural knowledge in a transitional Europe, for instance, requires the requestioning of the role of the intellectual and the academy, and how they can serve the cause of a viable democratic society.

WAR IN THE NEW EUROPE/WAR IN THE GLOBAL VILLAGE

Modern war seems to occur between two parties and ends up involving the whole world. This shows our economic, military, and political connectedness and not unfortunately ideological, moral, and ethical connectedness. At this point I would like to present a brief critique of Yugoslavian director Emir Kusturica's 1995 Cannes prize-winning film *Underground*. The film depicts chaos, will to power, and betrayal in a land that goes through rough times—World War II, fascism, and then ethnic strife and genocide. The film is a brilliant allegorical tale of modern Yugoslavian history. What may seem like a web of stormy relationships between the central characters—Blacky, Marko, and Natalijia—is really the story of intrigue, deceipt, and guile used by one friend against another to first win over his girlfriend (Natalijia), and later seize control of the politics of the country. Blacky and Marko's tactics seem to resemble the authoritarian and criminalized politics of Slobodan Milosevic and Radko Mladic.

The war scenes in the film take on a realistic aura with a closing commentary that goes something like this: "A war is not a war unless a brother kills a brother." In this instance, Kusterica comments directly on the breakdown of human morality and familial connection during conflict: a time when the social fabric is too weak to provide succor and redress to its communities. The last scene, however, is of friends and family reunited during a marriage party when the piece of land they rejoice on breaks from the mainland and floats away. This powerful image of fragmentation and unity leaves the audience without a sense of closure and finality. Not only is this film an allegory for Yugoslavia, but it carries an allegorical message for most modern, multicultural societies that face conflict today. The allegory can certainly be extended to the Chechnya crisis in Russia or the Taliban insurgency in Afghanistan.

Authoritarian principles of global unity can only serve to suppress local particularities that are constantly vying for attention.

DIFFERENCE IN CULTURAL STUDIES AND FEMINISM: CONTRIBUTION TO CRITICAL PEDAGOGY IN INTERCULTURAL COMMUNICATION FOR A EUROPE IN TRANSITION

The role of the academy at a time of social, economic, and political change is to recognize *difference* at every level. Cultural studies and its commitment to radical, critical intervention has created a special space for dialogue on *difference*, or its more popular form, *politics of difference*. Politics of difference debates within cultural studies emerged in recognition of the importance of critical dialogues between spheres of existence that had scarce prior interaction. The middle and latter part of the 20th century has seen major upheavals: such as dissolution of imperial and colonial power in parts of Asia, Africa, and South America. Also, the successes of feminist organization globally have almost forced recognition of issues concerning culture(s), race(s), and feminism(s) upon the field of culture and communication. As an outcome, dominant (specifically white male, imperialistic) discourses were urged to reevaluate their applicability, dominance, and relevance in an ever-evolving, pluralistic, polyphonic academic world. The oppressed (read: feminine, ravaged by war) can no longer be relegated to a position of *otherness* in relation to the valorized, masculine self. The absence of voices of women and minorities now refuse to conform to the *culture of silence* that had muted the stories of their lives for centuries. I present *difference* as an evolving term and concept, used in current literature to identify those who oppose dominant ideologies presumed upon the cohesivity and homogeneity of the modern West.

As a concept, difference in the past has rarely been used as a tool of creativity to question multiple and ongoing forms of repression and dominance. Rather, difference has been used as a tool of segregation, to exert power on the basis of racial and sexual essences. A difference that divides not unites sunders, not mends.

Gender, class, and race are formulated as *sites of difference* in contemporary theory. After Foucault's articulations on power, these categories must be seen as *sites of power*. These particular categorizations, which are so politically laden, have been accompanied in history by brutality, control, and lynchings of the powerful against the oppressed. Gayatri C. Spivak (1990) writes that third worldism as a phenomenon is willingly appropriated by Western academe. If you are poor, black, and female, you get it three ways, reminds Spivak. It may be interesting to see how these categories of race, nationality, and ethnicity reconfigure themselves with the balkanization of Eastern Europe.

Being part of a university, as a student and teacher, I am aware of the incredible diversity that a school of learning attracts. Minority and women students are learning and writing from the margins as they aspire to enter into the symbolic (dominant) order of the university. Marginality, with respect to the dominant center, has given minorities a vantage point to critique racist, sexist, and classist hegemony and also to visualize and create a counter-hegemony (hooks, 1984). By recognizing the order of things, we affect a dislocation of power, and enable student writers and scholars to (re)invent themselves, to inscribe *difference* inside academia. Difference in our lives cannot be simply celebrated, but rigorously thought through so that we fully realize what living with difference actually involves.

For a transitional Europe, the *imperative* for an aware pedagogy in culture, conflict, and communication is to study and/or recognize *difference* or multiculturalism in order to scrutinize race, gender, and class as constructs that are political and not naturally occurring. In this way, multiculturalism can become an effort to overturn the chronic tendency in academics to deny, suppress, or distort the cultural systems of thought, now considered to be in the minority, or marginal, in order to maintain the "fiction of scholarly disinterest" (Said, 1978/1994, p. 325). As in *Orientalism*, I suggest as imperative for the European institutions of socialization and higher learning, to raise a set of questions that are relevant in discussing openly the problems of human experience: "How does one represent another culture? Is the notion of a distinct culture (or race, or religion, or civilization) a useful one, (when one discusses one's own) or hostility and aggression (when one discusses the *other*)? Do cultural, religious, and racial differences matter more than socio-economic categories or politicohistorical ones?" (Said, 1978/1994, p. 325).

REFERENCES

Anderson, B. (1991). *Imagined communities: Reflections on the origin and spread of nationalism*. London: Verso.

Burrell, G., & Morgan, G. (1988). *Sociological paradigms and organizational analysis*. Portsmouth, NH: Heinemann.

Cook, S. P. (1990). *Coming of age in the global village*. Russellville, AR: Parthenon Books.

Gudykunst, W. B., & Kim, Y. Y. (1984). *Communicating with strangers: An approach to intercultural communication*. New York: McGraw-Hill.

Gudykunst, W. B., & Nishida, T. (1989). Theoretical perspectives for studying intercultural communication. In M. F. Asante & W. B. Gudykunst (Eds.), *Handbook of international and intercultural communciation* (pp.17–46). Newbury Park, CA: Sage.

hooks, b. (1984). *Feminist theory: From margin to center.* Boston, MA: South End Press.

Kristeva, J. (1991). *Strangers to ourselves* (L. S. Roudiez, Trans.). New York: Columbia University Press.

Kusturica, E. (Director). (1995). *Underground* [Film].

Martin, J., & Nakayama, T. K. (1999). Thinking dialectically about culture and communication. *Communication Theory, 9*(1), 1–25.

McLuhan, M., & Powers, B. R. (1989). *The global village: Transformations in world life and media in the 21st century.* Oxford and New York: Oxford University Press.

Pilotta, J. J. (1983). The phenomenological approach. In W. B. Gudykunst (Ed.), *Intercultural communication theory* (pp. 253–258). Beverly Hills, CA: Sage.

Rogers, E. (1999). Georg Simmel's concept of the stranger and intercultural communication research. *Communication Theory, 9*(1), 58–74.

Said, E. (1994). *Orientalism.* New York: Vintage Books. (Original work published 1978)

Spivak, G. C. (1990). *Post-colonial critic: Interviews, strategies, dialogues.* London: Routledge.

West, C. (1992). The post-modern crisis of black intellectuals. In L. Grossberg, C. Nelson, & P. A. Treichler (Eds.), *Cultural studies* (pp.689–705). New York: Routledge.

chapter 2

Economic, Sociocultural, and Technological Contexts in the New Europe

Anna Lubecka
Jagiellonian University, Krakow, Poland

CHALLENGES FOR POST-COMMUNIST
NATIONS IN TRANSFORMATION

S ince the fall of Communism, the countries of the New Europe have been faced with the challenging task to define their new politico-economic status and their sociocultural identity. Many changes that are visible nowadays have been intentional choices; others, often unconscious, have resulted from the necessity to adjust to and to follow the worldwide phenomena of globalization, technicization, and customization. Both positive and negative outcomes of these changes mark various domains of social and private life and make individuals and institutions look for solutions to previously unknown problems or treat issues already existing in a new way. The costs—economic, social and psychological—the East- and Central-Europeans pay in the process of transition are high, making some of them long for the past. Although most of them looked forward to the fall of the restrictive Communist political regime and the inefficient economic system, and greeted the changes enthusiastically when they happened, at present they find the economic reality too hard and too threatening to cope with. The result is, for many people facing totally alien situations, to often function as 'domestic strangers' in the transformed context.

Most of the changes that are either direct results or byproducts of the switch to the free-market economy have been experienced by Western societies, as these phenomena are inherent to this socioeconomic formation. The developed countries have not been free from their negative impact (for example, unemployment due to new technologies) although many would argue that the impact is, however, smaller and less acute. The pressure to have all the changes implemented is very strong and the standards to meet are Western standards, which rarely consider the culture-specific differences between the West and the New Europe. An important difference is the time factor. Unlike West-Europeans and Americans, people in this part of the world do not have the luxury of several generations in the race to catch up with economic and political world powers and to become their partners. The position of East- and Central-Europeans is also less advantageous when it comes to the use of modern technologies, especially in communication, where access to information and the speed with which it is sent and received often determines political and economic success or failure. Both economic, technological, and time factors limit the number of research projects and assistance programs to help people overcome the "transformation" problems. It is also apparent that many programs successful in the West do not apply to the same extent in the post-Communist cultures and societies when directly transferred without necessary adaptations. It is often felt that only a limited number of the foreign aid programs are really useful, while their majority is overly simplistic and fails to produce valuable effects, despite being very costly.

Efforts to implement economic changes are paralleled by efforts to transform the post-Communist societies into modern democracies. This is the most challenging and the most difficult task as East- and Central-Europeans have none or very limited experience in building democracy in modern times. Moreover, a switch from a totalitarian to a democratic system involves deep changes in systems of values, of attitudes, and of life philosophy on both a public and a private level.

HISTORICAL SOURCES THAT IMPACT THE LACK OF CONTEMPORARY CIVIC DISCOURSE

It is important to stress the fact that most post-Communist countries have rather quickly embraced the free market economy, have managed to successfully hold free elections, and have created modern and liberal constitutions. However, these successes are not paralleled by a successful civic discourse between citizens and governments, which will give impetus to a democratic consolidation of the whole country. The reason is that there is a very poor tradition of civic discourse in this part of the world because of politico-historical factors. They are possible to understand only by looking back at the history, both the most recent and more distant, of the East- and Central European nations (compare Linz & Stepan, 1996).

The turbulent history of Poland, for example, shows how the impact of the events that happened as long as 200 years ago is still felt in modern times. When in 1792 Austria, Russia, and Prussia partitioned Poland among themselves, and the country stopped existing as an independent country for nearly 200 years, citizens' virtues were endangered. Although the situation was similar in each partition, these were the Russians who enforced passivity because under their rule "Poles had no chance whatsoever of political self-organization and very limited activity for economic activity" (Janowski, 1997, p. 119).

The recent history of Central and Eastern Europe is marked by the legacy of Communism and people's perceptions of society and of social duties and roles. Andrzej Korboński (1995, pp. 143–144) writes that the "Poland in the 1970s and 1980s was characterized by the predominance of private values and virtues at the expense of public ones." He argues "This was a reaction to Stalinism...which two decades earlier had managed effectively to destroy and atomize the public sphere." In his attempt to define the Polish society after 1989, Janowski (1997, p. 122) claims that the Polish people still see the society divided into "we ordinary, decent people" and "them, people in power."

Presumably all the factors that influence the present state of democracy in Poland can also be applied to most post-Communist countries. In Russia, for example, the tradition of civic discourse is very weak. Westernized under Peter the Great, Russia became politically strong, but its strength resulted in an even bigger despotism of the ruler than ever before. Similarly, political pluralism was nonexistent under such autocratic emperors as Catherine II and Alexander I. The recent history of Russia and of the countries created after the fall of the Soviet Union has been marked by nepotism and an anti-democratic legacy of Communism. Although democratic principles are claimed to be at the basis of the countries' administrative structure and the governments' decisions, it can be argued that the old *nomenklatura* is still in power. Political and economic reforms serve the ex-Communist elite, now transformed into what can be called a "mafiocracy" or a "kleptocracy," to benefit from new economic opportunities for their own interests. The authoritarian, political post-Communist system keeps continuing its totalitarian character: not much has really changed as most civil liberties continue to be disrespected, the civil society feels weak, and, consequently, the development of democracy shows a serious deficiency.

It is interesting to notice that Gorbachev's idea to create "a common European house," earlier expressed by Jelcyn as his strong hope that Russia would become "a normal country," a democratic and economic partner for the developed countries of the Group of Seven, was strongly criticized by Russian nationalists and their leader Stankievicz (Huntington, 1988, p. 201). What is a natural consequence of a lack of a democratic foundation of the nation is the citizens' poor awareness of the need for legal order, and their conviction that the legal system is not for the whole nation and that an average person should learn how to bypass the law. The process of democratization in the whole ex-Communist bloc is hindered by private interests, passivity, lack of experience in self-organization, a very limited opportunity for economic activity, and even less experience in self-government, in political activity and in citizenship, which develops public virtues to work for the common wealth of a civic society.

An alienation toward public life results, to a big extent, from the type of education received in schools. Teaching curricula, which are inherited from the past, do not prepare for an active participation in the politico-economic and social life of the country. In Poland, for example, the educational system is in a painful process of change as the old-type schools offer neither instructional materials on democracy and market economics nor teachers who can teach self-government. Since many teachers themselves are often products of indoctrination and a tool of political selection for the Communist regime, they tend to have very little understanding of the implications of a civic discourse for education. This situation is not only typical of Polish schools, but of all schools where a Russian type of authoritarian and politicized pedagogy was used. Thus, a comprehensive civic education reform is one of the most challenging and urgent projects. Civic education began in Poland in 1994 with the project of Education for Democratic Citizenship in Poland (EDCP). Since 1995, the project has been realized with the help of the Ohio State University's Mershon Center, within the program of Civitas: An International Civic Education Exchange Program. The Czech Republic serves as another example of a country that gives much importance to civic virtues in the process of building a new society. The Czech educators, in cooperation with the University of Iowa, work on ways to increase democratic awareness among Czech students. Also worthy of mention is the initiative to make Russian teachers a part of a preservice teacher education course entitled "The School in a Democratic Society." It is supported by funding from the Soros Foundation, which allows for some parts of the course to be translated into Russian.

The newly empowered local governments show much interest in creating citizens who value and understand democracy, its privileges and duties, and who, because of participatory competencies, help bring in reforms. Media provide significant support to create a new awareness of acting "civis." Although most programs given to a discussion of crucial social issues, for example, the television series *Young People Vote*, *Civis Polonus*, *The River Speaks*, which are directed at school-age children, reach a much bigger public (Remy & Strzemieczny, 1997). The program *Civis Polonus* is an interesting form of international cooperation, as its participants are teachers and students from 16 Polish schools, seven Lithuanian schools, and two American schools. Communication is possible because of the use of modern technologies: through e-mail and a web site. Modern technologies play a very important role not only in promoting economic and technical progress, which is obvious, but also in accelerating the processes of democratization. Various democratic issues become less abstract notions as they can be discussed and experienced on a personal level. This communication paradigm corresponds to the preferred communication scripts of East- and Central-Europeans. Moreover, a personal touch is very important for two reasons: it validates the information received and it teaches an active and responsible participation in change, which is one of the skills to learn in East and Central Europe.

The River Speaks is a program that touches upon the global dimensions of civic issues. Considering the multicultural, multiethnic, and multinational nature of all contacts across the world, it is not enough to approach democracy merely from a local perspective. This is a new experience for East- and Central-Europeans, who, as members of a global society, have already been forced to start the process of becoming carriers of multiple identities and users of transcultural competencies. The second reason why programs that teach a global aspect of democratization are important are internal changes within each post-Communist country: the role and the duties of each state toward its citizens have undergone significant changes and so have supranational institutions, which are meant to function as guardians of citizens' rights and obligations.

It should be stressed that in the age of globalization, democracy is no longer an issue of any one country. The question that all countries aspiring to democracy have to ask, but that is especially important for emerging democracies, concerns the concept of *civic discourse on an international, global scale*. Three Eastern- and Central-European countries have joined NATO and they will eventually become members in the European Union (following the prognostics, some countries from the first wave of applicants, which are the Czech Republic, Estonia, Hungary, Poland, and Slovenia, might become members by the year 2006).

Economic and technological inclusion of East- and Central-European countries is linked with the global diffusion of Western values. How will this fact impinge on an understanding of democracy? What will it mean for an average Czech, Estonian, Hungarian, Pole, or Slovenian? How will global citizenship influence his/her local citizenship? Which local values will be spared and which ones will be replaced in the process of an inevitable homogenization in most spheres of life? How will new democracies in often newly constituted countries (such as the Czech Republic, Ukraine, Lithuania, and others in the region) build their national identity, preserve their cultural heritage, and participate in the global future? Will global democracy give local communities the right to decide in matters that affect them or will the "democracy" be only for those who can support it by economic means? These and many other issues, for the moment left unsolved, are the worries of the ex-Communist countries. Their rich cultural heritage and a very distinct cultural identity give them strength and are their greatest values, which they are afraid of losing. This may explain the fact why nationalistic movements grow on popularity in post-Communist countries. Nationalism is often prompted by the use, or rather misuse, of many pre-Communist period's national symbols that were revived to strengthen national identity and remind them of its roots by cutting off from the totalitarian past (for example, the eagle on the Polish national emblem got back the crown of which it was deprived by the Communist regime). Many young democracies say "yes" to modernization but "no" to Westernization.

ECONOMIC FACTORS, TECHNOLOGY, AND CIVIC DISCOURSE

The civic inertia of an average citizen, which replaced his/her strong will to participate in the process of building civic societies observed in the years immediately after the defeat of the Communist regime, can be explained by an economic situation. Economic hardships have had the most powerful effect on all the spheres of social and individual life. The most conspicuous and portent result of these difficulties in the ex-Soviet bloc countries is the development of social stratification, or rather polarization, into the minority who has and the majority who has not. The gap between the salaries in private and the state-owned sectors—public schools, health care, and administration—is immense, to the disadvantage of the latter. Despite the fact that having two or three jobs tends to negatively affect the quality of performance, most of the state-sector workers seek desperately for alternative sources of income, for example, tutorials often undeclared to tax offices. With the social policy of the state less well developed, as was true under Communism, household budgets are not big enough to cover even basic expenses. For example, nearly 50 percent of the people in Poland live at or below the minimum living wage, even though Poland is considered one of the most economically privileged Central-European countries, the other three being Slovenia, the Czech Republic, and Hungary. Moreover, it is Poland where the prognosis about the dynamics of further reforms seem to be the most optimistic in the whole ex-Soviet bloc ("Czwarta potęga swiata," 1998). An economic instability of the majority makes people feel cheated by leaders, politically indifferent, and too tired with everyday problems to get involved in public matters and to develop citizens' virtues.

The economic change is so difficult to accept, as under Communism the division was of a political origin, independent of personal skills and talents of individuals. All the decent people formed one classless and equally poor group. The social divide was clear: a poor underground elite, usually in the political opposition to the government, which, even added to its elitist character, and the official elite (bourgeoisie rouge), wealthy but despised by the nation. Now the dividing line between the rich and the poor is not political but based on free-market mechanisms. A new thing for ex-Soviet bloc people is that they themselves are responsible for their life and their position in the social hierarchy. Many are not able to take this challenge, and social gaps become more and more visible and more and more difficult to cross.

More and more often, economics functions as an inclusion or exclusion factor of participation in all forms of social life. Thus, the social groups that suffer from unemployment are automatically marginalized and their access to intellectual and economic goods is partly or totally denied. It is too early to speak about their ghetoization but economic ghetoization, whose many examples can be found in the free-market economy countries, with its all sociopsychological consequences, is a real threat. Although Manual Castells analyzes Western societies, his observations sound very true when applied to the post-Communist societies in transition. He claims that "our societies are increasingly structured around a bipolar opposition between the Net and the Self" (1996, p. 3). These are the new technologies that play an essential role in creating global networks of wealth and power, which can "selectively switch on and off individuals, groups, regions and even countries according to their relevance in fulfilling instrumental goals" (p. 3).

It is obvious that the position of post-Communist countries is less advantageous than that of the established Western powers. The rate of psychological breakdowns, suicides, and divorces due to loss of work and to economic instability is significant in this respect. The sociopsychological impact of unemployment, for example, is twice as difficult for East- and Central-Europeans as for Westerns for the simple reason that it is a totally new phenomenon for East- and Central-Europeans. People do not know how to cope with unemployment, as in the past they were used to having a job for a lifetime and to being protected by the social policy of the state. The unemployed tend to picture themselves as failures, unfit to meet new challenges, or of social roles, which are still perceived as important, especially among older people throughout the entire ex-Communist bloc. Many men, traditionally breadwinners, find it shameful to admit in public that they are jobless and they do not register for unemployment benefits or retraining. The figures are even less indicative for women who register in work centers less often than men. Even so, their number exceeds the number of unemployed men. The worst situation exists in rural and industrially underprivileged districts, where collective farms gave work to many people. For most of the economically underprivileged people, civic discourse is an empty term, a luxury that they cannot afford now as they must fight for survival. Notice that nearly all the strikes in the post-Communist countries are undertaken to improve economic conditions, not to fight for civic rights.

The processes of privatization and of developing new technologies, when taken together with the free market rules of supply and demand, play an important role in shaping the scope of unemployment and the sectors where it is the most strongly felt. New technologies have a double impact on the process: on the one hand, they significantly reduce the number of work posts, on the other, they offer new opportunities, as computerization of all domains of life has become a *sine non qua* condition of progress and of economic growth. Many young, technologically astute people that are independent, adventurous, and full of entrepreneurial spirit and initiative open their own businesses. The free-market reality has much to offer to them and they take the opportunities with both hands. They learn the difficult lesson on how to be assertive, make the best of the skills and abilities they possess, take responsibility for their own future, and make sensible choices and decisions. Competitiveness, drive, "workaholism," perfectionism, work ethics, an acute sense of ownership, and so on, are slowly becoming the values of East- and Central-European "yuppies," although these values are not traditional values of their mother cultures.

Careers of people in private, computer-based businesses illustrate the process of ideational changes prompted by a strong need to achieve professional success in the economic niche, which suddenly opened up on the market. Bulgaria is an example of this economic phenomenon.

Since in the past the Soviet technology initiatives were housed there and students had good access to computer technology, at present, many young people could develop their own hardware and software businesses. Internet service is also widely spread and the number of its users and providers increases every month. Even for many East- and Central-Europeans, communication without e-mail seems to be impossible.

However, many working in the Internet service providers (ISPs) and other technology-based businesses work illegally. They have gone underground from where they provide their services, for example, tapping into the official ISPs to double on accounts or tapping into others' telephone lines. At this stage of "computer culture," "phreakers," "hackers," and "crackers" have gotten the status of heroes, who are admired mainly because of the practical value of their skills. Moreover, it has to be remembered that, in Poland, for example, breaking into a computer system or producing systems with 'viruses' is qualified as a criminal act only according to the new legal code. Compared with the U.S., the punishment is very mild in Poland (from three months to five years in prison).

Another controversial issue is the protection of authors' rights and of intellectual property. Illegal studios tend to produce thousands of CDs, tapes, and videos. Illegally copied computer programs and software can be purchased on the black market at very attractive prices. The computer "black market" promotes new technologies by making them available to a wide public, especially youngsters, who otherwise, considering the prices of legally offered goods, would not be able to afford them. Not only the existence itself of the "black market" but also its prosperity can be explained by the fact that the new technology and its products have gained the function of new status symbols in post-Communist countries. This is particularly true now that the economic abundance of goods and services available on the market has stimulated consumption appetites. Identification through objects is a common practice of all consumption cultures and economic constraints limit the number of those who can participate in the process of this kind of a symbolical identity formation.

It can be argued that the economy-motivated, unequal access to modern technologies adds to the factors that create a significant gap between differences in socioeconomic status. It not only strengthens the already-existing *big power distance* in the post-Communist countries, but enhances it as well. Since modern technologies serve as an instrument of control, it can be observed that the polarization of societies gets bigger and bigger. The chance to use the Internet opens up thousands of new opportunities to become an active part of the global society (through such Internet services as IRC, interactive web sites, and e-mail). The Internet can be a real link with the world, which also promotes a development of civic discourse by raising a new kind of global awareness. For many East- and Central-Europeans, Internet replaces a direct experience of the West that, under the Communist regime, appeared as a mythical, promised land, a symbol of civic virtues, and a warranty to have them implemented in the New Europe. When the West became within immediate reach, it looks more real, although less glittering and tempting than before.

New technologies are a great chance, especially in the communities lower down on the sociocultural and economic hierarchies. Those who can benefit from new technologies get better education, knowledge, and understanding of worldwide and local issues. However, new technologies can also be used to the detriment of poorer social groups if they play the role of selection factor, an instrument of inclusion and exclusion. As discussed earlier, there are these who have access to information and to the world and those who are deprived of it, with all the sociocultural and politico-economic consequences of such a divide. The so-called "electronic democracy" is in fact another example of an economic marginalization of some social groups.

Within this context, the black market offers an interesting alternative to the official trade centers. It becomes a buffer, whose role is to reduce the real and perceived power distance based on economic inequality. It is more so that most customers find nothing improper in the black-market practices. The point is that the notion of intellectual property is very vague for most East-and Central-Europeans. For many of them, breaking either authors' rights or intellectual property rights does not qualify as a crime. Moreover, in many countries, there are no legal measures to regulate these spheres of activities. The two examples clearly show that the development and use of modern technologies must be assisted by a development of proper legal regulations in order not to hinder the growth of democratic societies in the aggressive race for economic growth.

CIVIC DISCOURSE AND CULTURAL REALITY IN TRANSITION

Living in the period of post-Communist transition is very complex and controversial because the system of values, norms, and culture-specific paradigms is in a process of constant flux. Two or even three value systems coexist, making East- and Central-Europeans feel insecure, vulnerable, and confused. The culture in the period of transition is an amalgam of three distinct, culture-specific influences (compare Lubecka, 1995): national cultures, culture of imposition, and culture of adoption.

First, *national cultures*, which are at the heart of each culture and which make each culture a unique entity, distinct from any other culture. National, culture-specific values helped to preserve national identity throughout history (compare the bloody events in 1956 in Hungary, the underground opposition in Poland in the years before 1989, and the dissidents' movement in all ex-Soviet bloc countries) by teaching citizens' virtues that consist of putting public matters before private interests (as a great Polish poet says "country is a common duty") (Nowicki, 1995). These were the national values that placed the protection of civic rights at the heart of the discussions about the future democracies. Second, the culture imposed during the years of the Communist regime, the so-called *culture of imposition,* endangered the national culture values by promoting disrespect for authority and private property, lack of work ethos, and existence of a double ethics, one for the official use in accordance with the party ideology, and another stemming from purely human values. Third is the most recent trend, the culture of the Western world, for which I suggest the name of *culture of adoption.* Its attractiveness, mainly economic, made East- and Central-Europeans, especially in the years immediately after the fall of Communism, strive for an uncritical identification with the values of the West, often very superficial, commercial, and totally opposed to respective national cultures.

The natural consequence of the clash between the Western and the East- and Central-European cultural paradigms was an ideational conflict and a feeling of inferiority. Germany is a good example of how confrontational the unification can be. Even now, nearly 10 years after the fall of the Berlin Wall, many frictions and conflict-engendering demands of culture-specific origin between the East and the West Germans can still be observed. On the other hand, a slow process of indigenization of culture can also be observed (Dore, 1995). This process consists of a switch toward the mother culture and the values it engenders, which happens when the country progresses economically.

The young democracies in Eastern and Central Europe are challenged not only by the necessity to define their identity in relation to the West, but also to delineate their policy to many minorities that either emerged in the process of state formation or started voicing their presence. One of the major tasks consists of an opening to any kind of diversity, be it ethnic, gender, religious, racial, and so on. A burning issue is to create proper conditions that will enable a civic discourse among all different groups whose existence becomes more and more conspicuous but which, because of being different, feel endangered, especially by growing nationalistic movements, in their civic rights. It is right to say that the citizens' liberties of ethnic minorities test the value of democracy.

None of the post-Communist countries is ethnically homogeneous and ethnicity has existed as an important sociopolitical and cultural issue since the end of World War II, which resulted in a shift of borders. Consequently, some ethnic groups became nearly automatically excluded from the new territory of their previous country, while others were included in it (for example, changes in the territory of Poland). Formation of new states after the fall of the Soviet Union gave a new political value to ethnic minorities whose support is sought by political party leaders in their race for power. In the Ukraine, for example, playing on the electoral power of the minority voters, the policy of some parties resembles the 'carrot and stick' game, which may often generate hostility toward the ethnic group temporarily privileged. This concern is also evident in the situation of the Polish minority in the Ukraine or in Lithuania, which feels endangered in their rights to cultivate Polish language, culture, and history.

Despite a worldwide crisis of religion, Catholicism, Protestantism, and Orthodox religions have strengthened their position in this part of the world. Church played the role of a political power opposed to the Communist oppressor and of a moral support to the opposition. Its depolitization has become a controversial issue after the fall of Communism. Although there are no longer conditions for it to play the role of a political and moral leader (especially in Poland), its influence on human life is still immense and religion belongs to the top values. A revival of the Orthodox Church in the European part of the former Soviet Union and of Islam in its Asian republics is an interesting sociopolitical phenomenon that can be explained by three correlated processes. First, the fall of the Communist ideology left thousands of people in an ideational void and made them face identity crisis, which could be overcome by looking for cultural roots. Orthodox religion, along with Islam, is a very powerful identity link between the present and the past of Russia. Second, restoration of the traditional religion is possible only because of the development of democracy (Huntington, 1988). Third, nationalism finds its strength and social acceptance by means of returning to the religion that was a part of the pre-Communist past. Eagerly accepted not only by East- and Central-Europeans, religion becomes a new desecularized ideology.

Coexistence of different religions within each of the Central- and Eastern-European countries reflects how successful the civic discourse is among its multiethnic inhabitants. In Poland, for example, where Catholicism is a dominating religion, ethnic minorities of Germans, Ukrainians, Tartars, Jews, Karaims, and so on, can practice their religion freely and this fact does not cause any social tensions. On the other hand, the political opening of this part of the world has also resulted in an unprecedented activity of many religious sects and churches, such as the Bahai, Krishna, and Bodiharma. If in the first years of the 'crusades' to the 'virgin land' they gained social approval or at least indifference, now most people are against their practices, which, in some extreme cases, threaten even the life of their followers, such as the case of the Sect of Heaven. In many cases, religion has become again a controversial issue, although in another sense than in the past.

NEW MINORITIES IN THE NEW EUROPE

All the operating sociocultural changes within the New Europe are generated and sped up by a proliferation of new minorities. Some of them have always existed, but now they want to be heard and they look for a place within the social structures. Women, handicapped people, and gays and lesbians, to mention the most active to fight for their rights, challenge the sense of tolerance of Central- and East-Europeans.

In the common opinion, East- and Central-European women seem to be enemies of themselves in their fight for equality. Feminism is not popular in this part of the world where a rather strict division of social roles assigned on the basis of gender differences is questioned neither by women nor by men. The social perception of women is, first of all, mothers and housewives, whose vocation is to bear children and to create a happy family. This is also their self-image; they do not seem to want to change, although women are discriminated at work and the concept of a *glass ceiling* applies to them in the free-market reality—they get smaller salaries for the same work and lose in the race for top jobs. Their chances to be employed when they are after 40 years of age are very small. How can this inertia be explained? Under Communism, women had access to all professions, as professional equality was the policy of the system. They were even encouraged to become miners, crane operators, and builders, and to challenge men in their jobs. Currently, nearly all women are professionally active and additionally they have to fulfill their family duties. Considering social and economic factors, women have neither experience nor time to fight for rights that they have suddenly lost.

One of the burning issues is the situation of another minority: the handicapped. A visitor to the New Europe could mistakenly believe that this group does not exist. They are invisible in streets, schools, universities, offices, and so on, unless they appear as distinct groups with nurses and volunteers. There are hardly any facilities to make them a part of the mainstream society and to lessen the painful feeling of being ghetoized. This state of affairs is not only because of economic problems, but also because their voice is neither heard nor listened to. Despite some slow improvements (some buildings have access ramps, a very small number of flats are adopted to the needs of the handicapped), society does not seem to be ready to cope with this type of diversity, which is the most difficult barrier to overcome.

Gays and lesbians' concerns are still a taboo topic. They do not manifest their difference as openly and even aggressively as in the West because social pressure and a negative judgment are very strong; an innocent act of buying their newspaper from a kiosk engenders at least suspicion, not to say hostility and moral contempt. A very powerful stereotype presents homosexuals as HIV-positive, lazy, and immoral drug addicts. The two worlds of homosexuals and of heterosexuals avoid getting in touch with one another: different clubs, bars, socializing events, press, books, and so on, keep them apart. They have their own pages on the Internet that help them to exchange various information and to create the feeling of togetherness within their own circles. This is also a means to offer an alternative image, more positive than the commonly accepted one about the social "outsiders," the different ones.

Ethnicity- and race-related problems existed before, but they used to be treated as internal problems of a given country. Now many of them are still limited to individual countries and are the matter of internal policy, but others have an international impact. The Hungarian minority in Romania, for example, wants to come back to Hungary. In Poland, after the recent changes in the ownership law, many Germans are interested in buying farms in the Upper Silesia region. This resulted in a defensive reaction of Polish people who are afraid of becoming a minority there. Jewish concerns are still unsettled and raise controversies, such as the vehement protest of the Jews, who oppose the idea that a cross, a symbol of the Catholic religion, should be put at the entrance to the Auschwitz concentration camp to commemorate the martyrdom of all prisoners.

An unprecedented mobility,[1] coupled with economic differences among the ex-Communist countries, especially the underprivileged situation of the former Soviet republics and of Romania, have resulted in many ethnic conflicts, which affect interpersonal relations by strengthening an ethnocentric attitude and developing negative stereotypes. For example, although most beggars in Polish streets are Roma, people tend to define them as Romanians and ascribe to the whole nation the vices of only this ethnic group, together with a whole range of negative feelings and behaviors they engender. A similarly negative attitude is often observed in relations with the so-called 'commercial tourists' from the former Soviet bloc. These people usually come in organized groups with their own bodyguards, as they are often a target of their own or of Polish mafia. Even if attacked and robbed of their possessions, they hardly ever report to the police, as they know that what they do is illegal. Thus, opening of the borders has contributed dramatically to the growth of criminality, both organized and individual. The previously, rather underused term "mafia" has become a basic vocabulary item in all Slavonic languages and a part of reality in these countries. Accidental passersby are often victims of wars among mafias, where acts of violence are endless.

The New Europe has also become very important on the map of drug routes from Asia to Western Europe, which has moved the activity of international drug gangs to this part of the world. Drugs have become easily available everywhere in the New Europe. School children and students are the highest risk groups. Especially among the young, consequences of drug addictions, such as delinquency and a high rate of AIDS, call not only for social preventive actions, but for developing a new attitude of people toward this phenomenon. The most common reaction across societies is contempt, intolerance, and fear, all of which stem from a lack of knowledge.

Emigration is a marginal problem, although it adds to these new phenomena, which have to be dealt with. I do not mean the economic emigration form the ex-Communist countries to the West. Its peak is over, as the political changes created new economic opportunities. Central Europe has become a waiting room for illegal emigrants from Asia to Western Europe. Although this is not a mass phenomenon, emigration centers must be founded and some special services provided. This situation applied to the Polish government, for example, which has signed the convention on emigrants and whose responsibility it is to deport them to their country of origin.

The second type of emigration is chiefly typical of Poland. After World War II, Polish borders were changed and many territories on the East became a part of the Soviet Union. Moreover, many descendants of Polish deportees live in Siberia. Now they can come back to Poland, which, apart from economic problems (the local government usually provides them with a house, a job, and some financial help), is a long process to both newcomers and local society to integrate.

Multiculturalism, with all the challenges it brings to young democracies, is a fact of life in Central and Eastern Europe, although it is different than its Western counterpart. The multitude of new issues and their complexity makes the search for a new identity a painful and long-lasting process. Question marks, vague and ambiguous ideas, and doubts and uncertainties proliferate in civic discourse. The operating changes have overpowered many people, made them helpless, shy, and disappointed with life. In their case, their dreams have come true, but they themselves have also become overgrown by reality. For others, success, usually professional and economic, has become a motor to speed up changes and to ensure their implementation. Economic transformations have resulted in significant sociocultural changes. The latter are even more difficult to accept than the free-market mechanisms, as changes of mental states, level of awareness, and cognitive paradigms are time- and energy-consuming. They also presuppose development of new social skills and abilities to relate to previously unknown, often controversial, culture-specific groups, to listen to some *silent minorities* and to preserve one's own values in the multitude of various norms and lifestyles. New Europeans have so much to offer to themselves and to the rest of the world. They should not hesitate to do so.

NOTES

1. Mobility of the citizens from the former Communist countries is without precedence, as illustrated by the example of Poland. The most numerous groups of foreign tourists to Poland are: Czechs (15,102,100), Slovaks (4,351,100), Germans (47,172,200), Belorussians (3,275,400), Lithuanians (1,210,400), Ukrainians (4,735,700), and Russians (2,313,000) versus the U.S. (2,01,5), Italy (171,900), and France (321,200). Moreover, it must be observed that New Europeans travel very inexpensively: an average daily amount of money (in US dollars) spent in Poland per person is as follows: American and French tourists spend $40 and $27 respectively, while Lithuanian tourists spend $14 and Slovakian tourists spend $15.

REFERENCES

Castells, M. (1996). *The rise of the network society.* Oxford, England: Basil Blackwell.

Czwarta potęga świata—Gospodarka Polski na tle Europy środkowo-Wschodniej. The fourth power of the world. (1998). *Dziennik Polski, 146,* 1, 3.

Dore, R. (1984). Unity and diversity in contemporary world culture. In H. Bull & A. Watson (Eds.), *Expansion of international society* (pp. 56–68). Oxford, England: Oxford University Press.

Huntington, S. P. (1988). *Zderzenie cywilizacji* [The clash of civilizations and the remaking of the world order]. Warsaw, Poland: Warszawskie Wydawnictwo Literackie "Muza."

Janowski, A. (1997). Specific nature and objectives of civic education in Poland: Analysis and reflections. In A. Fraczek (Ed.), *State and perspective of citizenship education in Poland* (pp. 115–132). Warsaw, Poland: University of Warsaw and Ministry of Education.

Korbónski, A. (1995). Poland. In Z. Volges & I. Volges (Eds.), *The legacies of Communism in Eastern Europe* (pp. 138–159). Baltimore, MD: Johns Hopkins University Press.

Linz, H. J., & Stepan, A. (1996). *Problems of democratic transition and consolidation: Southern Europe, South America, and post-Communist Europe.* Baltimore, MD: Johns Hopkins University Press.

Lubecka, A. (1995). Teaching English in Poland: A socio-cultural perspective. *Language and Intercultural Training, 15*(3), 7–9.

Nowicki, J. (1995, March). *Central and Western Europe: Confrontation of cultural paradigms.* Paper presented at the SIETAR Europa Conference, Prague.

Remy, R. C., & Strzemieczny, J. (1997). Education for democratic citizenship in Poland. *International Journal of Social Education, 2*(12), 47–59.

chapter 3

Intellectuals' Civic Discourse in the New Europe: Konrád and Cultural Responsibilities of a Civil Society

Noemi Marin
University of Maryland, College Park

T hroughout the years, the role of opposition in European societies has been played by the educated elite. Their critiques and participation in the cultural discourse of their countries question obsolete social, political, and cultural paradigms. Similar to other moments in European history, in the last decades of the 20th century, intellectuals from Eastern and Central Europe posit a challenge to cultural discourse as they operate within active social and political opposition in their societies. Searching for boundaries that reflect civil society, these public intellectuals pursue an understanding of social and political structures within specific historic and geographic contexts. More specifically, they become politically active participants in deconstructing Communism in countries that before 1989 formed the Iron Curtain.

Public dissidents like Vaclav Havel, Adam Michnik, or George Konrád, among many others, continue to create in their works cultural and political appeals to inscribe critical intellectuals within a unified European public sphere of the 1990s. Tismaneanu (1995) acknowledges the public discourse of Eastern- and Central-European critical intellectuals as inherently contributing to the "destruction of Leninism" (p. 16). And yet, the fall of the Communist curtain seems to mark the end of these critical intellectuals' role as participants in the social, cultural, and political reconstruction of European society.

The significant cultural and sociopolitical contribution of these elites to new democratic societies fires never ending debates in post-Communist times. Critical intellectuals, former dissidents, and even present-day exiles, like Slavenka Drakulić, all continue to write and speak, after 1989, against Communist relapses, against anti-democratic and nationalistic politics, against the faces of a "human Communism." Questions about the role of intellectuals changing over time, about their discourse validating political and sociocultural choices for the populations of these countries, or about their contribution to democratic values resonate within the new discourse of Eastern and Central Europe. Does, then, critical intellectuals' participation in civic discourse of societies in transit remain a challenge for the newly democratized states? If so, what role and responsibilities should these elite intellectuals have in the newly reconfigured Europe?

George Konrád, one of the best-known dissident intellectuals of Central and Eastern Europe, constitutes an emblematic case. As a critical intellectual from Hungary, an internal exile for over 16 years banned to pursue any professional career in literature, a samizdat writer of the underground, Konrád (1994) creates discourse, before and after 1989, juxtaposing personal public action and critical commentaries of social and cultural conditions of Eastern and Central Europe. His writings form a cultural and rhetorical nexus for sociocultural and political tensions in current Hungary.

In 1994, Konrád published a collection of essays, *The Melancholy of Rebirth*, and in one of the works comprised in the volume, "More than Nothing: The Role of the Intellectual," he specifically addresses the above-mentioned questions. Thus, the article explores critical intellectuals' role in the newly liberated Eastern and Central Europe. Providing a cultural critique of the speech, this chapter argues that critical intellectuals' appeals for moral values open up the cultural arena for a new civic discourse in academia. First, I briefly examine who are the critical intellectuals after the revolutions of 1989. Second, analyzing Konrád's essay, I explore the author's cultural and critical perspective on public intellectuals' role in new democracies. And last, I offer some cultural implications on these elites' participation through discourse to the new technological era in the New Europe.

CRITICAL INTELLECTUALS IN CENTRAL AND EASTERN EUROPE

Eyerman, in *Between Culture and Politics: Intellectuals in Modern Society* (1994), views European intellectuals as an integrative part of the historical process in which "human actors reinvent cultural traditions in different contexts" (p. 4). Called intellectuals, critical intellectuals, intelligentsia, elite, counter-elite, academia people, scholars, dissidents, universal professionals, and/or specialized professionals, these social participants reflect a juxtaposition of public and local roles in the Europe of the 1990s. Their participation in the public arena of discourse reflects a complicated social and cultural texture of democratic appeals for a new civil society (Bauman, 1991; Said, 1991; Tismaneanu, 1992).

In Communist times, the official elites Echikinson (1990) identifies as "nomenklatura" or "apparatchiks with degrees" coexist in the same public sphere with academics and personalities like Havel, Sakharov, Kundera, or Konrád, which belong to the social group of the counter-elite (p. 88). Contending that such nonofficial social groups engage "in conflict and collective action and political thinking," Jorgensen (1990) redefines their role as social and political participants, through their discourse, in reinscribing civil society values within their cultures (p. 35). For example, in Czechoslovakia before 1989, the discourse of critical intellectuals was not constituted only of singular names, rather, the entire community of critical intellectuals consisted of participants in the Prague Spring of 1968, of dissidents, and of the signing members of Charter 77. In social and political synchronism with Hungary and Poland, intellectual opposition in Czechoslovakia acts as representatives of "the wrong side of history; its victims and its outsiders" (Kundera, 1984/1991, p. 221). Thus, identified by their social, political, and cultural critiques of Communist societies, critical intellectuals bring within their discourse sociopolitical tensions in contemporary contexts of Central Europe.

As Havel describes in *Summer Meditations* (1992/1995), critical intellectuals of Central Europe create public discourse in order to "de-ideologize" the public sphere and fight against the power of legitimated officials (p. 34). These elites write and speak from the political site of the *under* or *below*, from inside social and cultural movements such as KOR, Charter 77, the Prague Spring, or from samizdat underground (Tismaneanu, 1992). Generally, these public intellectuals posit their discourse between power structures and the "powerless," between local arenas of universities and immediate communities, between newspaper headquarters and larger public participation. However, since their discourse addresses the fall of Communism, do these counter-elites continue to preserve a cultural and political site of opposition after 1989? If so, how does their public role change in discourse from a sociopolitical and cultural perspective?

As mentioned, Havel (1979/1991), Konrád (1984/1996), Michnik (1985), Milosz (1981), and Sakharov (1975) all write about legitimacy of

voice within the public sphere of their countries of origin. Inscribing themselves as participants in the discourse of democratic opposition, these public heroes are located at the very core of the 1989 events. Claiming moral
responsibilities for free and democratic societies, they create powerful discourse that intertwine rhetorical actions with social and cultural duties for
the benefit of a new civil Europe (Tismaneanu, 1992). Advocates of human
rights and democracy reveal to audiences all over the world dimensions of
Communist oppression unknown before. Within the cultural and political
context of Central and Eastern Europe, these intellectuals' contribution to
the post-Communist public sphere becomes invaluable.

After 1989, most of these critical elites maintain their social and political responsibility to proclaim the values of civil societies for the benefit
of these countries' citizens. Counter-elite and former dissidents intertwine social and political roles in their public discourse. They posit
themselves at the intersection of former censorship, underground public
sphere, and current nationalistic views. Thus, in addition to maintaining
their nexus of free and anti-political speech, these intellectuals contribute to the development of moral responsibilities among the population
of newly liberated countries. Their task is "self-critical," as they have to
"create, preserve, and transmit both culture and social goals" coming to
function as "a class," and thus subordinating "its cognitive activity to its
own class interests" (Konrád, 1984/1996, p. 179).

How, then, does the discourse of critical intellectuals continue to
emphasize opinions of social responsibility and legitimation after 1989?
Writing initially from an underground position, Konrád argues that critical intellectuals need to assist in recreating a moral and responsible free
existence within the framework of a civil society, for all citizens of Central and Eastern Europe.

GEORGE KONRÁD: A VOICE OF
RESPONSIBLE OPPOSITION

Author of novels like *The Loser, The Case Worker, The Feast in the Garden*,
and mostly quoted for his famous essay "Antipolitics," George Konrád
was an inherent part of the underground literary and democratic resistance during Communist times. One of the most influential democratic
figures among critical intellectuals in Eastern and Central Europe, Konrád was silenced for two decades in the "official" political arena in Hungary. His voice of the Other, however, could be heard loud and clear in
the underground public sphere (Konrád, 1994). Putting his life and his
family at risk, bringing to oppressed population a glimpse of personal
strength and powerful beliefs in democratic values, Konrád's dissidence

became a public action, an inspiration for his audiences both in Eastern and Western Europe (Heim, 1994).

Konrád contributes to the Eastern and Central European resistance movement in a special way. He is a dissident by profession, an internal exile, comfortable with his identity as critical intellectual and moral evaluator of Hungarian society. As he describes his own existence during the 1970s and 1980s, he "fell under a total ban" due to his writings, publishing in "independent, underground, samizdat press, that is, for a highly discriminating audience but one that numbered no more than a few thousand" (Konrád, 1994, p. x). After 1989, a year-threshold in terms of Communist dissidence, Konrád became a constant public presence in the pro-democratic Hungarian arena. Obtaining national and international recognition as a writer and as a spokesman for democratic values, Konrád became an active part in Hungarian reconstructive strategies for civil society. In 1994, he published *The Melancholy of the Rebirth*, a collection of essays written after the fall of Communism.

Gathering some of his most important public speeches and participation, Konrád's volume presents a writer grappling with moral, social, and cultural problems of post-Communism. As mentioned, Konrád, in these essays, views the transitions happening in Eastern and Central Europe with a vigil eye, as he advocates the values of civil society and democracy. Thus, he chooses not to forget his former banned existence and revisits it in discourse. His works continue to emphasize critical practices of dissidence as the necessary sociocultural and political measure for democratic progress. Konrád's (1984/1996) outsider and antipolitical look into the public arena of post-Communist societies in transit attempts to capture all the tensions of a complex political context as he writes that:

> [A] society does not become politically conscious when it shares some political philosophy but, rather, when it refuses to be fooled by any of them. The apolitical person is only the dupe of the professional politician, whose real adversary is the antipolitician. It is the antipolitician [with whom Konrád identifies himself] who wants to keep the scope of government policy (especially that of its military apparatus) under the control of civil society.... The antipoliticians—and in secret there are many of them—want to free biology and religion, rock music and animal husbandry from the pathological bloat of political state. (pp. 179–180)

THE MORAL RESPONSIBILITIES OF INTELLECTUALS

In "More than Nothing: The Role of the Intellectual," Konrád writes from the position of author and intellectual as dissident, sharing with his audiences a moral duty: to become critical commentator(s) of the socio-political events in Eastern and Central Europe. Like Brodsky, Konrád considers writers and critical intellectuals of having the function to tell "about oppression" and to warn "any thinking man toying with the idea of an ideal society" (Brodsky, 1987/1994, p. 11). Speaking in front of Western intellectuals at the Conference for German University Chancellors, in Frankfurt, in 1991, Konrád argues in favor of the moral and responsible existence of academic elite within the framework of a civil society. In doing so, Konrád illuminates how language and sociocultural responsibilities converge and assist critical intellectuals in creating critical commentaries on the newly changed conditions of existence. Thus, according to Konrád, academics and critical thinkers need to engage themselves more responsibly in the public arena. Interestingly, across the Atlantic, speaking to an American academic forum, Schiappa (1996) makes similar arguments in a call for civic action among academics.

Emphasizing mainly the cultural and political dimensions of intellectuals' role through discourse, Konrád reinscribes both himself and his critical group within the social paradigm of civil order current in Europe. Hence, locating himself at the crossroad between private and public arenas, Konrád begins his speech with a call for civil responsibilities citizens need to have in a free(d) country. "Responsible for their own acts," with a rationale of existence posited centrally, the critical minds are called to establish a "symbiotic relationship" with societal goals (Konrád, 1994, pp. 79–80). Transcending "integration and compassion" and "politics and public relations," these elites are challenged by their claim to the "profession of understanding" (pp. 81–82). For Konrád, intellectuals have power and legitimacy, exercising a significant role in all compartments of social and cultural existence. Konrád writes that:

> [T]he intelligentsia is the keeper of legitimacies; it provides grounds for morality, allegories for ethics, and analysis for politics. In other words, intellectuals peddle clear consciences and guilty consciences. All people have cultural values to guide them and justify their existence.... Those values are in the hands of the intellectual. (p. 82)

Konrád separates "ivory tower intellectuals," to keep Bourdieu's (1993) terminology, from the critical minds involved in the public social and cultural arenas of civil societies of Central and Eastern Europe. Thus, "true intellectuals," for Konrád, are more than just professionals in universities, they are critical thinkers implicating themselves in the civil responsibilities the society demands (p. 83). Invested with authority, these social elites have a major social task to accomplish, as "their wisdom is their debt to the world, their duty; understanding is their profession" (p. 83). Making distinctions among different groups of intellectuals, Konrád explores in his discourse the social and cultural powers invested mainly in critical elites. For Konrád, these participants in universities and other public arenas embody social power at both individual and professional levels for the benefit of an entire society. Therefore, while some professionals in universities seek glory and sacrifice "their lives for a name," the "true" educators respond to a public duty," going beyond technical and professional expertise (p. 83). For, in a civil society, "our times call for the knowledge of the initiate," and critical initiates need become commentators and guardians of social and cultural values in Central and Eastern European countries (p. 83).

Konrád (1994) opens the local arena of intellectual work—the universities—to the public realm, in order to specifically create "an antidote to the world" (p. 85). Universities become, then, a dynamic site of discourse where any responsible intellectual need learn about social and cultural responsibilities in a civil society. Since "universities transmit values" and consequently, "it is not enough for them to turn out apathetic specialists," Konrád reflects upon the new roles of educators (p. 85). He states that, "if by some strange quirk of fate I were to find myself on a podium, I would spend less time teaching my students the tricks of the trade than inculcating in them a feeling of personal responsibility" (p. 85). Hence, in Konrád's view, along with providing understanding and expertise, universities should serve a social function, fighting against "career-oriented intellectuals designed to fit reigning political cliches" and offering the power of freedom for individual thinkers (p. 85). Universities, then, need to promote intellectual ideals, fighting the taras of Communist or oppressive education, as Konrád argues:

> [I]ndifference, conformism, a lack of professional ideals, an impersonal readiness to do anybody's bidding as long as the technology is available— people have to be taught these things for major crimes against humanity to take place. (p. 85)

While Western critique emphasizes the lack of collective responsibility and social involvement in intellectuals' work of contemporary times (Schiappa, 1996), Konrád (1994) reverses the individual and collective paradigm of moral involvement in his part of the world. Coming from the Hungarian experience of over 45 years of Communism, "collective responsibility" translates for the author in "collective irresponsibility" (p. 86). The political umbrella under which civil accountability was performed during Communist times claimed collective benefit of the "people." With the help of antipolitics to preserve "moral criticism of politics," Konrád underlines that intellectuals as gatekeepers have a moral obligation to shift their responsibilities from a collective level to a "personal" level (pp. 86–87).

Looking back at the Communist regime, Konrád (1994) identifies "two collectivisms" for "the vulgarizers and organizers on stage" who banned genuine artists and promoted pseudo-intellectuals" (p. 88). As long as they were active solely at the professional level, without presenting any personal responsibility other than a life-long pledge to the Party, intellectuals remained safe. In reponse, Konrád's appeal examines precisely this sociocultural and political tension critical elites need to use in a civil society. Thus, Konrád shifts the role of intellectuals from mere professionals to "idealists," to people who believe in democratic values and ideas, and whose "personal responsibility take the place of collective responsibility" (p. 86). Konrád maintains:

> [L]ooking backward, we must keep in mind that communist censorship did more than prohibit.... Even its first-person singular was essentially a first-person plural.... State functionaries during the communist period had no idea how much their every move was conditioned by the state, how much the one-party-state, first-person-plural-mentality had permeated their consciousness. (pp. 90–91)

Searching to offer solutions for a civil society, the author acknowledges the difficulties a new and changing social order brings about in public discourse. "The entire East European region is pregnant with new antinomies ready to burst into the world" warns the author, alluding to nationalistic and authoritarian tendencies merging in the newly liberated countries (Konrád, 1994, p. 91). For, "whether the authoritarian state uses communist or fascist rhetoric is less interesting than whether it is in fact what we have now, whether all that has happened is that the flatterers and liars have regrouped" (p. 92). He thus opposes the gloomy image of a possible fall back into authoritarian societies to a technologically optimistic view on democracy. Technology might be, in Konrád's final paragraphs of his speech, one of the most significant solutions against oppression.

The information era brings about a "paradigmatic challenge," just like the unification of "two Europes in Germany" did several years ago (Konrád, 1994, p. 95). Hence, Konrád views the new culture of technology as contributing and developing civic discourse, engaging individuals to responsible public actions. Here is what Konrád writes at the end of his speech:

What I would tell my students, then, is: Don't identify the responsible individualism of the twenty-first century with the numbing, consumer-driven
mass individualism of the twentieth. You have nothing coming to
you...nothing but the whole world, and your calling as students is to formulate a worldview based on your own, first-person experience. (p. 95)

Adding to it, and empowering Europe as "an electronic network of
distinct entities," the writer opens the doors to technology as a possible
new answer to civil societies in Central and Eastern Europe. For technology might provide a new engagement of discourse; a new way for critical
thinkers to liberate the public arena of their countries by exposing it to
the world.

TECHNOLOGY: THE NEXT QUESTION
FOR THE NEW EUROPE

Whether Konrád's solution to address moral responsibilities lies within a
technologically savvy audience represents an implied answer from the
former dissident. A technologically equipped Eastern and Central
Europe seems to be the cultural response to the former, pre-1989 era of
Communist propaganda, thus creating democratic dialogue in any, for
that matter, civil society. In spite of the possibility to view the technologization of discourse as a problematic context for academics, as Fairclough (1996) announces for the Western world, the information access
to international and antipolitical cyberspace should be celebrated in the
universities of Central and Eastern Europe. The fact that intellectuals
can post their articles and writings on the Net, or that universities are
constructing web pages in order to open a transnational dialogue with
the world, represent immense cultural and social contributions to the
civic discourse in this part of the world. For, in spite of the continuing
debates on the role of critical intellectuals in post-Communist Europe,
the access to information on democratic discourse is available for all
audiences. In addition, information about the realities of Eastern- and
Central-European academia is also open to a much larger public discourse. Whether information is related to specific universities in Hungary—for example, the Technological University of Budapest (http://
www.khmk.bme.hu), the Budapest University of Economics (http://
www.einet.net/hytelnet/HU003.html), or Central Europe University
(http://www.ceu.hu)—where Konrád offers lectures, or listervs (for example, VirtualHungary.com, 1998), the democratization of discourse is taking place right now. Even some of Konrád's work is posted on the Web
either in the format of paying a birthday tribute to an old friend, Profes-

sor Ivan Szeleny at UCLA (Simpson, n.d.), or sampling *The Case Worker*, his first novel (San Francisco Jewish Community Publications, 1998). To list just a few sites related to Konrád's very own collection of essays presented in the article, other web sites offer yet another speech, "Revolution or Reform" (WGBH Educational Foundation, n.d.) or a review of the same book, by W.L. Webb (Hungary Network, 1996). Konrád's recent opinions are posted in an interview (and a recent book) by Michael Blumenthal (Pleasure Boat Studio, 1999). As for the ongoing debate on the role of critical intellectuals in civil societies of Central and Eastern Europe, one might be interested to take an active participation by checking pages such as the Czech position on the same social and cultural problem of moral responsibility in Culik (1996).

Consequently, is the role of critical intellectuals enhanced by the technological advancements in the New Europe? Can citizens from this part of the world become more responsible in their civil societies by accessing transnational venues of information on democratic values? According to Konrád, the answer is affirmative. And who can say he is wrong?

REFERENCES

Bauman, Z. (1991). Ideology and the Weltanschauung of the intellectuals. In A. Kroker & M. Kroker (Eds.), *Ideology and power in the age of Lenin in ruins* (pp. 107–123). New York: St. Martin's Press.

Bourdieu, P. (1993). *Sociology in question* (R. Nice, Trans.). London: Sage.

Brodksy, J. (1994). The condition we call exile. In M. Robinson (Ed.), *Altogether elsewhere: Writers on exile* (pp. 3–12). San Diego, CA: Harcourt Brace. (Original work published 1987)

Culik, J. (1996). *Intellectuals and their position in the Czech Republic now* [Online]. Available: <http://www.arts.gla.ac.uk/Slavonic/staff/article3b.html> [1999, March 29].

Fairclough. N. (1996). Technologisation of discourse. In C. R. Caldas-Coulthard & M. Coulthard (Eds.), *Texts and practices: readings in critical discourse analysis* (pp. 71–84). London: Routledge.

Echkinson, W. (1990). *Lighting the night: Revolution in Eastern Europe.* New York: William Morrow.

Eyerman, R. (1994). *Between culture and politics: Intellectuals in modern society.* Cambridge, England: Polity Press.

Havel, V. (1993). *Summer meditations* (P. Wilson, Trans.). New York: Vintage Books. (Original work published 1992)

Havel, V. (1991). The power of the powerless. In G. Stokes (Ed.), *From Stalinism to pluralism: A documentary history of Eastern Europe since 1945* (P. Wilson, Trans.). New York: Oxford University Press. (Original work published 1979)

Heim, M. H. (1994). Translator's afterword. In G. Konrád, *The melancholy of rebirth: Essays from post-Communist Central Europe, 1989–1994* (M. H. Heim, Trans.; pp. 191–196). San Diego, CA: Harcourt Brace.

Hungary Network (1996, Summer). W. L. Webb, winning the millennium match. *The Hungarian Quarterly* [Online serial], *37*(142). Available: <http://www.hungary.com/hungq/no142/p143.html>

Jorgensen, K. E. (1990). The end of anti-politics in Central Europe. In P. G. Lewis (Ed.), *Democracy and civil society in Eastern Europe* (pp. 32–61). New York: St. Martin's Press.

Konrád, G. (1996). Antipolitics. In G. Stokes (Ed.), *From Stalinism to pluralism: A documentary history of Eastern Europe since 1945* (E. White, Trans.; pp. 173–180). New York: Oxford University Press. (Original work published 1984)

Konrád, G. (1994). *The melancholy of rebirth: Essays from post-Communist Central Europe, 1989–1994* (M. H. Heim, Trans.). San Diego, CA: Harcourt Brace.

Kundera, M. (1991). The tragedy of Central Europe In G. Stokes (Ed.), *From Stalinism to pluralism: A documentary history of Eastern Europe since 1945* (E. White, Trans.). New York: Oxford University Press. (Original work published 1984)

Michnik, A. (1985). *Letters from prison and other essays.* Berkeley, CA: University of California Press.

Milosz, C. (1981). *The captive mind.* New York: Vintage Books.

Pleasure Boat Studio. (1999, February 3). *A conversation with George Konrád* [Online]. Available: <http://www.pbstudio.com/blumenthal/konrád.html> [1999, March 29].

Said, E. (1991). Criticism, culture and performance: An interview with Edward Said. *Performing Arts Journal, 37*, 25–28.

Sakharov, A. (1975). *My country and the world* (G. V. Daniels, Trans.). New York: Vintage Books.

San Francisco Jewish Community Publications. (1998). *The case worker* [Online]. Available: <http://jewishsf.com/bk980130/suppacas.htm>

Schiappa, E. (1996). Intellectuals and the place of cultural critique. In J. F. Reynolds (Ed.), *Rhetoric, cultural studies, and literacy: Selected papers from the 1994 Conference of the Rhetoric Society of America* (pp. 21–29). Hillsdale, NJ: Lawrence Erlbaum.

Simpson, R. (n.d.). *On Iván Szelényi's birthday by György Konrád* [Online]. Available: <http://hi.rutgers.edu/szelenyi60/konrád.html> [1999, March 27].

Tismaneanu, V. (1992). *Reinventing politics: Eastern Europe from Stalin to Havel.* New York: The Free Press.

Tismaneanu, V. (1995, October). Knowing and doing. *Village Literary Supplement,* 15–18.

VirtualHungary.com. (1998, November 15). *Universities and colleges in Budapest* [Online]. Available: <http://virtualhungary.com/lists/universi.htm> [1999, March 27].

WGBH Educational Foundation. (n.d.). Revolution or reform (with Iván Szelényi) [Online]. In G. Konrád, *The melancholy of rebirth: Essays from post-Communist Central Europe, 1989–1994.* Available: <http://www.nmis.org/Gate/themes/Konrád.html> [1999, March 28].

chapter 4

The Internet and the Public Sphere: What Kind of Space is Cyberspace?

Jon Mided
University of Sussex, England

I t is difficult to completely appreciate the manner in which the digitization of communication media is affecting our culture. New technology has created a web of virtual communities of people from around the globe sharing information within an amorphous and ungovernable space.

But what kind of space is cyberspace? History offers us few examples of environments in which the public has been able to exercise political influence outside of the traditional means of voting, lobbying, and petitioning. Perhaps the only comparable space is that detailed by Habermas (1962/1989), who postulates the concept of a political public sphere arising from the initial encapsulation of public opinion as a new tool of the emerging middle class in the late 17th and early 18th centuries.

Habermas's (1962/1989) description of the political public sphere in its original form is predicated on the notion of informed citizens reaching consensus through open debate. Within this framework, citizens are united against the common foe of the state, and through their insurgency, that act as a limiting influence upon the powers of that state. The public sphere is a body of individuals which remains outside of official government, but acts as a controlling force upon the powers of the state.

The existence of the public sphere in its original and idealized form is consigned to a period of history during which social and economic circumstances led to the embodiment of public opinion as a political entity. The conditions that allowed for this development were specific to the particular era, and could not be sustained when the consequences of the general public becoming politically empowered became extended throughout a larger slice of the community. From the outset, the public sphere represented only a specific group of individuals. "Citizens" were narrowly defined as educated members of a reading public, albeit that this included significant numbers of the middle class. They would meet in coffeehouses or similar establishments and would debate topics of political interest. The coffeehouses and salons of the 18th century provided a meeting space for these forums, which, despite their somewhat limited representativeness, encompassed a newly politicized and less status-based social grouping.

Habermas (1962/1989) provides us not only with a description of the circumstances that led to the creation of the public sphere, but also with an analysis of how the public sphere was diffused and ultimately disenfranchised. The public sphere was structurally altered when the notion of what constitutes being a citizen was enlarged to include a greater cross-section of the general public. The transformation continued as public opinion became seen as part of the process of government, and in this way started to be hegemonized into the bureaucracy of the state. The development of the mass media furthered the co-opting of the public sphere into the apparatus of government by fuelling the commoditization of political discourse.

PARALLELS ACROSS HISTORY

To examine what possibilities the Internet offers to provide a basis for a new public sphere, it will be necessary to look for historical parallels between the circumstances that led to the creation of the public sphere in the 18th century and those that the Internet may provide.

At first glance, it would seem that there is no correlation between the limited definition of a citizen in the 18th century, and the huge cross-cultural membership of the Internet community, but this differentiation may not be as it appears. Although today's reading public is a more diffused group than that of the 18th century, there are still limits to the Internet's accessibility. Ownership or access to a computer and to an Internet connection, while growing on a huge scale every day, remains an obstacle to participation for much of the world's population. While education has been extended across class lines, other economic factors continue to segregate the public.

A key element in the creation of the original public sphere was the development of the coffee house as a forum for political discussion. Of particular importance was how it embraced "a wider strata of the middle class, including craftsmen and shopkeepers" (Habermas, 1962/1989, p. 33). These meeting places bear strong similarities to the newsgroups, mailing lists, and chatrooms, which can be found on the Internet. The "universal access" of citizens to the coffeehouse is directly comparable to that found in the newsgroups of Usenet.

Other factors that were important in the inception of the original public sphere were its emphasis as an oppositional force on issue-based politics, and its fomentation of small political publications. Similarly, the Internet is characterized by activist politics and its spawning of private publishing in the form of home pages on the Web. The use of the Zamir network during the war in Bosnia is an example of this type of activism. Set up in 1992, Zamir is a regional network providing interest groups and individuals with a means to campaign for peace in former Yugoslavia. A wide variety of anti-war groups used this forum, including the Centre for Anti-War Action in Serbia and the Anti-War Campaign in Croatia, as well as women's groups, ecology groups, and humanitarian agencies (Stubbs, 1998). The political journals of Addison & Steele are closely paralleled by e-mail, ezines (online magazines), and online publications written by people from outside the traditional schools of journalism.

THE TRANSFORMATION OF THE PUBLIC SPHERE

Habermas (1962/1989) details a number of points that led to the downfall of the political public sphere: a widened body of citizens, convergence with the apparatus of the state, and commercialization fueled by advertising and the mass media. If the Internet is to be viewed as a new public sphere, then it must be seen to overcome the circumstances that led to the downfall of its predecessor. While it is essential to draw comparisons with the past, it is also necessary to somewhat redefine these criteria to encompass the viewpoint of a mediated culture.

Citizenship in the New Europe

The Internet plays host to a community of such a potentially huge scale that it would appear to immediately deny the condition of a consensus-forming citizenship limited to an educated public. On a large scale, this supposition is undoubtedly true: the number and diversity of Internet users, coupled with the accessibility of entry, is clearly an obstacle to achieving consensus. However, it is more useful to look at the Internet as a cluster of many different communities than as a single entity. One of the Internet's distinguishing characteristics is its provision of thematic and issue-oriented forums such as those found on Usenet or in topical mailing lists. These groupings offer new possibilities for information exchange, less limited by time and distance than their predecessors. The amorphous nature of virtual community allows for easy and discreet membership across a range of ongoing debates. Computer-mediated discussion is further enhanced by the threaded nature of its dialogues, which benefit from previously unavailable storage and retrieval capabilities. The entire nature of online discussion is distinguished as a new, written form of discourse, widely accessible and diversely configured.

One must also not underestimate the limitations that still exist to becoming a citizen of the Net. The cost of ownership of computer equipment and the subscription to a dial-up network is beyond the means of most people in the world. Access to network connections is not universally available. While there are laudable civic projects that seek to place Internet connections in public buildings and libraries, these projects cannot address deeper socioeconomic problems, which ultimately limit who can get online. Nonetheless, Jonathan Peizer ("First Monday," 1999) argues that the focusing of resources available to the public in Central and Eastern Europe does provide the basis for social progress: "To create open societies when there were none before, you must concentrate on those sectors most involved in fostering civil society and give them the necessary tools to achieve that end."

Convergence with State

The Internet cannot converge with the state because its architecture denies the structure of the state. The multifaceted and transnational character of the network itself defies state control. Nevertheless, the pervasiveness of the apparatus of the state may continue to hold significant influence over the Internet. In fact, the very foundation of the Internet, the ARPANET military network, was created by the U.S. government.

It is questionable whether Habermas is correct in viewing the original public sphere as a body wholly separate from the state. Almost certainly, whatever truth exists in this assertion is specific to the initial inception of the public as a body of opinion, and it is therefore problematic, having passed this historical node, to present this as a criteria against which to measure the formation of a new public sphere. In this regard, it is more useful to examine ways in which the Internet can act as an influence upon the state where other media have been less successful.

Commercialization and the Mass Media

Habermas (1962/1989) argues that the advertising-driven entertainment served to us by the mass media acts to exclude the public from political debate:

> The mass press was based on the commercialization of the participation in the public sphere on the part of a broad strata designed predominantly to give the masses in general access to the public sphere. This expanded public sphere, however, lost its political character to the extent that the means of "psychological facilitation" could become an end in itself for a commercially fostered consumer attitude. (p. 169)

There are fundamental differences between the Internet and the mass media. The Internet is an information-based medium, mass media are entertainment-based. The Internet is interactive, the mass media are not. The mass media comply to a centralized broadcast model, the Internet is decentralized. Despite these distinctions, the Internet cannot be seen in isolation from other media. The influence of commercialization on the political nature of our culture pervades and intersects with all aspects of the Internet. As Mark Poster (1997) puts it, "It appears that the media, especially television but also other forms of electronic communication isolate citizens from one another and substitute themselves for older spaces of politics" (p. 207). Habermas (1962/1989) himself says something similar: "The world fashioned by the public sphere is a public sphere in appearance only" (p. 171).

Does the commercialization and expansion of the Internet over the last few years offer a similar threat to the concept of a new global public sphere? On one hand, the answer has to be yes. Looking back, there seems to be a strong correlation between the early days of the Internet, prior to the explosion of the World Wide Web, and Habermas's description of coffeehouse debate. Both worlds are peopled by a group of educated and informed individuals, and like the original public sphere, there is at least a degree to which the Internet community can be mobilized to act as political force opposed to a common enemy. One of the clearest examples of such action occurred in 1996 with the success of the Blue Ribbon Campaign in helping to challenge and defeat the Communication Decency Act, a draconian piece of legislation put forward by the Clinton Administration as a regulatory tool for the Internet. However, as the Internet has grown, it has become increasingly commercialized, with inevitable implications for its ability to foment political action.

Commercialization, argues Habermas (1962/1989), has changed the very nature of public discussion:

Discussion, now a "business," becomes formalized; the presentation of positions and counterpositions is bound to certain prearranged rules of the game; consensus about the subject matter is made largely superfluous by that concerning form.... Thus, discussion seems to be carefully culti-vated and there seems to be no barrier to its proliferation. But surrepti-tiously it has changed in a specific way: it assumes the form of a consumer item. (p. 164)

These "prearranged rules" cannot be escaped from simply by using a new medium. It is possible that in the course of time, the Internet will help break down these rules, and that the nature of dialogue can be extracted from the language of exchange.

TOWARD A NEW GLOBAL PUBLIC SPHERE

Digitization is the technological foundation for a new world order. At least that is the hype. While it has become fashionable to predict sweep-ing cultural change as a result of new computer-based technologies, in truth we have nothing to measure these predictions against. Yet while it may be foolhardy to second-guess the future, there are still many useful conclusions that can be drawn from considering the possibilities offered by new technology.

The reduction of old and cumbersome industrial equipment into the binary code of a software package that can run on any desktop has reduced the cost of market entry and production to such a degree that the paradigms of ownership and power, which we have all grown up with, are experiencing a revolutionary shift. Digitization has led to radi-cally cheaper and more flexible methods of communication, which all but deny traditional economic and social boundaries. Some of the effects of this revolution are already apparent, in particular its globalizing influence. Take, for example, the issue of censorship. In the past, peo-ple's limited exposure to ideas and images from outside their own cul-ture meant that a relatively common set of values was maintained within a particular community or country. The advent of the mass media, and in particular television, had a globalizing effect upon the world, as words and images could be broadcast across national boundaries with great ease. However, the nature of broadcast media is such that it is not terri-bly difficult for governments to limit the intrusion of these signals into their countries through legislation. The emergence of the Internet has created a new communication topology that decentralizes power and turns everyone with a computer into a potential publisher. The Internet is often characterized as an anarchic and dangerous place for good reason: the decentralized network denies the power of the nation-state. Today's governments are fighting to find legislative means to control content on the Internet, but the fact is that the topology of the network makes this aim an impossibility. Countries that have successfully controlled content have only been able to do so by severely restricting their connection to the network, but even in the least democratic of nations, the process of technological development has the potential to undermine this control. Over time it seems inevitable that the sovereignty of the nation-state will undergo a radical realignment, but it is of critical importance to view the influence of the Internet within a wider context of globalization and cultural convergence. Just as the public sphere originally emerged from a gradual shift toward representative government, so too can the globalizing forces of the Internet be seen to have further empowered an already existing tendency.

The Internet is an individuated medium. Every user uses the network differently. Of particular significance is the emphasis on areas of interest that transcend regional and localist politics:

> The development of communications technologies has vastly transformed the capacity of global civil society to build coalitions and networks. In times past, communication transaction clusters formed among nation-states, colonial empires, regional economies and alliances—for example, medieval Europe, the Arab world, China and Japan, West African kingdoms, the Caribbean slave and sugar economies. Today new and equally powerful forces have emerged on the world stage—the rain forest protection movement, the campaign against the arms trade, alternative news agencies, and planetary computer networks. (Frederick, 1992)

THE NATURE OF DEBATE

The political influence of the Internet has a decidedly activist nature to it. Partially, this is a result of the empowerment of individuals as publishers in a decentralized network, but also it derives from the fragmented nature of discussion. There are over 20,000 newsgroups on Usenet, each playing host to an unmoderated topical discussion. There are literally millions of web pages, and a vast number of chatrooms on IRC or other networks. Users are forced to be highly selective in what spaces they frequent because it is simply impossible to survey all of the possible areas of one's interest.

Issues debated on Usenet need to fall into specific subheadings to enable users to find them. While there may be no limit to the diversity of opinion that can be expressed, this structure serves to somewhat limit the breadth of discussion. In order for any specific political issue to gain attention across a wide range of sites, it will need to be of interest to a significant body of users, but since the Internet is so diversely populated, there are unlikely to be many issues that can meet this criteria. Hence, activist politics such as civil rights and environmental issues come to the fore. The Blue Ribbon campaign against the U.S. Communications Decency Act (CDA) of 1996 highlights the strength and weakness of these conditions. While political discussion was able to be much more widespread than it could have been via traditional media, the elevation of the CDA as a topic of debate occurred because it directly affected the Net community. While other legislation may have been fiercely debated in various corners of the network, the CDA had a potentially direct effect on every online user, and was therefore extremely widely published and discussed. An issue such as the European Commission (EC) regulation of grain imports is unlikely to attract such attention.

Another way in which political activism develops on the Internet is through the influence of other mass media. Take, for example, the case of the independent Yugoslavian radio station B92. Radio B92 was closed down by the Serbian government at the start of the 1999 NATO bombing, but a B92 website and a campaign to allow the station to continue to provide news and information were made available on the Internet by a group of Dutch-based activists.

VIRTUAL COMMUNITY

A virtual community is a community of people who have never met, who may be hiding behind false identities, and who meet in spaces that don't exist in substance. The strength of a virtual community is summed up as follows: "Experientially, community within cyberspace emphasizes a community of interests, usually bounded by the topic under discussion, that can lead to communal spirit and apparent social bonding" (Fernback & Thompson, 1997).

But this is only half the story. While an idealized virtual community offers progressive and useful discussion in which the participants can speak freely under the cloak of anonymity, the reality is more ambiguous. It is worth returning here to Habermas's original public sphere to compare the nature of coffeehouse debate with that of newsgroups and mailing lists. To begin, let us look at the demise of the coffeehouse:

> Regular denizens of particular coffee-houses, presumably becoming self-satisfied and uninterested in the views and news of less-regular participants in the discussion, began to withdraw into backrooms. As early as

1715, according to William Thomas Laprade, "the bluff democracy of the public rooms in earlier coffee-houses [was gone as] men of note withdrew and did not court the common crowd. Select assemblies gathered in private rooms." Such "select" assemblies led to the rise of the private club. (Knapp, 1997, p. 176)

The notion of separate societies emerging within the public sphere can be seen on the Internet everyday. Individuals who express opinions that upset other members of the group are often "flamed" by those participants. "Newbies" who ask inane and simplistic questions are generally directed to a group's FAQ (Frequently Asked Questions). When newbies begin to dominate a group, more sophisticated users may move into private chatrooms or other less accessible areas, or they may lose interest altogether. On a moderated list, contibutors can be removed by the moderator without reason or recourse. To some degree, the anonymous nature of a virtual community allows participants to act less responsibly toward each other. Rather than increasing social spirit, the virtuality of a virtual community might give free reign to our intolerance.

The other area in which the Internet fails to meet Habermas's criteria is in its failure to provide conditions for consensus forming. The activism espoused on the Zamir network may amount to a consensus, but that consensus was not formed solely on the Internet. As Paul Stubbs (1998) states: "...using *zamir* was one part of the repertoire of the alternative or oppositional *scene* in Zagreb, linking explicitly with specific real events, such as petitions, actions, demonstrations, or happenings, and often being covered by, or prefiguring coverage in, the alternative journal *Arkzin*." Equally, television and newspapers may act to draw an audience to an issue, and that audience may consequently use the Internet as a communication tool. While the Net offers "something for everyone," its fragmented nature is not fertile ground for the unifying of divergent points of view. The Internet provides a campaigning platform, but its debates are more likely to produce cyclical arguments or ideological standoffs. While the information on the Net can enable researchers to delve widely into their subject matter, political discussion exists predominantly in the form of discourses between individuals with set opinions.

PROBLEMS OF DEMOCRACY

Perhaps the strongest argument in favor of the Internet as a new global public sphere is seen in how it gets used to publicize issues in much the same way that Habermas (1962/1989) describes "publicity" as the central tool of the original public sphere.

For example, the Zapatista rebels in the Chiapas region of southern Mexico have been using websites and newsgroups to call for support in their struggle for land support. Jose Angel Gurria, Mexico's foreign minister, recently acknowledged that the government had been forced into half-hearted negotiations with the insurgents only because of the power of local and global public opinion mobilized by the Net (Barbrook, 1995).

While such political influence allows us to genuinely embrace the Internet as a force for global democracy, there are also strong arguments that suggest that the Net may serve to diminish certain freedoms. One potential threat is that the Internet could be used by the government or corporate entities to gather information about individuals, which can later be used against them. In this scenario, the storage and retrieval mechanisms that enable threaded discussion and fast referencing of archives contribute not to the improved quality of dialogue, but actually undermine our privacy. Howard Rheingold (1994, p. 292) makes this very point:

> All of the information on the hypothetical mass-dossier disk is available from public sources; it is in their compilation, the way that information is sorted into files linked to real citizens, that intrusion is accomplished. On each CD-ROM disk will be a file that knows a lot about your tastes, your brand preferences, your marital status, even your political opinions. If you contributed to a freewheeling Usenet newsgroup, all the better, for your political views, sexual preferences, even the way you think, can now be compiled and compared with other information in your dossier.

Much play is currently being made by politicians about "open government." The White House has an e-mail address and governments throughout the world are publishing legislation on the Web. For those involved in the fabric of government, or for lobbyists or students engaged in research, this allows for much faster access to information. But who else is going to read a 200-page technical report? Governments are not proclaiming to publish information that they would previously have kept secret, and in some ways Web publishing might even serve to further obfuscate information. As Clifford Stoll (1995) remarks, "Hey— these reports and regulations have always been printed and distributed. Once on-line, that paper trail may partially disappear, replaced by a digital archive" (p. 34).

THE TRANSFORMATION OF THE INTERNET

On a technological level, the Internet offers us a means to reinvent democracy. It presents us with an ideal in which every man, woman, and child could actively participate in government. The model of the electronic town hall sees citizens debating issues and voting on a regular basis. But it is through looking at this ideal that the concept of a new global public sphere shows serious flaws.

The Internet faces a crisis of information. While businesses are increasing their online presence, they are also increasing their online status. The days when a home page offered more useful information than a commercial page are fast receding. The perception that the Internet offers a level playing field in which private publishers are not outgunned by the resources of huge corporations is simply untrue. While individuals may have far more publishing power, and thus a voice that they have never had before, it is increasingly difficult to compete with big business. Corporations have the resources to run their own servers across high-speed dedicated connections, often linking complex database functionality to their sites. They have a team of staff to maintain and update their pages, which means that they can produce far more up-to-date information than most individuals. These are big advantages. Of equal importance is their ability to promote themselves through a combination of brand-awareness, financial muscle, and market influence. The holy grail of increased bandwidth promises to vastly increase the multimedia content of the Web, and this convergence with broadcast media may well reduce the Internet to being another promulgator of sound bites and public stances. Since its inception, the Internet has been primarily an information medium, but it clearly faces the threat of being overwhelmed by entertainment content.

The shift that Habermas describes from critical debating of culture to the consumption of it can only have increased in an age where the commodification of images has reduced our politicians to being agents of public relations and advertising. John Perry Barlow (1996), while referring to his viewing of the Kennedy–Nixon debates, expands on this idea with reference to television:

> The most striking realization that came to me as I watched the tapes was that Kennedy was not so much elected president by television—that strange projection from which most Americans have since derived their map of reality. He also, in some sense, participated in a process whereby television became president. Since then this medium has defined the national agenda in ways that were often at odds with what might have been dictated by either sense or experience with unmediated reality, until

we are left today with what I call Government by Hallucinating Mob. (p. 54)

This thinking inevitably leads to more profound and unanswerable questions about the nature of reality. Does "unmediated reality" really exist? Baudrillard argues that our language has developed into a form that hides reality and ultimately goes further and hides the absence of reality. If we accept this hyperrealist critique, then we must accept that the Internet can only serve to reinforce the unreality that we have fashioned for ourselves through the traditional mass media:

> Hyper-realists see the use of communications technologies as a route to the total replacement of the natural world and the social order with a technologically mediated hyper-reality, a "society of spectacle" in which we are not even aware that we work all day to earn money to pay for entertainment media that tell us what to desire and which brand to consume and which politician to believe. We don't see our environment as an artificial construction that uses media to extract our money and power. We see it as "reality"—the way things are. (Rheingold, 1994)

Or to put it another way:

> But in our media-dominated culture the virtual reality of the television image is so powerful that "media-reality" is more real than actual experience and the majority of humanity is invisible, appearing only sporadically in connection with some natural catastrophe, war or revolution. (Adrian X, 1997, p. 87)

The users of the Internet live in a mediated world, and in these circumstances the Internet cannot provide us with a new political public sphere.

THE NEW PUBLIC SPHERE IN THE NEW EUROPE

In the narrow sense of Habermas's original conceptualization, the Internet cannot offer a new political public sphere, but it does clearly offer a new kind of space that presents an opportunity for dialogue to take place which may not have been previously possible. While there are political consequences to some of this dialogue, the participants remain subject to other circumstances and media, and so cannot seem to be acting outside of the influence of the state. Consensus forming through rational argument may occur in certain circles, but much of the discussion found on the Internet is in the form of individuals exchanging pre-conceived arguments.

The new public sphere engendered by the Net takes a form more social than political. A virtual community of support groups and common interest forums has arisen outside of the gamut of traditional processes. Existing not for financial gain or on the basis of volunteer work, individuals have used newsgroups to participate in an arena of mutual assistance, particularly during the crises in Yugoslavia, Bosnia and Kosovo. From academic research to the sharing of health-related problems, people have helped each other through the sharing of knowledge and experience. Enabled by threaded discussion and instant publishing, the Internet has ushered in a new social public sphere.

REFERENCES

Adrian X, R. (1997). Infobahn blues. In A. Kroker & M. Kroker (Eds.), *Digital delirium* (pp. 84–88). Montreal: New World Perspectives.

Barbrook, R. (1995). *Electronic democracy—politics in cyberspace* [Online]. Available: http://www.wmin.ac.uk/media/VD/elecdem.html [1997, December 3].

Barlow, J. P. (1996, September). The powers that were. *Wired, 4.09,* 53–56, 195–199.

First Monday interviews: Jonathan Peizer [Online]. (1999, March 25). Available: http://www.firstmonday.dk/issues.issue4_2/interview [1999, March 25].

Fernback, J., & Thompson, B. (1997, December 3). *Virtual communities: Abort, retry, failure?* [Online]. Available: http://www.well.com/user/hlr/texts/VCcivil.html [1997, December 3].

Frederick, H. H. (1992). Computer networks and the emergence of global civil society: The case of the Association for Progressive Communications (APC) [Online]. Available: ftp://ftp.sunet.se/ftp/pub/global-net/global_society.txt [1997, December 19].

Habermas, J. (1962/1989). *The structural transformation of the public sphere.* London: Polity Press.

Knapp, J. A. (1997). Essayistic messages: Internet newsgroups as an electronic public sphere. In D. Porter (Ed.), *Internet culture* (pp. 181–200). New York and London: Routledge.

Poster, M. (1997). Cyberdemocracy: Internet and the public sphere. In D. Porter (Ed.), *Internet culture* (pp. 201–218). London: Routledge.

Rheingold, H. (1994). *The virtual community: Surfing the Internet.* London: Minerva.

Stoll, C. (1995). *Silicon Snake Oil.* New York: Doubleday.

Stubbs, P. (1998, September 30). Conflict and co-operation in the virtual community: Email and the wars of the Yugoslav succession. *Sociological Research Online* [Online serial], *3*(3). Available: http://www.socresonline.org.uk/socresonline/3/3/7.html. [1999, March 25].

chapter 5

Alone in the Crowd:
The Politics of Cybernetic Isolation

John Horvath
Telepolis, Budapest

C enturies ago, mapmakers in both China and Europe drew imposing monsters on the "unknown lands," which then made up a greater part of the world. Now, in the age of computer-mediated communication (CMC), it is hard to imagine that such areas exist. Indeed, the notion of Internet-based civic discourse carries with it the embedded virtue of opening societies once closed by the rigid political ideologies of the past.

The New Europe provides a case in point. Even so, after almost a decade of social, political, and economic change, knowledge about the region appears quite sophomoric. What is more, despite the potential of digital technology to encourage international discourse among regions and nations, the New Europe is still a "terra incognita" to many—both within and without the region.

This chapter seeks to provide an overview of the state of civic discourse within the New Europe on a regional level. It opens with a brief look into the nature of Internet-based civic discourse from a general standpoint, for this provides the structural framework upon which civic discourse is usually based. Next, a historiographical analysis of common assumptions held about the region will be presented. Many of these assumptions are due to a lingering bias, which views the region as a homogeneous whole. Subsequently, it will be revealed that this "bloc" attitude, a vestige of the cold war era, is not only unfounded, but misleading.

With both the nature of civic discourse and assumptions about the region clarified, the chapter then delves into the issue at hand. First, the social and technological challenges faced by the region are discussed, followed by an examination of various restraining influences that act as additional impediments to civic discourse. Taking all of this into consideration, present and future implications are then evaluated.[1]

The chapter concludes by noting the precarious state of civic discourse within the New Europe. It warns that if present trends are left to continue and certain changes are not made, the problems that exist will be reinforced and carried over into the third millennium. Moreover, gaps that are already apparent between "east" and "west," not to mention within the region itself, will deepen and may, if left unchecked, become insurmountable later on.

THE NATURE OF CIVIC DISCOURSE

The advent of the Internet has been accompanied by a myriad of euphoric promises. One of these is in the area of a greater participation of the citizen in the democratic process. Extensive civic discourse is seen as a natural result of what is frequently referred to as a "many-to-many" communications medium.

In Europe, the European Commission (EC) has envisaged civic discourse to be an integral part of what it terms the "information society." Indeed, through the process of convergence, as described in its Green Paper (European Commission, 1997a), the information society is seen as more than just a technological revolution, for it carries with it a variety of implications—legal, social, industrial, and economic: "The truth is that the debate on the implications of this unification is only the beginning. It is bringing new ways of communicating, of learning, of *acquiring culture*, of looking at yourself, of doing business, and of functioning in a democracy" (original emphasis, European Commission, 1998b, p. 26).

The notion of "acquiring culture" will become important later on; for now, it is apparent from the above quotation that the EC sees civic discourse evolving along with the technological changes taking place. For Central and Eastern Europe (CEE), this is important. Since the region is making preparations to become a part of the European Union (EU), commonly referred to as the "New Europe," all policy objectives of the EU will naturally be taken up by the accession states. One area in which this can already be seen is the participation of Central and Eastern European states in the Fifth Framework of the Telematics Programme

(1998–2002). The Fifth Framework Programme is the latest in a series of structured R&D activities supported by the European Commission. Formally established in 1987, this latest program differs from its predecessors in that countries from Central and Eastern Europe are able to take a more active part in wider-range projects, projects that usually have their focus on the telematic aspects of education, health, and administration.

The idea of increased civic discourse brought about by such initiatives as the Fifth Framework specifically, and media technologies generally, has been advocated for some time, mostly in the U.S. In fact, the concept of "civic journalism"—a change in basic journalism culture, converting cynicism into civic exploration—is the latest approach among many attempting to draw citizens into public discussions about community life. Ellen Hume's research, "Tabloids, Talk Radio, and the Future of News" (1995), provides a veneer of such "civic journalism." However, instead of providing an opportunity to express new ideas to a potentially more interactive audience, websites of leading publishers usually just mirror what can already be found in print.

Some are not only skeptical about this, but the myriad other potentials of new technologies as well, arguing that the promise of increased civic discourse through such media is a delusion. Robert McChesney, in his research on policy debates surrounding the Internet and telecommunication, points out that there is simply no public debate about the use of the medium for the public good (Corporate Watch, n.d.). Felix Stalder (1998) goes deeper, analyzing the nature of "techno-discourse" itself. He demonstrates that it is, basically, the use of something that sounds good, ripping it out of any context, blowing it up beyond proportion, and then declaring it absolutely new (or at least revolutionary). Accordingly, he explains that "this will do two things at the same time: first it will sell the product and second it will make any discussion about what is really happening impossible because most of the critiques will accept those inflated terms and simply try to denounce them."

In the realm of art, similar, common assumptions are held about the liberating power of the new media. Many believe that new media art will break down traditional "art delivery systems" and replace them with an open, pluralistic anarchy run by artists. Such optimism is rejected by Stephen Pope (1999), who argues that technology has changed our relationship to the arts for the worse. His view is that art has shifted from a medium of creation to one of excessive archiving and consuming, bringing with them new art forms or aesthetics that are of little significance. "The problem that I see," writes Pope, "is that the new media do not seem to be helping to solve the crises of aesthetics, audience relations, social relevance, and economic power in which the arts find themselves today—crises that were created, or at least exacerbated, by the media of broadcasting and recording."

Alexei Shulgin (1996) is even more blunt. He observes that the reliance on the medium obscures the content of what is being transmitted. As a matter of consequence, he sees digital media art in terms of a struggle for power instead of communication. The emergence of media art is thus characterized by a transition from representation to manipulation. The country of Albania provides a striking, albeit extreme, example. As Eduard Muka (1996) notes, in the struggle between representational and conceptual art, the controversy grounding the struggle is not an artistic debate, but rather simply a matter of power.

In the face of all this, the traditional art world continues to take an isolationist approach, simply refusing to acknowledge other media environments as a viable context for art production and distribution. Carol Duncan (cited in Pope, 1999), writing in the *Socialist Review*, sees this in the context of a historical process of adaptation: "Art and discourse in the 19th century distorted and idealized the external world and celebrated it as Beauty. Modern art celebrates alienation from that world and idealizes it as Freedom."

It must be kept in mind that all forms of Internet-based civic discourse, whether in the form of art or community networking, is not simply dependent on a computer and Internet connection. The way in which computers are integrated within society (especially at work) is also important. Furthermore, telematic alternatives, such as teleworking, contribute significantly to the nature of civic discourse.

For instance, the annual report of the European Commission's Information Society Forum (1996) identified different social and legal frameworks for the development of teleworking within the EU. Among them, one was identified as the "rights of access to domestic premises for employers and relevant work inspectors despite the basic principle of the sanctity of the home" (p. 59). Without the ability to relate such issues to a particular environment, civic discourse naturally becomes stunted. According to the European Commission's *Status Report on Telework* (1997b), "in terms of awareness of teleworking, the situation is that this new way of working is virtually unknown in CEE countries" (p. 45).

On an even more basic level, the problem of civic discourse has not so much to do with the technology as with the basic philosophical foundations upon which Western society itself is based, where a severely weakened state of civic discourse is maintained by a predominant neo-liberalist political climate. According to Thomas Bridges (1998), modernist liberal philosophy for the past century actually encouraged the neglect of civic culture, for "it promoted universalist and essentialist misconceptions of liberal moral ideals that today actually have the effect of positively weakening civic culture."

These philosophical foundations can be easily observed in Western views towards the "east," where a totalizing cultural perspective operates as a universal axiom. This, coupled with the missionary-like fervor with which the new media are being introduced to Central and Eastern Europe, adds weight to Bridges's (1998) observation that

> where a liberal democracy lacks the cultural resources to make citizenship intelligible to citizens and to motivate them to achieve liberal moral ideals, there will be no citizens and, eventually, no liberal democracy—even if political philosophers finally come up with a knock-down proof that liberal ideals of civic freedom and equality are written into the foundation of the world.

As a result, the belief in the inviolability of a consumerist democracy has led to a growing rejection of traditional political categorizations (see, for example, De Pauw, 1997; Kunzru, 1997), as if the political and economic realities of the past (and present) are no longer relevant. The overall effect of this is a growing myth toward social injustice, one akin to "blame the victim."

In terms of civic discourse, Robert Weissman (1998) notes that the U.S. National Commission on Civic Renewal, in the release of its final report entitled "A Nation of Spectators: How Civic Disengagement Weakens America and What We Can Do About It," muddled the issue when it came to dealing with corporations. According to Weissman, "better to blame the citizens for inactivity than commend them for actively opposing corporate power."

Also, the move away from the political realities of the past disengages people from sociopolitical activity by putting issues out of focus and relegating them into abstraction. Hence, sociopolitical activity—marching in the streets, attending rallies and volunteer work as opposed to "surfing the Net" and checking out the websites of activists—is no longer seen as an effective means to elicit change (see, for example, Rijs, 1996; Schultz, 1996).

As Stoller (1996) aptly put it, "They see what is, not what is possible" (p. 15). Therefore, despite appearances and the euphoric promises of a greater expression of democracy and extensive civic discourse through new media technologies, it is clear that the medium has the reverse potential to drown the message—especially since civic discourse in and of itself is in a fragile state. The challenges for those in the east, meanwhile, are multiplied, for, in addition to these shortcomings, the standards by which their societies are judged are often not even met by those judging them.

THE FUTURE IN THE LIGHT OF THE PAST

A mistake often made when dealing with the New Europe is to treat the entire region as a homogeneous whole (see, for example, Arns, 1998). This was done frequently during the cold war era, when the entire area was known to many simply as the "East Bloc." Unfortunately, according to Dr. Andrzej Ziolowski, a Vienna-based writer and academic, this misreading of Central and Eastern Europe still continues (cited in Skyring, 1998). This should come as no surprise, since the philosophical underpinnings that were responsible for the cold war in the first place, as elaborated by Bridges (1998), are still present in today's post-cold war world.[1]

The misreading of the New Europe in the present has a lot to do with erroneous assumptions about the region's past. Some of these assumptions are important in trying to understand not only the history, but also the nature, of civic discourse within the region.

One of the most common Western assumptions is that under the previous regimes, civic discourse was nonexistent. The media in Central and Eastern Europe was seen as nothing more than a perpetrator of lies, a weapon of the cold war used indiscriminately by the Communists. Yet many Westerners who lived in the region during those years were usually surprised to find that those on the "other side" of the Iron Curtain were at times better informed than those in the West. Even for artists, the dark period was not everything as the "west" made it out to be. Concerning the dark period, János Sugár, a Hungarian artist and filmmaker during the period, states:

> It wasn't so dark. Only access by the general public and mainstream media was censored, not production. Public culture was strongly controlled: censorship, bans, but a vital underground art scene (the second public) existed—art shows, pop and contemporary music, performance, samizdat etc. Having no space for the ambitions, no practical perspectives, we had lots of time. For me as a young artist, it was an idyllic training—everyone was approachable, ready for dialogue. (cited in Lovink, 1998a, p. 14)

During the 1960s and 1970s, when most of the Communist states of Central and Eastern Europe had undertaken programs to "liberalize" their regimes, the way in which the media—and intellectuals in particular—were treated changed. Although they could never be fully independent, the media were nonetheless given a quasi-independent status, in which little was expected of them in return for a limited amount of freedom to pursue their interests and concerns through themes related to national and sociological issues. In Hungary, for instance, Sugár (cited in Lovink, 1998b) explains that "[this kind of] censorship was based on three principles: support, tolerance, ban. Practically, the Communists used the system intelligently—banning a few, tolerating a lot and continuously playing with dissolving previous bans." As a result, while the media still served as a form of social control for the government, it also served as an outlet that enabled the intelligentsia to criticize the government in a tacit sort of way. By allowing the intelligentsia and media together to deal with their favorite subjects (such as suicide in Hungary and alcoholism in Russia) semi-independently, the Communist governments throughout Central and Eastern Europe were able to elicit their passive support.

Even in the realm of art and entertainment, mild criticisms of the regime could be heard.[2] "There is always a dialogue in art," writes Sugár, "the hard core avant-garde was somehow still present" (cited in Lovink, 1998b). In Hungary, films such as Péter Bascó's *A tanu* (*The Witness*, 1968) and rock group Illés' song "*Sárga Rózsa*" (Yellow Rose), all contained messages that implicitly and explicitly were aimed at Communist society and even the government. Indeed, with Bascó's film, a parody on Stalinist show trials, became a cult film within the country. Even though it was officially banned by the government, almost everyone, if not having seen it, at least heard about it.

As for those on the receiving end, people eventually perfected the art of "reading between the lines," a skill that is still largely absent in the West, since everybody is under the illusion of a "free press." Because people were aware of inconsistencies and inaccurate information they received from the media, accentuated by their increasing contacts with foreigners, people tended to be more skeptical and were less likely to take what they read, saw, or heard at face value. Knowing that their governments not always told the truth, or at least hid it from view, it can be said that many people within Central and Eastern Europe were more free than in the West, since they knew they were not "free" and were subsequently not under any illusions of a "free media."

Instead of trying to understand these dynamics that operated in the past (and to a great extent still exist) within the region, the concept of "change" that has accompanied the fall of the Berlin Wall and Iron Curtain has become a euphemism for cultural denial. As mentioned earlier, the EC regards the "acquiring of culture" (that is, U.S. and western European cultural values) as one of the implications of technological development that Central and Eastern Europe will have to accept. More importantly, however, is the acceptance and implementation of an underlying economic framework that is, in many ways, in conflict with the social and cultural values of the region. American-style free-market capitalism, envisioned as the backbone of an emergent global economy and the driving force behind technological change, has come out as the "victor" of the cold war era and, because it outlasted the others, has by default become the guide to the 21st century.

Consequently, "the east is least and the west is best" is a motto that has come to summarize the attitude many people have toward the region. In more diplomatic language, it is usually put in this way: "Yes, we do have a great democracy [referring to the U.S.], one I appreciate all the more as I visit other countries" (Dyson, 1997a, p. 1). Such attitudes are merely examples of what Bridges (1998) termed "the closed open mind," where "there is no real point in seriously investigating other cultural world views or in critically examining their own."

A case in point is the overworked issue of nationalism. According to Nicholas Negroponte, director of the MIT Media Lab, one reason why the so-called "information society" is less developed in Europe as compared to the U.S. is because in the latter, there is less arrogance about history and self. "In many ways," observed Negroponte, "they [the U.S., Canada, and Nordic countries of Europe] suffer less from the baggage of history" (European Commission, 1998a, p. 28). Applying this meme to the New Europe, the broad concept of "nationalism" is seen as the main restrictive factor to Internet development and, subsequently, Internet-based activities such as civic discourse. Negroponte stressed this point during the 1997 European Information and Technology Conference and Exhibition (EITC-97) in Brussels. Viewing himself as an employable product of Western digital culture, he described himself as 50 percent European and "without a nationalistic bone" in his body (Negroponte, 1997). Others view his lack of "nationalistic bone[s]" rather differently. Ian Grigg (1999) translated and posted a Dutch commentary on Negroponte on the media theory list Nettime, which read, "Negroponte is just like any ordinary rock star, he gets out of the plane and when he walks down the stairs he still doesn't know which country he is in."

Thus, despite the potential of digital technology to encourage international discourse among regions and nations, the New Europe remains, to many digerati like Negroponte, a "terra incognita." Furthermore, because of lingering bloc attitudes toward the region, differing approaches to sociotechnological development and the diverse levels of progress that exist are frequently masked or misunderstood. The paradigm of modernist liberal philosophy is mainly responsible for this, for "liberal moral ideals became identified with a cultural perspective that claimed to embrace all humanity" (Bridges, 1998). To this extent, pundits claim that "culture" can be simply "acquired." The assumption that naturally follows is that the "negative" aspects of a given culture can likewise be just as simply "discarded."

In short, diversity within the New Europe is leveled to the point of naive simplicity, to the extent that regional issues and concerns are swept away or ignored by Western observers as relics of the past. This, in turn, reinforces existing communication gaps between "east" and "west" and, in some cases, even widens them. This stands true not only of politics and economics, but of technology as well.

SOCIAL AND TECHNOLOGICAL CHALLENGES

Although the New Europe is usually treated as a single entity, there are communication gaps within the region. It is apparent that there are at least two different speeds to the development of the new technology within the region: on the one hand, there is a "fast" lane that is comprised of countries such as the Czech Republic, Estonia, Poland, Hungary, and Slovenia. On the other, there is a slower lane that is comprised of countries such as Romania, Bulgaria, Russia, and the Commonwealth of Independent States (CIS).

To a large extent, this dichotomy mirrors the state of technological development that had already existed toward the end of the Communist era. For example, much of the information infrastructure of the former USSR was located in the Baltic region because of its proximity to neutral countries such as Finland and Sweden, which acted as relay centers to the outside world (Folkmanis, 1995). Hungary, meanwhile, specialized in DEC, PDP, and VAX machines, producing clones that ran on unlicensed operating systems and software; indeed, by the end of the 1980s, Hungary already had a limited Internet connection (Bodoky, 1996).

The state of technological development has further political significance in the present. If one takes the number of Web hosts per population as an indicator (European Commission, 1997a),[3] we can see that the groupings closely mirror the division of Central and Eastern Europe states between those that have started accession talks with the EU and those that are not in the first round of EU expansion. Generally speaking, the development of the Internet within the New Europe is foremost dependent on the economic and political developments of the region.

In addition to this, Internet use is a reflection of not only the pace of change that Central and Eastern Europeans are going through, but also the attitudes that they have toward this change. For some, their approach to the problems they face is to insist at the outset that the situation is hopeless. Such overriding apathy is one of the main reasons why the Internet has had a different impact on different countries within the area. In conjunction with this is a sense of insularity, which isolates the various nations within the region from one another. Each country still talks about "going to Europe"; using Hungary as an example, Carlson (1998) notes that their attitude is one of "If it didn't happen here, it didn't really happen."

Compared with western Europe and North America, overall knowledge of the Internet is at an elementary stage throughout Central and Eastern Europe. Where it is used, it is relied upon mainly to cull information; meanwhile, the skills needed to exploit the information at hand are clearly lacking. Although no reliable statistics exist, it is estimated that at least three-quarters of Central and Eastern European users have access to the Internet through a university or educational institution. Moreover, the majority of users live in large urban areas; most are male and under 30 years of age, with the biggest single group of users working in the fields of engineering and computer science.

Knowledge about the Internet is based more on hearsay rather than on any sort of change people are experiencing in the way they communicate or procure goods and services. For most, the "information revolution" is only something that is heard through the mass media—and not experienced. In addition to this, many live their lives from day to day; as a result, most of their plans are short-term, so they are wary of trying anything new unless financial rewards are high and immediate.

In light of this, the most daunting task facing the region is, without a doubt, problems related to access. Underdeveloped telecommunication infrastructures are the biggest problem. Although the region is doing its best to upgrade its telecom infrastructure, in places like Romania, Bulgaria, Russia, and the CIS, work has been among the slowest. There, people still wait years for a phone to be put in and most of the analog networks haven't been changed yet to accommodate for data communications. According to some estimates, it will take at least a decade to replace existing analog switches and lines with digital fiber optic ones.

As a result, most individuals in these areas gain access to the Internet through academic networks. Many students after graduating still retain their accounts and then continue to use them as private accounts. Some even share accounts, since most Internet activity is in the area of e-mail communication. Internet providers are few and far between, and those that do exist are quite expensive. Furthermore, since phones are not as commonplace as in the West and the quality of service is rather poor— especially in rural and remote areas—it is difficult for users to work from home.

Yet even in some of the more telematically advanced countries of the area, much work still needs to be done in order to foster an efficient information infrastructure. In Hungary, for instance, the local Internet community is being retarded by a handful of social and economic factors, in spite of the fact that Hungarians appear enthusiastic about computers and computer technology. As Carlson (1998) notes, a recent study revealed that 91 percent of the population agree it is important their children or grandchildren become familiar with computer technology (see also Nyiro, 1998).

Many of the social, economic, and other obstacles to the expansion of the Internet in the New Europe—weak and lopsided telecommunication infrastructures, language (despite software localization, most online software content is still dominated by English), government censorship and regulatory control, and impoverished and uneducated people who cannot afford to buy or use computers—are already well known. What is less acknowledged, however, is the obvious clash of cultural values between "east" and "west."

Americans and other Westerners are much more independent-minded (or at least appear to be so) as opposed to Central and Eastern Europeans. As a result, the latter tend to view the former as more aloof—sometimes even cold—with the feeling that they do not really understand nor are emphatic to their problems. To make matters worse, some Western companies have set up operations in Central and Eastern Europe with a view to making a short-term killing rather than to make a more long-term, or even permanent, investment. Further, Central and Eastern Europe has been used as a dumping ground for faulty and redundant technology (Horvath, 1997c). As a result, many end up making the erroneous assumption that Central and Eastern Europe is simply one big, homogeneous market or region, as opposed to a mosaic of more than a dozen unique cultures and societies.

For the majority of users in the New Europe, the Internet is being adopted as an entertainment phenomenon rather than an economic one. The economic aspect of the new media does not entail merely the buying and selling of goods and services over the Internet (better known as e-commerce), but also includes other activities as well, such as telework. This does not mean the economic dimension does not exist or has not become an important factor. Indeed, as an increasing number of jobs require computer skills, not to mention knowledge and experience of the Internet, the economic motivation to learn about the new media has become more pressing.

Nevertheless, the economic face of the Internet as it develops in Central and Eastern Europe is in many ways different from that of North America or western Europe, due most in part to the region's differing social, political, and economic structures. Failure to properly understand this has thus led to technological challenges that are not being dealt with on a regional level. This, in turn, has had a detrimental effect on the development of civic discourse within Central and Eastern Europe.

SELECTIVE DEVELOPMENT

As mentioned above, the development of the Internet within the New Europe can be broken down into two groups, one on a fast lane and another one on a slow lane. This dichotomy is one of the foremost stumbling blocks to the development of civic discourse within the region. The political aspirations of Western, developed countries, meanwhile, augment this situation through a process of selective development. Resources and support have been selectively given to certain countries in order to consolidate post-cold war political gains. At the same time, new spheres of influence between western Europe and Russia have been tacitly agreed upon. A case in point is the slide of Belarus toward the east; the Baltics, meanwhile, have moved toward the west.

The Baltics provide a clear example of the politics of selective development. All three Baltic states have become the center of a lot of investment by the EC seeking to develop its information infrastructure. Consequently, the region is being developed at a much faster rate than all other areas of the former Soviet Union, including Russia. A regional forum for cooperation between Estonia, Latvia, and Lithuania was established in 1992 through the Council of Baltic States (CBSS). This was soon followed by a pilot action initiated by the EC in May 1994, called the Baltic Information Infrastructure Pilot (BIIP). The purpose of this pilot action, according to the EC, was to strengthen information services in the Baltics and begin to opening such services more widely to Western users (Folkmanis, 1995).

In essence, the BIIP was expected to fill the gaps that are present in the existing networks throughout the Baltic region. In conjunction with this, in April 1996, the EC launched the Baltic Sea Regional Initiative (BSRI), with the intended aim to better coordinate and concentrate EU activities in the area. The BSRI is expected to provide a lasting framework for strengthening cooperation among CBSS members, by means of overall coordinated planning and the financing of large infrastructure projects.

All this does not mean that Russia and other CIS members are being neglected or ignored. They have also received aid and technical assistance from the West, but not at the same technical level nor as proportionally as in the Baltic States. For example, the EU approved an "action plan" for Russia. Unlike the BIIP or BSRI, however, the objectives of this action plan are mostly to promote economic reforms, with technical assistance mainly in the area of energy and nuclear safety, the environment, and the modernization of production systems.

Despite this, some work has been done to upgrade the educational aspect of networking in Russia. UNESCO set up the STACCIS project (Support for Telematics Applications Cooperation with the Commonwealth of Independent States), which hopes to further research and development activities in the field of telematics-based education and training in Russia and other CIS states. With the help of the STACCIS project, more people are likely to be exposed and acquainted with the new technology through the schools, thus enabling CMC to slowly expand to a wider section of the population.

Critics of this and other such projects, however, say that it is too much too fast; basically, the New Europe has to learn how to walk before it can run. There is a fear that if governments spend too much time and money on the advanced aspects of infrastructure development, other, more basic areas (such as telephones and roads) will be neglected, thus leading to a lopsided infrastructure. In addition to this, it threatens to widen regional differences, since such infrastructure development would benefit mostly the big urban centers and the western part of East Europe.

Counteracting the disproportionate initiatives of governments and other political bodies, there have been some independent efforts aimed at developing the civic aspects of digital information infrastructure. The most prevalent of these are the activities of George Soros and the Open Society Institute (OSI).

Aside from his general philanthropic activities in the area (for example, supporting educational and cultural activities and institutions), the biggest project launched by Soros has been a special five-year program signed between him and former Prime Minister Viktor Chernomyrdin in the spring of 1996, which will see 32 Russian provincial universities all hooked up to the Internet. Part of this project was also the development of the digital backbone in Moscow, a plan to link commercial and academic providers and institutions to the city's telephone switching centers.

Similar plans have been adopted in other areas of the former Soviet Union as well. In Belarus, work has begun to set up a powerful IP backbone network in Minsk that would make Internet access possible for a large number of organizations throughout the country. In addition to technical assistance, the OSI in Belarus has set for itself the task of introducing and spreading Internet culture and ideology as a means of bringing together large, diverse communities of different users (Tavgen, 1996).

This is an ambitious project, especially taking into account the political situation in Belarus. Yet, this is one of the unique aspects of Soros's activities. Unlike others, Soros can be found in the most politically volatile areas of the former Soviet Union and Central and Eastern Europe—including Bosnia and Serbia. In Albania, for instance, the OSI organized a exhibition of paintings in 1992, which was the only known medium at the time (Muka, 1996). Meanwhile, in Moldova, the OSI has been involved in a computerization program for secondary schools, as well as teacher training programs and other related activities. Not surprisingly, many government-sponsored programs and organizations have cut back their support to Central and Eastern Europe. This also includes the OSI. However, unlike others who have moved further east, feeling that their job in the region is done, Soros has pledged to still remain very active in those places where the civic aspects of sociopolitical change are still clearly lacking, such as in Slovakia and Belarus (OSF NF, 1998).

The philanthropic activities of Soros and the OSI are not welcomed by everyone, however (see, for example, Horvath, 1997a). One area in which Soros has been making a controversial impact is in the setting up of ISPs, which, according to some, have been stunting the growth of commercial ISPs. The OSI has given enormous amounts of assistance to academic networks, which, in turn, provides some commercial companies with access, which is usually free or well below commercial ISP rates.

While in the more "advanced" areas of Central and Eastern Europe such activities are no longer considered to be an issue (Carlson, 1998), elsewhere (in places like Romania and Bulgaria) such philanthropy has prompted some to wonder how much good the OSI is actually doing in the region—and for whom.[4] The OSI is sometimes seen as doing more harm than good because it gives a seemingly unfair advantage to those who happen to work for the OSI or are the direct recipients of Soros's philanthropy. More importantly, many feel that such development should be left up to the market. In much the same way, those involved in building the commercial aspect of the Internet within Central and Eastern Europe feel that the civic aspects of digital infrastructure (that is, art, education, and so forth) should likewise be market-driven.

All these different approaches (political, philanthropic, and business)—which are not always complimentary—have led to unequal support, thus reinforcing the fragmented state of regional development. Subsequently, civic discourse among the countries of Central and Eastern Europe is likewise fragmented, for some continue to speed ahead on the "information superhighway," while others are left to make their way as best they can. Indeed, it appears the prime objective of most countries within the region is to zoom down the highway as fast as possible in order to "catch up" to Europe, without regard for others on the road or those left behind.

RESTRAINING INFLUENCES

While some nations speed ahead and others are left behind, the fragmented political environment left over from the fall of Communism, coupled with the region's unique ethnic mosaic, has isolated communities from one another and cultivated feelings of insularity, which makes any sort of constructive political dialogue between groups near to impossible. Furthermore, restraining influences unique to the area, attributable to a mix of history, culture, and language, are being strengthened and, in turn, have become a further hindrance to the development of civic discourse.

As noted previously, the underdeveloped state of digital infrastructure is one of the foremost technological challenges that the entire region faces. As a result, access has become a primary restrictive factor to the development of civic discourse. But it is not merely a question of obtaining physical access—a problem mostly shared by rural areas—but also the high cost of access in those places where access is available. In Hungary, for instance, to access the Internet for an average of five hours per week at a reasonable time of day (that is, between 6:00 pm and 10:00 pm) it would cost approximately $20 (U.S.; 1998 rates) in telephone charges alone. This represents more than 10 percent of an average Hungarian's salary (that is, before taxes). Thus, bandwidth is very expensive, and therefore scarce; the nation's largest ISP is connected to the rest of the world by just 10 megabytes per second.

Consequently, most users do not have Internet access at home. Only 34,000 people, representing a mere 14 percent of the online population in Hungary, have commercial access. This is less than half the number of users in the Czech Republic, who have domestic Internet access. In terms of overall penetration, just 0.7 percent of Hungarian households are connected to the Internet, compared to a European average of 4 percent.

In order to stimulate domestic Internet use, there has been pressure to reduce telephone costs. However, the Hungarian telecom giant, MATÁV, has so far reacted half-heartedly, encouraging increased use without actually reducing rates. For instance, a special weekend "discount" for April 1998 was introduced in which a price cap was put on any domestic call exceeding a certain limit. The limit, however, was set at such a high level that a person would have to make a local call for at least 200 minutes before any savings could be had.

The high cost of online access makes civic discourse not only prohibitive, but renders it an elitist activity. Consequently, any discourse that does exist is usually limited in scope.[5]

Language is another restricting factor. For many countries within the New Europe, the preservation of their cultural identity is often expressed through the vehicles of linguistic chauvinism. Language is a major component of their identity and "cultural baggage"; hence, the fear of corruption of their language finds expression in terms of cultural preservation. This is particularly so in Hungary, where Hungarians tend to regard both their language and culture prone to corruption (Glenny, 1993). Despite assurances that low barriers to entry will mean producers of native language content will always have a void to fill on the Internet (van Dusseldorp, 1998), the fears and concerns within Central and Eastern Europe toward the preservation of national languages remains. These fears are not entirely groundless, for historical precedents do exist. The most recent was during the Soviet occupation, where the Russian language was incorporated within the education curriculum of many nations within the region.[6] Even prior to that era, concern over the preservation of minority and national languages was apparent, for many linguists of the time from outside the region adopted a negative view toward the language mosaic of Central and Eastern Europe.[7]

Closely related to the issue of language is that of education. Most analysts agree that Central and Eastern Europe's secondary grammar schools, designated for a smaller, more elite group, is a restrictive factor (Langenkamp, 1996). Moreover, traditional, teacher-centered approaches to learning, coupled with paternalistic views toward education in general, are further obstacles to the development of Internet-based civic discourse, for they sustain an underlying fear and mistrust of computer technology. Many teachers feel that computers will replace them in the same way that workers in other sectors of the economy have been replaced. In conjunction with this, they are unable to appreciate the new roles that the new media will create for them, since traditional teaching methodology views knowledge acquisition as a top-down process.

Meanwhile, in those places where new media technologies have made inroads, the problem is that computers and telematic systems are relied upon as a mere substitute for a book rather than as an additional tool available to both students and teachers. As a result, computer-assisted instruction (CAI) within Central and Eastern Europe has become nothing more than an empty shell into which content is simply poured in to give it substance, with the quality of education being directly proportional to the quantity of the content it holds. As a reaction to this problem, "edutainment" has become a looming threat. A hybrid of education and entertainment, it is fast becoming an alternative educational method. The threat edutainment poses is that it tends to undermine the educational value of the media in which it is contained (Horvath, 1997b). Consequently, the various government programs aimed at "wiring" schools to the Internet are improperly focused. These programs merely introduce students to the technology; they are not taught nor encouraged to make any sense of it. As a result, the Internet has become a pseudo-educational medium, as Johnson (1995) had warned. To this extent, civic discourse has been compromised; the Internet has been introduced to the young within Central and Eastern Europe as simply a medium for market-based entertainment in all its forms.

Outside the field of education, the problem is not that much different. As with educators, "tradition" generally acts as a restricting factor for many—especially the older generation. Much of this has to do with the legacy of Communism, which still influences the way in which people think and do things (Gulyás, 1998). This is further accentuated by the archaic methods employed by various ISPs as well as the business practices of state-run telecoms.[8]

Aside from questions related to computer technology and its penetration, there is a more basic factor restricting civic discourse that, in turn, is magnified through the new media. This has to do with the isolation of groups and individuals from each other and often manifests itself in the form of an "island" mentality. Much of this has to do with events of the recent past. For decades, many believed that they had come from "great nations," undertaking a historical experiment in social justice and equality. With the collapse of the Communist system, and the utopian image it had created, many had to reassess their past and their values. In Russia, for example, one of the biggest and unpronounced effects of the cold war—the illusion of Russia as a superpower—has left Russians with a strong and painful sense of isolation and the feeling of being deprived of moral support and understanding (see, for example, International Organization for Migration, 1994).

Civic discourse is not only hampered by an "island feeling," but also a social malaise that permeates the region. According to Petrovics-Ofner (1993), this is attributable in large part to a feeling of "learned helplessness"[9] (p. 6), an inhibition to assert oneself that had been left over from the Communist regime and that is still slow in being overcome. Hence, many of the problems and issues that people are forced to deal with are either avoided or simply internalized. To illustrate this, Glenny (1993) argues that Hungarians are brought up amid a series of cultural traditions that pull fiercely in opposing directions, leading many to suffer from a crisis of identity as they attempt to either reconcile or choose among these conflicting traditions. Not surprisingly, Hungarians are considered to be the most pessimistic within the New Europe, which also explains why the country consistently has one of the highest suicide rates in the world.

While this "learned helplessness" hypothesis helps to explain some aspects of sociopolitical behavior, it nevertheless falls short of the mark. Beyond communism's enduring social and political legacy is the fact that people within Central and Eastern Europe just do not want to take risks; in fact, they are a little tired of change. They had already taken enough risks at the beginning with the change in system, and for many the promises of a better life have been slow in coming or unfulfilled altogether. Others are torn between feelings of gratification and dissatisfaction, for they are not sure that the advantages of the post-cold war era outweigh the disadvantages. Furthermore, the new factors on which their place in life now depends are uncertain and not clearly understood. Hence, talk about Internet-based civic discourse is fine when there is a margin to spare—a margin for risk. However, since most in the region do not have this margin to play with (or if they do, then it is quite slim), and that there is a measure of risk in anything that is untried, many feel more comfortable in sticking with something that is certain.

In addition to all this, change is habitually feared within Central and Eastern Europe, not only because of the risks involved, but because of the region's tragic history of change. The underlying premise of Western industrial societies is that change is identified with new and better ways of producing or organizing things. This means not only tangibles (such as commercial products), but includes other things as well, such as ideas. Hence, modern ideas of civic discourse are trapped within this Western, industrial paradigm; as with capitalism, it has formed an article of faith that surmises that the whole community unquestionably benefits from the advance of change.

Yet, for the countries of the New Europe, change has come to mean something entirely different. For centuries, caught in a vice between the ambitions of empire builders from east and west, change has traditionally meant that someone at one time or another had seized land, exacted rents, and levied taxes, all for the enrichment of an outsider—at their expense.

This being the psychohistorical experience of change in the New Europe, it should come as no surprise, then, that many are wary of trying anything new. Indeed, many feel the historiographical process of domination continuing unabated: foreign capitalists have now replaced the empire builders of old. Hence, the present economic climate acts as a further deterrent to civic discourse. Although the smug minority on the Internet can afford to be outspoken, there are many others who are afraid to do so because of the fear—both real and imagined—of losing their jobs if they express unorthodox opinions. For those who dare to dissent in today's economic climate, they may easily find themselves out of a job, socially ostracized, and economically strangled.

Finally, it must be recognized that due to a process of thwarted nationhood (Rady, 1990), democratic traditions—the basis for civic discourse—have not had the chance to develop properly. Moreover, the present concept of civic discourse is uniquely American in character: the practice of writing, faxing, and calling your congressperson—activities that are all enhanced by new media technologies, and constitute the basis of modern conceptions of civic discourse—is a practice that is not only lacking within Central and Eastern Europe, but within the EU as well. Indeed, many of the democratic traditions highlighted by Alexis de Tocqueville (1835/1998) over 150 years ago still remain unique to the North American democratic experience.

To sum up, restraining influences to the development of civic discourse are many and varied, and thus cannot be attributed to simply one or two factors—be it the cost of access or the legacy of the region's Communist past. Apart from technological considerations and the economics of access, historic inhibitions based on language and identity, coupled with a lack of democratic traditions, all exercise a negative impact on the development of civic discourse within the New Europe.

PRESENT AND FUTURE IMPLICATIONS

Given the restraining influences that exist, it is commonly assumed that there is no interest at all in the New Europe about the issue of Internet-based civic discourse. The Internet and Politics conference held in Munich at the beginning of 1997 provides a concrete example. According to Christa Maar, one of the main organizers of the event, invitations to the conference were sent to various people from Central and Eastern Europe, but none had decided to attend. As a result, a talk on the Internet in Eastern Europe was given by Esther Dyson (1997b), who spoke more about the economic opportunities available for entrepreneurs going east rather than regional issues related to civic discourse.

The conclusion to be drawn from this is misleading. The absence of participants from Central and Eastern Europe at the conference has more to do with the inability of conference organizers to seek appropriate speakers than with a disinterest toward, or regional inexperience of, democracy and the electronic media. For example, the MetaForum series of conferences within Budapest, organized by the Media Research

Foundation, should have provided them with ample opportunities to find participants. Almost none of those from the New Europe who had participated in these conferences (in total, three conferences over three years) were consulted by the organizers of the Internet and Politics conference.

Furthermore, discourse that does trickle from the region is usually considered to be insignificant or is treated in a condescending manner. In fact, in many cases, it's foreign observers who connect Central and Eastern Europe to the world in terms of communicating information from and about the region.

In conjunction with this, a lack of solidarity within the New Europe is being sustained by the region's Internet "elites." As already mentioned, these elites suffer from an "island" complex and are thus often isolated from one another. Moreover, since each region is in competition with one another as they race down the information superhighway, cooperation and empathy is often missing. Most have acquired a worldview that is an adaptation—on a regional scale—of a modernist-liberal philosophy, as described by Bridges (1998). Hence, Tamás Bodoky's (1996) smug claim that Hungary is neither "data rich" nor "data poor," but occupies a certain position in the middle—a kind of "data middle class" (that is, not quite like the "west," but definitely not "east" either), despite much evidence to the contrary (Nyiro, 1998).

For this reason, most online discourse lacks a truly civic focus—both locally and interregionally. Whereas elsewhere, discussions range from how the Internet can strengthen local communities by addressing urban decay and social breakdown (that is, community networking) or invigorating democratic politics, Central and Eastern Europe governments and online communities alike are more concerned with building a "market," warning the public that they have to change or they will be left out of the economic benefits of an "information society."

A direct implication of this is that global issues with a regional impact, such as the Multilateral Agreement on Investment (MAI), are not discussed to a marked degree within regional and local forums. In turn, globally coordinated action is limited. For instance, during the "Global Days of Action Against 'Free' Trade and the WTO" conference, held in May 1998, groups from only four countries within Central and Eastern Europe initiated some sort of protest, as opposed to over 10 from the rest of Europe.[10]

Such neglected civic discourse not only affects the population at large, but also has a detrimental effect on ethnic minorities. Particularly affected are the Roma (gypsy) populations of Central and Eastern Europe. The worsening situation for the Roma is not only perpetuated, but even magnified, since the educational and economic resources needed to maintain an online presence is clearly lacking.

The adoption of overt (and often excessive) market-based discourse also has a negative effect on how digital media art articulates "new" cultural and creative "freedoms" once "forbidden" by the Soviet regime. In many ways, artistic expression is more limited now than before. In the past, expression was allowed, yet dissemination was prevented (Sugár, cited in Lovink, 1998b); at present, it is the reverse. It's simply a question of economics: "because there is no mass market for it, and no social power associated with it, art is being marginalized and replaced by entertainment" (Pope, 1999). As Sugár (cited in Lovink, 1998b) laments, "with the dismantling of the Iron Curtain, it has changed: a sort of cultural protectionism emerged between the former Socialist countries and Western Europe. We are not anymore picante Easterners but weak competitors with a bad infrastructure."

CONCLUSION

Civic discourse in the New Europe is limited to an elite minority, who hold values and discuss issues that are usually closed, and have generally little relevance to the public at large. This is mostly due to an inherently weak state of civic discourse worldwide, which is reinforced by a predominant neo-liberalist political climate. Despite appearances and the euphoric promises of a greater expression of democracy and extensive civic discourse through new media technologies, the medium has so far exercised a reverse potential to drown the message.

Added to all this is a chronic misreading of the New Europe by the West. A lot of this has to do with erroneous assumptions about the region's diversity, which is leveled to the point of naive simplicity. This is done to the extent that regional issues and concerns are merely swept aside or ignored as obstructive ghosts of the past. Consequently, the social and technological challenges that are faced by the region are not properly understood, thus leading to a process of selective development.

Selective development represents one of the foremost stumbling blocks to civic discourse within the region. It exasperates restraining influences, which are based on a unique mix of history, culture, and language. These restraining influences are many and varied, and are a hindrance to not only the development of civic discourse on a regional level, but within the larger framework of a "New Europe" as well.

The implications of this are that discourse with a truly civic focus, which is in its embryonic stages within the New Europe, runs the grave risk of being stillborn. If present trends continue, congenital feelings of insularity will be merely reinforced and thus carried over into the third millennium, thereby threatening to increase gaps that already exist between "east" and "west," as well as within the region itself, in terms of communication, economic development, and even minority rights.

This does not mean, however, that the situation is hopeless. Yet, in order for progressive change to come about, the nature of civic discourse in and of itself must first change. At the same time, the homogenized and often faulty perception toward the "east" needs to be overcome. Additionally, less emphasis should be placed on the marketing aspect of new media technologies. An effort should also be made to have children in school understand the technology they use and apply it to their everyday experience in more student-centered approaches. This would mean transcending the image of computer-mediated communication from its present status as a purely entertainment form of media.

Unless such change is forthcoming, many within the region will continue to feel isolated. Meanwhile, statistics on all aspects of Internet development will keep on painting an optimistic picture of a digital future. However, these images will be mostly superficial and cosmetic, for against this backdrop individual users will feel that they and their problems are not properly understood by others in the outside world—that somehow they are alone in the crowd.

NOTES

1. While the underlying issues of this chapter remain relevant, much has changed since it was written. This is the challenge of dealing with a rapidly changing subject like technology. For current concerns in Hungary, and elsewhere in the New Europe, please see my articles in *Telepolis*, found on the Internet at http://www.heise.de/tp/english/default.html.

2. Writing in the late 1970s about Hungarian cinema, Graham Petrie laments that "despite the fact, however, that Hungarian cinema of the past decade has long been acknowledged as the most consistently interesting in Eastern Europe and one of the most significant features in European cinema as a whole, much of the best work has been seen only intermittently in the English-speaking world and, when seen, it has often been misunderstood or misinterpreted." Petrie explains that "part of this can be attributed to the notorious laziness, or blindness, or arrogance, of Anglo Saxon society: it has long been taken for granted that, outside Great Britain and America themselves, the only cultural traditions worth taking seriously are those of France, Italy, Germany, Spain, and Russia." He goes on to conclude, "where Hungary is concerned, the problem is compounded by an extremely difficult (and to a foreigner, almost unpronouceable) language, and by the fact that many of the best Hungarian films take their starting-point in historical

events that are only vaguely known to, or comprehended by, outsiders" (1978, pp. 1–2).

3. As Bridges (1998) observes, a theoretically legitimated set of political arrangements were presumed to be universally valid and normative—the set of political arrangements that all nations should or eventually will adopt. Only this sort of modernist conception of the cognitive task of political philosophy could have produced the bizarre intellectual phenomena of the cold war—a struggle between two totalizing social and political systems, systems whose claims to legitimacy rested on conflicting philosophical demonstrations of the conformity of those systems with the objective nature of things.

4. See also the survey by Baltic Media Facts called "Usage of Computers and Internet Among the Population in Estonia" (1997). According to this survey, 10 percent of all inhabitants from Estonia, between 15 and 74 years of age, along with 36 percent of all computer users within the country, have used the Internet during the first six months of 1997. This represents about 116,000 persons. The weekly reach of the Internet, meanwhile, is 6 percent of the Estonian population aged 15 to 74 (about 64,000 people). It is interesting to note that Estonia also has the highest number of mobile phone users within Central and Easern Europe, with a penetration of more than 7 percent of the total population.

5. Gordon Cook, author and compiler of *The Cook Report on the Internet*, a monthly review of computer and Internet-related issues, revealed in a January 1995 report on the case of the Moscow backbone dispute, in which a Soros foundation turned something that was much needed and welcome into something highly controversial. In this dispute, the Soros foundation refused to share administration of the Moscow backbone with Realcom, one of the principal partners in the project, to the extent that two separate backbones within the Russian capital were being built. What appears to have happened in Moscow was that the backbone became a victim of power politics. As Cook succinctly put it in his report of the situation: "You are either a friend or an enemy of [the] ISF and are treated accordingly" (pp. 18–19).

6. As further proof of the lack of true civic discourse and the elite nature of online communities in the New Europe, the Hungarian Net community had "averted" a strike at the beginning of January 1999, when MATÁV introduced its latest round of price increases. While those within the Internet elite claimed some sort of victory through the proposals they made to avert the strike, the truth of the matter is that it had no effect for society as a whole. Indeed, the solutions proposed by the self-appointed "representatives" of Hungary's Net community merely reaffirms the status quo of high-cost access, one that leaves the average Hungarian unable to afford the use of computer-mediated communication at home (see, for example, Horvath, 1999).

7. The forced teaching of the Russian language under the Soviets was in part based on N. Ya Murr's theory of the evolution of a universal language under Communism. According to Murr, a Georgian scholar, archaeologist, and ethnologist writing in the 1920s, language was a class phenomenon

related to a nation's cultural superstructure, which is, in turn, derived from an economic base. As a consequence of socialism's leveling effects, Communism would inevitably lead to the emergence of a universal language (see, for example, De Jonge, 1986).

8. For instance, Antoine Meillet, professor at the College de France, in a book written shortly after World War I, entitled *Les langues dans l'Europe nouvelle*, regarded the linguistic map of Europe as simply absurd (Kosztolányi, 1987). An interesting criticism of Meillet can be found in an open letter published by Dezsō Kosztolányi (1987), one of Hungary's leading literary figures of the 20th century. This, coupled with the feeling that Hungary was being misunderstood by both the English-speaking world (namely, the U.S. and Great Britain) and the French intellectual elite, prompted leading Hungarian intellectuals and politicians during the interwar years to counter what they saw as anti-Hungarian propaganda. The *Hungarian Quarterly* was a direct result of this apparent need for Hungary to assert itself through literary means (Frank, 1993).

9. For the situation with MATÁV in Hungary, see Haas (1998); for the situation with the Committee on Posts and Telecoms in Bulgaria, see Basmadjiev (1998); for the situation in Croatia, see Spigel (1998); and for the situation in Russia, see Kolesnikov (1998).

10. This idea is based on Goldstein's original theory of learned helplessness, where forlorn behavior can be ingrained within the consciousness. Goldstein experimented with dogs, exposing some to pain they could not escape from and others that could. He found that the dogs that could not escape from the pain ended up in a helpless state and continued to be so even after the pain was removed. Meanwhile, those dogs that could volitionally escape the pain remained healthy (Petrovics-Ofner, 1993).

11. Of those countries that participated within Europe ("east" and "west"): Austria, Belgium, the Czech Republic, Estonia, Finland (Helsinki, Turku), France, Germany (Berlin, Darmstadt, Dresden, Frankfurt, Freiburg, Gorleben, Göttingen, Gunkelrode, Heidelberg, Hildesheim, Karlsruhe, Mainz), The Netherlands (The Hague, Utrecht), Russia, Slovenia, Spanish State (Avilés, Barcelona, Durango, Iruña, Lugo, Sevilla, València), Sweden, Switzerland (Aarau, Basel, Bern, Geneva, Gössgen, Hindelbank, Offtringen), and the United Kingdom (Birmingham, York). (See also PGA Bulletin, 1998.)

REFERENCES

Arns, I. (1998, Summer). Editorial: New media cultures in Eastern, Central and South-Eastern Europe. *Convergence: The Journal of Research into New Media Technologies, 4*(2), 5–7.

Baltic Media Facts. (1997, September). *Usage of computers and Internet among the population in Estonia* [Online]. Available: <http://www.bmf.ee/internet98_1/> [1999, February 14].

Bascó, P. (Director). (1969). *A tanu* [Film]. Available: <http://www.interj.data-net.hu/comser/tanu.html>

Basmadjiev, B. (1998, March 10). *Initiator of "regulation of ISPs" thread on Online Europe mailing list* [Online]. Available: <http://www.isys.hu/online-europe> [1999, February 13].

Bodoky, T. (1996, December). *Fear and loathing in Hungary*. Presentation at Data Conflicts: Eastern Europe and the Geopolitics of Cyberspace Conference, Potsdam, Germany.

Bridges, T. (1998, April 19). *Consequences of the modernist liberal abandonment of classical conceptions of practical philosophy, philosophy and civil society* [Online]. Available: <http://www.chss.montclair.edu/civsoc/homepage.html> [1998, September 2].

Carlson, S. (1998, March 31). *We have to build this market* [Online]. Available: <http://www.isys.hu/online-europe/current/0411.html> [1999, February 5].

Cook, G. (1995, January 15). *The COOK Report on the Internet* [Online]. Available: <http://www.cookreport.com/> [1999, February 13].

Corporate Watch. (n.d.). *Towards a democratic media system: Interview with Robert McChesney, Corporate Watch* [Online]. Available: <http://www.corpwatch.org/trac/internet/corpspeech/mcchesney.html> [1999, February 6].

De Jonge, A. (1986). *Stalin and the shaping of the Soviet Union*. Glasgow, Scotland: William Collins & Sons.

De Pauw, J. (1997, January 22). *Nettime: Reacting to "What Kind of Libertarian"* [Online]. Available: <http://www.nettime.org/nettime.w3archive> [1999, February 13].

van Dusseldorp, M. (1998, April 3). *English vs. local language* [Online]. Available: <http://www.nettime.org/nettime.w3archive> [1999, February 13].

Dyson, E. (1997a, January 19). And now, a word from some fellow Americans. *Washington Post*, Outlook Section, p. 1.

Dyson, E. (1997b, February). *The Net in Eastern Europe—From state restrictions to auto-regulation*. Presentation given at Internet & Politics: The Modernization of Democracy Through the Electronic Media, International Conference of the Burda Academy of the Third Millennium, European Patent Office, Munich, Germany.

European Commission. (1997a, December 3). *Green paper on the convergence of the telecommunications, media and information technology sectors, and the implications for regulation: Towards an information society approach* [Online]. Available: <http://www.ispo.cec.be/convergencegp/greenp.html> [1999, February 11].

European Commission. (1997b). *Status report on telework: Telework 1997* (# DG-XIII-B). Brussels, Belgium: Author.

European Commission. (1998a, March-April). A wired worldview. *RTD Info, 18*, 28–30.

European Commission. (1998b, March-April). The unknown factors of convergence. *RTD Info, 18*, 26–27.

Folkmanis, A. J. (1995, October). Baltic information infrastructure—A first step. *I&T Magazine, 18*, 6–9.

Frank, T. (1993, Spring). Editing as politics: Jozsef Balogh and the *Hungarian Quarterly*. *The Hungarian Quarterly, 34*(129), 5–13.

Glenny, M. (1993). *The rebirth of history: Eastern Europe in the age of democracy.* New York: Penguin.

Grigg, I. (Trans.). (1999, February 10). *How DigiCash blew everything* [Online]. Available: <http://www.desk.nl/~nettime> [1999, February 6].

Gulyás, Á. (1998, Summer). In the slow lane on the information superhighway: Hungary and the information revolution. *Convergence: The Journal of Research into New Media Technologies, 4*(2), 76–92.

Haas, M. (1998, April 8). *Reply to the "We have to build this market" thread on the Online Europe mailing list* [Online]. Available: <http://www.isys.hu/online-europe/current/0426.html> [1999, February 6].

Horvath, J. (1997a, March). Geschlossene Gesellschaft: Das Soros-Netzwerk. *Telepolis: Soft Life, 1,* 128–138.

Horvath, J. (1997b, Spring). Access is not enough. *Convergence: The Journal of Research into New Media Technologies, 3*(1), 20–24.

Horvath, J. (1997c, June/July). The virtual dumping ground. *Toward Freedom, 46*(3), 29–30.

Horvath, J (1999). *The great Hungarian sellout* [Online]. Available: <http://www.heise.de/tp/english/inhalt/te/1761/1.html> [1999, January 14].

Hume, E. (1995). *Tabloids, talk radio, and the future of news: Technology's impact on journalism* [Online]. Available: <http://www.annenberg.nwu.edu/pubs/tabloids/tabloids08.htm> [1999, February 6].

Illés. (1967). *Sárya rózsa* [LP]. Budapest: Qualiton.

Information Society Forum. (1996, June). *Networks for people and their communities: Making the most of the information society in the European Union. First Annual Report of the European Commission from the Information Society Forum.* Brussels, Belgium: European Commission.

International Organization for Migration. (1994). *Reports on transit migration within individual Central and Eastern European countries (Romania, Poland, Bulgaria, and the Czech Republic, respectively).* Budapest, Hungary: Migration Information Programme.

Johnson, J. (1995). *The information hypeway: A worst-case scenario.* Paper presented at the Conference on Computer-Human Interaction (CHI '95), Association for Computing Machinery, Denver, CO.

Kolesnikov, A. (1998, March 10). *Reply to the "regulation of ISPs" thread on the Online Europe mailing list* [Online]. Available: <http://www.isys.hu/online-europe> [1999, February 9].

Kosztolányi, D. (1987). The place of the Hungarian language on the earth. In E. Tóth (Ed.), *Today: An anthology of contemporary Hungarian literature* (pp. 21–37). Budapest, Hungary: Corvina Press.

Kunzru, H. (1997, January 5). *Rewiring technoculture* [Online]. Available: <http://www.nettime.org/nettime.w3archive> [1999, February 9].

Langenkamp, D. (1996, May 20). Hungary's graduates face the real world. *The Hungary Report* [Online serial], *1.50.* Available: <http://www.isys.hu/hrep/> [1999, February 12].

Lovink, G. (1998a, Summer). Intermedia: The dirty digital bauhaus—A e-mail exchange with János Sugár. *Convergence: The Journal of Research into New Media Technologies, 4*(2), 14–19.

Lovink, G. (1998b, February 26). *Intermedia: The dirty digital bauhaus—A e-mail exchange with János Sugár* [Online]. Available: <http://www.desk.nl/~nettime/> [1999, March 14].

Muka, E. (1996, October). Media art in Albania, first steps, an interview conducted by Geert Lovink during the "V2_East" meeting, DEAF Conference, Rotterdam, Netherlands. In *zpk 3* (p. 198). Budapest: metaforum.

Negroponte, N. (1997, November). Keynote address at the European Information and Technology Conference and Exhibition (EITC-97), Brussels, Belgium.

Nyiro, A. (1998, March). *Hungary is falling behind on the Net* [Online]. Available: <http://helyzet.internetto.hu> [1999, February 6].

OSF NF. (1998, May 5). OSF NF letter [Online]. Available: <http://www.desk.nl/~nettime/>

Petrie, G. (1978). *History must answer to man: The contemporary Hungarian cinema.* Budapest: Corvina.

Petrovics-Ofner, L. (1993, July-August). A cure for "learned helplessness." *Budapest Week, 3*(21), 6.

PGA Bulletin. (1998, June). *Peoples' global action against "free" trade and the WTO* [Online]. Available: <http://www.agp.org/pga>

Pope, S. T. (1999). Proceedings of the Salzburg Symposium on Arts and the Internet. Mozarteum Academy, Salzburg, Austria. *Computer Music Journal, 23*(1) [Online serial]. Available: <http://mitpress.mit.edu/e~journals/Computer-Music-Journal/CMJ.html> [1999, September 10].

Rady, M. (1990). The present in the light of the past. In D. Jones (Ed.), *And the walls came tumbling down: Eastern Europe after the revolutions* (pp. 5–10). London: Broadcasting Support Services.

Rijs, B. (1996, December 2). *The revolution in Serbia begins with a homepage on the Internet* [Online]. Available: <http://www.xs4all.nl/~opennet/8.html>

Schultz, P. (1996, December 4). *Response to "The Revolution in Serbia Begins with a Homepage on the Internet"* [Online]. Available: <http://www.xs4all.nl/~opennet/8.html>

Shulgin, A. (1996, October). Art, power and communication. *Proceedings from the Metaforum 3 Conference*, 153–154.

Skyring, K. (1998, July 9). *Interview with Andrzej Ziolowski* [Online]. Available: <http://www.via.at/fobdr> [1999, February 12].

Spigel, I. (1998, March 10). *Reply to the "Regulation of ISPs" thread on the Online Europe mailing list* [Online]. Available: <http://www.isys.hu/online-europe> [1999, February 13].

Stalder, F. (1998, April 8). *Response to the "Interactivity" thread on Nettime* [Online]. Available: < http://www.nettime.org/nettime.w3archive> [1999, February 11].

Stoller, J. (December 1996/January 1997). Rebels without a clue. *Toward Freedom, 45*(7), 13–15.

Tavgen, I. (1996). *Internet program information sheet.* Minsk, Belarus: Belarus Soros Foundation.

de Tocqueville, A. (1998). *Democracy in America* (F. Bowen, Trans.). London: Wordsworth Editions. (Original work published 1835)

Weissman, R. (1998, June). *A nation of spectators? Focus on the corporation* [Online]. Available: <www.essential.org/monitor> [1999, February 5].

Part II

Concerns and Challenges in the New Europe

chapter 6

Mediated Concerns:
The New Europe in Hypertext

Dina Iordanova
University of Leicester, England

I recently received an e-mail message from a Ph.D. student at the American University in Washington, D.C., who wanted to consult me on the choice of her dissertation topic. The dissertation was to deal with East European media, and the student was considering writing a thesis on deregulation in television, but was getting more and more hesitant, as studying television, she wrote, seemed to be so completely out-of-date. Today, she said, no one works on anything but the Internet.

Are other media obsolete and is the Internet the only viable subject for research nowadays? Things certainly may look this way from the point of view of an American graduate student, but was this the case indeed, I wondered? Most recent studies on media in various Eastern European countries and on the region as a whole do not include considerations of the growing online communications, as if the Internet has not yet become part of the mediatic reality of these countries. This is the picture with important writings by Goban-Klas (1994); Gross (1996); O'Neil (1997); Paletz, Jakubowicz, and Novosel (1995); Sparks (1997); and Splichal (1994). In a 1998 study, John Downey even claimed that "the discussion of new information and communication technologies is not of central importance for understanding what is happening in Central and Eastern Europe" (p. 54). In the West, many scholars working at the cutting edge of communication research more and more often turn to studying the Internet, often approaching it along the lines suggested by Richard MacKinnon (1995), who used the metaphor of Hobbesian *Leviathan* to describe it. At the same time and in spite of the growing literature, communication scholarship has not yet produced an authoritative study that would become a milestone for this new and dynamically growing field.

At the same time, in many East European countries, basic postal communication is an unresolved issue; and let's not even mention telephony. Shouldn't we then expect that media scholarship would focus on these aspects first and foremost? How important is it to look at the Internet in the context of the New Europe? Can we continue ignoring the information exchange carried out via the means of online communications in the mediatic environment of the countries in Eastern Europe?

I do not think we can. The New Europe uses the Internet to mediate its concerns in no lesser degree than the other means of mass communication. Its presence on the Internet is substantial, and its mode or existence in hypertext is of no lesser validity or intensity than the one it has in print or broadcast media.

To acknowledge the growing importance of the Internet for the New Europe is just the first step, however. The next one is to critically examine the contradictions that come along with it. It is of particular importance to recognize that the enthusiastic view of the future of the Internet is seriously counterbalanced by a pessimistic one, and to recognize that besides the rich opportunities for dialogue, there are valid dangers of dependency. Only if we consider opposing interpretations will we be able to offer a balanced outlook for the future.

CONFLICTING VIEWS

The burgeoning developments of computer networking at large cannot leave communication scholars indifferent, and many have undertaken to look into the claims that we are living in an age of revolutionary changes in the ways we communicate. While some are overtly optimistic, however, others remain pessimists.

On the one hand, there are the enthusiasts. They recognize that the Internet is, and most likely will long remain, an elite medium in many regions, but they stress that it still has a powerful potential for solving many of the faults of the existing information infrastructure, as it allows for unprecedented access to an endless wealth of information choices, and empowers economic entrepreneurship and various other undertakings in culture and politics. To them, the explosive expansion of the Internet is a unique configuration of political, economic, and cultural factors, undermining rigid structures and entrenched management attitudes and creating new situations where technological innovation, if properly handled, could enhance opportunities of unprecedented access to information and create new freedom in personal communication. MIT's Media Lab director Nicholas Negroponte (1996), for example, does not see the division between information-rich and information-poor countries as essential. He stresses on the generational divide in the use of the Internet, and believes that this is par excellence the communication tool of the young generation. Esther Dyson (1997), one of the most active Western entrepreneurs in the New Europe and a high profile promoter of the Internet and new technologies, is also enthusiastic about the future. Her experiences in Eastern Europe have made her realize that ensuring access to information and creating a solid legal infrastructure are necessary preconditions for the development of market economy and therefore these need to be resolved first and foremost. The tendency to be mistrustful that Dyson encounters amidst East Europeans is a legacy from the Communist past, in her opinion. Creating a new culture of trust in information, however, is an essential building block in Dyson's design for living in the digital age.

Others are skeptical about the chances of new technologies to democratize communication, and they point at examples of global inequalities in accessing the Internet, at imperial-type dependencies, and at resulting exclusion and limitations. Peter Goulding (1998), for example, believes that the Internet will follow the fate of other new technologies, whose promise of shared abundance has been dissipated by corporate greed and political failure. Goulding, who believes that the real divide around the Net is a class one, stresses the ongoing corporate takeover of the Internet and claims that its exponential growth is driven not as much by the real needs of democratic communication, but rather by the big corporations' need to expand markets. "What we are witnessing," he writes, "is the 'mediatisation' of the new technologies, as they follow past scenarios of commercialization, differentiated access, exclusion of the poor, privatization, deregulation and globalisation" (p. 148).

If we transfer these conflicting views to the reality of the Internet in Eastern Europe, we will most likely have to choose a middle ground between the optimists and the pessimists. On the one hand, we cannot deny that the Internet has allowed its East European users unprecedented access to information and has helped to overcome the isolation from the rest of Europe. In spite of the limited access, the medium still has great inclusion potential, and it is a tool that could enhance the public sphere and could provide a vehicle for progressive politics and ideals. On the other hand, the commercialization is there and it cannot be denied that within the context of the New Europe the concepts of capitalism and democracy have been quite often uncritically used as synonyms. We also have to keep in mind that 10 years in the transition, Eastern Europe is an area that can no longer be considered an entity, within which we see internal contrasts. Within the last decades, incompatible extremities have appeared—on the one hand, we have countries such as Yugoslavia, which is torn by war and ruled by an oppressive political regime, and on the other hand, countries such as Hungary or the Czech Republic, which can be described more or less as emerging democracies. It is logical to expect that within such a diverse region we will come across different examples of the uses and misuses of such a new communication tool as the Internet.

In spite of all the differences, there are common features that apply to all countries of the new Europe in regard to the Internet:

Economy. Western economies control all cutting-edge developments in hardware, software, and networking. In the lesser developed countries of the New Europe, the existing hardware and networks are often inadequate, and foreign investment is of crucial importance for any development.

Social. The proliferation of new technologies is still characterized by substantial imbalances, even within the Western world. Referring to the high speed of technological development and innovation generated by the U.S., Jaques Santer, the president of the European Commission, recently claimed that even West Europeans were in danger of becoming "hitchhikers on the information superhighway" (qtd. in Barnard, 1995, p. 12). In Eastern Europe, the Internet is still an elitist medium and mostly international and Western, rather than local, organizations are committed to providing it; computer literacy is still relatively low, even among highly educated people.

Regulation. Issues of the information superhighway have been on the political agendas in the most developed Western countries since 1993. Most governments in Eastern Europe, however, do not have a clearly defined position on the issues of the information society, and issues of Internet access and regulation have not yet become an integral part of their media and telecommunication policy.

Technological Innovation. Like for most countries around the world, in the New Europe, technological innovation and state-of-the-art equipment that is essential for computer networking is almost exclusively an issue of import and enhances dependency. Technological innovation that originates in the New Europe is recognized domestically only if first sold to the West.

Usage. While in the countries of the north and the west, access to the Internet is part of everyday life, in the New Europe, only a relatively small number of academics, social activists, media professionals, and businessmen regularly use the Internet for online research and for dissemination of information. The Internet has not yet become an integral part of everyday life.

DIALOGUE OR DEPENDENCY

The Internet came into being and became a global mass medium only in the 1990s. As it exists today, it is a communication tool that is by definition independent and decentralized. It creates unprecedented opportunities to access information, it can transcend national boundaries, thus empowering new types of political and human rights activism, and no central authority has control over it.

If the powerful communication tool of networked computers had existed during the years of *real socialism*, it would have been classified and made available only to a narrow circle of members of the nomenklatura. The advent of the Internet as a profoundly new communication tool coincided, however, with the period in which the New Europe reemerged and took up the struggle to overcome the isolation of the cold war. In spite of that, the Internet is, and most likely will long remain, an elite medium in the region, having the powerful potential for solving many of the faults of the information infrastructure of Communism. This is why it is worth looking into the question if the expansion of the Internet in the New Europe leads to a dynamic dialogue or if it creates new dependencies.

The situation in electronic networks in Eastern Europe presents us with a different picture with regard to a whole set of social, political, and economic issues than the other mass media in the region. Unlike these other media, the computer networks do not need to be transformed, privatized, made independent, democratized, decentralized, and staffed with better-educated professionals—tasks to which scholars attribute primary importance in the process of post-Communist transformation (Jakubowicz, 1995). The issues that we need to look into in regard to the Internet concern accessibility and rate of use, and invite an investigation into the role which this new tool can play within the context of globally oriented personal and organizational communication in education, government, economy, and culture. As is the case with other media in the New Europe, the developments around the Internet reveal situations where we see examples of intensive exchanges in which East Europeans engage within the new global community. At the same time, we come across examples suggesting that specific dependencies are coming into being as well. I will discuss situations that combine the two.

Clear examples of potential dependencies can be found if one looks into the hierarchies of national and international networks. Most Bulgarian connections pass via Greece and the Netherlands, Macedonia depends on Slovenia for all of its international connections, and in other East European countries, the connectivity depends on backbones located in Austria and Switzerland. As in telephony, this situation makes some question the security of data transmission. One can expect that issues of the location of connectivity backbones will increasingly become a concern for governments. But these questions have not been explicitly raised yet, desspite the global trend toward establishing national infrastructures, which "is characterized by active support from governments to build and maintain national backbones, and to help provide gateways to other nations" (Goodman, Press, Ruth, & Rutkowski, 1994, p. 27). A rare instance of computer network-related legislation from the region that can be seen as an early expression of these concerns was Yeltzin's decree on encryption, which was passed in 1995 (Coudenhove, 1995; Dyson, 1996; Safire, 1995). To many, passing such a bill seemed quite irrelevant, as e-mail communication was still rather scarce in Russia. The fact that such a decree was passed, however, suggests existing security concerns.

Until recently, Albania was the only East European country that did not have IP connectivity or servers. Nevertheless, Albania was present on the World Wide Web, with several home pages featuring information about the country. All of them were maintained by ethnic Albanians living in the West—either in the U.S. (Cana, 1995) or in Italy. In the case of countries like Bulgaria and Macedonia, some home pages are carried by local servers maintained by Western organizations (AUBG, 1995; Macedonia, n.d.), but their number is far smaller than the number of home pages about the same countries that are being maintained at foreign institutions. The discrepancy in the number of domestic and foreign servers is not so drastic in the case of East Central Europe. The balance is gradually changing in favor of local servers, but still more information is carried by servers that are physically located in the West than by domestic ones.

Users' online statistics clearly suggest that Western users access the home pages featuring East European information far more often than do local users, according to Craig Plumlee, Web-master of the Russian and East European Network Information Center (REENIC) at the University of Texas at Austin (1994). The information on these home pages is intended mostly for promoting the countries to potential visitors and to providing news to members of the diaspora. Only incidentally does it target the international business community, although some recent developments suggest the opposite, such as the Polish Business Consultants Group home page (n.d.). Home pages that target primarily end users within the country are seen only in the case of Hungary: a large number of servers are located in the country, and most of the information is in the Hungarian language (Hungarian, n.d.). In the case of all other East European countries, as the information is obviously intended for foreign users, it tends to be predominantly in English. The best web search sites featuring comprehensive East European information are maintained not by East Europeans, but at U.S. universities, most notably REESWeb at the University of Pittsburgh (1995) and previously mentioned REENIC at the University of Texas at Austin (1994).

More and more frequently, home pages with international scope are maintained at a Western server and simultaneously mirrored at servers in Eastern Europe or Russia. Such as, for example, the Friends and Partners (1994) home page, run jointly by Greg Cole of the University of Knoxville, Tennessee, and by Natasha Bulashova in Pushkino, Russia. Besides the home page, they maintain an e-mail mailing list, and are targeting users in Russia with useful information, such as health-related links.

The Internet has already become a proven tool for dissemination of news. In 1996, the former Radio Free Europe/Radio Liberty (RFE/RL, 1997) site, which was now renamed Open Media Research Institute (OMRI), launched new services, such as Web analytical briefs, newsletters featuring business information, and e-mailing lists for sale. OMRI was restructured once again at the end of 1997 and took back its older name, RFE/RL, continuing to produce a significant news and analytical output that is disseminated via e-mail and their website. Other specialized news services on the Internet have proliferated and have played the twofold function to inform the members of the new diaspora as well as to provide information to people with online access in the region as well as to researchers elsewhere around the globe. The existence of such specialized news services and cites is a guarantee for the liberties of independent media, which is of primary importance in the case of Serbia and Croatia, for example (Bogart, 1995). The Sarajevo journalism project, which was launched via a site in France in the spring of 1995, was meant to encourage dialogue between ethnic groups driven apart during the 43-month civil war (Sarajevo Online, 1995). Numerous Internet sites launched in 1998 by all sides involved in the conflict provide information and interpretation on the Kosovo situation (Istina o Kosovu, n.d.; Kosovo Information Page 1998; Situation in Kosovo, n.d.).

Western scholars and businessmen who are involved in area studies or business ventures with Eastern Europe have established and take part in various electronic communities such as listservs or bulletin boards (for example, *EE-Business*, *Online-Europe*, *CEEMAN*, *CERRO-L*, *Mideur-L*,

Poland-L, and *Slovak-L*). These forums have a number of participants from Eastern Europe, but still a prevalent number of subscribers are from the West. The author of this study has been running the *EEMedia* listserv since 1994. In 1997, it had nearly 500 subscribers from around the globe, with about 65 percent of the subscribers being physically located in Western countries, and around 35 percent of them located in the countries of Eastern Europe. At least half of these 35 percent, however, were Westerners working in the New Europe.

Usenet newsgroups also feature a variety of discussions on East European topics and issues. There are more than 40 discussion forums dealing with various aspects of the region (groups such as *soc.culture.polish*, *soc.culture.slovak*, *soc.culture.bulgaria*, and *alt.news.macedonia*). Again, the majority of discussion participants are physically located in the West rather than in the country that is the subject of discussion, although often they are displaced nationals of the country in question. Due to restricted Internet access, it is an extremely rare occurrence that subscribers from the discussed country itself would appear online and make postings to the newsgroups. An unpublished study of *alt.news.macedonia*, which I conducted over a period of four months in 1994 and 1995, indicated that out of 3,667 postings to the group, not a single one originated from an end user physically located in the country that was the object of such a heated Usenet discussion (averaging 30 postings a day). The most active participants in the discussion were posting out of Melbourne, Toronto, San Francisco, Calgary, Tokyo, and Munich. When observing this virtual activity, I could not help having the feeling that this was another whole parallel world that coexisted with the real Macedonia, and yet it was not present in its reality in any way.

The conclusion that can be drawn from these examples is that we can no longer discuss online communications without taking into consideration the migrations of the last decade that characterized the countries of the New Europe, which resulted in the creation of a large number of new diasporic communities over a short time span. Migratory movements and geographical dispersal are no longer disruptive to the communication process. On the contrary, the Internet makes it possible to turn the displacement and deterritorialization from limitation into an advantage. Enhanced by the new communication tool, new exchanges become possible and new communities come into being.

GROWTH/USAGE/ACCESS

Since 1989, media in the New Europe have caught up to the West in every respect. Today, they feature violence, advertising, soaps and sitcoms, talk and quiz shows, and free opinions. The Internet has become a topic covered by the media, but is not yet a part of everyday life in Eastern Europe (Dyson, 1996). Coverage on the Internet appears mostly in the media sections that deal with gossip or in reports on technology. The 1995/96 U.S. debate over banning child pornography on the Internet, for example, was diligently taken up by gossip columnists, while information pertaining to the release of the new Netscape version at approximately the same time appeared only in specialized technical publications—no wonder, since such information would appear obscure to wider audiences.

Things are gradually changing, however. While just a few years ago many journalists only knew of e-mail and had no access to the whole range of other Internet features, toward the end of the 1990s, many East European journalists who work for major print and broadcast media have had the chance to attend demonstrations and to undergo Internet training, and have started using a range of websites in their own work. Some yearly events regularly take place, such as, for example, The New Media for New World annual workshop for journalists in Moscow, run by a Seattle-based organization, and a number of similar workshops run by the ProMedia advisors in the countries of East Central Europe.

Although the picture is changing very rapidly, Eastern Europe is not living in the digital age yet. In Russia, providers such as GlasNet and Relcom appear to Americans to offer very inexpensive services (Specter, 1994), but these services are not affordable for many ordinary Russians. Data from early 1996 set the rate of connectivity growth in Russia for the last quarter of 1995 at 68 percent. Still, if looking at the absolute volume of the use of computer networks, computers and modem connections are not a part of the lives of the ordinary people in Eastern Europe and the former Soviet Union. Looking at general numbers provided by computer merchants, sales are booming, but East European societies at large remain still relatively undercomputerized ("Computers," 1996; Dizard & Swensrud, 1987; Specter, 1995). In fact, as noted by Specter, "most users rely on first-generation IBM-PC clones of the type that Americans long ago consigned to yard sales or donated to charity, and most modems work like molasses at speeds of 2,400 bauds or less" (Specter, 1994, p. C1). An expression of rapid development, computers have now appeared in different spheres of everyday life where no electronics were present just a decade ago, but are still not widely used at all levels of business, administration, and education. Hardware prices are comparable and often higher than in the U.S. and in the EC countries, and the networking market is far from developed. The growing competition amidst connectivity providers suggests that there is more supply than demand, and getting online is not on the immediate agendas of many organizations that would be the potential clients for Web designers and Intranet developers.

The circumstance in the current structure of telecommunications adds difficulty to the situation of computer networking, since most links depend on phone line dial-up access. Numerous reports on traffic jams at the Internet's international lines often refer to the inadequacy in the speed of transmission and reception of data (Butler, 1996; Fick, 1996). Major investments and reconstruction efforts have been directed toward addressing the poor condition of telephony across Eastern Europe, but improving online connectivity has rarely been a priority. The privatization undertakings in telecommunications have led to clashes of interest among North American and European telecommunication giants such as Sprint, Northern Telecom, Siemens, Erickson, and Alcatel, who all hold stakes in the newly opening East European market (Cane, 1995). A number of large international meetings, most notably in Warsaw and Prague in 1995, are sponsored by Western governments and corporations to promote the export of telecommunications equipment and services to Central and Eastern Europe ("TDA to Hold," 1995). The growth of computer networks, however, is not part of the official telecommunication policies of most East European countries, and it is often not clear which government structure (if any) is directly responsible for it.

Large software companies expanding into Eastern Europe have made efforts toward securing the profits and establishing a permanent presence in these emerging markets. Microsoft, for example, had programs translated into Russian, Czech, Polish, and Hungarian to facilitate penetration to the relevant markets. State-of-the-art upgrades are not available, due to simple economic factors—namely that businesses, organizations, and regular people cannot afford them. Thus, only companies and educational institutions that have some form of foreign involvement or receive grants from abroad can claim they actually have access to adequate platforms and applications.

Most Internet users in Eastern Europe are academic research centers and commercial enterprises. Students at higher education institutions are being given demonstrations about what the Internet is, but hands-on access is limited and many of them lack basic computer skills and command of networking software. While at some American universities, Internet-mediated interaction with students has increased so much that it has caused a backlash against the excessive use of networks (Wilson, 1995), only larger universities in East Central Europe give their students the opportunity to have a personal e-mail account. Even then, not all students take advantage of this opportunity, mostly because they have neither regular access to computers that are properly equipped with networking software nor the Internet connectivity that would allow them to browse the World Wide Web or read the Usenet newsgroups. Neverthe-less, the number of students who use the Internet is steadily growing, and a number of interesting student-run projects can be found on the Web.

The situation is not very different for some educational professionals who could make great use of the networks. Librarians, for example, often know very little about the growing online resources, in spite of the fact that the situation is changing as a result of numerous exchange pro-grams offered by Western institutions, like the one offered specifically for East European librarians by the library at the University of Illinois at Urbana-Champaign.

Training on the basic features of the Internet, where available, is insufficient. Lately, however, some high schools in East Central Europe and Romania have engaged in computer-mediated teaching projects that will hopefully bring higher network literacy to the younger genera-tion (Horvath, 1997). While the universities and public institutions usu-ally control "the national backbone" (if there is one), the commercial users are usually foreigners, businesses, and international institutions, "although domestic demand increases as local citizens encounter the new resource" (Woodard, 1995a, p. A21).

Academics are still the group most interested in having access to the Internet, and in all East European countries they have more or less secured themselves this access. State funding for undertakings such as the Information Infrastructure Program (IIP) in Hungary is one of the few examples of clear government involvement in sponsoring computer networks (Gulyás, 1998; Woodard, 1995b). In Macedonia immediately after independence was proclaimed in 1991, steps were taken to use the University of Skopje computer network as a basic infrastructure. Educa-tional undertakings seem to attract most interest, and academics throughout Eastern Europe more and more often engage in personal, professional, and political computer-mediated networking that would promote better education for various causes—democracy, concepts of responsible citizenship, and other civil concerns. Some occasional attempts to commercialize Internet access have been confronted with criticism within academia ("Rate Increases," 1996).

Eastern Europe as a whole is expected to become a boom zone for Western communications suppliers, although for now their endeavors are most suitably described with words such as "potential" and "patience" (Dougherty, 1995). Selling connectivity has proven very lucrative, and Westerners claim that East European markets are boom-ing, even in times when the economy is not exactly in great shape (Lewis, 1995). Thus, alongside the emerging local Internet service pro-viders, Western companies continue maintaining their interest in East

European markets. Eunet, for example, which is being run out of Western Europe, has regional branches in several East European countries.

Growth, however, is encouraged by the West, as long as it is accompanied by a growth in the market for Western products. Many Western businesses have expressed a legitimate concern about extensive copyright infringement involving pirated software and CD-ROMs in the countries of the New Europe. At the same time, some Western software designers have claimed they have lost a substantial part of their business and have sought legislative protection against East European "offshore software development services" provided by Web-based entrepreneurs in the East to Western clients (Lewis, 1995). It is a classical situation of unfair competition resulting from cross-border inequalities, as programmer wages in Russia and Eastern Europe are, on the average, about one-fifth of those in the U.S. ("Analysis," 1995).

CIVIL ORGANIZATIONS AND GRASSROOTS ACTIVISM

In Communist times, when oppressive regimes had an iron grip on all mainstream information channels, many people were involved in cross-border smuggling of underground publications or tape-recorded texts. The broadcasts of cross-border radio stations were jammed and members of the pubic needed to be fairly inventive if they wanted to listen to their programs. Today, however, all activities that may involve the transmission of information or messages that would be considered subversive by the powers-that-be are diverted over to the Internet. In addition, the new medium has the capability to also link the centers of resistance with each other, creating an unprecedented dynamic interaction between global and local levels.

Strengthening civil society across the countries of the New Europe is believed to be of utmost importance for the transition, particularly in regard to the changing mediatic environment (Ganley, 1996; Jakubowicz, 1995; Splichal, 1994). Fewer scholars have recognized the importance of the Internet for enhancing civil society. A decade since 1989, however, the information superhighway has proven to have been of definite use to various alternative political movements, be it oppositional political voices, ethnic minorities, or gay rights activists—all these and many more grassroots movements have established a visible presence on the Internet.

Civil society activists of the West have actively helped their East European counterparts in using the Internet (Butts, 1995). One of the first comprehensive reference books on East European Internet resources published in the West was the *Guide to Grassroots Organizations and Inter-*

net Resources in the Newly Independent States (Green, 1996). Many of the post-1989 organizations, most notably the ones dealing with issues of human rights advocacy or environmental protection, now have websites, and many are linked to international human rights gateways, such as One World (1995) or Network of East-West Women (NEWW, n.d.). A database of all private voluntary organizations working in the Ukraine was available as early as 1993 ("Database," 1993). So were databases featuring the Internet public access sites in Russia and Central Asia ("Kazakhstan," 1994; "Public Access," 1994), and databases featuring information on various other NGOs.

Whereas in the past it was extremely difficult to communicate human rights abuses or projects detrimental to the environment to the outside world, now, with the advent of e-mail connections, this reporting has become much easier and civil organizations are among the first to take advantage of the new technology. Researchers have shown that this was also the case with citizens' activism in the West (Bozman, 1991; Downing, 1989) and that promoting nonprofit networking, with initiatives such as The Electronic Frontier Foundation, The Institute for Global Communications (formerly Peace Net), Hands Net, and the Center for Media Education, is still at the center of pubic attention ("Nonprofit Networking," 1994). More and more civil organizations across the New Europe now have e-mail addresses, especially those where urgent action may be required, like in monitoring human rights and the treatment of minorities, or humanitarian aid and various social work projects.

Public activism on the Internet often develops within a regulatory vacuum—in most cases, governments do not exercise rigid control over the online dimension of the work of these organizations, but no clear regulations are in place. East European governments are only moderately interested in the possibilities that the new information infrastructure can offer. With a few exceptions, politicians here do not try to control or regulate the developments of the new information infrastructure imposed by the invasion of new technologies. They do not commit to promoting it, either (Dyson, 1996).

At the end of the millennium, a large variety of visions on the future of the digital age had been created by various governments (the U.S., Japan, the European Union, among others), and the most important visionaries of technology (for example, Masuda, Attali, Toffler) had given us their comments on the information society (Inkinen, 1995). In the U.S., and lately in Western Europe, questions concerning technological innovation in communication have become an integral part of strategic planning and politicians are expected to include in their official platform a statement on their attitudes on the Information Society. In the United States, the Clinton/Gore administration set the trend by declaring a firm commitment to moderately regulating and promoting the information superhighway. Al Gore's (1995) concept of the Global Information Infrastructure is a key element in determining the policy of encouragement for new technological developments. Some American social scientists even spoke of an "emerging electronic republic," where the roles of citizenship and political leadership would be redefined and where the Internet would make the representative form of democracy obsolete, since it will allow direct participation of each citizen in politics, like in the times of the Athenian democracy (Grossman, 1995).

Politicians in Eastern Europe have their own, different priorities. In countries where even the mail service does not function properly, one can barely expect to see the expansion of computer networks on the top of the agenda of communication executives. Top priority is usually given to improving the structure and quality of telephone connections and the data transmission capacity of phone lines. Improving telecommunications and telephony, however, does not mean that computer networking should be left behind. While Hungary, for example, is still struggling to improve its obsolete telephony, it is simultaneously working to make the most out of its presence on the Internet (Woodard, 1995b).

The current regulatory situation has negative and positive sides. While in other spheres of communication delayed deregulation is regarded as an obstacle to further developments, in the case of the Internet, the obstacle is a lack of government action and commitment. In this context, the indifference toward technological innovation becomes a specific means of control. Why bother controling something to which most people have no access to? Why commit to something that could cause unforeseen headaches?

The lack of government commitment and thus the nonexistent control over civil networking, however, allows for a most intensive growth in the grassroots usage of the Internet. An organization that has been taking full advantage of this situation since 1993, for example, is the internationally oriented Network of East-West Women (NEWW, n.d.). It is part of their program to promote the usage of Internet connections as a tool of empowerment for women, and they work on numerous projects in that area. The national Helsinki Committee, which branches across the Balkans, work together and maintain an extremely useful and information-rich website featuring studies on hate speech and ethnic minorities' rights across the Balkans via their Greek counterpart, Greek Helsinki Monitor (1998; see also Lengel, 1998).

There is more and more evidence of the increasing importance of e-mail connections for people in zones of conflict. One of the most widely featured examples of using computer networking for activism that shaped the international public opinion was Wam Kat's *Zagreb Diary* (Cooke & Lehrer, 1994; "Pioneering," 1993). Working for a Danish relief organization in Croatia in 1992 and 1993, Kat had been regularly transmitting to his friends via e-mail diary entries about his experiences in the war zone. The diary postings were then further distributed by users around the world. In spite of all the problems with poorly functioning phone lines, and in spite of the fact that Wam Kat's e-mail connection was passing through Denmark, the *Zagreb Diary* became a prominent source of information and had a major impact within the international community of relief workers and beyond.

Since the early 1990s, the importance of electronic e-mail links for people in war zones has been extensively discussed and studied. Many share the opinion, for example, that good Internet connectivity helped Slovenia to achieve independence from former Yugoslavia faster and easier than it would have had it not been so wired because Slovenian academics flooded the Internet with messages asking for support and thus created a favorable international public opinion (Baker, 1994; Bollag, 1994). The independent Croatian publication *ZaMir*, which had an e-mail connection, had turned into a major site serving Bosnian refugees who were using their terminal to send out messages from Zagreb (Daly, 1995). *ZaMir* was involved, among other projects, with an international modem-gathering endeavor that would allow more people in the war zone to go online (ZTN InFo, n.d.). Other projects and details about *ZaMir* are presented by Amy Herron and Eric Bachman in Chapter 15, in this volume.

Due to the turbulent events in Bosnia, the country has attracted the most international activities and traffic on the Internet. There are Bosnian home pages hosted by *The New York Times* (DiNucci, 1996), Web pages that carry daily information about the developments at the International Tribunal at the Hague, and sites that feature military organizations in Bosnia (Schmitt, 1995). Most useful links are located at the Bosnian Home Page at CalTech University (1995). Many in the former Yugoslavia use the Internet as a tool for innovative political action— exemplary websites are the ones of Serbia's Radio B92 (Hedges, 1996).

When discussing the New Europe at large, one can give numerous examples of governments trying to control print and broadcast media, directly or indirectly. In the case of electronic networks, however, there is little evidence of systematically attempted control, and it seems that the growth of networks is "more limited by cost considerations than by political or security controls" (Goodman, Press, Ruth, & Rutkowski, 1994, p. 27). Governments do not seem interested in having a monopoly over the computer networks or in practicing strict control. A classical example for this lack of interest is the 1991 Russian coup, when computer links were not cut and e-mail messages became a key means for reporting on developments in Moscow to the outside world. Although the August 1991 coup example is usually given as an illustration of the empowerment potential of computer networking, it actually illustrates the extent of ignorance and neglect displayed by the coup organizers, who easily could have cut the computer messaging systems if they had known more about these new communication channels (Bonnell & Freidin, 1995; Goodman et al., 1994).

In 2000, however, one can no longer claim that governments are oblivious to the added leverage that this new channel of communication gives to civil organizations. Earlier in the 1990s, authorities in Serbia had made attempts to shut down the independent Belgrade radio station B'92. However, its members were never deprived of e-mail access, which allowed them to effectively communicate to the outside world the news of any repressive action taken against them. In 1998, however, as part of the crackdown on independent media, the Serbian government restricted connectivity and banned websites.

CULTURE

Needless to say, many writers, artists, musicians, and simply fans from around the globe have made the Internet their meeting point. The East Europeans are not absent from the party, either, and if one wants to get acquainted with the culture of any of the countries of the former Communist block today, one can do it fairly easily by taking a tour of websites that carry both samples of high art and of popular entertainment.

The Gutenberg project of posting literary texts in electronic format may be limited for now to the classic works of the Western tradition, but today one can find numerous examples of East European poetry, short stories, and literary criticism from all the countries in the New Europe on sites scattered all over the World Wide Web. There are websites created by those involved in theater, featuring photographs from performances and profiles of theater companies, as well as reviews and promotional material about the actors. The sites that carry sound files proliferate rapidly, and besides the traditional sites that feature audio files of Slovenian popular music ("Music," n.d.), it is possible to download sound bite samples of virtually all of the most popular pop and rock groups from the region. For those who want to learn more about film, there are home pages devoted to East European cinema (East European Media and Cinema Studies, 1994), a Polish film database (Polish Cinema Database, 1995), a Hungarian film production and distribution site (Media Guide Hungary, 1996), a Zagreb animation festival home page (13th World Festival of Animated Films, 1998), a Kieslowski home page frequented by his fans (Kieslowski, 1995), and even a commercial site that sells Polish movie posters to Americans (Blind Moon Grafika, 1994). And this is just a small part of what can be found on the Web, where the art and entertainment landscape is constantly changing, getting richer and more diverse every week. A multimedia online magazine, which will be promoting awareness of recent avant-garde developments on the East European arts scene, lists a number of Web events across Central and South-Eastern Europe (ArtMargins, 1998), and reviewers write about various cooperative Web art undertakings in Slovenia, Hungary, and other countries (Arns, 1998; Peternák, 1998).

When one looks around for examples in fine arts, one comes across an interesting Web gallery selling the famous naivist pictures of three generations of painters from the Generalic family in Croatia (Gallery Josip Generalic, 1997). Even artists in besieged Sarajevo had an outlet that allowed them to showcase their work to the world—an online exhibit of Sarajevo painter and artist Muradif Cerimagic, for example, can still be found on the Web after many other exhibits that took place have been withdrawn since the war officially ended (Ceri Magic Art, n.d.).

Working out of war-torn Sarajevo, the innovative design work of Bojan and Dada Hadzihalilovic (a.k.a. TRIO) came to be known all over the world with its bold combination of commercial and popular images with messages that besieged Sarajevo. Although they had many opportunities to continue work outside Bosnia-Herzegovina, TRIO chose to remain in Sarajevo throughout the war, despite the obvious hardships of life in a city under siege. Their computer design work depended on the availability of electricity, which was often in short supply. Nevertheless, TRIO managed to put together an extensive collection of graphic art aimed at raising awareness of the plight of their city throughout the world. They became famous for the series of reworkings of well-known advertising and pop-art images—well-known commercial designs like *Enjoy Coca-Cola* (which became *Enjoy Sara-Jevo*), *Absolut Vodka* (which became *Absolut Sarajevo*), or the title sequence of *The Twilight Zone* series (which became *The Sarajevo Zone*). They modified accordingly the logo of Spielberg's *Jurassic Park* (which became *Sarajevo Park*), used Andy Warhol's painting of *Campbell's Soup* (with added bullet holes in it), and adapted famous posters, such as *Some Like it Hot*, *Your Country Needs You*, and *Wake Up America!*. TRIO's pop-art designs were exhibited on a site maintained by the media department at the University of Westminster in London (ARTSUNDERTHESIEGE, n.d.).

The story of the Croatian feminist group NONA is closely intertwined with the growing use of the Internet by its members. NONA, named after the Croatian term for grandmother or granny, originally started as a Zagreb-based gallery and center where refugee women could come for art therapy sessions, and where they would hold poetry readings, exhibits of photographic work, or of pottery they had crafted and of drawings they had created while healing war-time traumas. NONA's work came to the attention of feminist groups from Chicago, who helped build a website that features information about the struggle of refugee women and that carries several ongoing exhibits, and hosts a collection of poetry and essays. Hosted on free Web space provided by a corporation, NONA is a site for active international networking for women. In 1997, when funding for many of the club-based activities maintained by NONA in Zagreb was no longer available, the group closed down the center, but still maintains a visible presence online, at their virtual site NONA international (1995).

Art work shows and interactive multimedia exhibits from the New Europe are becoming a frequent and prominent activity on the World Wide Web. This type of cultural events coexist with other art exhibits, seminars, or film series organized cross-culturally to showcase the artistic output of the countries of the New Europe. Marking a decade worth of transition within the New Europe, special East European seminars and film series have been organized across the western Europe throughout 1999, opening with the *After the Wall* film series at the Rotterdam Film Festival in February and continuing with an extensive series of events at Stockholm Museum of Modern Art in October and November. Within this past decade, Internet-based showcasing of artistic achievement and diversity has become an inseparable part of the international cultural exchange.

THE FUTURE: ENTHUSIASTIC IN MODERATION

I am one of those who believe that the advent of the Internet is a revolutionary watershed in communications. This new communication tool has unique features that profoundly change the way we communicate. First, it is the first medium that combines in one the ability to broadcast (mass communication) and simultaneously be a tool for personal communication. The interactive potential of the Internet is enormous and it creates unprecedented opportunities for the formation of new communities. In such acontext, location begins to matter less, which is particularly important in the context of the ongoing migration processes.

Second, the convergence within the Internet itself toward the Web is clearly visible from the history of development of the networks (Salus, 1995), and the further convergence of other mediatic aspects toward the new multimedia environment (which now includes text, sound, image, and moving image) makes it a universal medium that brings together all modes of communication. The development of hypertext subverts the traditional hierarchies in human knowledge and encourages unprecedented epistemological creativity.

This potential is sufficiently strong to counterbalance the otherwise very valid concerns of various inequalities, which we addressed earlier. In the context of the New Europe, the Internet could provide a radical solution to the shortage of social information. Since it is deregulated from the onset, it could bring a substantial change in the mechanisms of access to information, it could spare printing and distribution costs, and it could provide selective information that is more and more often needed. Organizations could post their information to networks, businesses could be greatly assisted in searching foreign markets and cross-border opportunities, and educational institutions could make full use of the new possibilities in distance learning and multimedia. Individuals could freely access whatever information they deem necessary for achieving their personal goals.

Given this huge information potential, however, we have to recognize that the growth that we see is not as dramatic as it could be, and the impact is not as substantial as it could be. All evidence of explosive growth in percentages does not yet signify the advent of computer networks as tools for a new information revolution, and Eastern Europe is still far from riding the information superhighway. A series of developments in various fields has yet to take place in order to facilitate the further expansion of the Internet. First of all, in the field of technology, an improvement in the telecommunications infrastructure must take place, and one needs to secure availability of hardware and software and access to computer networks. In the social sphere, a campaign for computer literacy not just among teenagers but among adults as well is a task of primary importance. And last, but not least, the governments have to explicitly commit to promoting use and access of the new information infrastructure.

While technological advancement is taking place, there is little evidence to suggest that the literacy is growing at the same speed or that policymakers are getting more conscious of what is expected from them. As most of the technological innovations have come into existence only during the past few years, most mid-career professionals and decision makers just do not possess relevant knowledge, as it could not have been taught to them during the time they have been in a period of active formation. Hence a resistance to the unknown, which in addition seems intimidatingly complex. This constraint is easy to overcome and it is a matter of an elementary learning effort to improve one's technological literacy. There are several obstacles to these processes, deeply grounded in the philosophy commonly shared by decision makers across the New Europe, and they need to be made explicit.

The first commonly raised objection against the wider introduction of online communication is the concern of exclusion—as some will not have access to advanced Internet features, they are likely to be marginalized in a hi-tech environment, therefore encouraging the growth of this type of communication tools would mean legitimizing exclusion. This argument often remains one-sided and does not look at the other side of the issue—the enormous inclusive potential of online communication, which brings to remote locations the potential of accessing the same up-to-date and high-quality materials that are currently available to people in the countries enjoying the highest life and educational standards.

The second popular argument against new technologies has its roots in the luddist tradition of fear of enslavement through technology, which is usually enhanced by the fact that technology is often represented in a mystified and intimidating light, as something awfully complex and unintelligible. At the same time, it is becoming increasingly easier to operate in an online environment and no special technical expertise is needed in order to do it. A third important consideration is the change in generational relations that the advancement in computer-mediated technologies brings about. Writing in the late 1960s, in her *Culture and Commitment* (1970), Margaret Mead first talked of changing patterns of knowledge transmission that she saw as basic characteristics of the generational gap, which sociologists were observing at the time. She noticed that unlike in traditional cultures where the body of knowledge is in possession of the older generation and is gradually transmitted to the younger one, in modern times people were more likely to learn from their peers rather than from their elders, a trend that had a subversive effect on traditional social relations and produced a generation gap. Mead predicted that later on the acceleration of technology and the rapidity of change would lead to the establishment of what she called a "prefigurative culture," in which the older generation was to learn from the younger one.

While Mead only projected such development, we see it happen all around us, and it is more than obvious in the field of new technologies. It would be enough to just quote names like Mark Andreissen, the 23-year-old inventor of Netscape and Jerry Yang, who started Yahoo as a 21-year-old undergraduate student at Stanford University. Microsoft's Bill Gates was 40 in 1999, and Steve Jobs, the creator of the Macintosh computer, was only 44. We see the same picture across the New Europe, where the majority of the most active promoters of the technological advancement and computer-enhanced communication environment are in their 20s or early 30s. It is they who currently mediate the concerns of their countries, cultures, and immediate groups in hypertext. It will be their responsibility to continue speaking for those who remain excluded, and their struggle to make sure everyone is able to join in the future.

REFERENCES

13th World Festival of Animated Films [Online]. (1998). Available: <http://animaf-est.hr/> [1999, March 8].

American University in Bulgaria (AUBG) [Online]. (1995). Available: <http://sun.iccs.acad.bg/> [1999, March 10].

Analysis. (1995). *Computer Finance, 6*(1), 23.

Arns, I. (1998). Pioneers revisited: Documenting aspects of the first two decades of media art in Germany. *Convergence: Journal of Research into New Media Technologies, 4*(2), 110–113.

ArtMargins [Online]. (1998). Available: <http://www.gss.ucsb.edu/artmargins/>

ARTSUNDERTHESIEGE [Online]. (n.d.). Available: <http://www.worldmedia.fr/sarajevo/arts.html> [1999, March 8].

Baker, R. (1994). *Summer in the Balkans. Laughter and tears after Communism.* Hartford, CT: Kumarian Press.

Barnard, B. (1995, April). Europe gets up to speed on the information super-highway. *Europe,* 12.

Blind Moon Grafika [Online]. (1994). Available: <http://www.mjwebworks.com/webworks/amg/> [1999, March 8].

Bogart, L. (1995, Summer). Media and democracy. *Media Studies Journal,* 1–11.

Bollag, B. (1994, June 29). The "great equalizer": Users from Tokyo to Tashkent meet in Prague to discuss the Internet. *Chronicle of Higher Education,* p. A17.

Bonnell, V. E., & Freidin, G. (1995). Televorot: The role of television coverage in Russia's August 1991 coup. In N. Condee (Ed.), *Soviet hieroglyphics* (pp. 22–52). Bloomington, IN: Indiana University Press.

Bosnia Home Page at CalTech [Online]. (1995). Available: <http://www.cco.caltech.edu/~bosnia/bosnia.html> [1999, March 10].

Bozman, J. (1991). Peacenet usage soars as war erupts in Iraq. *Computerworld, 25*(3), 84.

Butler, D. (1996, April 4). Packet jams clog international highways. *Nature,* 379.

Butts, R. F. (1995, June 23). Many blueprints for democracy. *The Christian Science Monitor,* p. 18.

Cana, M. (1995). *Mentor Cana's home page* [Online]. Available: <http://menger.eecs.stevens-tech.edu/~cana/> [1999, March 10].

Cane, A. (1995, October 3). Survey of international telecommunications. *Financial Times,* p. 1.

Ceri Magic Art (n.d.). *Virtual gallery of works of Bosnian painter and artist Muradif Cerimagic* [Online]. Available: <http://members.aol.com/Cerimagic/home.htm> [1999, March 8].

Computers: Who buys them? (1996, March 7). *Moscow News*, p. 9.

Cooke, K., & Lehrer, D. (1994, January-February). Who will own the information highway? *Utne Reader*, 107–111.

Coudenhove, S. (1995, June 2). State control over electronic data feared. *The Moscow Times*, p. 3.

Daly, E. (1995, January 7). Internet provides electronic window out of the siege for Sarajevans. *Ottawa Citizen*, p. C1.

Database of PVOs working in Ukraine goes on-line. (1993). *NetTalk. Civil Society - East and West, 1*, 1–2.

DiNucci, D. (1996, November-December). Bornia: Uncertain paths to understanding. *New York Times*, Print, 6, p. 33.

Dizard, W. P., & Swensrud, S. B. (1987). *Gorbachev's information revolution: Controlling glasnost in a new electronic era*. Boulder, CO: Westview Press.

Dougherty, J. (1995, December 5). U.S. computer firms target obstacles to success in Eastern Europe. *Deutsche Presse-Agentur*.

Downey, J. (1998). Full of Eastern Promise? Central and Eastern European media after 1989. In D. K. Thussu (Ed.), *Electronic empires: Global media and local resistance* (pp. 47–63). London: Arnold.

Downing, J. D. H. (1989). Computers for political change: PeaceNet and public data access. *Journal of Communication, 39*(3), 154–163.

Dyson, E. (1996, October 18). Toward a more mature Internet. *Transition, 2*(21), 6–12.

Dyson, E. (1997). *Release 2.0: A design for living in the digital age*. New York: Broadway Books.

East European Media and Cinema Studies [Online]. (1994, September). Available: <http://www.utexas.edu/ftp/pub/eems/main.html> [1999, March 10].

Fick, B. (1996, October 18). The Internet lurches forward in Russia. *Transition, 2*(21), 12–17.

Friends and Partners (F&P) [Online]. (1994). Available: <http://www.friends-partners.org/friends/> [1999, March 8].

Gallery Josip Generalic [Online]. (1997). Available: <http://pubwww.srce.hr/generalic/gal.htm> [1999, February 19].

Ganley, G. (1996). *Unglued empire: The Soviet experience with communications technologies*. Norwood, NJ: Ablex.

Goban-Klas, T. (1994). *The orchestration of the media: The politics of mass communications in Communist Poland and the aftermath*. Boulder, CO: Westview Press.

Gore, A. (1995). *Global information infrastructure*. Washington, DC: Government Printing Office.

Goodman, S., Press, L., Ruth, S. R., & Rutkowski, A. M. (1994, August). The global diffusion of the Internet: Patterns and problems. *Communications of the ACM, 37*(8), 27.

Goulding, P. (1998). Worldwide wedge: Division and contradiction in the global information infrastructure. In D. K. Thussu (Ed.), *Electronic empires: Global media and local resistance* (pp. 131–152). London: Arnold.

Greek Helsinki Monitor [Online]. (1998). Available: <http://www.greekhelsinki.gr/>

Green, S. W. (1996, November 1). The post-Soviet handbook: A guide to grass-roots organizations and Internet resources in the Newly Independent States. *Library Journal*, 62.

Gross, P. (1996). *Mass media in revolution and national development. The Romanian laboratory.* Iowa City, IA: University of Iowa Press.

Grossman, L. (1995, Summer). The electronic republic. *Media Studies Journal*, 163–169.

Gulyás, Á. (1998). In the slow lane on the information superhighway: Hungary and the Information Revolution. *Convergence: Journal of Research into New Media Technologies, 4*(2), 76–92.

Hedges, C. (1996, December 8). Serbs' answer to oppression: Their web site. *The New York Times*, Sec. 1, p. 1.

Horvath, J. (1997, Spring). Access is not enough. Computer assisted instruction in Central and Eastern Europe. *Convergence: Journal of Research into New Media Technologies, 3*(1), 20–24.

Hungarian Home Page [Online]. (n.d.) Available: <http://www.fsz.bme.hu/hungary/>

Inkinen, S. (1995). Internet, "data highways," and information society: A comment on the rhetoric of the electronic sublime. *Lahikuva, 1,* 5–34.

Istina o Kosovu [Online]. (n.d.). Available:<http://www.decani.yunet.com/kip.html>

Jakubowicz, K. (1995). Lovebirds? The media, the state and politics in Central and Eastern Europe. *The Public, 2*(1), 75–93.

Kazakhstan and Kyrgyzstan NGOs on-line. (1994, February). *NetTalk. Civil Society - East and West, 2,* 3.

Kieslowski [Online]. (1995, March 27). Available: <http://www-personal.engin.umich.edu/~zbigniew/Kieslowski/kieslowski.html> [1999, March 8].

Kosovo Information Page [Online]. (1998). Available: <http://www.decani.yunet.com/kip.html> [1999, March 8].

Lengel, L. (1998). Access to the Internet in East Central and South-Eastern Europe: New technologies and new women's voices. *Convergence: Journal of Research into New Media Technologies, 4*(2), 38–56.

Lewis, J. (1995, July 20). Raising the iron curtain. *Computing,* 28.

Macedonia [Online]. (n.d.). Available: <http://www.soros.org.mk/mk/>

MacKinnon, R. C. (1995). Searching for the Leviathan in Usenet. In S. G. Jones (Ed.), *CyberSociety: Computer-mediated communication and community* (pp. 112–127). London: Sage.

Mead, M. (1970). *Culture and commitment. The new relationships between the generations in the 1970s.* New York: Anchor Books.

Media Guide Hungary. (1996). *International directory of film productions, television, video & multimedia programs* [Online]. Available: <http://www.mediaguide.hu/> [1999, March 8].

Music of Slovenia [Online]. (no date). Available <http://www.ijs.si/slo/country/culture/music/> [1999, March 8].

Negroponte, N. (1996). *Being digital.* London: Coronet.

Network of East-West Women (NEWW). [Online]. (n.d.). Available: <http://www.neww.org/> [1999, March 8].

NONA International [Online]. (1995). Available: <http://www.applicom.com/nona/> [1999, March 8].

Nonprofit networking, resources for the rest of us. (1994). *Info Active. The Telecommunications Monthly for Nonprofits, 1*(2), 1–5.

O'Neil, P. (Ed.). (1997). *Post-Communism and the media in Eastern Europe.* London and Portland, OR: Frank Cass.

One World [Online]. (1995, January). Available: <http://www.oneworld.org/> [1999, March 8].

Paletz, D., Jakubowicz, K., & Novosel, P. (Eds.). (1995). *Glasnost and after: Media and change in Central and Eastern Europe.* Cresskill, NJ: Hampton Press.

Peternák, M. (1998). Three years of Internet-art in Hungary: An annotated list of sites and events. *Convergence: Journal of Research into New Media Technologies, 4*(2), 119–124.

Pioneering the electronic frontier. (1993, December 6). *U.S. News and World Report,* 57–62.

Polish Business Consultants Group [Online]. (n.d.). Available: <http://www.PolBizNet.com/> [1999, March 8].

Polish Cinema Database [Online]. (1995). Available: <http://info.fuw.edu.pl/Filmy/>

Public access e-mail sites in Kazan, Novosibirsk and Vladivostok. (1994). *Net Talk. Civil Society East and West, 2*(5), 1–3.

Rate increases in Poland questioned by Polish Internet organization. (1996, February). *Internet Society Newsletter,* p. 71.

REENIC [Online]. (1994). Available: <http://reenic.utexas.edu/reenic.html> [1999, February 19].

REESWeb [Online]. (1995). Available: <http://www.ucis.pitt.edu/reesweb/> [1999, February 19].

Radio Free Europe/Radio Liberty (RFE/RL) [Online]. (1997, December 1). Available: <http://www.rferl.org/> [1999, March 10].

Safire, W. (1995, June 8). Lubyanka lullaby. *The New York Times,* p. A29.

Salus, P. H. (1995). *Casting the Net: From ARPANET to Internet and beyond.* Reading, MA: Addison-Wesley.

Sarajevo Online [Online]. (1995). Available: http://www.worldmedia.fr//sarajevo/index.html> [1999, March 9].

Schmitt, E. (1995, December 15). Military puts Bosnia on the Web. *The New York Times,* Sec. 4, p. E14.

Situation in Kosovo. (n.d.). *U.S. State department briefings* [Online]. Available: <http://www.state.gov/www/regions/eur/kosovo_hp.html> [1999, March 8].

Sparks, C. (1997). Post-communist media in transition. In J. Corner, P. Schlesinger, & R. Silverstone (Eds.), *International media research: A critical survey* (pp. 96–123). London: Routledge.

Specter, M. (1994, March 9). Russians' newest space adventure: Cyberspace. *The New York Times,* pp. C1/C2.

Specter, M. (1995, May 1). Russia awakens to the world of computer. *The New York Times,* p. C1.

Splichal, S. (1994). *Media beyond socialism. Theory and practice in East-Central Europe.* Boulder, CO: Westview.

TDA to hold "Global Information Summit" in Warsaw. Warsaw meeting aims to increase U.S. telecommunications exports to Eastern Europe. (1995, May 17). *PR Newswire*.

Wilson, D. L. (1995, December 1). Internet users face lines at computers. Colleges can't accommodate the growing student demand for access. *Chronicle of Higher Education*, p. A35.

Woodard, C. (1995a, June 9). The Internet international. Network's expansion is a boom for universities in Central and Eastern Europe. *Chronicle of Higher Education*, p. A21.

Woodard, C. (1995b). The Internet's explosive expansion. *Transition, 1*(18), 84–90.

ZTN InFo. (n.d.). ZaMir peace network in the war zone [Online]. Available: <http://MediaFilter.org/MFF/ZTN_InFo.html> [1999, March 8].

chapter 7

Organized Innocence and War in the New Europe: On Electronic Solitude and Independent Media*

Geert Lovink
Adilkno, Amsterdam

Nietzsche would be laughing about Europe. He would not be complaining about the impending loss of national identity or the power of the Brussels bureaucracy. He would look down disdainfully at the bumbling, pompous Euro-citizens who, confused and without Witz or Idea,[1] are trying to sidestep their own history. Europeans have the greatest difficulty putting into words the current dialectic of construction and demolition that manifests itself around them. The last intellectuals are still doing their best to characterize the post-1989 juncture, but they are not succeeding. The amalgam of the war in former Yugoslavia, the strange new media, capitalism without an enemy, the Economic Tigers in Asia, grassroots neo-liberalism, Shell Oil's platform, the Brent Spar and French nuclear tests, foreigners and refugees, the devastation of Chechnya—it is all impossible to grasp anymore. One group believes it has arrived in the 21st century, as others are catapulted back a couple of centuries. What one sees as progress spells sheer destruction for another. We observe developments with worry, but can

---

*This chapter was translated by Laura Martz. An earlier version of this chapter was presented as a plenary lecture at the Sixth International Symposium on Electronic Art, September 20, 1995, in Montreal.

no longer associate them with conclusions. But that is no longer necessary, for what occupies Europeans most of all is the development of one's own lifestyle. And no one is laughing at the little worries of the middle classes.

In my talk at the 1994 International Symposium on Electronic Art, I introduced the work of Adilkno, the Dutch group to which I belong. Adilkno, the Foundation for the Advancement of Illegal Knowledge, is an association of nonacademic theorists who bumped into each other in the early 1980s, in what were then the autonomist movements. In 1994, a first English translation appeared: *Cracking the Movement,* a book about the Amsterdam squatters' movement and their dealings with the media (Adilkno, 1994). Although Adilkno has been writing about the media since 1984, this theme has become increasingly important since 1989. The result is the book whose working title is *The Media Archive* (1998). After five years of devoting ourselves with great pleasure and abandon to speculative media theory and potential media figures such as the data dandy, lately we act as if the media have lost their dynamism. To begin with, the introductory phase, "the short summer of the media," now lies behind us. The commercialization of the new media brings with it a relapse into old, familiar patterns. The rapid expansion of the info-universe leads to an implosion of the power of imagination. The media are once again "the others."

While hordes of young businesspeople lap up the "digital revolution" and chase visions of a utopian world full of communication, the cultural situation in fact looks very different. Apart from the aggressive information elite, named the "virtual class" by Arthur Kroker (Kroker & Weinstein, 1994), the intellectual climate has taken on a defensive character. People are preparing for "Cold War II," or what Jeltzin warned would be a "Cold Peace," and secretly looking forward to a new period of stability (Lepor, 1997). They are prepared to accept its accompanying stagnation as part of the bargain.

In retrospect, the year 1989 turns out not to have been a moment of liberation. For Westerners, Glasnost ultimately became synonymous with the deadly radioactive cloud of Chernobyl, solely out to destroy the health of Western Europeans. At the fall of the Berlin Wall, emotions were conspicuously scarce. Skepticism and disbelief prevailed, and the Eastern neighbors met with a cool reception. Romanians' certainty in early 1990 that everything would stay the same could not be refuted, and is now generally accepted, even in the West. The old officers returned to the political stage as neo-Communists, nationalists, or Thatcherites. Their transformation caused decreased income, the breakdown of social services, unemployment, radical privatization to the point of simple robbery, war, genocide, and hatred. What is going on in the

East in an extreme form (and at an increased speed) is also happening on a similar scale in Western Europe. But it is not resulting in resistance or protest. An anti-war movement, as in the Vietnam era, a solidarity movement like the one for Nicaragua, or a peace movement like the one against nuclear weapons in the early 1980s, once again seem light-years removed from us, thus unimaginable. In a strictly medial sense, Western citizens remain observers, letting in information from the Wild East according to a voracious ecological media appetite, so as not to be further numbed. Even the viewers see themselves as victims—if not of events, of information, which has been set before them everyday for years. Everyone is in the race for the most-favored-victim status.

In Adilkno's recent writings, the concept of media is no longer used as a dumpster where all fantasies are deposited and retrieved. We now see media more as a part of broader cultural phenomena, such as tourism, shopping, sport, commerce and sex. For Europeans, the abstract media sphere is not merely a consumable product. Though the ideology of the market is raging, the media remain part of a metaphysical terrain, where Western "culture" is thought to be located. However, in contrast to the (still?) open concept of "media," which, if we follow German post-structuralist Friedrich Kittler (see, for example, Kittler, 1992; Kittler & Johnston, 1997), has mainly a technical connotation, the concept of "culture" plays a crucial role in the dominant ideology of the West, which is gaining in importance, and in which rightist-elitist notions are mainstreamed into a collision of tele-evangalism and tele-communion.

The West German pop theorist Mark Terkessidis, formerly of the monthly *SPEX*, shows in his book *Kulturkampf* (1995) that the oft-cited "swing to the right" is playing out mainly in the sphere of "culture." According to media-makers and intellectuals, social conflicts are determined no longer economically or ideologically, but culturally. As in American conservative Samuel Huntington's *The Clash of Civilizations and the Remaking of World Order* (1996), the West must defend itself as a "minority." The supposed "cultural hegemony" of the left-liberal 1968 generation in the media, in schools and in universities must be broken, especially in the area of (national) culture. There is a harkening back, says Terkessides, to the late 18th-century German romantic Herder, who defined culture in defensive terms, as an ethnic identity that only really fulfills itself in the exclusion of others. As blacks rediscover their own culture, Europeans must rediscover their "Eurocentrism." "The ideology of culture," with its mix of symbols, and life and ethnic differences, offers a paradigm for exclusion (Terkessidis, 1995). And that is what "purified ethnocentrism" seeks: protection from Third World refugees, immigrants, Islam, and last but not least, the first full-scale war in Europe since 1945, in which everything revolves around the definition of ethnicity. Terkessides sees it as a mistake to consider culture as an issue of power, as was done in the 1970s and 1980s. He even suspects a "deal" between the establishment and its erstwhile critics: "If you'll let us govern in peace and stop bringing up the power question, then you can have culture" (1995, p. 47). The result of this transformation of politics into cultural lifestyles was that "cultures" were no longer seen in their social context. Even "subversion" and "autonomy" ran aground in the early 1990s. The strategy of "confusion, ambiguity and spectacle" (p. 48) still works, but political content is no longer discernible in it, as is the case with techno, ambient, and jungle. "Independent" thought has ended in "self-satisfaction, stripped of any consequence" (p. 48). Postmodern strategies of difference, heterogeneity and complexity resulted in a "transformation of culture, of which one no longer knows what direction it is taking" (p. 47).

Behind slogans like "Not right, not left, just culture," Terkessides (1995, p. 12) sees a very nearly fascist *weltanschauung* lurking, and reconstructs its intellectual history. He considers it necessary to place contemporary media culture in a "materialistic perspective," so that struggles on the terrain of culture, in music, multimedia, computer networks, and so on, are again placed in a social, political, and economic context, without relinquishing culture's autonomy. What is happening is clear: with no successors to Guattari and Foucault, and with Parisian intellectuals getting more conservative and/or simplistic by the day, there is a retrieval of neo-marxism and its attempts in the 1970s to foreground "ideology critique." Since the mid-1980s, we have been seeing a return to precisely the kind of leftist theorizing that the "Parisians" tried to leave behind. Foucault's "non-fascistic practice" is no longer discussed. Derrida's project to save philosophy has run aground in an interminable defense of Heidegger. Paul Virilio is seen as an anti-media, worried deacon, who has ended up in his own "raging stillness" (compare Wilson, 1997). People find his radical critique of cyberspace and the Net merely excessive. They see the Net as an enrichment and can only imagine what Virilio meant by an "accident of reality," disturbing the perception of reality (Wilson, 1997, p. 42). And if the Gulf War did not take place, then Jean Baudrillard no longer exists either (after Baudrillard's "No reprieve with Sarajevo," there is "No reprieve with Paris").

Terkessides (1995) identifies a "void in which people seem to consent to everything" (p. 49). It is precisely this empty space that Adilkno wishes to investigate in the New Europe. It is tempting to suspect an extreme-right, reactionary body of thought behind this void, in which "culture" has replaced "race." Terkessides dwells at elaborate length on the anti-parliamentarist legal philosopher Carl Schmitt and his influence on the contemporary conservative elite in Germany. Adilkno makes do for the moment without such a constructed, imaginary enemy, such as "new right" thinkers. We concern ourselves at present with the following artifacts: almost-engagement, advanced disinterest, touching vagueness, cold passions, the fun of meaninglessness, advanced confusion, the colors of boredom, the out-of-context, electronic solitude, IKEA as cultural ideal and collective forms of disappointment. We see an ascending ideal of a society without ideas, with a "Net without qualities." Here, "comfort" has become a human right and one delegates as much as possible to professionals in order to be rid of bother.

There was amateurism enough in the 20th century! The split between success and failure has arrived in the social sciences and cultural criticism, as is apparent in the following fragment from Adilkno's ode to the Parisian media theorist Guy Debord.

THE SOCIETY OF THE DEBACLE

After a fascination with Evil in the 1980s, we are now in the midst of an interest in Failure. We no longer read about Seduction, Simulation, Perfection, Glamour, and Passion as pure self-expression. Evil had to snuff out all the Good of the 1960s, and it succeeded smashingly, as evidenced in the breakthroughs of 1989. But then something else happened. The triumph of the dialectic, the historical synthesis of market and democracy, did not occur, and not even a new anti-thesis could be found. Good Socialism rightly gave way to the Capitalism of Failure. The system and its slaves underwent a revaluation of all values, and meanwhile nothing has changed. An indefinable situation in which nobody bothers any longer to put into words the World or the own Ego (or anything related to these). Chaos rules, and this does not lend itself to unlawful visualization. Timeless struggle takes place in the form of destructive private enterprise amid rotting cement and bankrupt government structures. The heroic radiance of the declaimed end of history is missing. The society of the spectacle has plunged us unexpectedly into the Society of the Debacle. We can learn from Guy Debord.

A heathen faith in new media, project management, surveillance, flexible scheduling, retraining, improvisation, image, and identity is the tried and true method of introducing new technologies. In the beginning there is amazement that all the strange machines and concepts function. But once they start to become widespread and really work, attention shifts to the moments at which the technologies fail, and they are written off. Once grounded in the realm of normalcy, any cybertechnology loses its sparkle and has to be routinely usable. Once hardware and software begin to fail, the consumer's rage turns against the

Machine and its makers. How lovely to unleash your Rage and throw all the malfunctioning machines out the window into the street en masse! Grunge and Generation X have mobilized the authenticity of elementary failure against the Lycra sheen of revoked success. The breakthrough of stagnation is the surprising turn history has taken since 1989. As long as the end of progress was being announced, nothing happened. But Fukuyama the liberation philosopher couldn't foresee that bungling would get the upper hand. To be sure, self-organizing principles like chaos, artificial life, fractals, the Internet, complexity, Biosphere II, and turbulence are moving optimistically forward, but they will get stuck in their advertising hype. No consequential cancerous metastasis will be achieved—these things will remain models. Failure, on the contrary, is in principle not a model, nor a strategy. In this respect it distinguishes itself from everything that the 1980s provided in the way of ideas. Failure is not a fate: fate approaches from outside, while fiasco comes from within, impossible to program in advance. The inherent disappointment that unfolds is not a bug that can be removed from the program. In the age of overorganization and a social surplus of experience, success-thinking has got bogged down in flop prevention. They tried to redefine failure as an educative moment, but Intel's Pentium chip, Microsoft Windows 5.1, the Philips CD-i, nuclear power, the hasty reunification of Germany, and peace in Europe were all strong concepts, lacking nothing in persuasive power, and yet they went nowhere.

In order to survive, one dons a mental armor. No longer a sexual armor, as described by Klaus Theweleit in *Male Fantasies* (1989), but an inconspicuous set of behaviors and precepts bent on avoiding all warm passions; a refined method and technique for dealing with "reality overload." This is "organized innocence": a phenomenon mirroring "organized crime," and one that just as invisibly embodies modern-day Evil.

ORGANIZED INNOCENCE

With the emergence of the privileged middle class, innocent existence came within everyone's reach. The middle was no longer a class that strove for a historic goal, such as revolution or fascism; it had arrived in a cold period, henceforth to be without passions. While outside it stormed and change followed change with alarming speed, one put one's own life in "park." Without regard to history, fashion, politics, sex, and the media, time could take its course. The innocent caused no problems, indeed they hated problems: "Just let things take their course." Regular folks considered themselves cogs in a larger whole, and all in all they were unashamed of it. They made sure the trains ran on time and turned homeward in the evening for a hot meal.

In place of old barriers like caste, sex, and religion, innocence brought in conversation-killers like tolerance, openness, and harmony. Positivism became a way of life. Positive criticism served the reconstruction of politics and culture. One enjoyed oneself, was dynamically busy, and had plenty of work to do. The picture of reality was simple and clear. The innocents did not embody the Good, they simply had no plan, but nor did they lack a sense of values. They never got around to crime either. And so they unintentionally became the object for strategies of Good and Evil. We speak here of a life without drama, urgency, *Entscheidung* (meaning efficiency, functionality). There will never be a close race. There need never be a decision. You need not break away just to be yourself. As the Dutch say: act normal, that's crazy enough. Innocents thrive on the rituals of everyday; these make them happy. A broken washing machine can drive a person crazy: the thing should just work.

The complaint against things is that they break down, falter, fall apart, act strange, and cannot be unobtrusively replaced. The promise of undisturbed consumption is that nothing will ever happen again. In this unproblematic existence comfort is so taken for granted that it goes unnoticed. The innocent consciousness is characterized by a narrow, small-scale thinking that calls forth a universe where personal irritations erupt at the least little thing: stoplights, traffic jams, late trains, red tape, bad weather, construction noise, illness, accidents, and unexpected guests and events are a repeated assault on the innocent existence. One becomes involved nonetheless in matters that one had not been expecting. This disturbance-hating mentality, which devotes itself to work and career, shuts out all risk and has elevated practicality as its sole criterion. The ideal of a wrinkle-free, spotless life presumes, touchingly, that literally everyone is pursuing it. Innocence is under continuous treatment by the doctor, the therapist, the beauty specialist, the acupuncturist, the garage manager. Innocence likes to be tinkered with. It sees it as a duty to develop itself, and retrain itself if need be. One takes a course; attends a lecture; visits the theatre, concert hall, and exhibition; reads a book; follows the arrows on a walk in the woods; engages in muscle sports. Innocence is a universal human right that extends to animals, plants, buildings, landscapes, and cultures. This is the condition under which the planet can finally still be saved: neither utopian nor fatalistic, but functioning normally.

You can lose your innocence by committing murder, joining a motorcycle club, choosing art, or going undercover, but the entertainment underworld offers no solace. Only the crossing over to war and genocide is still an option that we hear much about. Yet there is no escaping the agglomeration and its dictates. Mountain bikes, cool t-shirts, clever children's clothes, computer games, graffiti, bumper stickers, sloppy sportswear, brightly colored backpacks, hair gel: these are the *objets nomades* of Jacques Attali's Europe (1999), on its way to a stylized uniformity. Innocence cannot be neutralized or counterbalanced by its opposite. The only thing it cannot stand is the spoiling of the atmosphere. This rotting process within normalcy offers no alternative, commits no resistance and performs no act. And innocence finds it exhausting. One cannot always be fresh and cheerful and sweep away the fog with constructive thinking. Innocence is in no danger of being wiped out by revolution or reaction. It can only decline, sink into poverty, and slowly disappear from the picture. In a stagnating relationship one drags up a trash container, dumps the accumulated innocence in it, rebuilds the interior and makes a fresh, wild new start. The politicization of the private a generation ago managed to clear out some of the innocence, but it has regrouped stronger than before. "Grungies," "generation X'ers," "trancers," and other young people search in vain for a footing that sets themselves apart in a format other than fashion or media, the new organizational forms of innocence. The Dutch government itself seems the most anti-racist, anti-sexist, anti-fascist, anti-housing-shortage, anti-everything that a well-intentioned rebel could be against. The only thing innocent new generations can unleash their rage upon is organized innocence itself, in all its forms. Material enough to start a massive social movement and get to work in countless spheres, and then discover that all those disparate groups have something in common. "Boycott all forms of insurance, storm the stores full of obnoxious baby clothes, set fire to all those superfluous cute gift shops—there is a whole consumer paradise to destroy!" But let's not get excited. We will let innocence ebb away, grow silent, we won't talk about it anymore.

INNOCENT EUROPE AND THE WAR

So this is the Europe of genocide. In Belgrade, Kosovo, Zagreb, Sarajevo, Tuzla, people bravely try to join in and desperately keep believing that they are part of "Europe." David Rieff, in his book *Slaughterhouse: Bosnia and the Failure of the West* (1995), argues that those in the Balkans thought that, as Europeans, they would be protected from the devastation of war. The citizens of former Yugoslavia could not believe that the "CNN effect" would not occur in their case. They waited in vain for a live broadcast of the arrival of a rapid intervention force, come to set them free. However, Rieff acknowledges that the debate is long over now and the West has chosen to do anything but intercede. It chose, on the contrary, to contain the crisis, anticipating the Cold War II paradigm that an imposed stagnation produces some positive effect. The West did not want to save the Bosnian Muslims. After he has witnessed a genocide, Europe is, for Rieff, no longer a civilized space. The question is, why does even this message fail to get through, 50 years after Hiroshima and Auschwitz? For the first time, the mental armor of the Europeans triumphed over the daily bombardment of information. According to Slavoj Žižek (1993), the Balkans are a new site for Western fantasies. They are an imaginary glacis for the defense of a culture, full of communication and global dreams. They reveal the end of the age of the media, the accompanying games of perception included.

With whom could the average Westerner identify? With no broad anti-war movement, oppositional culture in former Yugoslavia is completely left to itself. The only thing that counts anymore is survival. In the long absence of political confrontations, the rage against the war machine expresses itself in a vital, ironic, high-grade cynicism. Not a nonchalant indifference, rather a form of stylized despair. The survival artists in Kosovo, Belgrade, Sarajevo and Zagreb are averse to purism, and every expression of political correctness comes across as foolish pettiness. It is not a protest that begs for sympathy or solidarity. The help offered by international organizations causes consolidation rather than breakthrough, and offers no prospect of liberation from oppressive and dismal nationalism. In a situation in which all parties define themselves as victims, it makes no sense to identify with this or that group. Once involved one automatically arrives in a gray zone. One becomes part of the black market, smokes homegrown pot, sells relief goods, is ruined by cheap heroin, or finally manage to escape to Paris, London, New York, or Amsterdam.

On the scene we become acquainted with the techno-existentialism of the few who have stayed behind. They no longer need bid farewell to modernism, as Western postmodernism has believed for decades it must do. The dominant discourse is indifferent to attempts at deconstruction and merely leaves the intellectuals to muddle on. Their supposed power is ancient history. The minuscule opposition, which maintains itself under the yoke of repressive tolerance in the shadow of power, expresses itself in a number of so-called "independent media."[2] By this is meant merely that they are not property of the state or under direct influence of the governing party, which in the former Eastern Bloc is already quite a feat. Just as in Western Europe, the subculture has its own radio stations and weeklies, organizes techno parties, makes videos, posters, rock-and-roll, and theater, and communicates via faxes and computer networks. Technologically speaking, the lag behind the West is remarkably small. New hardware and software get around with lightning speed, and in this respect there is scarcely a difference anymore in Europe between a Western center and a periphery in the south and east. An example of this is the ZaMir Transnational computer network, with almost 2,000 users, which has been providing e-mail contact between cities like Prestina, Belgrade, Zagreb, Tuzla, and Ljubljana since 1992. Mail is sent and received several times a day. Network traffic runs through Germany. Five hundred users reach nearby capitals and the rest of the world from Sarajevo by e-mail, and anti-war groups from Zagreb and Belgrade maintain contact through the network.

The underground magazine ARKZIN is published in Zagreb; there are several free radio stations in Skopje; the weekly VREME and the radio station B92 are based in Belgrade; Radio ZID broadcasts the sounds of the opposition in Sarajevo (and criticizes the Bosnian government); and the independent Albanian weekly KOHA is published in Prestina, despite heavy Serbian repression of the Albanian majority in the province of Kosovo. Here, in "Old Serbia," President Milosevic's media campaign began in 1989—a stroke of propaganda many see as the fatal beginning of the war. Milosevic still controls the state media and manipulates them to stay in power. These include several influential newspapers and the national radio and TV channels, which can be received everywhere, especially in the backward countryside, in contrast to the independent media with their inadequate distribution. In Croatia, the situation is the same, and in Bosnia-Herzegovina, too, the party of Izetbegovic has authority over radio and television. Even the heroic daily newspaper *Oslobodenje* cannot be spoken of as independent.

The war will only be over when the warlords and their small armies have laid down their weapons and the war profiteers who are now in power are voted out in a democratic manner. But the anti-nationalist, non-Communist opposition is still too weak to take the helm (as is the case in other Eastern European countries). To support such an opposition from the West, it is first of all necessary, as Žižek says, to make one's own power analysis of the Balkans, one that is based on history and that views the role of the media in correct proportions. It will also be necessary to make a clean sweep of the UN's quasi-neutrality and the Europeans' humanitarian aid, the slow nonintervention force. One would also have to ridicule the 19th-century diplomacy and the half-hearted support of one of the warring sides.

Now that the war has acquired its own dynamic, we must not overestimate the power of the media. The so-called "independent media" cannot bring down the ruling tribe. At most, they are the germs of a democratic movement that has had enough of hatred, robbery, and genocide. But they are no longer breeding grounds for dissidents with clear-cut principles. European innocence must be conquered, the crippling identity of victimhood pushed aside. If, as Kroker maintains, in the New Europe, with its new, invisible, electronic war, everything is about "the bitter division of the world into virtual flesh and surplus flesh" (Kroker & Weinstein, 1994, p. 37), then it is up to the independent media like ZaMir, B92, and ARKZIN to ridicule this split, and in an ironic, existential manner, to give shape to the universal technological desire, cyberspace.

NOTES

1. The term "Witz" is German for joke. It also means spirit and lively ideas. As an adjective, *Witzig*, it can also mean funny or even strange. In some contexts, it can also mean "the great thing about this."
2. Information about the independent media in former Yugoslavia can be found (among other places) on MediaFilter, a New York-based website, at <http://MediaFilter.org/MFF/warzone>

REFERENCES

Adilkno. (1994). *Cracking the movement: Squatting beyond the media.* New York: Autonomedia.

Adilkno. (1998). *The media archive.* New York: Autonomedia.

Attali, J. (1999). *Labyrinth in culture and society: Pathways to wisdom* (J. Rowe, Trans.). Berkeley, CA: North Atlantic Books.

Huntington, S. (1996). *The clash of civilizations and the remaking of world order.* New York: Simon & Schuster.

Kittler, F. A. (1992). *Discourse networks, 1800/1900.* (M. Metteer, Trans.). Stanford, CA: Stanford University Press.

Kittler, F. A., & Johnston, J. (Eds.). (1997). *Literature, media, information systems.* New York: Distributed Art Publishers.

Lepor, K. P. (Ed.). (1997). *After the cold war: Essays on the emerging world order.* Austin, TX: University of Texas Press.

Kroker, A., & Weinstein, M. (1994). *Data trash: The theory of the virtual class.* New York: St. Martin's Press.

Rieff, D. (1995). *Slaughterhouse: Bosnia and the failure of the West.* New York: Vintage.

Terkessides, M. (1995). *Kulturkampf: Volk, Nation, der Westen und die Neue Rechte* [Fight for culture: Nation, the West and new rights]. Cologne: Verlag Kiepenheuer & Witsch.

Theweleit, K. (with Carter, E., & Turner, C.). (1989). *Male fantasies, male bodies: Psychoanalyzing the White Terror.* Minneapolis, MN: University of Minnesota Press.

Wilson, L. (1997). Cyberwar, God and television: Interview with Paul Virilio. In A. Kroker & M. Kroker (Eds.), *Digital delirium* (pp. 41–48). Montréal: New World Perspectives.

Žižek, S. (1993). *Tarrying with the negative*. Durham, NC: Duke University Press.

chapter 8

Cyber Hate: The Discourse of Intolerance in the New Europe

Elliot Glassman
Eötvös Loránd University, Budapest

Zvi Lando, list manager of the Hate-Hotline, argues "The re-emergence of racism, neo-nazism and neo-fascism is all around us. It wears many different costumes, it calls itself in many different names, and it speaks many different languages" (1995). Under "different names" and "speaking different languages," hate groups and hate speech have an extensive history, traced back to the bible, to tribal wars, and to the division of perceived nations. More recently, written communication spurred the growth of the dissemination of material laced with hate speech. The recipients of such verbal and written enmity often consisted of minorities in increasingly homogeneous countries, where they were perceived as inner enemies. At the dawn of the third millennium, the newest communicative phenomenon is the Internet, through which hate groups have an alternative to more traditional and costly communication campaigns that can reach a global audience in seconds. Such campaigns have been referred to as "cyber hate," "Net hate," or "cyber intolerance." Regardless of the name, the concern of hate speech has been analyzed by both opponents of these groups and advocates of free speech (see, for example, Anti-Defamation League, 1998; Fiss, 1996; Hentoff, 1994; Mendels, 1998; Miller & Andsager, 1998; Olson, 1997; Titch, 1996; Walker, 1994). Through critical analyses of World Wide Web content and primary research concerning hate discourse through newsgroups, this chapter focuses on cyber hate as it relates to the New Europe, either as emanating from the region or directed at the region.

BACKGROUND CONSIDERATIONS

Before examining cyber hate specifically in the New Europe, this chapter will analyze some key background considerations about the Internet generally and cyber hate globally. In contrast to hate speech, which has long been printed in "specialist" newspapers and magazines, the Internet can reach a vast amount of people without much effort. An e-mail "spam," a message reaching a vast number of people, can notify thousands on a particular server. For instance, a user hacked into a Texas A & M University professor's e-mail account and sent racist and anti-Semitic messages to 20,000 users in four states ("Hackers Racist Note," 1994; Simon Wiesenthal Center, 1995). In 1995, Greg Raven obtained the list of e-mail addresses for all the members of the History of the Holocaust electronic mailing list and proceeded to send them an e-mail message propagating his Holocaust denying material. Those who received the mail included hundreds of scholars, survivors, children of survivors, and others interested in Holocaust scholarship (Tel Aviv University Faculty of the Humanities, n.d.). If one posts a message on the Usenet, anywhere from tens to hundreds of thousands can read the disseminated discussion. Every server containing newsgroups makes the discussions and channels available without totaling the numbers of readers. Accordingly, it is virtually impossible to know how many readers can access a particular message. Even though some websites containing hate messages use counters to assess how many users accessed the sites, such counting mechanisms can be easily manipulated by the Webmaster.

The crossnational and multinational nature of the Internet brings concerns about freedom of speech and civic discourse. Each country has its own laws on free speech and that which may not be considered totally "free." If one country prohibits a site due to its content, the material can appear from another site in another country and infiltrate those from the original country that prohibited the site's material in the first place. Furthermore, if one site is blocked out, as will be discussed, the site can still be mirrored to other locations that are not blocked out. This means that a continuous website location change takes place in order to sideline those attempting to prohibit the site, and thereby new Web locations sprout up and close down very quickly in a perpetual cat-and-mouse chase. Additionally, many Internet providers do not examine the content of the sites they host, unaware of the hateful material. When the

Internet providers learn of the hateful content, in order to prevent negative publicity for their companies, many of them will shut down the intolerant websites, consequently causing the continuous disappearance/ reappearance scenario of intolerant sites.

While the Internet has been growing in fantastic proportions in the United States and Western Europe, due to reasons including relatively inexpensive user costs and technology-driven business ventures, access to the Internet remains exclusively for some of the upper echelons of society in East Central Europe, South-Eastern Europe, and the post-Soviet bloc. As a worldwide network, any web page can virtually be visualized anywhere, unless locked out, or "filtered" by an Internet service provider (ISP) or by other means. This filtering situation has taken place in Germany with pages that may incite violence and in China with sites deemed politically sensitive to the national government. Filtering foregrounds the issue that access to disseminating information on the Internet is the key to both those propagating hate and to those targeted for recruitment. Access to technology generally is a key issue in the New Europe (see, for example, Lengel, 1998). For example, in 1997, 300,000 Hungarian high school students gained access for the first time to unlimited resources of this technology through a government initiative to place computers with Internet service in the schools. Thus, they too may be prone to intolerant propaganda from those who can afford the Internet in the region and those elsewhere where use is quite inexpensive. This new government program is expected to be duplicated throughout the region, and has been a model for other governments.

Information emerging from the area or directed at the region may be in the native language and/or in another language that overwhelmingly tends to be English. Either way, the message can get through. The Anti-Defamation League (ADL) states, "Hate Group Recruitment On the Internet shows how extremists are exploiting the technology of the Internet, including the World Wide Web and USENET, to attract supporters, foster racial divisiveness, and promote their propaganda. Several extremists have actually posted strategies and tactics as a "how-to-guide" to recruit unaffiliated users into the neo-Nazi orbit" (Anti-Defamation League, 1998). The ADL statement demonstrates the controversy involved with the advent of this new technology. Nevertheless, those propagating the hate and their adherents do not comprise more than just a fringe number of Internet users. On the other hand, the possibilities for further recruitment through the Internet continues to grow as an alternative to printed material, such as newspapers or magazines in native languages.

IS IT CIVIC DISCOURSE?

Attitudes toward cyber hate are illustrated by such comments as: "If you don't look for it, you won't find it."; "These groups are on the fringe of society. No one listens to them."; "If you ignore them, they'll go away."; or "There are not too many of them, so what harm can they do?" Perhaps the most important concern is raising awareness and understanding of the potential dangers involved in complacency and indifference. As in the cases above, in discussion of the Institute for Historical Review and the sites denigrating the Roma, most Internet users who find these sites do not look for them, but stumble onto them. If the people are young and impressionable, then a real danger exists. People will listen to these groups as the numbers of them swell and their adherents continue to grow. If one ignores them, others will listen and begin to perceive what they say as fact. If hate groups remain unchecked, then their small numbers will begin to expand. Many ideas have emerged to combat this potential threat. While in a liberal philosophy, all groups have a political say, and some governments, companies, foundations, and individuals have taken measures to halt what many would argue to be an abuse of free speech.

Advocates of unconditional free speech call for a healthy atmosphere of allowing all political thought and freedom of expression, even if they do not agree with the content. After Rabbi Abraham Cooper of the Simon Wiesenthal Center asked 2,000 Internet service providers to stop customers from using their services to distribute racist and anti-Semitic material, one free speech advocate stated: "Any censorship of speech ultimately boomerangs to injure good speech, and one of the tenants of what I call the 'free speech rulebook' is that no-one—not the government, not Netcom, not the Wiesenthal Center—is godlike enough to decide for other people what speech may be heard" (Ethical Spectacle, 1996).

Others opposing censorship offer similar arguments. For example, Richard Petersen (1996) asks why there is an assumption, without evidence, that distribution of hateful content will have a "deleterious effect upon minors"? He denigrates the use of government censorship, saying that radio and television have "barely recovered" from this authority and accuses the government of trying to control the way people perceive the world. Petersen looks at "total free speech" theory and states how the Internet can serve this idea best, only against the interests of corporate advertising and the "ability of companies to continue to convince people that happiness can be had through more and more consumption." Petersen and others adhere to a belief of total and unfettered free speech. This school of thought carries much debate, but nevertheless holds a very important view throughout world governments in questions of constitutions and human rights. However, governments have clamped down on certain activities, for without control, chaos would reign. Does this mean that hate speech should be protected?

It should be noted that hate group leaders continually refer to upholding freedom of speech and expression. Hate group websites devote enough space to "portray themselves as victims of vicious attacks meant to keep them from spreading the truth" (Tel Aviv University Faculty of the Humanities, n.d.). The Institute for Historical Review always alleges that they are targeted by those trying to hide the "truth of the Holocaust" and claims to apply scientific principles to break down the "Hoax of the Twentieth Century." That is, these so-called scientists believe that the Holocaust did not take place and that it was indeed a myth created by Jew-friendly world leaders who owed their continued success to Jewish capital. Hence, the assertions to explain historical documents that would further their anti-Semitic cause.

MONITORING CYBER HATE

Many monitoring groups exist to examine Internet sites and check for hateful material. Individuals also host websites that investigate intolerant substance. At least 20 organizations currently act as monitors; the organizations include, but are not limited to, the Anti-Defamation League (ADL), Antifascist Web, the Coalition for Human Dignity, Germany Alert, the Gay Lesbian Alliance Against Defamation (GLAAD), Net Hate, and the Nizkor Project. All of these organizations are either American or Western European-based and have yet to precisely concentrate on post-Communist nations, where ethnic strife has had a large part in the continent's affairs for the past century in particular. One problem inherent in these organizations is that they do not critically analyze, but rather just condemn or list the sites so the person logged onto that monitoring site can hyperlink to those berated by these organizations.

One of these organizations, the ADL, recently stated that Web locations propagating hate are currently doubling every three months. In addition, more and more young people are "surfing the Web" for all sorts of information, not necessarily looking for hate material, but rather stumbling on it. For instance, one could be looking up information on the Holocaust, only to discover the Institute for Historical Review, an organization dedicated to denying the Holocaust via a charade of academic scholarship. Thus the problem with the Internet and its search engines lies in the question of context and content. Not only does the unsuspecting individual delve into a territory of hate mongers without understanding who these people are, but the person also falls victim to the propaganda such sites espouse. Moreover, as many contemporary Internet users are young, impressionable people, they can become prey for such propagandists. Much wrong information exists on the Net, and the targeted individual has no way of discerning what is truth and what is false. For example, one could try to find information about Rome, Italy, only to latch onto a site denigrating the Roma.

Several hate-monitoring organizations as well as international bodies have come up with various means of handling hate groups on the Internet. One school of thought rests on the idea that ignoring the hate will not bring attention to those "malicious" Web locations and that the only way for these "hate mongers" to continue lies in publicity of ill-repute, a task that brings together others of similar beliefs enabling their ideology to grow. However, by ignoring them, this trend does not even begin. Another belief is that by exposing the sites through educating the public to how they misrepresent cultures will render these groups ineffective. Hate monitors follow this path by listing the sites, quoting a few lines, and providing hyperlinks to the Web locations. Yet, by not conducting a full analysis of these sites, the hate monitors cannot accomplish their goals of "education." A full analysis means that a concrete investigation of each site with correct statistics and reports on inaccuracies, in addition to comparisons and contrasts, act as an educating force. A third solution comes down to making laws as a preventative measure or criminalizing it. Such a solution holds a strong hope that further publication of this material on the Web would be arrested. Yet, this measure brings strong condemnation by advocates of freedom of speech, as stated earlier. Finally, hacking the material would create difficulty for people to access the information by blocking specific Internet sites (Goldberg, 1996). Nonetheless, questions emerge such as "Who decides what we should and should not see?"; "Should someone decide for us what is incorrect content?"; How can anyone sort through the plethora of information already on the Net as well as the additional information added every single day?" And still more questions evolve: "Who will be alienated?" and "Will the freedom of speech be continuously eroded?" All of these questions relate to a higher liberty, yet in a time of technological breakthroughs, freedom of speech changes into other means.

These questions are being addressed by national governments, which are scrambling to update their laws in order to accommodate the Internet. For instance, in Canada, hate speech, be it disseminated through traditional or new technological means, is not protected. This falls under Section 13 of the Canadian Human Rights Act, which forbids hate discourse "by means of a telecommunication undertaking within the legislative authority of Parliament" (cited in Balkan, 1996). Similarly, German authorities recently ordered service providers to prevent subscribers from connecting to certain sites that are of "pro-Nazi" content. The European Parliament has drafted an extensive measure to fight intolerance and has called upon member states to take action against extremism. As an international network crossing borders, Articles 59 and 60 of the European Convention Treaty govern telecommunications and the Internet (cited in Balkan, 1996). Article 10, Section 2 of the European Convention on Human Rights states that national legislatures may enact exceptions to the freedom of expression when three factors are met (cited in Balkan, 1996). First, the law must provide a clear and precise exception. Second, an imperative social need must be addressed. Third, the law must be proportionate. A legitimate goal, such as "national security, crime prevention, the protection of morality or the protection of the reputation or rights of others" (cited in Balkan, 1996) must also be considered.

The European Parliament Committee on Civil Liberties and Internal Affairs has passed numerous resolutions condemning terrorism, racism, xenophobia, and anti-Semitism. The legislative body also recognizes the difficulty in imposing legal restrictions on the Internet and that "what cannot get through one channel will pass via another" (European Parliament, 1996, p. 14). A report by the Committee encourages self-regulation, as implemented in the United Kingdom with the Safety Net Foundation. This organization attempts to find "troublemakers" and ask them to expunge the illegal contents from the network. If the "perpetrator" refuses, the Safety Net Foundation will request the site manager to take action against the user and report the situation to the UK police. In Germany and the Netherlands, similar measures have been undertaken. Once informed, the ISP should initiate a process to remove the inflammatory documents from the server.

Some ISPs have created blacklists of sites and specific messages that will be refused for dissemination through their servers. Yet savvy Internet users can always go around the local server and connect to one that will allow access to hate material. The European Parliament Committee on Civil Liberties and Internal Affairs has suggested the method of monitoring as another means whereby a filtering process would occur. This process would result in disconnecting the user if certain keywords are used. The Committee report states that "problems ensued in the United States when America Online attempted to intercept words with sexual connotations, such as 'breast,' and mistakenly blocked a newsgroup that aimed to consult women with breast cancer. Such methods have become technologically insecure and problematic" (European Parliament, 1996, p. 15). The report then calls for a need of tracing users. This would in effect make individuals responsible for their actions, and if their words cause a certain hateful action like advocating an attack on a specific group, then the webmaster would face legal ramifications.

One form of control against "harmful material," as the report calls it, possibly would be parental control software in which minors could not stumble onto racist or neo-Nazi sites. Hence, parents would be able to use specialized software based on a filtering method. The report notes how online service providers favor parental control, essentially to relieve their culpability. Online services such as America Online and Compuserve already have an in-house parental control system. This process keeps government control out of the system, thus arresting arguments from free speech advocates. Three possibilities exist in this endeavor: Blacklisting, which prevents access to a specific site; whitelisting, which means that certain sites are authorized; and neutral labeling, which marks sites with a label or "moral rating," allowing the user to make the appropriate judgement on whether or not to access the Web. This last method is much like the rating system for television programming in the United States (European Parliament, 1996). In order to accomplish this last technique, new filtering technology called Platform for Internet Content Solution (PICS) is required. Thus, the PICS label and the special parameters set up by parents will guide young users. The report calls this solution, "the most comprehensive and ground-breaking means of dealing with problems of content on the Internet" (European Parliament, 1996, p. 16). In reference to certain neo-Nazi groups, which promote computer hate games, like KZ (Concentration Camp) Manager in Austria, or sell recordings from record companies like Resistance Records, a group distributing skinhead music that is both anti-Semitic and racist, neutral labeling becomes an ideal method.

CYBER HATE IN THE NEW EUROPE

In contrast to the racial, religious, and ethnic problems in Western Europe, the United States, and other regions discussed previously, East Central Europe, South-Eastern Europe, and the former Soviet bloc has been rife with ethnic intolerance for centuries. Most recently, the wars in Bosnia and Yugoslavia, and the crisis in Kosovo, aimed the world's attention once again at the complex and diverse cultures of the region. As the cold war ended and Communism melted away, a resurgence of the right began to unfold. Not only did the far right emerge for the first time since World War II, but prejudice became open and its inherent nature warned the West of new dangers to be faced. As a part of the transition to a market economy, many people remained impoverished, needing to place blame on someone. Hence, ethnic minorities became targets for a new generation of nationalism. This type of nationalism not only denigrated those who were different, but also looked to the "nation" as the sole entity to which to aspire. Thereby, in Slovakia, it became even more important to be Slovak and in Poland, more important to be Polish. Those not fitting within this preferential category bore the brunt of animosity held onto, yet not acted upon, in society for 40 years.

Suddenly, the first freely elected governments in the New Europe, with the exception of that in the Czech Republic, lost power during the next elections to new groups composed of former Communist Party members. Equally, the nationalism that had been used as the new political ideology also declined. As a result of the loss of power of the elected governments and increasing economic problems, parties of the right were poised to reemerge once again and began to gain in popularity. Elections from Poland to Hungary attest to this trend. At the same time, a small segment of the populations from the various countries garnered an incredible amount of wealth, while a large percentage remained considerably impoverished. Would the scene be right for the nationalist ideas to again reemerge?

HUNGARY

During the first wave of post-cold war nationalism, Internet discussion groups appeared focusing on various nations in the New Europe. Yet, most of these discussion posts were implemented by ex-patriates living in the West. For example, Andras Pellionisz, Istvan Csorna, Zoltan Egyed, and Andras Peter Nemenyi posted culturally insensitive statements on a Hungarian discussion group during the early 1990s. Csorna is presently a professor of physics at Vanderbilt University; his Ph.D. student is Egyed, who is now working for Pellionisz. Pellionisz allegedly hosts a list called Nemzet (nation) and heralds the "greatness" of Hungary.

The Hungarian posts also included HIX Forum, now under the name of HIX Szabad, where nationalist and racist material came together. HIX Moka, which now has a moderator on the channel, contained much anti-Roma sentiment. The main archives of HIX remained at hix.mit.edu, until it was shut down by its maintainer, Tibor Beke. Beke, upset with the tone of the Internet Relay Chat, returned the computer server to Jozsef Hollosi, a strong believer in free speech. This series of events illustrates the process of the appearance/disappearance/reappearance scenario of culturally insensitive groups on the Internet. It also shows the connection between a small group of "nationalists" living outside of Hungary, yet posting the information for themselves and for those with access in Hungary.

The U.S.-based Silicon Valley Net consists of many pro-Hungarian web pages, mostly written in Hungarian. This means that the targeted audience are those accessing the site from Hungary. Included are pages from Magyar Forum, the far-right wing political party MIEP (Hungarian Truth and Justice Party), and the March 14, 1996, speech by Hungarian Agriculture and Regional Development Minister Jozsef Torgyan rejecting foreigners, defined by Torgyan as both persons who are not Hungarian as well as Hungarians who do not fit the dominant norm, such as gays and lesbians.

THE CZECH REPUBLIC

In contrast to the Hungarian sites housed on the U.S.-based Silicon Valley website, the Patriotic Front site is actually located in the Czech Republic. This site uses nationalism and the "cultural and spiritual heritage" of proud Czechs to delve into an intolerant tone by arguing that "The national identity of the Czech nation is endangered by the contemporary cosmopolitan government" (Elnet, 1997). The organization's mission is defined on the site: "The Patriotic Front is a protector of our national identity against all of the cosmopolitan projects heading to mixing people and cultures. Far from racism and xenophobia, the Patriotic Front protects the Czech nation by prefering [sic] it to strangers and respecting its basic rights" (Elnet, 1997).

Moreover, Point 6 of its manifesto states the following: "We demand the first rate social policy for our nation depending of the values of our work. Canceling [sic] all of unqualified privileges for Gipsies. No national minority or group cannot be prefered [sic] at the expense of the Czech nation" (Elnet, 1997). If one neglects the grammatical and spelling errors found in many of these sites, it is apparent that the racist element does surface in contrast to the aforementioned denial of racism and xenophobia. Other points in the organization's manifesto also illustrate a right-wing philosophy, but do not show intolerance toward minorities. For example, Point 4 calls for an end to immigration, while Point 10 states, "Czech money to Czech firms!". The Patriotic Front site not only publishes its views in the Czech language, but also in English. The dual-lingual site thus can reach a far wider audience than merely within the Czech Republic.

POLAND, ROMANIA, AND SLOVAKIA

The far right-wing organization, International Third Position, located in London, hosts Web pages for many European far-right political parties.

Included among these are websites for Poland, Romania, and Slovakia. All of these pages are written in English, but advertise printed publications in the native languages for ordering.

Within the International Third Position website (n.d., a), one can find selected articles from its far right journal, *Final Conflict*. Links to these articles are also available via the Czech Patriotic Front site, illustrating how the nationalist sites support each other via links. In the Polish section entitled "Narodowe Odrodzenie Polski," brief news headlines are published using a nationalist tone. One such "news" item, "Jews Before Poles," announces, "The 'Restitution of Jewish property in Poland Bill' became law! The Polish Parliament (Sejm) approved the proposed bill on the 31st of May. Polish citizens are still waiting for their own reprivatisation law" ("Narodowe Odrodzenie Polski," 1996). Not only does this statement intimate that Polish Jews are not Polish, but tries to incite an animosity between the "two" peoples. The next headline is equally disturbing as it again forces a barrier between Jews and Poles, a reminder of the prejudice still present in the everyday life of Polish society.

Another "news" item, "Auschwitz," on the Narodowe Odrodzenie Polski site discusses how U.S. Congressman Dick Zimmer is opposing the building of a shopping center near the concentration camp site. The article notes, "Republican Zimmer is making every effort to gain the votes of Jewish electors (who usually vote for Democrats). He gave up after his assistants told him about the 700,000 Polish electors living in the New Jersey constituency. He decided to avoid any public debate" ("Narodowe Odrodzenie Polski," 1996). Both of the above headlines and the subsequent articles are not overtly anti-Semitic, indicating a tremendous difference in the American versus European sites. Even though this site technically is located in the United States, the International Third Position organization is based in London. The International Third Position supports all of these sites and fosters partnerships among the Webmasters from the various countries.

The Romanian website, as part of the International Third Position, is quite extensive. Online articles, reviews, and catalogues can be accessed. Subscriptions for the *Final Conflict* publication can also be ordered via a check or postal money order payable to *Final Conflict* in pounds at the address stated. The site lists subscriptions in English and in Romanian as well as links to other nationalist contacts (International Third Position, n.d., a). Many articles in English are available from this site. One link to the site, entitled "The Legion of the Archangel Michael," admits its stance as a "nationalist movement" proclaiming its ill-fated history as the fault of others: "With the help of political leaders and the Judeo-Masonic conspiracy, King Carol II abolished the constitution and assumed dictatorial power" (Gazeta de Vest, 1999). An article on the

Kshatriya (n.d.) site praises the deceased leader of the Legionaries, Corneliu Z. Codreanu. Yet this article and others actually link up to another site for the information. Some of the articles linked to the site are also in German, a way to easily bypass the strict German laws that prohibit cyber intolerance on their servers. In addition, the Romanian website contains articles on "Germany and its Place in Europe" one of which attacks Jehovah's Witnesses by calling them "borderless" in a demeaning manner (International Third Position, n.d., c). The site enables the computer user to read these articles under the guise of G. V. Compact, the Internet version of *Gazeta de Vest*, a far-right Romanian newspaper. The introduction from the editor announces that the newspaper is produced by a group of Romanian men and women, averaging 30 years of age, whose "job is to raise questions and search for the truth" (International Third Position, n.d., b).

The editor goes on to note how Romania stood as a bastion against the Ottoman Turks in defense of Europe and then lists various feats of the Romanian nation. Yet the issue of searching for the "truth" becomes the new bastion of the far right. Extremist groups tend to use this expression and reasoning. Here, the Romanian nationalists state that they are searching for the truth; most hate groups use the same line of argument.

CROATIA, SERBIA, ALBANIA, AND KOSOVO

Many World Wide Web sites denigrate the diverse cultural communities in the Balkans, where hate speech, disseminated through both traditional and new media "tends to become the standard" (B92, n.d.). Croats against Serbs, Serbs against Albanians, the sites are fertile with hate speech. Numerous reports on listservs and Web pages, as well as traditional media forms, use "'hate speech,' including the continuing use of insulting derogatives to describe Albanians in the Serbian state media, [which] continue to poison inter-ethnic relations" (International Helsinki Federation, 1999). The crisis in Kosovo has led to recent sites, such as one from the Serbian Unity Congress (Walsh, 1999). The author, Zora Walsh, argues "We are constantly pointing out that 90 percent of Kosovo's population are Albanians who, incidentally, entered Kosovo illegally from Albania. Now they demand independence." Elsewhere on the Serbian Unity Congress site, Stephen Rosenfeld (1999), writes,

> Once, and not so long ago, the Albanians in Kosovo were repressing Kosovo's Serbs and conducting a vile "ethnic cleansing." This is what gave an otherwise unremarkable provincial politician, Slobodan Milosevic, the

opportunity to become a champion of Serb nationalism, a position he parlayed into national Yugoslav leadership and international notoriety. It is helpful to keep this rarely mentioned phase of Serbia's story in mind at a moment when, in defense of Kosovan interests, NATO has just begun bombing Serb targets in Serbia and in its province of Kosovo. As recently as the '80s, the Albanians were the heavies and the Serbs were the victims. Now it has all turned around, with the Serbs becoming the heavies while the Albanians take their turn as victims.

While the status of "heavies" and "victims" may be debated by all sides in the Balkans, it is clear that the New Europe is faced with significant crises as ethnic minorities are targets for cyber hate on the World Wide Web. Other services of the Internet, too, are for cyber hate against cultural diversity in the New Europe. Unlike the World Wide Web, which is a relatively passive service of the Internet, Usenet provides much more active computer-mediated communication channels. Many newsgroups endure by drawing a large audience for those who post messages. Groups and individuals disseminating find newsgroups a very effective tool in the promotion of their ideas. Worldwide, a number of newsgroups, such as alt.politics.nationalism.white, alt.politics.white-power, alt.revisionism, alt.revolution.american.second, alt. skinheads, and misc. activism.militia, provide spaces for promoting sexism, racism, white supremacy, class difference, and homophobia. Some research has been conducted on cyber hate in computer-mediated communication (see, for example, Johnston, 1998; Sack, 1998). An important study in 1995, by Tali Tadmor-Shimony, used participant observation to distinguish among the participants of the talk.politics.mideast discussion channel within a four-month period, where he analyzed participants who spoke on a debate of Holocaust denial and anti-Semitism. In his study, Tadmor-Shimony divided the debate participants in the following categories: Anti-Semites (Professionals), Opponents, Neutrals, and Anti-Zionists opposed to anti-Semitism. Not only did Tadmor-Shimony investigate one channel that included 184 people for the short time period of four months, he also examined who participated in the debate and into which category those people fell. As experience shows, ambiguities exist and placing people within these categories may not be all that telling in such a short examination period. Moreover, this discussion group seems to attract those wishing to propagate anti-Semitic ideas and those wishing to oppose that agenda. In other words, outspoken activists on both sides of the debate flock to this channel in order to fight it out in words. However, this study does provide some understanding as to the propagation of cyber hate through newsgroups.

RESEARCHING NEWSGROUP CYBER HATE IN
POST-COMMUNIST NATIONS

Building on Tadmor-Shimony's (1995) research, I elicited information from users on newsgroups, which focused on issues in East-Central and South-Eastern Europe. My initial goal was to seek guidance on cyber hate websites in and about the region. The following message was used in each of the newsgroups:

To whom it may concern:
I am a researcher studying extremism on the net. I am looking for web sites dealing with nationalism and intolerance. Please post it or e-mail me as I am searching the entire area. Also, I am not trying to denigrate any specific country in any way, but there are far right parties in EVERY country. The question will be how those who can access the web be affected by these intolerant sites. My objective is to survey all the countries in the region, so please respond if you have any info.
Thank you.
Elliot Glassman
25 April 1998
Postings were placed on the following newsgroups[1]:

alt.current-events.ukraine
soc.culture.albania
soc.culture.belarus
soc.culture.bulgaria
soc.culture.croatia
soc.culture.czecho-slovak
soc.culture.magyar
soc.culture.romanian
soc.culture.slovenia
soc.culture.yugoslavia

One respondent wrote,

You want racism???????????---------go to New York or Alabama or perhaps even Texas...........but if you are trying to find red herrings in Croatia, good luck!!! I would suggest that you will find 1000 times as many racists in the US or in the UK, than you will in Croatia, in fact, we are one of the few countries that do not have a racist National Front style party that seems to be getting a steady stream of votes. (Usenet posting on soc.culture.croatia, April 26, 1998)

Other respondents posted long letters. For example, Eric M. wrote several anti-Serb statements, one of which follows:

Wartime Nazi movements in Croatia, Slovenia, Hungary and Romania have been amply studied. Serbia's home-grown brand of WWII nazism has not been—for three reasons. First, it hid under the mantle of slav nationalism. Because Serb nazis were anti-German they were exempt from censure. Second, Serbia was a close, useful ally of Britain, France, and Russia. Third, Serb nazism has always been amorphous, concealed in the shadows, and linguistically unintelligible to outsiders.

Serb slav nazism began around 1900 and flourished in the 1920's after the creation of unstable, mult-ethnic Yugoslavia. Numerous influential Serb writers and academics, notably Vaso Cubrilovic and Radivoje Pesic, proclaimed Serbs racial supermen, and Serbia the true cradle of western civilization.

Serb nazis urged ethnic cleansing of all "racially inferior" Hungarians, Croats, Jews, Albanians, Catholics, and Muslims from a purified Greater Serbia, stretching from Italy to the Aegean. Some elements of the Serb Orthodox Church eagerly cooperated—and still do—with these ideas. (Usenet posting on soc.culture.croatia, "The Last Nest of Nazis in Europe," April 26, 1998)

The above passage illustrates a deep-seated animosity about which many on the soc.culture.croatia also write. Other posts, such as the following, also illustrate cyber hate:

When Mr. Milosevic decided to attack Croatia in the summer of 1991, he used volunteers under the extremist paramilitary leader Vojislav Seslj. The Yugoslav Federal Army provided weapons, uniforms and transportation. The paramilitaries burned civilians alive and left the bodies as a message. (Usenet posting on soc.culture.croatia, "Shell them 'till they're on the Edge of Madness," April 27, 1998)

While such postings are not overtly racist, they do cite certain facts as "absolute truth," thus promoting these articles as those of mainstream reporting rather than just opinion. Political messages also were embedded in such postings. A few users inserted their own political philosophy, which has become the calling card of those opposing the new democracies in the region: "What do you mean by "extremism"? In my opinion, all mainstream media in Eastern Europe are extremist, for instance, because they consider capitalism as the undeniable basis of the whole cosmos...." (Usenet posting on soc.culture.bulgaria, April 28, 1998). Another example shows a similar belief: "Except that the proponents of Eugenics were considered liberal at the time. That goes to show that the Nazis and the Left are really two of the same ilk" (Usenet posting on soc.culture.magyar, May 5, 1998). Others perceive the research as an incitement in itself:

> Glassman is hoping to draw out some anti-Jewish demagoguery (sajnos vannak ilyen hulyek koztunk) [Unfortunately there are stupid people among us] and use it to smear Hungary and all Hungarians. He is an anti-Hungarian hate peddler, and I hope you all recognize him for what he is, and do not fall for his provocation. (Usenet posting on soc.culture.maygar, April 27, 1998)

While the above responses indicate evidence of cyber hate, other newsgroup users, who did not specifically respond to my research question, had similarly hateful commentary. Newsgroup postings such as "Racist Croat Cartoon" (soc.culture.romanian), an anti-Serb message entitled "Satan's Helper from Montenegro" (soc.culture.yugoslavia), and "Jews Love to Torture and How" (soc.culture.yugoslavia) are merely a few examples of the hate discourse that is disseminated in newsgroups.

CYBER HATE ON INTERNET RELAY CHAT AND LISTSERVS

Along with newsgroups, Internet Relay Chat (IRC) is another active service of the Internet, affording users to participate in a variety of discussions that may use racist tones. This can be carried on as if someone were speaking on the telephone through a party line. Virtually anything can be said, and unless the particular IRC channel is hosting a closed discussion, anyone can join. That also means that people who find the talk offensive can verbally fight back or simply leave. If the channel has a moderator, then a person can contact the moderator and complain so that the perpetrators will be blocked from entering that channel. However, this method does not completely work, in that new channels can easily be created or other moderators can let the perpetrator in again. Channels such as #nazi, #skinheads, #aryan, #whitepower, #kkk, and #racial_identity attract people from all over the world, rather than those designed to target any specific group. Anyone wishing to get onto such a discussion group has to join a server that supports them, as do some of the Undernet servers such as <okc.ok.us.undernet.org 7777> or <us.undernet.org 6669>.

Unlike the conversational approach of Internet Relay Chat, listservs are a more passive type of computer-mediated communication. Listservs, which afford the opportunity of reaching a group of users through their e-mail accounts, contain news or commentary on the subject of that list. Not many listservs produce cyber hate, but those that do are substantial. Perhaps more distressing is the fact that listservs are very difficult to monitor and remain more secret than other Internet venues because the list manager includes users who request to receive them and, undoubtedly, subscribe to the principles of the list. For example, HIX Moka, discussed earlier, is a Hungarian list that often contains messages that denigrate members of the Roma community through racial slurs and untrue "facts." Another vocal part of the right-wing listserv comes from Gotthard Saghi-Szabo, located at the University of Maryland, but aimed at a Hungarian audience after the political listserv of HIX ceased to function. Other cyber hate lists also exist, but are not specifically aimed at this region, such as the Stormfront article forum, Aryan News Agency, Resistance Records Electronic Newsletter, and Zgrams from the Zundelsite.

CONCLUSION

The New Europe is now experiencing a new phenomenon for civic discourse through technology. Often, this new technology can be misused by those wishing to propagate hate against others. The vast reaches of the Internet allow disseminators of cyber hate to recruit others to their philosophies. However, in order for these groups to recruit believers, their targeted audience must have access, access that is not yet widespread in the New Europe. Access, however, is growing in the region, due to the efforts of private firms (see, for instance, Chapter 18, in this volume) and governments in the region. Such efforts, particularly in countries such as the Czech Republic and Hungary, are allowing university and primary and secondary students to log onto the Net for free (see, for instance, Chapter 14, in this volume). Once access is achieved, students may fall prey to the intolerance. In an area with a history of ethnic strife, a resurgence of nationalism after the fall of Communism, and a return of political popularity for parties of the right, the New Europe remains ripe for intolerance to sweep the region.

Many of the cyber hate mongers are émigrés living in the West in a wealthier society where Internet access is relatively cheap. They tend to target their compatriots in the region, especially the young, who most readily use the Internet. These young are also very impressionable, and such propaganda can influence them, especially as the political system moves to the right.

While most World Wide Web sites coming from or focusing on the region do not contain anti-Semitic, anti-Roma, or other intolerant messages, those that do attract a high number of visitors. As hate monitor organizations have noted, hate recruitment on the Internet is continuing to double within a span of merely a few months. This is highly evident by looking at the number of hate sites from one year to the next. Cyber hate sites for the region are beginning to be written in native languages, yet are not overtly racist, a stark difference to sites created within the United States. Unlike the Web, Usenet, listservs, and Internet Relay Chat also contain ethnic intolerance, but the cyber hate disseminated through these more active Internet services constantly change through updates and deletions. When Internet service providers discover cyber hate sites that they host, many of them will discontinue their business relationships with those who placed the site there in the first place. However, with the issues of free speech and civic discourse involved, many will not deny the sites, even in the wake of increasing marginalization of those communities of color, women, and anyone outside the dominant norms of sexual preference, ethnicity, religion, and other types of cultural differences.

Several legislative measures have been developed, notably in Canada and Germany, but post-socialist national governments have yet to take a stand. Some special computer applications using PICS can also be obtained that will not allow access to minors for certain sites, although the technology still has a long way to go before complete reliability can be met. In spite of such technology, cyber hate disseminators will always be able to target their intended audience as they continuously mirror the sites from one server to the next, and eventually, they get through.

Much of IRC is unmoderated and therefore anyone can relate any message. This new forum stands as another means of free speech and assembly. Many racist sites have been blocked by numerous servers, but someone can always hook onto a server that does contain these sites.

The overall questions are whether people looking for these sites find them or whether people merely stumble onto them. Further, as messages will be written in native languages, a more specialized system will be in place. Will the governments in the New Europe act against hate mongers in special ways, or will they stand by free speech for fear that they may sink into the former regime's policies of preventing free speech? While these governments attempt to answer these questions, hate mongers continue to grow and use cyber hate to convince a technology-friendly youth to believe in their ideals. As Rick Goldberg (1996) lamented, "The Internet is the greatest thing that has ever happened to hate."

NOTE

1. Newsgroups for Macedonia, Bosnia and Herczegovina, or Poland could not be located.

REFERENCES

Anti-Defamation League. (1998, November 17). *Hate on the Internet: New ADL report reveals neo-Nazis and others exploiting technology* [Online]. Available: <http://206.3.178.10:80//./PresRele/ASUS_12/2609_12.html> [1999, February 24].

B92. (n.d.). *Spiral of "hate speech" in Kosovo* [Online]. Available: <http://www.rnw.nl/realradio/community/html/anem110199.html> [1999, April 10].

Balkan, D. (1996, November 22). *Communiqué. Canadian Human Rights Commission/Commission canadienne des droites de la personne* [Online]. Available: <http://insight.mcmaster.ca/org/efc/pages/doc/chrc-pr-22nov96.html> [1999, February 26].

Elnet. (1997, March 23). *The Patriotic Front* [Online]. Available: <http://www.elnet.cz/vf/english.html> [1999, May 2].

Ethical Spectacle. (1996, March). My letter to the Wiesenthal Center. *The Ethical Spectacle* [Online serial], *2*(3). Available: <http://www.spectacle.org> [1999, September 12].

European Parliament. (1996). *Draft report on the Commission Communication on Illegal and Harmful Content on the Internet* (COM(96)0487-C4-0592/96). Luxembourg: European Parliament Committee on Civil Liberties and Internal Affairs, European Parliament.

Fiss, O. M. (1996). *The irony of free speech*. Cambridge, MA: Harvard University Press.

Gazeta de Vest. (1999, January 7). *The legion of the Archangel Michael* [Online]. Available: <http://dialspace.dial.pipex.com/town/terrace/gir91/rom-in. html> [1999, February 27].

Goldberg, R. (1996, July 2). *Religion in the technological age: Dealing with antisemitism on the Internet* [Online]. Available: <http://www.yucc.yorku.ca/%7Erickg/academics/hatenet.html> [1999, February 26].

Hacker's racist note is sent on Internet. (1994, October 20). *New York Times*, p. B12.

Hentoff, N. (1994, March 1). Let all hate speech be heard. *Village Voice, 39*(9), pp. 16–18.

International Helsinki Federation. (1999, March 24). *Open letter to the Contact Group on Human Rights Violations in Kosovo* [Online]. Available: <http://www.ihf-hr.org/appeals/980324.htm> [1998, March 27].

International Third Position. (n.d., a). *Final conflict* [Online]. Available: <http://dspace.dial.pipex.com/town/plaza/rbg93/fc.html> [1998, May 3].

International Third Position. (n.d., b). *From the editor—Nice to meet you!* [Online]. Available: <http://dspace.dial.pipex.com/town/plaza/rbg93/rom-nm.html> [1998, May 3].

International Third Position. (n.d., c). *Germany and its place in Europe: The squanderer son* [Online]. Available: <http://dspace.dial.pipex.com/town/plaza/rbg93/rom-ge2.html> [1998, May 3].

Johnston, C. (1998, October 16). Racism challenge on Net. *London Times Educational Supplement, 4294*, p. 9.

Lando, Z. (1995). *Jewishnet Global Jewish Information Network. Jewish and Israeli Lists* [Online]. Available: <mofetsrv.mofet.macam98.ac.il/~dovw/jw/l/j1-0370.html> [1998, September 10].

Lengel, L. (1998, Summer). Access to the Internet in East Central and South-Eastern Europe: New women's voices and new media technologies. *Convergence: The Journal of Research into New Media Technologies, 4*(2), 38–54.

Mendels, P. (1998, November 12). Filter to block hate speech on Internet. *New York Times*, p. A21.

Miller, M. M., & Andsager, J. (1998, Summer/Fall). Protecting 1st amendment? *Newspaper Research Journal, 18*(3/4), 2–16.

Narodowe Odrodzenie Polski [Online]. (1996, August). Available: <http://dspace.dial.pipex.com/third-position/poland.html> [1999, February 27].

Olson, E. G. (1997, November 24). As hate spills onto the Web, a struggle over whether, and how, to control it. *New York Times*, p. D11.

Petersen, R. (1996, June 13). *Hate and freedom on the Internet* [Online]. Available:<http://dspace.dial.pipex.com/town/plaza/rbg93/short.html#s> [1998, August 10].

Rosenfeld, S. (1999, March 26). *Don't demonize the Serbs. Serbian Unity Congress site* [Online]. Available: <http://www.suc.org/politics/kosovo/html/Rosenfeld032699.html> [1999, April 10].

Sack, K. (1998, March 3). Hate groups in U.S. are growing, report says. *New York Times*, p. A10.

Simon Wiesenthal Center. (1995). *Perspective on hate on the Internet.* Los Angeles, CA: Author.

Tadmor-Shimony, T. (1995). *Antisemitism on the information superhighway: A case study of a UseNet discussion group.* Jerusalem: Vidal Sassoon International Center for the Study of Antisemitism.

Tel Aviv University Faculty of the Humanities (n.d.). *Anti-Semitism on the Internet. Steven Roth Institute for the Study of Contemporary Anti-Semitism and Racism* [Online]. Available: <http://www.tau.ac.il:81/Anti-Semitism/internet1.html> [1998, August 21].

Titch, S. (1996, February 12). Controlling the Internet. *Telephony, 230*(7), 52.

Walker, S. (1994). *Hate speech: The history of an American controversy.* Lincoln, NE: University of Nebraska Press.

Walsh, Z. (1999). *Kosovo is Serbia. The Patriot-News. Serbian Unity Congress* [Online]. Available: <http://www.suc.org/politics/kosovo/html/Walsh102198.html> [1999, April 10].

chapter 9

Gender and Technology in the New Europe

Laura Lengel
Richmond American International University in London

"Democracy without women is no democracy," announces Slavenka Drakulić, internationally known Croatian journalist and writer (Network of East-West Women, 1999a). Drakulić's statement is highlighted on the World Wide Web site of the Network of East-West Women, an international organization dedicated to empowering women and girls throughout the New Europe. This mission is crucial to women, both in the New Europe and elsewhere, as dominant discourses have tended to render women invisible or misrepresent them. Gender difference in the New Europe, in many ways, has become more problematic in the decade since the fall of the old regimes. Women's status in East Central Europe, South-Eastern Europe, the Newly Independent States, and the Russian Federation is an ambiguous phenomenon and there is much work to be done to achieve gender equity in the future (I. Arns, personal communication, March 16, 1998). Barbara Einhorn, in her examination of women's movements and citizenship in East Central Europe, notes gender differentiation inherent in the region "has in practice operated as an exclusionary mechanism, hindering female entitlement to citizenship rights" (1993, p. 258). Similarly, Renata Salecl, in her study of feminism after the fall of Communism, maintains "Just as communist ideology erased the problem of patriarchal domination, today's post-socialist societies also erase the problem of sexual inequality. The post-socialists act as if emancipation of women is not an issue for them at all" (p. 26). She notes, "The only force addressing the status of women is the nationalist right, although its major concern is, of course, to help women rediscover their 'natural' mission" (1994, p. 26).

Dominant discourses encouraging women's "'natural' mission" and "authentic culture" of homemaking and child rearing (Petrova, 1993, pp. 22–23) have emerged throughout the region. Dimitrina Petrova argues that the 1989 so-called "revolution" "left the patriarchal system of power intact, transforming its more superficial manifestations from bad to worse" (Petrova, 1992, p. 3).

WOMEN, WORK, AND TECHNOLOGY DURING AND AFTER COMMUNIST RULE

In the decade since the fall of Communist rule, the return to "family values" throughout the New Europe, coupled with a new emphasis on nationhood, is foregrounded in the search for new identity (Einhorn, 1993). Perhaps the "family values" discourse has emerged in conjunction with women's post-Communist work conditions. Under Communism, women benefited from job security, stable child care, and pro-woman welfare policies. After 1989, however, Minton Goldman argues that "women have been especially hard hit by the movement toward a free-market economy" (1997, p. 210). Goldman contends that women seemed "to be better off under communist rule. At least under Communism there was a pretense of fostering equality, with communist governments providing women opportunities to work outside the home and earn income that could help improve living conditions for them and their families" (p. 75).

An interesting case study to examine women's working conditions before and after the fall of communist rule is evidenced in technology-related professions. Female science and technology professionals, in such areas as mathematics, engineering, and aviation, were encouraged under Soviet rule. For instance, a women-only bomber pilot battalion, called the Soviet "Night Witches," fought the Nazis during World War II. However, Inke Arns, a Berlin-based media art scholar and curator, notes, after the war, "when 'times had changed', no one wanted to hear about what these 'equally heroic' women did during the war" (personal communication, March 16, 1998). The silencing of the Night Witches' achievements in late Stalinism, Inke Arns argues, reflects the challenge for a patriarchal society to accept the image of a woman fighting rather than raising children and managing a home.

Just as the success of the Soviet "Night Witches" was silenced after World War II, contemporary women in the New Europe are faced with problematic tensions between traditional and professional ways of life, whether or not they hold careers in technology. As evidenced by the research I have conducted in the New Europe, I have heard women attest to the contemporary gender inequality inherent in technology, both in working and learning conditions (M. Danova, personal communication, April 25, 1997; K. Merdjanska, personal communication, April 24, 1997). Women argue that they are "outsiders," "isolated from the world" that hails both advances in technology and advances for women. However, that is not to say that there have been no improvements. Czech women, who are now professors of computer technology, were in the vast minority of their university computer science classes 15 to 25 years ago (Z. Telnarová, personal communication, December 18, 1998). Current educational and professional initiatives in computing technology have developed since the fall of Communist rule, as discussed elsewhere in this book (specifically in Chapters 14 and 18, in this volume). Even so, women and girls have remained largely on the margins of technology. While many women under Soviet rule held high positions in technology-related fields, most women employed by Soviet owned-and-operated software and hardware firms were positioned in mundane factory-line positions, a situation consistent with women's low-level production work in the "West" and elsewhere (Malinowska, 1995). If not working to piece together computer chips, women were, in many cases, discouraged from more creative research and development-focused technology work.

Women in the New Europe are, however, moving out of the margins of technology. They see the possibility of using the Internet, for example, to participate in a previously oppressed civic discourse. Such participation, however, is hindered by gender inequality inherent in the local cultures. Barbara Einhorn notes that despite "improvements in the civil and political rights associated with democratic citizenship, in the short run at least" women in the region "stand to lose economic, social welfare, and reproductive rights" (1993, p. 1). For instance, Czech and Slovak women have been ignored by new political parties (Goldman, 1997), which distrust women and have "few incentives to address their concerns, much less share power with them" (Goldman, 1997, p. 133). In Poland, Goldman writes, "the Catholic Church has been a big obstacle to gender equality, having literally gone on a[n] offensive against the social and political advancement of women since 1989" (p. 41).

WOMEN, TECHNOLOGY, AND CIVIC DISCOURSE IN
THE NEW EUROPE

Women in the New Europe are fighting the political and religious offensives that try to send them back to their "natural mission" and "authentic culture." They are seizing opportunities to express themselves through politics, commerce, education, and the media. Compared to radio, television, and print media, "new media" often provide the most cost-effective and quickest means for women's voices to be heard by a wide, global audience. Where access is available, women are using "new media," particularly the Internet, to engage in proactive civic, nongovernmental, discourse.

Jean Brunet and Serge Proulx (1989) maintain that information and communication technology supports a grassroots model of civic discourse that women prefer over more formal communicative means. Other feminist scholars argue that this type of grassroots communication provides a strong basis for political activity and activism. Lynda Birke and Marsha Henry (1996) note that despite challenges of gender marginalization, the Internet "allows women to communicate and spread information across the globe; among other things, this mode of communication is relatively cheap and can dramatically expedite political actions by putting women quickly into contact" (p. 230). This contact, through communication technology, makes links between women's communities possible (see, for example, Plant, 1997; Spender, 1995; Voet, 1993).

These links are being made by individual women and women's organizations who are narrowing the gender and technology gap. Similarly, these women's links are narrowing the gaps between "East" and "West" through supporting dialogue, electronic information exchange and activism for women's issues. Through the websites of organizations like Magyar Nõk Elektronikus Lapjai (meaning Hungarian Women's Pages) (Hír-Nõk Információk, n.d.), Prague's Gender Studies Centre (1999), and the Free Feminists and Gender Project for Bulgaria (Network of East-West Women, 1999b), women have developed a growing presence on the Internet. This presence is critical, as more traditional communication channels such as print media and word of mouth limit the growth potential of women's organizations. For example, support for the Gender Studies Centre in Prague has been thin since its founding in 1991 by Jiřina Šiklová, a Charles University professor who, in 1981–1982, spent a year in prison and seven years thereafter working as a cleaning woman, charged with smuggling literature in and out of Czechoslovakia (Einhorn, 1993). Now women like Šiklová have the freedom to disseminate literature without threat of imprisonment. Alongside this freedom of information and political thought, there is currently a resistance to feminism. Einhorn (1993) notes "Šiklová feels there is a great need for education so that women overcome their misgivings about feminism and begin to understand some of the issues at stake" (p. 188).

Just as Šiklová and the Prague Gender Studies Centre are using the Internet to work against anti-feminist and anti-woman discourses in East Central and South-Eastern Europe, other women's groups are fighting these discourses. For example, NaNe! (short for Nők a Nőkért Együtt az Erőszak Ellen [Women Working With Women Against Violence]; n.d.) is an organization that is fighting violence against women. The organization, whose name means roughly "Don't do that!" in Hungarian, established Hungary's first telephone hotline to aid women and children survivors of violence, and organized an international conference on violence and democracy, to raise public awareness of domestic violence in Hungary. Éva Thun, lecturer in the Teaching Training College at Eötvös Loránd University in Budapest and creator of the Magyar Nők Elektronikus Lapjai and NaNe! sites, notes, "In Hungary discussing women's issues and advocating the importance of public discourse on women's lives and women's experiences are still not considered to be popular modes of thinking and action." However, she argues, "there is a growing number of women who are determined to foster changes and persistent and enthusiastic in their pursuit of making their voices heard and their demands met. By launching the HÍR-NŐK Homepage we would like to offer yet another (hopefully powerful) channel for discussion in order to be able to step out of invisibility" (Thun, 1998).

Women of the New Europe are also stepping out of invisibility through the Network of East-West Women (NEWW). With offices in Warsaw, Moscow, and Washington, D.C., the NEWW is creating links between women in East Central Europe, South-Eastern Europe, the Newly Independent States, and the Russian Federation with other women throughout the world. Because "post-communist countries have imposed a harsh life upon women in their societies," NEWW's mission is to bring a wide global understanding to users "directly, not via the mass media, the efforts of these women to abolish the injustices and inequalities they face in their homelands" (Network of East-West Women, 1999a). Updated frequently, the site has included an online discussion space, "Sister Links" to regional organizations, regional and global news relating to women's issues, links to listservs that address gender in post-Communist societies, and the On-Line Legal Resource Service, which concerns women's legal and human rights issues in the region.

The Network of East-West Women also supports other women's organizations through its site. For example, the website of "eFKa," a Krakow-based Polish women's foundation and Poland's only feminist group, is housed on the NEWW site. The "eFKa" site discusses its activities of the group, which are "aimed at changing stereotypes on gender, particularly by supporting women's solidarity and independence, anti-discrimination actions and a development of women's culture." It also focuses on the current projects "eFKa" is developing, which include a counseling and advice center for women and a hot-line run by female psychologists and lawyers (Kozak & Walczewska, n.d.). Another organization supported by the NEWW site is ZiF (Zentrum für interdisziplinäire Frauenforschung), founded in December 1989 by a group of East Berlin women academics from Humboldt University and the Academy of Science, the first women's studies center in the then GDR. Prior to the foundation of ZiF, the women academics had been doing research on feminist issues for over a decade, individually and collectively. "Up to today," the site announces, "the ZiF is one of the few examples of a successful institutionalization of women studies in East Germany" (ZiF, 1998). ZiF sets an example of collaboration both within and across women's organizations.

Developing collaborative "East-East networking links between women, as well as East-West dialogue," Barbara Einhorn (1993) notes, is critical in the "search for new understandings of women's situations both within and outside the region" (p. 13). The NEWW "Sister Links" exemplify how women in both the "East" and the "West" are engaging in dialogue and finding collaborative possibilities. For example, the Netherlands' Vrouwen ontmoeten Vrouwen (Women meet Women) project is a forum for women's organizations to disseminate news and discuss issues. Vrouwen ontmoeten Vrouwen was developed by a group of five women from Milieukwartet, a Dutch national organization concerned with women and the environment. The organization's aim is to implement results emerging from the Fourth World Conference on Women, in Beijing in 1995, on an international level. The Vrouwen ontmoeten Vrouwen website announces: "We think it is important that women support and have a stimulating role to achieve implemantation [sic] of the Platformme for Action. This project gives us the opportunity to exchange ideas and strategies with women" not only between East and West regions, but North and South (Loeffen, 1998). VOVNews, the organization's electronic newsletter, highlights collaboration between the International Women Centre in Nijmegen with discussion partners Lenka Prusova in the Czech Republic and Vashty Maharaj in Trinidad. Pauline Loeffen of Milieukwartet announces, "with the exchange of this information we hope to come to have a good contact in which we can learn from each others' experiences and start an interesting discussion. We hope this gives us more ideas on how we can improve the situation of women and how to deal with the problems we have to face" (Loeffen, 1998).

WOMEN ACTIVISTS IN KOSOVO AND THE BALKANS

Women activists have been facing the immense problems in the Balkan region online. One project, entitled Balkan Neighbors, has been developed by Mariana Lenkova. Lenkova is an editor of the Greek Helsinki Monitor, an online service from the Greek National Committee of the International Helsinki Federation, which provides information about the Balkans both within the region and "outside" to the world. Through support from ACCESS, a nongovernmental organization in Sofia, and funding from George Soros's Open Society Foundation, Balkan Neighbors promotes national and ethnic relations through the Internet. One of the Balkan Neighbors reports, "Balkan Neighbors: Positive and Negative Stereotypes in the Media of Seven Balkan Countries," has been distributed through a listserv since late 1996. The project analyzes the media representation of Balkan countries, including Albania, Bulgaria, Greece, Macedonia, Romania, Serbia, and Turkey. Lenkova prepares monthly regional summaries of the media analysis, including possible misrepresentation of the Balkan nations by the media. It also addresses issues such as racial and ethnic prejudice against Roma communities, attitudes to what she terms "internal minorities" within Balkan nations, and media coverage of Bulgaria's "mafia" (M. Lenkova, personal communication, October 24, 1997). The project also focuses on relations between Macedonia, Bulgaria, and Greece and diversity across the New Europe. These foci provide those outside the region with a deeper understanding that these nations are not monolithic entities but are extremely diverse, politically, economically, and culturally. With the focus on diversity across the New Europe and, in particular, the Balkan region, Lenkova is optimistic that computer-mediated projects like Balkan Neighbors can enact social change and, through dissemination of information online, raise awareness about the ethnic and nationalistic tensions within the region.

Recently, raising awareness about ethnic and nationalist tensions in the region have been at the forefront of women's organizations. In times of crisis, when voices are silenced by traditional media and other communicative means, the Internet provides a forum for women's activism. The crisis in Kosovo has moved women to organize and act against the atrocities that ethnic Albanians have experienced in their flight from their homes and nation. The organization of Independent Women Journalists in Kosova have posted their reports and photographs of the crisis on the Network of East-West Women site. Sevdie Ahmeti, Human Rights Director for the Center for the Protection of Women and Children in Prishtine, Kosovo, and a member of the of Independent Women Journalists in Kosova, posts a weekly "Kosova War Chronicle." Ahmeti

(1999h) writes "Kosova's future depends on the international community's will. Through this chronicle, the world will learn what the current dangerous situation is and how trapped Kosovar Albanians are!"

International Women's Day, March 8, should be a time for celebrating. However, the Kosova War Chronicle (Ahmeti, 1999g) indicated otherwise:

KOSOVA WAR CHRONICLE OF THE WEEK: 8-14 MARCH
...In the wake of the biggest Serb offensive in Kosova, where victims are flowing like a river, and where war has spread all over...

8 MARCH, 1999
In the Women's International Day, Ms. NAILE KALLUDRA (56) from Gremnik village of Kline is reported she died [sic] on Saturday at a police checkpoint at Dollc village because police prevented her from being taken to hospital. Naile was on her way to visit a doctor in Gjakove together with her husband BRAHIM, who was ill-treated for two hours in the police checkpoint. Naile died there "OF PAIN AND INDIGNATION OVER HER HUSBAND'S BRUTAL ILL-TREATMENT". The young girl GJYLE CUNAJ (15) is reported wounded with a bullet in the village of Gorozhub of the municipality of Prizren; she was staying with her uncle's [sic] when she was shot, probably from the VJ military positions along the Kosova-Albania border zone.

International Women's Day was not the first time that the Independent Women Journalists in Kosova reported the killing of ethnic Albanian women. Ahmeti reports that February 28, 1999, marks one year of war in the nation. "This day, one year ago, Serb police forces massacred 24 people in the villages of Likoshan and Cirez of Drenice. Among the massacred there were women and children, including pregnant RUKIE NEBIHU." Since February 28, 1998, Kosovans who had been peacefully resisting the Serb offenses now turned to war resistance. Kosovans had tried to "resist the violence through peaceful protests, but even those were 'calmed down' by Serb police forces with sticks, guns, tear gass [sic], arrests and all kinds of brutality used against the protesters. Women's Network organized a serial of 9 massive protests, but women were beaten up, injured and arrested" (Ahmeti, 1999f). The Independent Women's Journalists in Kosova report also notes how the international community ignored the crisis at this point, leading the nation to defend itself.

Other reports by the Independent Women Journalists in Kosova indicate additional murders of women and children (Ahmeti, 1999c, 1999d, 1999e), a mass grave of women and children (Ahmeti, 1999a), women and children being held at gunpoint (Ahmeti, 1999b), and the attempted murders of humanitarian aid organization members who have helped women and children. Ahmeti (1999d) reports that members of the Save the Children Foundation and Centre for Protection of Women and Children "were shot at when they tried to reach Ratishe village of Decan and do assessment on the current situation of children and women. The shot came right after passing the traces of tanks in the right side, where they were deployed. According to the negotiations with the police in Irzniq village, they admitted that it was them who shot and warned these two organizations not to continue."

The Independent Women Journalists in Kosova were reporting on the crisis in Kosovo long before it made the front pages and opening stories of Western print and broadcast news. On International Women's Day, 1998, the journalists' group reported a call to action from the Network of Women of Kosova for Kosovan women to protest the violence against their communities:

Date: 08 March 1998
NETWORK OF WOMEN OF KOSOVA
We invite all women of Kosova on March 8, 1998, at 12 noon to protest against the violence and terror with the motto "WE STAND FIRM IN FRONT OF OUR DOORS." The form of protest is such as: Women of Prishtina protest in front of the USIS office in Prishtine, and women of other parts of Kosova stand still 15 minutes in silence in front of their doors, to manifest the protest against violence, life threat and the denial of collective rights. Each woman is going to keep on her hand a blank white paper sheet with the message that we are for peace, and that we do not have any human and national rights.

On the occasion of March 8, the International Women's Day, all women around the world organize protests for their rights due to the UN conventions and CEDAW. Therefore, women of Kosova shall be part of the women's protests worldwide.

Being aware that at the United Nations in New York the Commission for the Status of Women is on its way, in these tragic moments for Kosova, where even a pregnant woman was slaughtered in front of her door, we invite women worldwide to solidarize with our demands for peace and women's human rights.

Other efforts are being made on the Network of East-West Women website, and associated listservs "neww-rights" and "women-east-west". The "neww-rights" listserv is part of the NEWW On-Line Legal Resource Service, disseminating information about women's legal and human rights issues in the former Soviet Union and Central and Eastern Europe. The "women-east-west" listserv provides information concerning the development of grassroots women's movements in post-Communist societies. The "women-east-west" listserv disseminates the "Kosovo Human Rights Flash" reporting on the human rights abuses and murders in Kosovo by Human Rights Watch researchers in the nation. An example report indicates the compassion of a Kosovan woman who sacrificed her life to save her son:

> In the early morning of March 25, Serb forces found the ethnic Albanians hiding near a bridge where the railroad tracks crossed the stream. The families of Clirim Zhuniqi and Xhemal Spahiu, who were approximately fifty meters away from the main group of villagers, were the first to be discovered. Twelve members of the two families were summarily executed with automatic weapon fire, witnesses said. *There was one survivor: a two-year-old boy whose mother had protected him with her body.* (original emphasis, P. Lucchesi, listserv communication, April 18, 1999)

The "women-east-west" listserv also provides advice on how to contact family members in the region if they have been separated during the flight out of Kosovo, reporting on the services currently being organized by the International Committee of the Red Cross, the National Red Cross, and the Red Crescent Societies to restore family links in the Balkans (P. Lucchesi, listserv communication, April 17, 1999).

The Network of East-West Women website also provides a voice for the STAR Network of World Learning, which established the Kosovo Women's Fund. The Kosovo Women's Fund collects donations for emergency support to Kosovan women's organizations. "Within hours of their harrowing escapes," women leaders of the organizations "began to organize trauma, medical support and media centers to respond to the extraordinary humanitarian and human rights needs of deportees and refugees in Macedonia" (Stegall & Benderly, n.d.).

Along with reports from Kosovo, the Network of East-West Women website includes reports from Independent Women's NGOs in Belgrade and Zagreb. One prominent NGO, Women in Black, has condemned the NATO bombings, arguing that the bombings have made the situation far worse for ethnic Albanians in Kosovo. Another group, the Autonomous Women's Center Against Sexual Violence in Belgrade, reports on the Serbian shutdown of traditional media:

> The situation: Many women are affraid [sic] more or less. last night some of us have worked in the Womens Center until 9pm.... The serbian officials have cut electriciy [sic] in Pristina last night, and tuned in this morning. The cutting of electricity was clearly the act of producing more fear on the one already there. So you can imagine the mood in Pristina...The fact that enrages is that serbian regime has totally and absolutely [sic] taken the control of all the media. Which means that only few words come

in, and that language of hatred, production of "enemies" and vengeance politics is increasing every minute. Four TV stations fused in one and two others in the other one. The people who do not have satellite TV get few news per hour, about shelters and enemies, and nothing else. This is as well frightening. Many women did not sleep last night. (Mladjenovic, 1999)

The shutdown of broadcast and print news media in the Federal Republic of Yugoslavia, and other Balkan nations, left only the Internet to disseminate reports of the war. For instance, independent radio station B92 in Belgrade was shut down by the authorities, who cite that the station's "maximum deviation and breadth of the transmission exceed the allowed levels defined in the Book of Rules on Technical and Exploitation Conditions of Radio Diffusion Station on Frequency Modulated Broadcasts...the said power exceeds the allowed level of 300W. This constitutes misdemeanour defined in Article 141 Paragraph 1 Point 6" (Yugoslav Federal Telecommunications Ministry, cited in Independent Women Journalists in Belgrade, 1999). Despite this "misdemeanour," B92 used its Internet site (Radio B92, 1999, April 2) to disseminate its news in text, audio, and video rather than through traditional radio broadcast.

Women's organizations in the region have also used the Internet to articulate concerns about the dominant patriarchal ideology of war. The Independent Women Journalists in Belgrade, in their article "War In Kosova—The Logics Of Patriarchy" (1998) write:

Women's autonomous groups in Belgrade are comunicating [sic] publicly in order to condemn the violence of the Serbian regime in Kosova. The war in Kosova has begun. The violence of the Serbian regime in Kosova is the continuation of the apartheid policy which the regime is applying for the past ten years. And the present situation shows that the teritory [sic] is sacred, not the human life.
Where do we start from?
WE START FROM THE PATRIARCHY,
From the Patriarchy as the mechanism for maintaining men's violence against women for thousands of years. Women's movement is unmasking the patriarchal ideology which serves the violent men to perpetuate violence, so that women and children cannot be helped from outside to stop the violence. Patriarchy considers that men's violence in family is a 'family private matter'—this ideaology [sic] of privacy permits the violence in all other domains of society. When the SOS hotline for women and children calls the police to intervene in violent scene, a violent husband next to his bruised wife claims: "This is my wife, it is my issue". Policeman, also, with male understanding confirms that it is a "family matter". That is exactly the model how the first man of the ruling regime leads the war in Kosova:

"Kosova is an inner problem of Serbia". About which he decides alone. In that way the referendum too becomes his personal matter—family matter—whilst Kosovo has been for many years an international open problem.

Women in the war-torn Balkan region condemn the patriarchal tendencies of the war. Groups such as the Women in Black (1998) maintain "We are the women' peace group and we will never accept the war, we shall always raise our voice against war."

WOMEN'S ROLE IN THE FUTURE
OF THE NEW EUROPE

Through collaboration and activism, individual women and women's organizations in the region, and broadly through the New Europe, are finding new ways to raise their voices against war, patriarchy violence against women, and human rights violations. Women's collaboration efforts can foster both gender equity and, more broadly, the future growth of participatory democracy and peace in Kosovo, and other nations in crisis, both within and outside the New Europe. When other media are shut down by oppressive governmental forces, women can communicate through the Internet as active, vital dialogic agents. Women in post-Communist nations realize that there is much work to be done now to seize opportunities to participate in truly open, peaceful dialogue in the future, and that future rests on this collaborative spirit. Through this spirit, Dimitrina Petrova (1992) announces, "We can only try to keep the flame burning—the small flame of sympathy, of simple concern for the other. Sisterhood may play a powerful part in this commitment."

With the efforts of women's organizations online, collaborative contacts through the Internet benefit those both within and outside the New Europe. Collaboration, understanding, and change are key to the empowerment promised by information and communication technology. Participation in an open computer-mediated dialogue affords women of the New Europe a space to enact change. They are enhancing both local and global understanding of such important issues as national and ethnic differences, and supporting communities in crisis, such as the Kosovan refugees. With the growing interest of individual women and women's organizations who wish to voice their concerns to the world, the Internet creates a discursive space for women in the New Europe to act, collaborate, and achieve.

REFERENCES

Ahmeti, S. (1999a, January 4). *Mass grave with women and children* [Online]. Available: <http://www.neww.org/kosova/Sevdie's%20Articles/010399koso.htm> [1999, April 17].

Ahmeti, S. (1999b, January 9). *Kosova war chronicle of the week* [Online]. Available: <http://www.neww.org/kosova/Sevdie's%20Chronicles/010999koso.htm> [1999, April 17].

Ahmeti, S. (1999c, January 23). *Headlines on Kosova* [Online]. Available: <http://www.neww.org/kosova/Sevdie's%20Chronicles/012399koso.htm> [1999, April 17].

Ahmeti, S. (1999d, January 30). *Yet another massacre* [Online]. Available: <http://www.neww.org/kosova/Sevdie's%20Chronicles/013099koso.htm> [1999, April 17].

Ahmeti, S. (1999e, February 13). *Kosova war chronicle of the week* [Online]. Available: <http://www.neww.org/kosova/Sevdie's%20Chronicles/021399koso. htm> [1999, April 17].

Ahmeti, S. (1999f, March 6). *Kosova chronicle of the week: 28 February - 6 March 1999* [Online]. Available: <http://www.neww.org/kosova/Sevdie's%20Chronicles/030699ko.htm> [1999, April 18].

Ahmeti, S. (1999g, March 8). *Kosova war chronicle of the week: 8-14 March* [Online]. Available: <http://www.neww.org/kosova/Sevdie's%20Chronicles/031499ko.htm> [1999, April 17].

Ahmeti, S. (1999h, March 22). *Kosova war chronicle of the week: 15-20 March* [Online]. Available: <http://www.neww.org/kosova/Sevdie's%20Chronicles/032299bko.htm> [1999, April 17].

Birke, L., & Henry, M. (1996). The black hole: Women's studies, science and technology. In V. Robinson & D. Richardson (Eds.), *Introducing women's studies: Feminist theory and practice* (2nd ed; pp. 220–230). London: MacMillan.

Brunet, J., & Proulx, S. (1989). Formal versus grass-roots training: women, work, and computers. *Journal of Communication*, *39*, 77–84.

Einhorn, B. (1993). *Cinderella goes to market: Citizenship, gender and women's movements in East Central Europe*. London: Verso.

Gender Studies Centre. (1999, February 14). *Centrum pro gender studies* [Online]. Available: <http://www.ecn.cz/gender> [1999, April 16].

Goldman, M. F. (1997). *Revolution and change in Central and Eastern Europe: Political, economic, and social changes*. London: M.E. Sharpe.

Hír-Nők Információk. (n.d.). *Magyar Nők Elektronikus Lapjai* [Hungarian Women's Pages] [Online]. Available: <http://www.tfk.elte.hu/hirnok> [1999, April 10].

Independent Women Journalists in Belgrade. (1998, May 22). *War in Kosova: The logics of patriarchy* [Online]. Available: <http://www.neww.org/kosova/Belgrade/0522belg.htm> [1999, April 18].

Independent Women Journalists in Belgrade. (1999, March 24). *Yugoslav Federal Telecommunications Ministry report cited in Radio B92 banned, its chief editor detained for questioning* [Online]. Available: <http://www.neww.org/kosova/032499bel.htm> [1999, April 18].

Kozak, B., & Walczewska, S. (n.d.). *Women's foundation "eFKa"* [Online]. Available: <http://www.neww.org/ceewomen/efka.htm> [1999, April 10].

Loeffen, P. (1998). *Experience of a Dutch partner: Milieukwartet. Vrouwen ontmoeten Vrouwen. Home page* [Online]. <http://www.vrouwen.net/ebg/ebg-cos> [1999, January 18].

Malinowska, E. (1995). Socio-political changes in Poland and the problems of sex discrimination. *Women's Studies International Forum, 18*(1), 35–43.

Mladjenovic, L. (1999, March 24). *From independent women journalists in Belgrade* [Online]. Available: <http://www.neww.org/kosova/032499le.htm> [1999, April 18].

NaNE! (n.d.). *NaNE! Women Working With Women Against Violence (Nők a Nőkért Együtt az Erőszak Ellen)* [Online]. Available: <http://kazy.elte.hu/personal-home/eva/women/medium/english/nane-e.html> [1999, April 17].

Network of East-West Women. (1999a, April 16). *Home page* [Online]. Available: <http://www.neww.org> [1999, April 16].

Network of East-West Women. (1999b, April 16). *Bulgaria. Women's Organizations* [Online]. Available: <http://www.neww.org/countries/Bulgaria/bulgaria.htm> [1999, April 16].

Petrova, D. (1992, December). *The farewell dance: Bulgarian women in transition.* Paper presented at the "Mary Wollstonecraft and 200 Years of Feminism" Conference, Sussex University, Sussex, England.

Petrova, D. (1993). The Bulgarian case: Women's issues or feminist issues. In N. Funk & M. Mueller (Eds.), *Gender politics and post-Communism* (pp. 22–32). London: Routledge.

Plant, S. (1997). *Zeros + ones: Digital women and the new technoculture.* London: Fourth Estate.

Radio B92. (1999, April 2). *Radio B92 closed down and sealed off* [Online]. Available: <http://www.b92.net> [1999, April 2].

Salecl, R. (1994). *The spoils of freedom: Psychoanalysis and feminism after the fall of socialism.* London: Routledge.

Spender, D. (1995). *Nattering on the Net: Women, power and cyberspace.* Melbourne, AU: Spinifex.

Stegall, L., & Benderly, J. (n.d.). *Kosovo Women's Fund* [Online]. Available: <http://www.neww.org/kosovawomenfund.htm> [1999, April 18].

Thun, E. (n.d.). *"Welcome," Magyar Nők Elektronikus Lapjai (Hungarian Women's Pages)* [Online]. Available: <http://kazy.elte.hu/personal-home/eva/women/medium/english/index.html> [1998, February 19].

Voet, R. (1993). Women as citizens and the role of information technology. In C. Beardon & D. Whitehouse (Eds.), *Computers and society* (pp. 15–26). Oxford, England: Intellect.

Women in Black. (1998, May 4). *Against the war on Kosovo* [Online]. Available: <http://www.neww.org/kosova/0502bel.htm> [1999, April 18].

ZiF. (1998). *Zentrum für interdisziplinäire Frauenforschung* [Online]. Available: <http://www.neww.org/ceewomen/zif.htm> [1998, November 5].

chapter 10

Online Orality: The Internet, Folklore, and Culture in Russia*

Bruce McClelland
University of Virginia

T he Internet is a strange phenomenon in the history of technology: unlike its immediate technological predecessors, namely the
press, telephony, and mass media, the Internet does not actually
exist. That is to say, it does not have any boundaries, any definable
physical existence or shape, nor does it have an owner, a designer, or
even a representative. It is not necessarily a commercial enterprise, nor
is it necessarily noncommercial. Despite its history, it does not belong to
a single nation, political group, or ethnolinguistic group. Its motions
and development are certainly not controlled by any identifiable individual. Its future is not being centrally planned, nor is it clear that anyone is capable of specifying the social roles the Internet will some day
play. It even transcends our usual notions of a network, because in fact it
is a virtual network of networks.

It is this aspect of "virtuality" that makes the Internet enigmatic,
something that by its very nature forces us to realize that we are dealing
with a different sort of animal than we have had in the past. The Internet is still mysterious, to the extent that it appears to be self-creating,
while at the same time it forms something of a community. Or, analo-

*An earlier version of this chapter was presented at the St. Petersburg State
Academy of Culture, St. Petersburg, Russia, in February 1998.

gous to its quality as a network of networks, it can be thought of as a community of communities.

The communal aspect of the Internet is today more difficult to discern than it once was, thanks to all the personalized home pages, advertisements, texts, and so on, that have deluged the World Wide Web in recent years. But once upon a time, in the early to mid-1980s, when the Internet was just expanding beyond the borders of the United States, the Internet was indeed a small community.

Begun as a mechanism for exchanging text-based technical information between major research universities and technologically oriented private enterprises with links to the United States government, the original DARPANet served only a handful of scientists and engineers working on a limited number of projects. It is safe to say that most of the people on the Net in its earliest years knew each other, either personally or by reputation. But gradually, the network, whose abilities to connect computers across vast spaces became more important as the personal computer began to be developed, expanded to include other faculty and students at those same universities, as well as nonclassified employees of the commercial firms that held nodes on the Net.

Thus, the Internet was once a very specific tool for a very specific purpose, and as such, was not of much interest to anyone who had no need to use its capacities (which at the time did not go far beyond e-mail). But as the Internet extended its reach to individuals who had nothing more in common with each other than their affiliation with a particular set of institutions, its purposes became more undefined, and the network began to take on the aspects of a larger, more diverse community— approximating a "real" community, like a city or even a country, with all the diversity such analogies imply. As people came onto the network with their home computers or from publicly accessible networked computers at universities, they encountered other "citizens" on the Net ("netizens," in Internet-speak), about whom they knew very little. At the same time, new text-based technologies began to be developed that would enable people to have more dynamic, interactive conversations with each other: the UNIX-server command "talk," or, more recently, Internet Relay Chat (IRC) and ICQ ("I seek you"), for example, enabled people to have real-time conversations with each other by using their keyboards (Reid, 1991).

This brief early history of the Internet is provided here merely to point to a time when the Internet began to exhibit characteristics that moved it beyond the domain of earlier communications technologies. The model for the development of the Internet in subsequent years has been somewhat analogous to the telephone, which is noncentralized and multiplexed (information flows in more than one direction, in multiple "layers") (Poster, 1995a). This is because existing phone lines were adapted to the transfer of digital information. However, the Internet is often perceived as a medium more akin to broadcast media, partly because of its "televisual" appearance (requiring a display screen) and because, in recent times, it has become capable of transmitting multimedia objects (including video, music, and computer programs), but primarily because it also possesses broadband characteristics: one person can send the same message to a large number of people without much additional effort. Unlike broadcast media, to date the content on the Internet has not been closely controlled or regulated by nation states or by conglomerates and public utilities. The uniqueness of the Internet is precisely this: that its development has so far been decentralized and "democratic," yet its power to influence and distribute information makes it seem more like a medium of mass information, and thus a desirable object to be owned and controlled, or at least "regulated."

PROBLEMS FOR THE INTERNET COMMUNITY

Unlike either the telephone or mass media, then, the Internet started out as, and continues to be, a kind of community—despite its rapid growth. As Mark Poster writes, distinguishing the technology of the Internet from other technological developments with which we are familiar, "the Internet is more like a social space than a thing so that its effects are more like those of Germany than those of hammers. The effect of Germany upon the people within it is to make them Germans; the effect of hammers is not to make people hammers..." (1995a, p. 3). The emergence of the Internet community was accompanied by problems similar to those encountered by physical communities, especially those where urban planning is absent: traffic jams, pollution, and the formation of social hierarchies and rivalries. As the number of people on the Net increased, so did (it would seem) the need to establish behavioral protocols. The Internet, by attracting people with different backgrounds, levels of education, and levels of expertise with a computer, not to mention different attitudes toward the nature and function of the network itself, began to get less controllable. The actions of any particular individual using the Internet became less predictable, although we must remember that these actions were primarily verbal, since aside from viruses, it is currently difficult to cause physical action or bodily harm directly across a telecommunications channel.[1] The incursion of obscenity, insults, anger, and other emotionally charged contributions to the previously peaceful community of the Net was viewed as antithetical to the goals of the group constituting the Internet.

What is odd about all this, historically, is that a community was being formed among people who had never seen each other, and in fact more often than not had absolutely no idea with whom they were conversing (Poster, 1995b). The "blindness" resulting from being limited to typing in text at a keyboard had the unusual side effect of permitting network citizens, conversing perhaps across thousands of miles, to represent themselves in any way imaginable. Short people could describe themselves as tall; engineers could become movie producers; men could become women or even children (Poster, 1995b). There was, and currently is, simply no way to tell the truth. Put another way, the very notion of social identity (with such trappings as gender and race) ceased to have the sort of stability we have become used to.

For some reason, the natural processes of community formation took place without any regard for the curious, *virtual* nature of the Internet. That is to say, the boundary between the actual and the virtual began to become blurred. As more people signed on to the Internet, primarily to find out "what all the fuss was about," those who had been on the Net for a longer amount of time began to express the need for rules governing behavior as a way of legitimating their heritage as old-guard users. A new class system was clearly in evidence: those with more experience with the network fancied themselves to have a certain authority over newcomers, and those whose user IDs (e-mail addresses) were associated with the ".edu" domain tended to consider their prerogatives greater than those accessing the Internet through a commercial node (".com"). (Even Internet server domain names are not free of cultural associations: domains registered in the U.S., for example, are the only ones free of a country designator: UK, IT, RU, and so on. Thus, the American genetics of the Internet are always implicit.)

The broader community of the Internet now of course has grown to global proportions. As with the spread of electricity and telephone service earlier in this century, the Internet, too, is reaching into remote (from urban centers) and sparsely populated areas around the world. There are fewer and fewer places without some form of access to the Internet, even if restricted by cost or some other means. Meanwhile, many of the pragmatic and political problems of coordinating a multiplicity of interacting cultures have analogues in the Internet universe. Aside from the obvious practical difficulties posed by language, currency transactions, security, and so forth, a relatively unstudied problem is that of cross-cultural fit, that is, how the cultural predispositions of the Internet (information retrieval, interface, resources, costs, and so on) are interpreted and dealt with in a new cultural context. Certainly, both electricity and telephony carry with them certain presumptions about methods and extent of distribution: relative affluence, population density, need, and similar factors are involved in the distribution of these technologies, as is also true of the distribution of computers, televisions, and so on. But unlike these more neutral technologies, the Internet is by nature associated with additional presumptions: the *lingua franca* used on the Internet is English, a de facto decision that never involved consultation with prospective users, yet whose consequences are still unassessed; the ability to duplicate and transmit "objects" such as photographs both presumes a value to such distribution and challenges traditional notions of production and intellectual property; the ability to communicate or interact across political boundaries almost seamlessly is a feature of the Internet's architecture that could only have been developed in circumstances where openness was considered a social benefit. In other words, the presumptions about the possible uses/abuses and social consequences of the Internet within a poorly defined and rapidly changing community continue to go unexamined, even by those who purport to deconstruct the Internet as a social phenomenon.[2]

THE PROBLEM OF PUBLIC SPACE IN RUSSIA

It is certainly not our purpose here to elucidate all the cultural assumptions that are embedded in the current set of Internet technologies. It is important, however, to understand that the Internet makes possible a "public space," which seems to be an abstraction, a "virtual recreation" of actual public spheres: "the *agora*, the New England town hall, the village church, the coffee house, the tavern, the public square, a convenient barn, a union hall, a park, a factory lunchroom, and even a street corner" (Poster, 1995a, p. 1). It is equally important to recognize that these spaces listed by Poster to suggest the public sphere are not nearly so commonplace in cultures with a shorter history of democratic institutions than the Anglo-American sphere.

Neither the village church, nor the coffeehouse, nor even the tavern was the sort of public space that was easily accessible to the average Russian before the fall of the Soviet Union. Therefore, as we can imagine, the Internet (since it virtually embodies all those metaphors for community) might have a different value for people in post-socialist nations (the concept of nation itself being challenged by the transactional complexities induced by the Internet). The uses to which the Internet is put, especially when it first enters a culture, are in large part dependent upon the availability and suitability of existing analogous services (for example, postal system versus electronic mail) and upon which functions have not been previously available or accessible. Indeed, the potentially democratizing effects of the Internet's incursion represent a possible wedge between those who would immediately apply the Internet's capabilities to decentralize power and the distribution of knowledge and information, and those who, seeing the Internet as conceptually homologous to instruments of mass media, would seek to restrain it.[3]

THE INTERNET AS A FOLKLORE SPACE

Folklore is communicative behavior whose primary characteristics, by one definition, are that (a) it doesn't "belong" to an individual or group (as a corollary, there is no way one can intentionally create folklore), and in the modern context therefore transcends issues of intellectual property; and (b) it is transmitted spontaneously, from one individual (or group of individuals) to another under certain conditions, frequently without regard for remuneration or return benefit. As it is transmitted, it often undergoes modification, according to the inclination of the retransmitter. Folklore, it must be pointed out here, is merely a label applied to certain types of cultural productions according to a given definition, which may vary from culture to culture. Indeed, there is absolutely no reason that a particular culture should have such a concept at all, even if there are many productions in that culture that we might want to term "folklore." What constitutes folklore in one circumstance might be considered "art" in another, or religious activity in yet another. The purposes of folklore itself, moreover, may be interpreted differently: from the Marxist-Leninist perspective, for example, folklore is "a reflection and a weapon of class conflict" (Sokolov, 1971, p. 15).

The English word *folklore* and the Russian word *fol'klor* tend to designate conceptual categories that do not completely overlap. The American usage demands that it must be primarily oral or performative; that is, subject to change with retelling or a new performance, as opposed to relying upon an invariable text or script. Second, folklore tends to not be ascribable to an individual creator or author. Finally, folklore and literary art are clearly distinguished. Thus, Gogol's story, *Vii*, for example, a short story about an errant priest, a vampiric witch, and a demon from Ukrainian folklore, would be construed as literature. Oral *skazki* (tales) about the *vii*, on the other hand, are folkloric. From the Russian perspective, the study of folklore is less a subdomain of anthropology, and may be closely linked with the study of theatre, dance, literature, and music (Sokolov, 1971).

Now, by my own definition, I would not technically be able to include jokes that are passed on the Internet in the category of folklore, because they are, for the time being at any rate (and we must remember that we are still at a very rudimentary stage of Internet technology), printed and reproduced by e-mail. At the same time, because of the Internet's ability to disseminate information broadly and quickly, current events may immediately produce a spate of Internet-based jokes, and this collective response we would want to include under the rubric "folklore." Such responses certainly are neither art nor literature, nor even news. The origin of the jokes is unimportant, and indeed the most common types of jokes that are sent over the Internet are lists and compilations, which suggests multiple authorship. For example, the number of jokes pertaining to Bill Clinton and Monica Lewinsky that were passed around the globe in a single year is perhaps uncountable. As jokes get translated and cross cultural boundaries, however, often the point gets lost. The mechanisms of transmission of this type of folklore via the Internet are as yet little understood. That is, no one has yet studied extensively how such materials as jokes get sent from one person to the next: what, for example, are the parameters for familiarity, how closely do you have to know someone in order to feel free to send jokes, which may be offensive, to someone else on the Net? How are the cultural boundaries for a given instance (for example, a joke) determined, and how does the Internet influence those boundaries?

The use of the Internet to transfer within a given community instances of jokes, gossip, legends, and even out-and-out lies depends upon the technical and personal ease with which such objects can be transmitted. In Russia and most of the former Soviet republics, for example, the cost of access to bandwidth sufficient to permit unhindered use of the World Wide Web is still somewhat high. Not only that, but in these environments, information technologies possessing the degree of openness that characterizes the Internet have not, historically, been widely available. Consequently, the use of the Internet for purposes that are not pragmatic or goal-oriented (research and information seeking; publishing; commercial activity) is understandably rarer.

FABULATES AND URBAN MYTHS

Folklore frequently crosses the boundary between the private and public domain. Tales that are passed from one individual to another in a private space, such as a face-to-face or telephone conversation, are usually told with a particular motive, whether to impress, frighten, amuse, prove, and so on. The motive of the original teller, however, can eventually become supplanted as the tale is retold, either in private or in public. Along the way, such a narrative can change to accommodate the new intentions of the teller. In the case of a certain subgenre of folklore, the so-called *fabulate*, a tale is usually told with some sort of confirmation of its veracity. "A neighbor of mine swears she saw this..." a story might begin, and frequently the teller may also believe that the story is true.

Because the Internet is still frequently perceived to be a space where what is printed is true (that is to say, the distinction between unverified or unedited information on the Internet and edited information such as that in newspapers and journals is not rigorously maintained), it is a likely medium for the transmission of folklore of the fabulate type. This is especially the case where the substance of the folkloric message involves the need for broadcasting to a large audience. Two recent examples come to mind.

The first occurred in the aftermath of the TWA flight 800 disaster in 1996, in which a jet exploded shortly after takeoff from JFK airport in New York. Some weeks following the incident, while there was still no well-understood reason for the explosion, the once well-known political writer and adviser, Pierre Salinger, claimed to have evidence of an attack upon the plane by a U.S. Navy rocket, and that the investigation, which was getting nowhere, was in fact a coverup of the truth. This information was eventually published and republished on the Internet, causing the investigators to have to publicly deny any such coverup. In our modern age, where technological and informational complexity itself has become a type of demon, conspiracy theories constitute a very common form of folklore. As Derrida observes (1995), "Contrary to what is normally thought, technological modernity doesn't neutralise any-thing; it causes a certain form of the demonic to re-emerge" (p. 35). The Internet, with its ability to obscure the usual tests for truth-value by eliminating or leveling the mechanisms for assigning value (such as edi-torial discretion or cost), is a superb medium for promoting and expressing social anxiety, hysteria, and so forth.

A similar but more widespread type of Internet folklore in the U.S. takes the form of so-called "urban legends." Urban legends, a term coined by the folklorist Jan Brunvand, constitute a genre of lore in which a story about a plausible but unlikely event, usually reflecting uncertainties about the modern age, is passed from person to person as if its truth were beyond question.

For example, the now-famous story of the Neimann-Marcus cookie recipe has recently been passed to possibly millions of people on the Internet. Neimann-Marcus is a large store in the U.S. that is known for its expensive, high-quality items it sells. A message passed around the Internet in recent years contains a recipe for chocolate chip cookies, and an accompanying story about how Neiman-Marcus charged the credit card account of a customer $250.00. The charge was supposedly the hid-den price of the cookie recipe, which the hapless customer believed cost only $2.50. The ostensible intention behind publishing the recipe on the

Internet was to deflate the value of the recipe so that Neimann-Marcus could not continue to overcharge customers in the future. The tale, which is of course untrue, is nevertheless believable at first glance. We can infer that the social motive for this type of Internet folklore is to express disapproval of the ways in which large, wealthy corporations infringe upon the limited rights of the individual: the free distribution of the ostensibly valuable recipe of course would make the recipe worthless, and thereby eliminate Neimann-Marcus' ability to dupe unsuspecting customers with exorbitant credit card charges.[4]

These types of easily reproducible narratives, such as jokes and urban legends, are the simplest forms of folkloric materials that can be moved from the domain of the actual community to the virtual community without much loss. The Internet adds nothing in these cases other than rapid and inexpensive reproduction to a form of social dissemination. However, as new technologies develop—in particular, those facilitating so-called virtual reality—not only will new forms of interaction develop, but the boundaries between online productions such as art, literature, theater, and folklore will blur. At the moment, outside of certain technically advanced areas, the ability of the Internet to transmit video and sound images in 'real time' is still quite limited. However, it is important to understand that folklore will assume whatever forms it wants if the means for doing so becomes available.

Games, which are distinguished by the presence of fairly explicit rules, are another form of behavior that fits some of the parameters of folklore. The emergence of virtual reality, first as a text-based environment controlled by a complex of programs residing on a central computer, later as a more distributed and visually representational phenomenon, enables interaction in imaginary or virtual spaces among people who have no face-to-face knowledge of each other.

Most of these games generally presume a certain fantastic background setting, such as a mythical, medieval Europe or some futuristic world. One such category of games is known as MUSH, an acronym for Multi-User Shared Hallucination. Each player must be on the Internet, of course, and creates the general outlines of a persona or character that will be injected into the ongoing, unending narrative of the MUSH-space to interact with other characters. The "game" is going on all the time, and often involves people from various parts of the world (although the games originating in the U.S. are usually conducted in English only). Aside from the fantastic setting, some of the characters can also eventually acquire fantastic or supernatural attributes, becoming magicians, vampires, or werewolves or other creatures. However, most of these games prohibit the newcomer from acquiring advanced attributes such as magical powers, shapeshifting, and so on, until the

character has been in the game for a while and has successfully interacted with other characters—who, in fact, have the power to virtually
"kill" him. These "powers," in reality, represent access to certain functions of the computer program controlling the game, and can best be
described as an increase in the ability to control "virtual objects," including other characters. Thus the rules of the game mimic those of real
society, in which social powers are conferred by the group on the basis
of familiarity and appreciation of certain acceptable qualities.

One very popular set of RPGs has the title "Vampire: the Masquerade," because it is based upon a book of the same name. In fact, Internet RPGs are based upon the same types of games that are played in
nonvirtual spaces. In these games, there are two basic classes of beings,
ordinary "mortals" and "vampires" or "immortals." Curiously, those who
aspire to become vampires are not regarded as monstrous aberrations or
murderers, but are in fact esteemed because of their "powers" and their
quality of being immortal.

The elaboration of this game, its rules, and what I take to be its meaning I will have to leave for another time. And, indeed, the question
arises as to whether such games constitute a form of folklore or instead a
new form of theater, since they require players to play roles with general
scripts (any virtual behavior that is completely unsynchronized with the
fantasy behind the game is considered to be outside the accepted script
and is therefore chastized by other players). But because it is construed
as a game, because it has a social purpose, because there is no definite,
repeatable performance, and because it occurs in a public space into
which anyone is admitted, it also can be included under the heading of
folklore. What is especially intriguing about these games is that there is
the potential for a certain psychological danger that results from the
elimination of a distinction between the actual and the virtual Self.
There are reports—and some of these reports themselves may also be
folklore—of players who have become depressed or even suicidal
because their roleplaying personae were outcast or abused. A recent case
in the U.S. involved a group of teenagers who imagined themselves to
be vampires. Several of the members of the group had been involved in
playing vampire-based RPGs. This group was held responsible for the
murders of the parents of a girl in the group. Although the Vampire
RPG was not considered to have played a significant role in the murder,
the loss of distinction between real and imaginary domains, exaggerated
by the increase in our ability to quickly generate manifestations of collective fantasies, was responsible for a horrendous act (Linedecker,
1998).

THE INTERNET AS A SPACE FOR
"FOLKLORIC PROTEST"

In the foregoing descriptions of some of the folkloric activities that can
be adapted to or generated on the Internet, we have not mentioned a
number of significant questions concerning how these new or modified
forms of folklore might operate cross-culturally. In Russia, as we have
noted, questions arise not only around technical parameters such as
computational power and bandwidth, but around the purpose of a powerful technology like the Internet. Many of the folkloric (and other creative) activities that take place on the Internet in Western countries
assume that the Internet is not by any means a scarce resource. Neither
is the time it takes to "surf the Web" considered particularly valuable,
since on average, the relative costs of usage with respect to personal
income are minimal, and the potential for freedom and openness that
Internet technologies imply does not appear threatening. The use of the
Internet for creative, nongoal-directed, even frivolous and excessive pur-
suits in fact is taken for granted by Western corporations wishing to
secure profits from the users of the Internet.

The adaptation of such incautious, apolitical, and excessive activities
in the former Soviet Union is likely to be complicated. Russia has, by
and large, taken the promise of the Internet very seriously: its use as a
publishing vehicle, for example, is valued quite highly, to judge from
the rapid growth of Web hosts supplying literature, art, bibliography,
news, and so on. Unlike the U.S., where access to the Internet has been
largely subsidized (a fact that is not promoted abroad), in countries with
less stable economies, the Internet appears to be more of a commodity,
that is, something that obeys rules of supply and demand, and therefore
is less likely to be used without premeditation or purpose—at least
among the older generation. Furthermore, the idea of an unwatched,
open community is still regarded with skepticism and ambivalence by
many Russians, and thus the casual use of the Internet may take longer
to develop than in the West. At the same time, as it becomes realized
that the Internet cannot be subjected to the same sorts of controls that
the state security organizations have enforced in the past, folk uses of
the Net should become more apparent. But this, of course, implies having a critical mass of the "folk" online.

CONTROLLING THE PAST?/CHARTING THE FUTURE

We see, then, that the Internet currently has the ability to do something
that the mass media cannot do: because everyone potentially creates or

modifies its content, it provides a mechanism for "folkloric protest," since the Net does not represent a coherent vested interest. Whereas television and radio stations are usually owned by an individual organization or a government, which makes it hard for unedited or uncensored information to be broadcast, the Internet provides a means for individuals to post information that may or may not be reliable, accurate, or even politically correct. The cost, however, of this leveling is that the economic or use-value of information currently available on the Net is difficult to determine. As the old adage has it, "You get what you pay for."

While we have certainly not described all the potential and actual forms of folklore on the Internet, we can confidently state that the Internet, regardless of its past and future directions, currently constitutes enough of a human community to accommodate all kinds of human verbal and nonverbal activity, including folklore. It is unlikely that this quality of the Internet as a self-creating technology owned by no one and controlled by no one will not be eliminated, despite its promise, especially for societies where freedom of expression is not taken for granted. Humans have a tendency to want always to possess for themselves what is seen to be an advantage to everyone, and the Internet represents just such a target. In the meantime, we have an opportunity to try to understand this new phenomenon by looking at the processes by which areas of human ritual and communication become adapted as the technology develops.

The eventual obliteration of the absoluteness of truth—an unexpected consequence of the technological drift toward total digitization, and therefore total reproducibility—will mean that one can no longer be sure that a given piece of information, be it a photograph or a legend, represents historical or perceptual fact. And as we gradually learn that photographs and newspaper stories have no greater claim on reality or truth than an urban legend, we might eventually free ourselves from the need to control the past.

NOTES

1. Regarding analogies to our traditional notions of 'harm' occurring over the Internet, however, see Dibbell, 1993.
2. Mark Poster (1995a) acknowledges the preponderance of "white maleness" in the development of the features that are developed for the Internet, yet does not question his own assumptions regarding the relative importance attributed to the Internet in different cultural settings.

3. In this regard, the governments of both the United States and Russia are equally misguided, even hypocritical. The U.S., for example, on the one hand has spent millions of dollars trying to make the Internet accessible to Russians who have returned to Russia after studying or working in the U.S., while at the same time it maintains a continuing attempt to legislate tariffs and to restrict access to portions of the Internet for some U.S. citizens.

4. For more details on the history of this Internet legend, see Goldin, 1994.

REFERENCES

Derrida, J. (1995). *The gift of death* (D. Wills, Trans.). Chicago: University of Chicago Press.

Dibbell, J. (1993). *A rape in cyberspace, or how an evil clown, a Haitian trickster spirit, two wizards, and a cast of dozens turned a database into a society* [Online]. Available: <ftp://ftp.lambda.moo.mud.org/pub/MOO/papers/VillageVoice.txt>; <http://www.hnet.uci.edu/mposter/syllabi/readings/rape.html> [1999, March 21].

Goldin, D. (1994, August 19). *Foodlore/recipe exchange* [Online]. Available: <http://hazel.ddb.com/Sweets/neiman.marcus> [1999, March 27].

Linedecker, C. (1998). *The vampire killers*. New York: St. Martin's Books.

Poster, M. (1995a). CyberDemocracy: Internet and the public sphere. In D. Porter (Ed.), *Internet culture* (pp. 201–217). New York: Routledge.

Poster, M. (1995b). *The second media age*. London: Basil Blackwell.

Reid, E. M. (1991). *Electropolis: Communication and community on Internet Relay Chat* [Online]. Available: < ftp://ftp.lambda.moo.mud.org/pub/MOO/papers/electropolis.txt> [1999, March 21].

Sokolov, Y. M. (1971). *Russian folklore* (C. Smith, Trans.). Detroit, MI: Folklore Associates.

Part III

Contexts and Practices in the New Europe

chapter 11

Video as Civic Discourse in Slovenia and the Former Yugoslavia: Strategies of Visualization and the Aesthetics of Video in the New Europe*

Marina Gržinić
Slovenian Academy of Science and Art, Ljubljana, Slovenia
Scientific and Research Center

T his chapter attempts to address how the video medium, as artistic, cultural, and discursive practice, faced its second birth in Eastern Europe in the 1980s. In particular, it will focus on how video as a specific art practice and form of visualization inscribed itself in the social and political corpus of Eastern Europe, simultaneously producing some distinctive aesthetic visual features. This chapter is the first attempt to write simultaneously about the general history of electronic arts across Eastern Europe, while focusing on the particular history of the media condition in ex-Yugoslavia, and more specifically in Slovenia, in connection with the underground and/or alternative movements in Eastern Europe (Gržinić, 1992, 1993a, 1993b, 1995). Finally, this chapter examines video in the 1990s, as the New Europe moved toward free-

*The author thanks Ms. Adele Eisenstein for her careful language revision of this chapter.

dom and democracy and the reformation of civic discourse through more recent technological developments.

TRACING THE HISTORY

Video gained a very particular status in the so-called "peripheral" totalitarian countries in the 1980s, where the Communist State apparatus (especially the most repressive ones) began to exercise looser control over artistic and cultural productions. This owed as well to the disintegrational processes that started to spurt out in the political and economic chaotic Eastern European reality of the 1980s. In spite of the differing Communist structures in Hungary, Poland, and especially ex-Yugoslavia, these countries succeeded to develop avant-garde film and art productions throughout the 1970s, and connected them to the video medium in the 1980s. Hungary connected the strong avant-garde film tradition to video, or at least, developed a conceptual approach to the medium through experimental film research. Poland connected the strong conceptual tradition in the visual arts with body art actions and happenings, performance and film productions. Ex-Yugoslavia, with its so-called Third Way into Socialism (that is, "nonaligned self-management socialism"), had already become a politically specific case (hi)story, which I will try to outline in detail later. The work shown at Western European festivals and cultural institutions in the 1980s were, in the first instance, video works by artists from ex-Yugoslavia, Poland and Hungary, in addition to the works of those who emigrated to Western Europe or North America in the 1960s and 1970s.

The so-called "first line" totalitarian socialist countries (that is, Russia/USSR, Romania, Bulgaria, East Germany, and so on) suffered a delay of a whole decade in developing art connected to the electronic media, including the use of the video medium as a social tool and civic technological discourse, in comparison with Poland, Hungary, and especially ex-Yugoslavia. This delay was due to the repressive nature of the Communist State in these countries, which executed an almost bloodthirsty control of art and cultural productions, not only over the written word, but over all instant visual reproductive media and technologies (for example, copy machines, VHS video technology, and even Polaroid photography). The severe censorship of literature was easily extended to cover visual reproductive technology. In this context, the underground film scene, which arose in St. Petersburg (at the time, Leningrad) in the mid-1980s, deserves special mention. The city had a strong underground scene known as the Necrorealist movement, which produced deconstructivist versions of the official Communist films on Super 8mm and 16mm film. Subsequently, in the late 1980s and 1990s, following the collapse of Communism, it proved impossible to stop the transfer of Necrorealist films onto video, facilitating their distribution and presentation at Western European art video, experimental, and media festivals.

On the other hand, the 1980s was an era of the shaping of a new scopic regime of contemporary reality, giving priority to works proceeding from the eye and intended for the eye. This oculocentrism can be applied to political and civic events, as well as to cultural and artistic ones. For example, throughout the 1980s, in the territory of ex-Yugoslavia, we witnessed the progressive disintegration of the watchful eye of authority. As an example, we may recall one of the most notorious trials in Slovenia, known as "The Trial against Four," which involved three journalists and a soldier of the then-Yugoslav People's Army. The Four allegedly stole a top secret army document in 1988. This trial may be perceived as an exemplary visual: the indictment of the Four was not founded on any actual offense. The Four were not indicted for the abuse of the document, but for having the knowledge of, or rather, for having an insight into the punitive, xeroxed, confidential army document. In this affair, it was the visual media and its technological gadgets that played a decisive role (Erjavec & Gržinić, 1991).

We must remember that the 1980s, in general, are defined as landmark in video art production worldwide, first and foremost, because of the changing relationship of video art and television. Video art was born in the 1960s as "prepared" television, as a personal medium and a counterculture tool for subverting the widespread dissemination of the televisual mass consumer ideology, initially in the U.S., and then globally. I refer here to Nam June Paik's works from the mid-1960s, which is considered by art historians and media chronologists to be the first video art sculpture. I do not intend at all here to summarize the history of the video medium worldwide. Furthermore, there are numerous accounts of the history of video and its various paths in the West, and only a few about its reality in the East. This chapter can be considered one of the first accounts of the history and theory of the video medium in Eastern Europe.

In the 1980s, video became fully integrated into television imagery through music video. The Music Television (MTV) Corporation not only radically influenced the rock and pop culture/industry, but also demonstrated how the consumer televisual culture, in an almost cannibalistic way, integrated experimental televisual video iconography. MTV's strategies of visualization derived largely from video art and experimental cinema. This MTV process is, on the one hand, tied with a whole revolution in the proliferation of cheap and accessible home video technology, and on the other, with the development of increasingly high quality, sophisticated video equipment, which opened up a variety of research fields in art, culture, science, and industry. Interactive video technology allows not only the fast development of video art as such (for example, video installations, interactive media projects), but also the research of other scientific and cultural fields. Moreover, with the inclusion of digital video technology in the film industry, the video medium and its technology became situated between mass home accessibility and high standard television/film industry performance. This has created a new social and technological status for video in the so-called industrialized world.

It is possible to detect a similar, if torsioned, logic in speaking about the second birth of video in Eastern Europe during the 1980s. Video, even in its most amateur form, via a nonprofessional home VHS video system, allows instantaneous replay of the recorded image. The instantaneous internal technological production (and post-production) principle proved crucial for the growth of the medium in Eastern Europe. Through the constant reproducibility of the totalitarian "original" image of power, cracks emerged in this original to the point that the replayed "copy" involved a decoding, which was not merely a pure, innocent, inner technological trick of the medium, but moreover, a political stance. The video medium's potential for incessant replay thus brought radical changes to the watchful eye of the Communist totalitarian system of power. These processes of replaying the video image may be perceived as a subversive mediatization of the social and political sphere in Eastern Europe, and, even more, as a process of developing specific ways of the forming of the so-called *societas civilis*; of including, through new media technology, its civic discourse in the process of state buildings and politics.

Therefore, to comprehend the second birth of the video medium in Eastern Europe, we must take into consideration this switch from the technologically produced replay to the political one, and to recognize that both forms of replay were carried out in Eastern Europe, within the social, political, and cultural underground.

LJUBLJANA'S ALTERNATIVE OR SUBCULTUR(E/AL) MOVEMENT

In this respect, the underground movement that arose in Ljubljana, Slovenia, in the 1980s manifests the exceptional underground collision of art, culture, and politics that allowed Slovenian video art to attain very specific and radical features, which colored video art with its significant and distinctive characteristics. It presented itself almost as an art media movement. We have to bear in mind that prior to the 1980s, when speaking of the media paradigm of Eastern Europe in general, the word *media* referred primarily to mass media channels, such as radio and television broadcasts, newspapers, magazines, and so on. To understand fully what came about, I will present the features of the Ljubljana cultural underground movement of the 1980s (the alternative or subculture movement) bearing in mind that, at the time, Slovenia maintained a very intense alternative organizational and structural physiognomy (Gržinić, 1993b). It was an exception, not only among the other underground cultural activities throughout the ex-Yugoslav republics, but likewise among Eastern Europe as a whole, where, in most cases, it was not possible to talk about a movement, but simply about sporadic and fragmented happenings, or a fusion of ideas and actions.

It is important to emphasize that the alternative or subculture movement was not simply a marginal movement that, ultimately, according to the logic of political isometrics, functioned as a reconfirmation of "the center as center." The most significant strategy of the Ljubljana alternative movement consisted of not in finding alternatives to the Communist system, but alternatives within it.

Within its relationship to the underground phenomena of the East European countries (for example, the Russian "Sotsart" and "Apt-Art" [Apartment - Art] movements, or Polish Post-Conceptualism), the Ljubljana alternative culture, or subculture, represented a metaphorical fight for the appropriation of the State legal cultural and artistic institutions, as well as for State funds, which were earmarked for investment in the so-called official socialist art and cultural productions. This was in opposition to other movements, which were characterized by the paradigm forming new artistic "practices" within private spheres that were completely removed from the State system and its institutions. The Ljubljana alternative movements went beyond the counterculture attitude of the 1970s, demanding new cultural, political, and artistic institutions and organizations to be formed, so to speak, within the very institutions of the socialist self-management paradigm of reality. In this way, the Ljubljana alternative or subculture movement clearly shows a deeper change in the actions of the underground movements of Europe, and more specifically, in Eastern Europe.

The end of the 1970s in Slovenia, commonly referred to as the end of authoritarian politics, marked a watershed for what had been until then an empty space in art. It was followed by the growth of a new youth subculture: "punk," which provided a noncompromising and critical energy, which evaluated and fed creativity in the 1980s. Punk culture and its artistic offshoots provided a critical energy, which provoked shifts in the medium of art in general.

In the beginning of the 1980s, the term "Ljubljana alternative, or subculture, production" was devised, and soon spread into the media. By naming itself from within, so to speak, and by recognizing itself on the basis of a common denominator, this production distinguished itself from other socialist cultural and artistic productions. By declaring itself a subculture, it dramatically displayed its limited material and media position. This position included a lack of financial resources and space, such as clubs, galleries, and centers. Via the means of minimal financial aid, the subculture was continually repressed by the State. As in most Socialist countries, with soft or hard totalitarian regimes, the position of "high" art was reserved for official art and culture.

Regardless of parallel events in America and Western Europe (for example, Dick Hebdige's cult book *Subculture, the Meaning of Style* [1979]), the Slovenian alternative culture was more than just a style, a passing fashion or trend. Fashion's tradition of never-ending surplus production was unknown under socialism, anyway. Instead, Ljubljana subculture signified a reconfiguration of the social and artistic arena. The Slovenian alternative movement of the 1980s introduced some very specific and autonomous productions and organizational forms of culture and art. These were developed independently, and in parallel to, the existing official, mostly impotent, cultural systems and channels. Hence, all alternative activity represented an intrusion into official cultural and artistic production, as well as a shift into the social and political sphere.

The alternative culture was not something that would place itself in opposition to the official, mainly rigid and often unimaginative culture and art of the 1980s in Ljubljana. Instead, it encouraged numerous new artistic practices and productions, and created a new referential background for their interpretation. In contrast with Slovenia's official culture and art, it was truly radical: radically different in thinking, necessitating an entirely different structure of language, self-organization, and self-reflection.

The alternative culture provided a relevant status to some artistic practices, such as performance, video, and popular theatre, and brought about a series of new socialization processes. These included new forms of social activity and nonformal institutional bodies, which decisively marked and defined the Slovene cultural scene. A network of clubs and public meeting places was created, as were new ways of accepting "deviant" social and artistic activities. The coming-out of Ljubljana's male homosexuals, and the constituting of a gay culture, also arose at this time. Ljubljana had the first organized movement of this kind in the then-socialist countries of Eastern Europe. In 1984, the coming out of Ljubljana homosexuals, the establishment of the gay social/art club Magnus, of a lesbian subgroup within the Lilit's section for women's issues in 1984–1985, and of new social movements (for example, the Section for a Culture of Peace at ŠKUC-Forum in 1985) were among the organizational processes that were part of Ljubljana's alternative movement. For all of the above, the 1980s also confirm that Ljubljana earned the title of an urban topos and fostered the creation of the gay culture in the 1990s in Eastern Europe.

The Slovenian alternative culture incorporated different artistic forms, media, theories, alternative forms of social behavior, and so-called "new social movements," which decisively changed the way art, as a more diverse production process, is perceived. It can also be viewed as contributing to the effort toward the establishment of a civil society in Slovenia. The alternative processes and projects demonstrate the exceptionally interwoven nature of culture and politics. From today's perspective, all subculture activity can therefore be regarded as a movement that radically marked the process of the "Slovenian Spring," which culminated in Slovenia's independence.

The alternative culture also defined art and culture as a cluster of "very real" institutions operating with "very real" money, having "very real" ideological effects and taking on the role of the legitimate institutions to promote and preserve certain beliefs and values. Finally, the alternative movement introduced a different notion of the relationship between art and politics. It was not interested in simple direct Leftist engagement, nor in partisan art (that is, utilizing and representing positive yet everyday political themes), but in the politics of representation and aesthetics.

As a cultural, artistic, and media phenomenon of the 1980s (at the time, organized primarily around the activities of Radio Študent, one of the first radio stations to become independent from State control in Eastern Europe, and the weekly journals *Mladina* and *Tribuna*), the Ljubljana alternative culture developed a specific context of culture, infrastructure, and organization. The Radio Študent broadcasting station was one of the few achievements that the students negotiated from the State at the time of the student riots in Ljubljana in 1968.

It not only tied itself to the existent international media configurations, but also established connections within the internationally independent distribution channels, especially in music (for example, the connection of the music group Laibach with Mute Records). The Ljubljana alternative culture built up its own network of audio, visual, and textual information, as well as its own network of international contacts and exchanges.

DEFINING LJUBLJANA ALTERNATIVE CULTURE THROUGH TECHNOLOGY

There are many elements that radically marked and in fact constituted the Ljubljana alternative culture. Those that are important to mention include the utilization of technology, such as photocopying and video, different forms of organizing and social gathering, and image (that is, style and poise at the same time). Changes occurred not only in representation (for example, new content imbued with sexuality and politics, graffiti art), but also in strategies and tactics of presentation (for example, outside galleries in underground rock clubs, presentations in private spaces), and through the embrace of instant visual technologies, such as Polaroid, Xerox, and, especially, video.

The Ljubljana alternative movement was organized around two student organizations in Ljubljana: the Students' Cultural and Art Centre (ŠKUC) and the Students' Cultural Forum Society (ŠKD Forum), as were Ljubljana's independent video production in the beginning of the 1980s. In 1982, both of these centers jointly established a video section, which became the basis of ŠKUC-Forum independent video productions. Nonprofessional VHS video equipment, with its simple handling and extremely fast production and reproduction, made video one of the most popular and radical forms of media for the 1980s generation. Access to video became a status symbol in itself. The second birth of the video medium in Slovenia was connected with the fact that the marginalized community of punks, rockers, and members of the underground perceived the video medium as an important technological tool, which allowed for personal expression and social engagement. It is important to note that video functioned as an integration transfer, which allowed for the formation of imagery and standpoints in a reflexive way.

The above does not apply at all to the situation of video art in the Yugoslavia of the 1970s, when only the productions of Nuša and Srečo Dragan and Miha Vipotnik from Ljubljana, and Sanja Iveković and Dalibor Martinis from Zagreb were known. In the 1970s, it was possible in Yugoslavia to acknowledge a wide practice of using the video medium primarily as recording technology, if we bypass for a moment the aforementioned artists. Video was used as a documentation tool for the recording of numerous body-art performances, art actions and happenings, as well as for the process/mental approaches to art and specific concepts. In this context, we must recognize the importance of the video works of Marina Abramović, which were recorded (some initially on film, then transferred to video) in the late 1960s and 1970s, when the artist still lived in her native town of Belgrade. Nevertheless, the importance of this video material does not lie in the video medium itself, as here video is used merely to record the performance, and not as an investigative medium, researching its possibility as internal to the medium. The importance of these video works should be recognized first of all, in that they captured and preserved the drama of the body-art happening. With only still photographic documentation of these actions, the wholeness of the work and process and its time-based quality would be lost.

It is essential to highlight that there was no such thing as "Yugoslav video." Video art productions were primarily the products of individual urban centers, mostly the capital cities of the respective Yugoslav republics: Ljubljana, the capital of Slovenia; Zagreb, the capital of Croatia; Belgrade, the capital of Yugoslavia/Serbia; Skopje, the capital of Macedonia; and Sarajevo, the capital of Bosnia-Herzegovina.

Kathy Rae Huffman, in her 1989 presentation at the New York Artists Space, clearly acknowledged this, referring to "video production from Yugoslavia." Huffman's presentation, entitled "Deconstruction, Quotation & Subversion," included video productions from the 1980s, which were the products of individual urban centers throughout the Yugoslav republics, such as Ljubljana, Zagreb, Belgrade, Skopje and Sarajevo. In 1990, Kathy Rae Huffman, who was then a curator and video producer at the Institute of Contemporary Art (ICA) in Boston, curated a few hour-long programs about the state of video art in Yugoslavia. At the time, it was the first comprehensive and detailed look into the complexity and diversity of video art production in Yugoslavia. The programs were presented in major American cities and cultural centers.

During the 1980s, Biljana Tomić and Bojana Pejić organized, under the auspices of the Student Culture Center in Belgrade, the international biennial art and media manifestation, "April's Meetings," showing video works by artists from Yugoslavia, as well as inviting internationally known video artists, curators, and critics. Within the framework of Radio/TV Belgrade, Dunja Blazević curated and produced the emission called "TVGallery," focusing on modern art, including video. Within the framework of "TVGallery," Blazević produced several art video works.

In the 1980s, the experimental video "The Happy TV," realized by Goran Gajić and Zoran Pezo in Zagreb, and produced by Croatian National TV, was a project that deeply echoed MTV pop characteristics.

At the end of the 1980s, Radio/TV Skopje (Macedonia) also started to produce video artworks, and, with other cultural partners, jointly organized a video workshop called "The Ohrid Video Meetings." By the mid-1980s, Sarajevo also joined in the video art manifestations, organizing international video meetings, of which the last edition was in 1991, the year preceding the inception of the war in Bosnia-Herzegovina. TV Sarajevo also produced programs similar to the American rock 'n roll late-night shows. These were produced just before the war escalated.

At this point, we can throw light on another ex-Yugoslav phenomenon. Numerous video artworks were produced in the 1980s by the so-called National Television production houses founded in the mid-1960s in each of the capitals of the respective ex-Yugoslav republics: Radio/TV Centre Ljubljana, Radio/TV Centre Zagreb, Radio/TV Centre Belgrade, Radio/TV Centre Skopje, Radio/TV Centre Sarajevo, and so on. The national television centers soon became the biggest production houses and, by the mid-1980s, the only real producers of video artworks. The former independent video productions centered around the student cultural centers soon reached the limits of nonprofessional VHS technology, as the Western video festivals started to show video programs on half-professional or high broadcast quality systems, using VHS video technology only as a preview system by the end of the 1980s.

The ex-Yugoslav national television houses were mainly established to fulfill regional cultural interests and art programming in each republic. In the 1970s, the news programs were entirely prepared and broadcast from the main television center in Belgrade. The main news, information, and political programs were kept uniformly under control. Following the death of Tito in May 1980, the uniformity of the prime-time news and its rigorously controlled distribution started to fall apart, as did Yugoslavia.

The engagement of the various television centers of each republic in video art production was not developed because the national "mother" television centers understood and propagated the experimental aesthetics of video art, but because this was the cheapest way to fulfill the socialist planning system, which depended on producing a fixed annual number of art and cultural productions. In comparison with similar television productions in the West, the artists were not really paid, while it was officially stated that the television center was "investing in the production of the work." The video artists who used the expensive technical facilities, which were rarely used for the daily television productions, were pioneers of sorts, pushing and testing the high-quality broadcasting facilities. After completing the production of the video work, the artists received the dubbed master copy to show freely in any noncommercial art festival or cultural institution. It is important to note that the copies of the work, and all other presentation expenses, had to be covered by the artists themselves. In the 1990s, National TV Slovenia slightly "changed" its politics with regard to video art production, and diminished the number of productions, due to the serious financial problems of maintaining the still-lingering socialist grandeur of its administration.

Thus, the shift from the notion of "Yugoslav video" to "Slovene video," which occurred almost overnight, when in 1991, Slovenia proclaimed its independence and seceded from Yugoslavia, was not a difficult changeover. In 1994, Kathy Rae Huffman, at that time an independent curator, media activist, and Internet artist, prepared the first comprehensive and detailed presentation of Slovenian video art production, a complex intertwining of styles, concepts, and approaches. Previously, Slovenian video art production had only been represented by individual artists, or with a much smaller selection of works. Furthermore, in the 1980s, video production within Slovenia was so radically different aesthetically, in comparison with local filmmaking and visual style, that the designation "Slovene video production" could not in any way allude to a "national" unifying style.

Video in Slovenia, while understood to be a form of "media technology" and media art, is still situated somewhere between the marginal and institutional. Judging by the productions, video art is an "institution," but the conditions under which it is produced are still largely marginal. Elsewhere, mostly in the so-called West, a solid network of private and public institutions, galleries, museums, festivals, and television programs, which include video art production, presentation, and distribution, has been established. While Slovenia has a few video producers, no one is involved in video distribution. Throughout the 1980s, ŠKUC Gallery (Gallery of the Students' Cultural and Art Center) ran local video productions and exhibited video installations. Numerous artistic and documentary video projects were carried out by ŠKUC-Forum, and also by the Cankar Cultural Center (Cankarjev Dom) in Ljubljana, within the framework of its video biennial, The International Video Biennial, which was initiated in 1983 and continued throughout the 1980s. The Information Center of the Modern Gallery in Ljubljana, established in 1990, continually shows international video programs, as does the newly re-established gallery of the Student Center, Gallery Kapelica. Both offered new prospects for the 1990s. The Soros Center in Ljubljana, as well as in all the former Yugoslav republics, and in all other Eastern European countries, is developing (through its media branches, and as part of its "open society postponed ideology") media programs, free Internet access, and educational research media programming. TV Slovenia is still one of the biggest producers in the field, and in the 1990s, it was joined by commercial private studios, which, from time to time, produced video artworks. Slovenia lacks a network of curators and/or editors who could represent video art within cultural institutions. For the moment, what we are left with are "weird" individual enthusiasts (mostly video artists), who, with much love and assiduity, cling to the field thath others consider rather eccentric. Video artists are therefore forced to be the critical and theoretical promoters of their own work.

STRATEGY OF VISUALIZATION AND THE AESTHETICS
OF VIDEO IN EASTERN EUROPE

Speaking in terms of aesthetic strategies and visual tactics of video art in Slovenia, we may state that video art productions reconstituted and created levels of history and creativity in contemporary art, culture, and social activities. Surprisingly, precisely what critics in the 1970s berated as lacking in official film productions and other visual media (for example, the absence of criticism, social engagement, and variations in political/social themes, as well as a lack of experimentation) began to appear in the 1980s through the video medium. In the 1970s, politicians and official State-controlled institutions repressed most of the films from the Yugoslav "black wave" film movement of the 1960s and early 1970s. The most important film directors from this period included Dušan Makavejev, Aleksandar Petrović, Bata Čengić, and Želimir Žilnik, some of whom are internationally recognized. These films, with their avant-garde and experimental approaches, filled with radical social and political stances, seemed to be for some nostalgic souls lost forever. In the 1980s, however, these concepts began to be reconstituted and reinvented through the video medium.

Video art succeeded to connect classical art productions with different levels of art, culture, and also technology, developing and articulating a specific civic discourse. Video based on the editing of various media (for example, theater, visual arts, literature, and music) made full use of the interdisciplinary potentialities of the medium. Due to these very possibilities, as well as video's connection with theater, film, performance, and music, exploration in form and content became extremely important. The boundaries of some traditional art and cultural practices were broadened, and the clear distinctions between them became blurred, forging new dynamics and a multitude of levels for interdisciplinary work.

One case in point is *Mongold* (1987), a video by Nuša and Srečo Dragan. In it, fragments from the film *Last Year in Marienbad*, by Alain Resnais, were reedited and combined with prose by Kurt Schwitters and Slovenian poet Aleš Debeljak.

Video artist Marko Kovačić is currently building his video universe, using elements from his own "plastic" art experience, intermingled with performance and theatre. In his video work, *American Dream* (1986), Kovačić connected elements of street theater, mime, and the burlesque, together with the replay logic of the video medium. The video replay is used in this work in a literal way. The historical visual material from the first session of State leaders who constituted the nonaligned movement—the Third World and ex-Yugoslavia among them—is (re)played in reverse. This subverts the historical balance; for example, politicians shake hands and sign documents with the wrong hand.

The mixed-media music group Borghesia has based its video creation in mass culture by working with found footage from the audio-visual material of national television. In these projects, music videos are used to relay visual and cultural information. In their music videos, for example, "Mud" and "No Hope No Fear," frenetic rhythms and emphasized textual criticism are intermixed with demented installation screenplays, psychedelic colors, and contents from the edge of society.

All this tells us that video production in Slovenia cannot be easily classified into categories such as "music video" or "video theater." Most of the projects could belong to many of these categories, particularly the works of Jasna Hribernik, Mirko Simić, Igor Zupe and Sašo Podgoršek, Nataša Prosenc, Marko Košnik, and Marko Peljhan. In the 1990s, technical imperfections in the field of the moving images are recreated by two nearly lost technological/narrative moments: the black-and-white picture and silence. Both are used convincingly by Mirko Simić in his works. By reusing and readapting amateur S-VHS video technology, Simić obtains an excellent source for producing the unstable, imperfect video image. Through "granulation and scratching" of the black-and-white surface of the image, the art video work clearly distances itself from the glossy mass media television image. Prosenc's video, on the other side, examines the contradictions of identity. In her video entitled *Tango for Fish* (1992), the twin couples acting in the video represent a real duplication of the body, and are somehow a substitute for the feasible technological duplication of the images in the video medium.

For example, the works of Peter Vezjak/Laibach, Borghesia, or the Hard Cord Punk Collective, due to their controversial political nature and borderline visuality, could hardly be considered to belong to only one category or genre. Rok Sieberer, one of the members of the tribal hard core punk community in Ljubljana—Hard Cord Punk Collective— challenged, to an almost absurd degree, the aesthetic and technical possibilities of VHS video technology in his video work *Crisis*. Sieberer created a frenetic video totality using the replay mode, mixing it with an almost neurotic TV zapping. In this work, two technological modes were employed: replay, which allows an almost intimate interactive research of the electronic image at home, and zapping, a new interactive modus for the viewers of mass-produced television pictures. *Crisis* is a crisis of genuine information, and the desperate longing for it, while it is only possible to achieve the fulfillment of the gaze and its symbolic voyeuristic orgasm with the information by constant (auto-) replaying, zapping, and rerecording instead.

In spite of the production gap, especially in the context of the post-1991 "war" in Slovenia (which took place for 10 days in June 1991 against the tanks of the Yugoslav government) and the post-independence economic crisis (Slovenia became an independent state in June 1991), thanks to the richness of strategies for visualization and narration, video art can be viewed as constituting an autonomous paradigm within art in Slovenia, a paradigm that may be defined and understood as a new economy of seeing.

Documentary video projects (realized by amateurs with VHS equipment, and by independent film and video groups with professional video equipment) captured different periods of political and social struggle in Slovenia: the "Trial of the Four" in 1988; the 10-day war in Slovenia in 1991 against the Federal Yugoslav Army; and protests against the attempt to abolish abortion rights in Slovenia at the end of 1991, following Slovenia's independence.

These nonprofessional documentary videos, often nonstylized and nonnarrative, also enable us to make a comparison with national television's interpretations of those same events and to relocate the responsibility of national mass media for particular versions of history. Within this context, video offers "authentic" historical, emotional, artistic, and political views on events, conditions, bodies, practices, languages, and topics, narrated through the perspective of its authors. Our knowledge is not only based on what we see, but also on what we can render visible.

DEMOCRATIZATION OF SLOVENIA: THE IMPACT OF THE NEW CIVIL SOCIETY ON VISUAL PRACTICE

The 1990s, with the democratization of the Slovene political spaces, are witnessing new forms of investigative journalism, which utilize documentary video material. In the 1990s, Jasna Hribernik, in collaboration with Peter Zobec and Studio Ljubljana/TV Slovenia, produced extremely provocative and critical documentary videos about the events in the ex-Soviet Union. The documentaries focus on Ukrainian underground art, culture, and politics, and were shot in Kiev and its surroundings in May 1991. These "video-tales" tell the story of Lenin's 273 coats, despite the intolerable poverty around him; about God, parapsychology, and revolution; and about gray faces, decaying cities, and the deformed human and animal fetuses five years after the Chernobyl nuclear catastrophe. We see the conscious disruption of both picture and text. The use of nonsense in the story, and in the process of editing, refuses to generate the illusion of reality. Similar concepts are raised in Hribernik's video artworks. Hribernik selects, records, and isolates actors, spaces, and objects, then slows them down (although throughout the video, we are impressed by the image of a timer). The result is a chronology of time that connects (paradoxically speaking) only spaces, even empty ones that oppose each other.

Thus, historically, from the mid-1980s into the 1990s, video films are not merely a means of expression, but also a method of documenting political events, despite the mass media usage of video equipment as surveillance in airports, banks, shops, on the streets, and even in toilets. Here, I refer to the supervisory episodes of installing video cameras in public toilets, where gay sexual activity was suspected. This situation is not only reserved for Eastern European State authorities, as the West does not lag behind in these matters. I refer here to similar events that happened in the 1980s in West Germany. In the 1980s, important documents about nonofficial art and cultural productions were preserved with the aid of VHS video equipment.

Establishing a new style of visual "writing" with video was a result of the conscious visual reconfiguration of an "original" socialist alternative cultural structure and civic society. This resulted in innumerable "explosive" contrasts and a series of "technical imperfections" (as I have termed them), which comprehend the outer and inner, sexual and mental, order and disorder, conceptual and political, original and recycled space and time. Furthermore, from such a point of view, we can detect and generalize two strategies of visualization in the video medium, which reflect two territories (elaborated in detail below): First, the body in connection with sexuality, and the social and historical corpus of the film and television medium and, second, history in connection with politics. These strategies can also be viewed as two fundamental approaches to the aesthetics of the video medium in Eastern Europe in general.

First, the 1980s in Yugoslavia witnessed the oversexualization of the video medium. This was not only a process of art/political reflexivity of the much-repressed sexuality under socialism and Communism, but the process of distancing and disassociating the video medium from its sisters: film and television. Throughout Eastern Europe, severe measures were introduced against homosexuals, whereby most were punished by law and imprisoned as criminals, or detained in psychiatric institutions. In the ex-Yugoslav territory, the laws banning homosexuality differed from republic to republic. There was a legal penalty for being a homosexual in Serbia, Bosnia-Herzegovina, Macedonia, and Montenegro. In Slovenia and Croatia, there was no legal ban of homosexuality; yet, they were blamed and marginalized in the mass media and in public. All the other "deviant" sexual orientations—transsexuals, cross-dressers, and transvestites—were not present (invisible?) in public life, nor discussed, except in a medical context.

Second, this process was carried out with the externalization of sexuality that had been adopted from the underground film tradition of Rainer Werner Fassbinder, Rosa Von Praunheim, Andy Warhol, and others, whose films were shown in the underground venues of Ljubljana in the 1980s. The externalization of sexuality took the form of overtly staged pornography and the gender confusion ("gender-bending") of gay, lesbian, and transvestite sexual attitudes. It was a process that can be simply explained: the sexual and civil rights stereotypes and prototypes were not only consumed in and by the underground, but immediately performed. In front of a VHS camera, in private rooms and bedrooms, a status of a political positioning of the sexual and social par excellence was acquired. In these works, the masquerade of reappropriation ensured not only the simple question of the formation of the identity of the artists or of the underground community, but also the process of negotiation to produce continually ambiguous and unbalanced situations and identities. Consider the video works in the beginning of the 1980s by the Slovenian groups Meje Kontrole and Borghesia.

The acquired hybrid and nonheterosexual positioning of sexuality, in the context of the remarkably impermeable gender boundaries of Communist Eastern Europe, was a way of overtly politicizing the sexual in socialism and Communism and fighting for civil rights. These processes of oversexualization, which can now be perceived as contemporary gender politics, are still performed in the 1990s, following the fall of the Berlin Wall, in all the other ex-socialist countries (for example, artists Mare Tralla [Estonia] and Andrei Ventslova [St. Petersburg, Russia]). Aesthetic strategies detectable in video art production in Slovenia in the 1980s, before the fall of the Berlin Wall, are found today in the works of other Eastern European artists. For example, Mare Tralla (b. 1967), a young Estonian video artist with a "new-age" image, has already aroused interest and rejection in Estonian society. She calls herself a "disgusting girl," and this is how she presents herself and her works before the international audience. In her short Hi-8 video work, Toy (1995), several Estonian girls appear, performing a home striptease in front of the camera. The girls, fat with cellulite, show themselves as almost totally transparent objects. The post-post-socialist bodies without makeup seem to function as subversive mirror images of the female body in the industrialized, post-modernist West, camouflaged by mass media and constantly redesigned. The works from the 1990s by Andrei Ventslova, a video artist from St. Petersburg, recreate stories about homosexuals; he juxtaposed images about homosexuals with heterosexual stereotypes, using elements of burlesque theater, as well as synchronized voices and lip-synching, similar to the foreign-language emissions on State Russian and Polish TV. Ventslova uses VHS nonprofessional equipment, and performs himself in his video works, acting in front of a still camera. His works remind us of the aesthetic developed a decade earlier in Ljubljana's alternative, or subculture, video and art scene.

In the 1980s, we also find several video projects that were created by copying, in most cases, the political broadcasts of the national television network. These copied sequences were then reedited and reinterpreted, taking into consideration the internal replay logic of the video medium. Selected television sequences on political events were combined with music, and reedited in vertiginous rhythmic repetitive works. Consider the video/film works by the Slovenian groups Borghesia and Laibach, and by Slovenian artist Peter Vezjak, as well as by Hungarian artist András Solyom. This resulted in an almost obscene uncovering of the internal mechanism of the everyday Communist political speeches and doctrine, which itself was based on the ritual of constant repetition. The thoroughly replayed and reedited political speeches began to reveal their internal repetitive logic; the shorter and shorter units of the recut political speech started to function as a pornographic act, which put the viewer in a position similar to that of a peep show. The discourse of the orderly politician was transformed through technology into an inarticulate striptease. Thus, a specific syncretism was produced, through which it was possible to detect similarities between different, until then incompatible, levels and expressions. This started to displace differences, not only between these incompatible levels and expressions, but also within them.

From this, we can formulate a thesis that in some cases video art took the position of the "B-movie" under post-socialism. We can also interpret these video works as kitsch, grotesque, absurd video films, impregnated with sex, politics, and rock 'n roll, similar to the "B-movies" or underground cinema of the West. This provides the video medium in the East with an additional historic dimension.

RENAMING AND RECLAIMING SLOVENE HISTORY

The functioning of socialist societies involved a painful recourse to a psychotic discourse, in an attempt to neutralize the side effects of pertinent interpretations and productions through hiding, masking, and renaming history. Recent political and social shifts represent a desire to retake possession of Slovene history. In the Slovene "post-war" period (post-1991), history has begun to play a starring role in art and culture, not as a means of retaking possession of the history of socialism (as deformed as it was), but in an effort to reject the blind retaliation, nationalism, and racism that can rise out of the "ruins of war." The effect of this phase of Slovene history on video is akin to an "interior multiculturalism" with international resonances. Through the video process of reappropriation and recycling of different histories and cultures, a multicultural condition has been constructed. The result of such procedures is the development of an imagery, which refers neither to the past nor the present, but to a potential time, somewhere between certainty and potentiality. The video image presents a persistent searching for the condensed point, which is simultaneously the past and the present. It is for this reason that one may define video art as providing an alternative history, which gathers the names and faces of forgotten or discarded cultures. It redefines their place inside a contemporary construction of power relations, which also feeds back to the status of video itself.

From this point, we can derive some significant generalizations about the status of video in Eastern Europe, with reference to the "technological switch of history." It is possible to draw a thesis that with the internal technological mode of functioning of the video medium, the replay in particular, video gained a new political context in the East. In the West, replay gained a mass presence in bedrooms and kitchens, where it is used for the repetitive performance of blockbuster films, porn films, and/or personal documentation. With the video replay in the East, on the other hand, we are witnesses to a process of detailed deconstruction and reconstruction of past history. Consider the video works of Hungarian artists Ildikó Enyedi and András Solyom, of Hungarian/Romanian artist Csilla Konczei, and the group SUBREAL, and of Polish artist Grzegorz Krolikiewicz.

Moreover, it is possible to say that video, via the technological process of encrustation, is developing a new destiny for historical documentary material. In the so-called post-socialist countries, video has, at the end of the century, developed into a specific vanishing mediator between history and the spectator in front of the television screen. As the third eye, video is enabling us to read history, to see through the surface of the film image, and possibly, to perceive the future. Consider the video works by the Slovenian artists Mirko Simić and Marko Peljhan/Brian Springer (a Slovenian/U.S. collaboration), Polish artist Jozef Robakowski, and Hungarian artist András Solyom. This is possible to understand in a literal, though twisted way, as the video blue-box system allows another image to be encrusted, or synthesized, through digitally produced blue holes in a single frame. Though both images are on the surface, the verité behind the image on the surface depends, metaphorically speaking, on the content of the image that will be inserted into the empty blue hole. The depth is, therefore, an effect of the content of the synthesized image, and not of the technological process itself.

Despite some rumors or prevailing opinions that it is not politically correct to distinguish between Western and Eastern Europe, it appears that new video productions in the 1990s in Eastern Europe are developing even more radically the strategies of visualization described a decade ago in the ex-Yugoslav territory, and, more specifically, in Slovenia. This refers to the Russian aesthetic and philosophical paradigm of 1990s contemporenaiety, coined in the 1980s as "Necrorealism." The nonmainstream video artworks in the East may be illustrated, for example, through the works of the Hungarian/Romanian video artist Csilla Konczei (b. 1963). In the Ceaucescu era, Konczei worked as an editor for Romanian TV; after the Romanian "TV revolution," she founded a VHS studio with some friends. In her video work *Abstract Knowledge*, she discusses the "third totalitarian eye"—the eye of the Romanian secret police: the Seguritate. Seguritate was, so to speak, present in every home, and made itself felt to every Romanian citizen, to the point of being almost an omnivoyeur, if a psychotic one.

TOWARD A THEORY OF THE SPECIFIC POSITION OF VIDEO IN THE NEW EUROPE

Not so long ago, I read that an electronic calculator can serve a capitalist as well as a post-socialist "world." Then why have I chosen such an ideological subtitle? Modern theories, which currently attempt to convince us that we are living in the best of all possible worlds, would provoke a similar question. Why can't we simply talk about ideology-free electronic instruments? I will try to address this dilemma and conclude by proposing a thesis with which to define how video and the electronic media in the territory once known as Eastern Europe can function as a system, or a model and a paradigm (Gržinić, 1996, 1997). This thesis will hopefully contribute to a future theory, concerning a critical and social discourse surrounding the new electronic art media condition in Eastern Europe, that will allow us to surpass the often superficial, romantic (sometimes not even specific) (hi)story-telling about the state of Eastern European art's involvement with electronic media. Hence, this rethinking of the Eastern European media condition does not end with the fall of the Berlin Wall. The Eastern European media condition is a tactic and a practice, and not a legal/political contract, nor a historical accident.

Interpretations attempting merely to explicate the national or ethnic media identity in the East miss, or consciously hide, the power structures lying beneath this supposedly innocent (and mostly Western) cultural pluralistic inquiry (or should I say, "Western tourism"?) (Fisher, 1996).

This "tourism," which defines the relation of inquiry practiced by Western culture in non-Western cultural spheres, masks the economic and political power relations inherent in such spheres. Here, according to Jean Fisher, we cannot talk about equality, since choice, primary discourse, and economic viability remain in the hands of the West.

Thus, I propose we enter a more philosophical dialogue by questioning the deep structures of "East" European relations with reality itself, and the immense role of the "media" and visual languages within such an inquiry. To clarify, one must ask what motivates the primary inquiry or interest in most instances of Western cultural tourism to the East. Such tourism is an examination of the "East," which focuses on the condition of human rights and the principles of autonomy, equality, and dignity, which have emerged in the Western world, or, more precisely, an examination of the regularity with which these rights are practiced and sustained in the "East." We must bluntly ask not only if these principles of autonomy, freedom, and humanity contain a special political, post-colonial interest for the West, with regard to the rest of the world, but importantly, we must ask whether these principles are still valuable. NO, they are not! We cannot conceive of a future today, for example, if we reflect on the war in Bosnia-Herzegovina, by adhering to these principles. The war in Bosnia-Herzegovina has, in my opinion, put into question the credibility of all the fundamental civil legislative relations in the world in which we live—not only the paradigm of the future, but the elementary supposition of humanism and the rhetoric of freedom, humanity, and civil rights developed in the industrialized Western world. Above all, this war raised a number of questions with regard to the theories of mass media, and the technology of new/old communications (radio-TV-satellite communications). For this reason, it not only called into question the role of the televised and printed information in (new) war strategies (in ascertaining the differences between wars before and after the invention of television), but also the methods of the redistribution of information in a technologically developed environment (the war in Bosnia-Herzegovina was/is taking place in Europe!). Consider the video documentaries and film/video works by the Bosnian directors Ademir Kenović, Mirza Idrizović, Zlatko Lavanić, and Srdjan Vuletić. This war could then be, speaking cynically, the first contribution of the ex-Yugoslavian territory, or, generally speaking, of the East European territory (not to forget Chechnya and the Kurds!) toward the theoretical conceptualization of the media condition in the West.

As Heinz Kimmerle (1996) stated, we are not after the end of modernity, but at its end. The dilemma, as Jean Fisher (1996) claimed, still remains: How does one express his/her worldview, with all the contradictory cultural inflections that inform it, without betraying his/her historical or geographical specificity, and without being caught in the web of signs that are all too consumable as mere exotic commodities? Perhaps one needs to think of cultural expression not only on the superficial level of the sign, but in terms of concept and deep structure: to consider a work's media condition through internal–external paths, and to define what governs different aesthetic media strategies.

NEW MEDIA IN THE "POST-SOCIALIST EUROPEAN PARADIGM"

This chapter does not seek to capitalize upon the reminiscence for a Western reader entitled "How We Survived Communism and Laughed," as writer Slavenka Drakulić (1993) formulated it. It is an attempt to show that all the big notions and goals of Western democracy, such as freedom and humanity, must be perceived in relation to the fall of socialism, and in relation, as I already stated, to the war within the territory of ex-Yugoslavia.

In this respect, Eastern Europe should be understood as a symptom (in a strictly psychoanalytical way) of the West, exposing to the West its proper internal borders. The same symptomatic reading can be applied to the territory of the new media in the East. The brutal, sexually perverse, and dehumanized form and content of the messages and media structures generated in and throughout Eastern Europe functioned as an inversed picture of what is yet to come in the media by the year 2000. Consider the video works by Russian artist Aleksandar Kuprin, Hungarians Gábor Bódy and Antal Lux, and Romanian artist Bogdan-Christian Dragan. I would like to add a small remark here, that this reverse picture might be as well-illustrated by the English commercial film *Trainspotting* (Boyle, 1996).

I wrote in the first part of this chapter that desire, obscenity, pornography, politics, and history appropriated the video medium in the East in the 1980s. It lost its innocence, becoming an index of time and subjective politics. The same happened in Russia, if we recall the spiritual state of Russia following the 1980s crackdown; according to Slavoj Žižek, the atmosphere was/is the atmosphere of pure, mystical spirituality, of the violent denial of corporeality on the one hand, accompanied by an obsession with pornography and sexual perversion on the other (see, for example, Žižek, 1991, 1993). Cynically speaking, the "perfect Western Europe" will have to include and subsume into its perfect image the "imperfect East." Consider the video works of Russian artist Oleg Kulik. In other words, it is as if the "perfect" itself needs the "imperfect" in order to assert itself. Such an interrogation is necessary because the

Enlightenment paradigm has fallen apart. This is also due, on the one hand, to the changed relations between the nation-state, citizenship and corporate power, and on the other, due to the effects of communications and computerised technology (see, for example, Žižek, 1985).

Even while thinkers such as Foucault (1982, 1984) and Deleuze and Guattari (1972) have offered a differentiated view of the workings of power, it is interesting to see that some aspects of the political crisis of postmodernism are linked to the ostensible impossibility of an alternative working of power (Asdam, 1995). Foucault differentiates between power relations, which in principle are reversible, and the domination of situations, which are one-sided, rigid, and marked by force. Wilhem Schmid (1995) argued that this differentiation between power relations and the situation of domination is significant, since it clarifies what is important for the individual in the art of living: the possibility of bringing a reversal of power relations into play. As long as this reversal is possible in principle, our concern is with the game of power, and not only with the condition of domination. Marxism never achieved this distinction between relations of domination and power relations. As a result, it offered only a symmetrical reversal of authority in political practice, which laid down a renewed, rigid order. Significantly, whenever an ambitious history of power is written, the aspect of individual power, and that which comes from the merging of individuals (such as citizens' initiatives and social movements), is systematically neglected (Schmid, 1995). Transposing this to the media art video situation in the East, we can claim that it is not only possible to establish such a history, but, if we want to draw upon it, we must establish it in such a way. The video medium in the East tries to subvert the very concept of politics. What it entails is a subversion of the body politic. The notion of (individual) politics, and of the politics of the medium in the East, goes beyond the mere question of resistance. Consider the works of Hungarian artist Ildikó Enyedi, and Croatian artists Dalibor Martinis and Sanja Iveković. Changes and new cultural traditions originating in Eastern Europe during the era of "real" socialism and prior to it—including cultural strategies/tactics and those of civil movements—should be taken into consideration when attempting to define a "new" European culture as a whole in the 1990s and 2000s.

One of the main topoi in new media is the problem of simulation, while the other is the speed of information exchange. The extreme velocity of communication leaves no time, according to Burghart Schmidt (1995), for controlling, or even thinking, about the information. The way of dealing with the structure of the video image, and with its political and sexual topics in Eastern Europe, is to develop strategies for slowing down the streams of communication and information though the creation of new values, meaning, and perspectives on information. Consider the works of Slovenian artists Jasna Hribernik, Marko Košnik, and Ema Kugler, Croatian artist Milan Bukovac, Polish artist Barbara Konopka, Hungarian artists Gusztáv Hámos and István Kantor, and Yugoslav-Hungarian artist Balint Szombathy.

I have tried to emphasize the key problem of how to maintain in contemporary international circumstances specific cultural contexts and avoid standardization, and to discover some key facts concerning the reflection of Eastern-European systems and specific historical, social, political, cultural, and artistic media and new technology experiences that were molded within these systems. Last but not least, I tried to define and include the *societas civilis* in it, so to speak, I tried to define and include "those citizens" or better to say, those civil forces (the subculture movement, media artists, intellectuals, gays, lesbians, and so on) who participated in the constructing and sharing of civic politics through new technology and electronic media. All these gave as the coordinates of a condition that, analogous to a great, postmodernist syntagm; I can name as "the post-socialist European paradigm."

It is quite telling that Eastern Europe would like to be perceived not only as an image, but also as an articulated actor of this world. The new actors that have emerged in Eastern Europe since 1991—if I refer to this artificially imposed year that today denotes without exception *le passage a l'acte* toward freedom and democracy—do not want to simply adopt the mask of either self or others, offered by previously dominant narratives of identity and politics. "They" ("we") insist on difference—a critical difference within and not as a special classification method marking the process of grounding differences, such as apartheid, as T. M. Trinh (1989) would say. The question of who is permitted to write the history of art, culture, and politics in the area once known as Eastern Europe has to be posed, along with the questions of how and when.

The simplified version of equilibrium between the East and the West, which sought an identification of the East with the West, is no longer possible. What we shall propose for the future is probably a restructuring of the East, which will undergo different and especially more profound changes than the West. This means to speak in favor of the materialization of "the post-socialist European paradigm" and in favor of strengthening and reformation of the civic discourse through the formation of necessary technological infrastructures, two-way communication, and independent data of information and interpretation.

ACKNOWLEDGMENT

The author thanks Ms. Adele Eisenstein for her careful language revision of this chapter.

REFERENCES

Asdam, K. H. (1995). The smallest deviation, the minimum excess. In H. Paetzold & N. Cacinovic (Eds.), *Contemporary culture and aesthetics* (pp. 5–15). Maastricht, Netherlands: Department of Theory, Jan van Eyck Akademie.

Boyle, D. (Director), & Macdonald, A. (Producer). (1996). *Trainspotting* [Film]. Available: Miramax.

Deleuze, G., & Guattari, F. (1972). *Anti-Oedipe*. Paris: Les Éditions de Minuit.

Drakulić, S. (1993). *How we survived Communism and even laughed*. New York: Harper.

Erjavec, A., & Gržinić, M. (1991). *Ljubljana, Ljubljana*. Ljubljana, Slovenia: Mladinska knjiga.

Fisher, J. (1996). The syncretic turn. In H. Paetzold & N. Čačinović (Eds.), *Contemporary culture and aesthetics* (pp. 65–74). Maastricht, Netherlands: Department of Theory, Jan van Eyck Akademie.

Foucault, M. (1982). *The archeology of knowledge*. New York: Pantheon.

Foucault, M. (1984). *The Foucault reader*. New York: Pantheon.

Gržinić, M. (1992). Video from Slovenia *Variant, 11*, 22–26.

Gržinić, M. (1993a). Video from Slovenia. In *Ostranenie* catalogue (pp. 183–186). Dessau, Germany: Bauhaus.

Gržinić, M. (1993b). *Art and culture in the 80's: The Slovenian case*. Koper, Slovenia: Loža Gallery.

Gržinić, M. (1995). Specific strategies in Slovene video art production in the present post-socialist period. In N. Czegledy (Ed.), *Insight media art from the middle of Europe* (pp. 20–28). Toronto: YYZ ARTISTS' OUTLET.

Gržinić, M. (1996). *Zur Situation der Medienkust in Slowenien und Ex- Yugoslawien* [Online]. Available: http://www.heise.de/tp [1996, June 22].

Gržinić, M. (1997). Video art in Slovenia and the territory of ex-Yugoslavia, or toward an electronic art media theory in Eastern Europe. *Mute, 7*, 3–4.

Hebdige, D. (1979). *Subculture: The meaning of style*. London: Routledge.

Kimmerle, H. (1996). Western philosophy and other cultures. In H. Paetzold & N. Čačinović (Eds.), *Contemporary culture and aesthetics* (pp. 15–26). Maastricht, Netherlands: Department of Theory, Jan van Eyck Akademie.

Schmid, W. (1995). Politics of the art of living with reference to Michel Foucault. In H. Paetzold & N. Čačinović (Eds.), *Contemporary culture and aesthetics* (pp. 15–23). Maastricht, Netherlands: Department of Theory, Jan van Eyck Akademie.

Schmidt, B. (1995). *The rest is utopian fiction: Art as showing of information, against pure information in acceleration*. In H. Paetzold & N. Čačinović (Eds.), *Con-*

temporary culture and aesthetics (pp. 37–41). Maastricht, Netherlands: Department of Theory, Jan van Eyck Akademie.

Trinh, T. M. (1989). *Woman, native, other: Writing post-coloniality and feminism.* Bloomington, IN: Indiana University Press.

Žižek, S. (1985). *Problemi teorije fetišizma.* Ljubljana, Slovenia: DDU Univerzum.

Žižek, S. (1991). *Looking awry: An introduction to Jacques Lacan through popular culture.* Cambridge, MA: MIT Press.

Žižek, S. (1993). *Tarrying with the negative.* Durham, NC: Duke University Press.

chapter 12

Building Global Community: U.S.–Russian Cybernetic Discourse on "Friends and Partners"

Margot Emery
Benjamin J. Bates
University of Tennessee

W riting in the preface of a volume of civic discourse analysis, Jean Bethke Elshtain makes the fundamental point that "words matter" (Elshtain, 1990). "The words with which we characterize our daily lives matter" including those that "live within, through, and alongside our daily existence" (p. xi). In 1993, Natasha Bulashova of Pushchino, Russia, and Greg Cole of Knoxville, Tennessee, met online and realized through their own discourse the power and value that words about everyday life could have in bridging the gap of understanding between citizens of Russia and the United States.

Although the World Wide Web was in its infancy, the two computer scientists envisioned creating an online center of information resources and community exchange that would integrate text and multimedia and operate in a distributed manner in which control and development were shared among a globally dispersed network of volunteer contributors. Using the computing facilities at the University of Tennessee, Knoxville, where Cole was based, the two launched "Friends and Partners" on January 19, 1994. Their idea caught fire, fusing with the new information technology and its new communication patterns and a world still sorting itself out in the wake of the sudden dissolution of the Soviet Union. In the first 24 hours, the initiative's server received 7,000 accesses of information from people around the world. By the end of the week, 300 people in 25 countries had signed up for its daily news distribution. Presently the initiative is still growing, with listservs that reach 9,000 subscribers, web servers that host over three gigabytes of material and, in the U.S., support more than 5 million Internet transactions a month with additional sizeable volume occurring on mirrored servers in Pushchino and Moscow—parameters that indicate the extent to which the initiative continues to engage people worldwide.

This chapter explores the development and social construction of "Friends and Partners," the forms of civic discourse it supports, and the implications they hold for transregional communication. As a foundation for that discussion, the effects of networking technology and its social uses on global communications flows are examined, as are the Internet's differing models of development in Russia and the U.S.

THE INFLUENCE OF COMMUNICATION STRUCTURES

Networks, more than most technologies, serve as barometers of underlying infrastructure, and their development reflects the condition of an array of connected factors, among them the availability of computer systems, trained users, and local and long distance telecommunications systems (Snyder, 1993). In a similar manner, the communication that flows across computer networks is affected by structural aspects of the network, the range of information technologies participants are able to choose from to conduct an exchange, and inherent cultural factors existing among sets of users that influence the messages they exchange (Gee, 1997). When considered at the aggregate level, these factors contribute to the structure of communications systems, influencing the individual and social impacts that the Internet and other technologies can have.

From the basic assumption of Marxist and criticalist theories that the ruling class constructs media structures to help maintain social control to McLuhan's famous line that "the medium is the message," there has been an indirect acknowledgment that the structure of media systems can have broad social impacts. Perhaps the most direct statement of that relationship can be found in Harold Innis's *Empire and Communications* (1972). In that work, Innis argued that the development and utilization of new media could be linked to the rise and fall of empires. Specifically, Innis (1964, 1972) argued that the structure of communication systems contained certain "biases"—that they promoted certain patterns of use and control by dominant groups. As new media systems came to predominate within a culture, their rise undermined previous power relationships and brought forth the potential for new groups of users to come to power through their ability to use and control the new medium and through their ability to take advantage of the changing social and information structures and relationships. With new media came new structures, new patterns of use and control, and, perhaps, new dominant groups.

A clearer statement of the mechanisms of how communication system structures can have broad social impacts can be found in Bates's (1993) "access, bias, control" model. This model argues, based on a synthesis of critical and social scientific theories of social effects, that the structure and operations of communication systems can have broad social effects through the operation of one or more of three basic mechanisms. The access mechanism is based on the notion that some social impacts come from a structure's inherent capacity to limit access to the communication system. The bias mechanism argues that structural factors can exert influence by favoring certain types of content, or certain uses of the communication system. The control mechanism examines the structural factors allowing or regulating the ability of outside groups to exert control of all types on the communication system, and through that control have influence.

These influences work, in essence, by helping to define and delimit relationships between various sets of users of the communication system. The approach is neither determinative nor definitive; rather, it attempts to provide a mechanism for examining patterns and relationships, both in the communication system and within the social systems that utilize them.

The Internet was developed in the U.S. as a test system for a cooperative, multisystem communications network, capable of supporting a wide range of communication uses and able to overcome system failures through a variety of routing mechanisms and paths. Its development in the U.S. and USSR illustrates the impacts access, bias, and control can exert on developing communications structures and, in turn, the dynamic social impacts that can be achieved when an inherently open technology collides with a constrictive political structure.

SOVIET NETWORKING AND THE RISE OF THE RUSSIAN INTERNET

Computer networks in the USSR and U.S. followed fundamentally different paths of development from the outset, which affected both the distinct uses, and user bases, of the networks in each nation.

In the U.S., network development was, at least initially, centralized and supported by the deep pockets of the Department of Defense. Arpanet began in 1969 as a research tool and the first wide-area network, and its development in the 1970s followed linear paths. At the same time, however, state and local educational networks were rising, and wide- and local-area networks were growing in the business sector. The parallel and distributed nature of this development allowed network connections, capacity, content, and social understanding of the technology to evolve simultaneously among significant clusters of the population, encompassing education, research, business, and even home users, who were actively linking their personal computers to a growing array of bulletin board systems (BBSs) and commercial networks. By the early 1990s, these diverse streams of development were converging on the Internet, aided by the emergence of Internet service providers (ISPs), increasingly affordable computer technology, and the privatization of the NSF backbone in 1995, which paved the way for electronic commerce on the Internet.

In the U.S., then, the Internet began as a medium for the military and academics in defense-related sciences, then expanded to include researchers and educators in other disciplines and the computer industry as a whole. Business and commerce followed, along with thousands of home users, each encouraging adoption by the other. This expansion was promoted by the designed structure of the Internet: a machine-independent, distributed network structure that facilitated access and limited control. This let users discover and define their own uses, moving the Internet away from its early military focus. And when the basic network was privatized in 1995, it removed the previous anti-commercial content bias, allowing for a similarly rapid expansion in business use and the emergence of e-commerce as a driving force in Internet development. In a similar way, the development of the HTML Web standards expanded the previous system access restrictions by reducing Internet literacy requirements, opening up the way for widespread public and home use. The basic designed structure of the Internet favors continued expansion of both users and uses and the inevitable globalization of communication, which, in itself, brings economic and political consequences (Pool, 1983).

In Central and Eastern Europe, the network was the early province of academics and dissidents, and it moved quickly from there to adoption for financial and business use. Many of the network developers made the leap as well, using the network as a tool for enterprise as they adapted to the political and economic changes underway in the late 1980s (Dyson, 1996). In the Soviet Union, research and commercial networks developed together and, until 1993, largely without any governmental support or funding (Platonov, 1994; Snyder, 1993; Snyder, Jarmoszko, & Goodman, 1991). And unlike the U.S., where networked computing was initially seen as a novelty (Reynolds & Postel, 1987), in the USSR, benefits of computer exchange were immediately obvious to everyone: In a sprawling region struggling with a broken and outmoded telecommunications system, unreliable posts, and a political system that discouraged open communication, the ability to send basic e-mail and files by computer from one city to another seemed like a miracle (Dyson, 1996; Lawton, 1993).

By the mid-1980s, a number of local- and wide-area computer networks were operating in the Soviet Union, the most significant at the Kurchatov Institute of Atomic Energy in northwestern Moscow, which used a Russian version of the UNIX operating system called Demos to link computers in a number of academic cities, including Leningrad, Novosibirsk, and Kyiv (Dyson, 1996). Its first connection to the West was through the Institute for Automated Systems (VNIIPAS) to a sister institute in Vienna and, by the summer of 1990, Kurchatov had formed a commercial service cooperative called Relcom and achieved connectivity to the Internet through a dial-up Usenet connection to a node in Helsinki (Lakhman, 1997a; Press, 1992). The system operator agreed to forward and receive messages between the Soviet Union. His activity was informally accepted by the European Internet hierarchy, EUnet, and in this way the USSR's connectivity became unofficially subsidized (Dyson, 1996). That same year, VNIIPAS joined with a Western corporation to create the first Internet provider in the Soviet Union, Sovam Teleport, while another Western-backed effort, GlasNet, was linking up nonprofit organizations. Meanwhile, connectivity to FidoNet, the worldwide network of BBSs, was also growing.

When the political tumult of 1991 began, the computer networks became pivotal channels of communication, both within the disintegrating USSR and with the West. In August, hard-line leaders attempting a coup on Soviet President Mikhail Gorbachev cracked down on media, but did not anticipate that the Russian networks could act as a mass medium (Lawton, 1993). What followed was a world lesson in the power of the new information technologies of fax machines and networks. Faxes were deployed both by Soviets and Westerners alike. The networks, through their ability to broadcast messages to groups as well as individuals, proved even more powerful. In messages to the Usenet newsgroup talk.politics.soviet, Relcom users announced the coup and continued throughout it to share news and reply to queries from the West. The Demos network routinely began posting English-language translations of protests and decrees by Russian President Boris Yeltsin and alerted world media to their availability (Press, 1992). Information from the West flowed across the same channels, much of it shared by everyday citizens, among them a group of sixth-grade schoolchildren in Salt Lake City, Utah, who downloaded news reports about world reaction to the coup and transmitted them to their keypals in Moscow, who quickly translated the reports into Russian and handed out copies to protestors in the streets (McCarty, 1995).

Arguably the most dramatic example of the power of the networked communication occurred on GlasNet, where news of the arrest and beating of three prominent Russian labor leaders was shared among GlasNet users. The wife of one of the detained men used the network to alert the deputy head of Russia's major labor confederation, who used the network to launch an international telephone campaign targeting the police station where the men were held. Within 30 minutes, calls from Japan, San Francisco, and other points around the world began flooding the switchboard. Witnesses reported that police, stunned and confused by the calls, first claimed the men had been freed and then, as pressure continued, released the three leaders along with several other political detainees (Leslie, 1994). The Internet was credited with saving their lives, and some made a similar claim regarding Gorbachev (Press, 1991).

This power of computer networks to subvert authoritarian control was not unanticipated. Social theorist Ithiel de Sola Pool (1983) foresaw these impacts almost a decade earlier, writing of the liberalizing effects of new information technologies. Stonier (1983) focused on the impacts of new information technologies on the Soviet Union and the Eastern bloc, suggesting specifically that the rise of "an extensive, powerful, yet leaky communication network" (p. 144) was driving democratization and leading to social upheaval. And in the summer of 1990, Gorbachev himself spoke of the implications of the new technologies in an address at Stanford University:

> We are witnessing a revolution of international relations toward increasingly open and mass-scale communication. And this greatly increases the role of creative and positive policies. But equally, it raises the price of mistakes—the price we must pay for adherence to outdated dogmas, routine and old thinking. (qtd. in Press, 1992, p. 1)

Through their access to the network, its bias for freedom, and inherent ability to overcome controls, Russian citizens found power through the Internet and the ability to communicate in structures that were previously unknown in the Soviet Union. Their ability to use the network to overcome a broken telecommunications system and other, more systemic barriers to communication and information exchange in Russia, was viewed as integral in the period following the coup and ensuing collapse of the Soviet Union, as Russia worked to establish a market economy and stabilize its social systems.

Early in the reconstruction period, a number of outside organizations provided grants and equipment to aid network expansion, most prominently the Hungarian-born philanthropist George Soros and his various organizations, which supported individual wiring efforts and later launched an ambitious $130 million effort in partnership with the Russian government to establish 33 university Internet centers throughout Russia by the year 2001 (Lakhman, 1997b). The Carnegie Foundation and the International Research and Exchanges Board (IREX) stepped forward to provide $100,000 in funding before the fall of the USSR to establish a connection to the European EARN network. These and dozens of other nongovernmental organizations, or NGOs, assisted in commercial and academic network expansion.

By 1994, it was generally understood that network development needed coordination. NATO hosted an Advanced Networking Workshop focused on Russia that involved 100 leading specialists in networking in Russia and the NIS in three days of assessment of issues and needs. Among the concerns cited were how to cooperatively carry commercial and educational/research content, strategies to work with NGOs in attracting grants and providing training and support, and, as always, how to address and work within the inherent problems of Russia's telecommunications system (*Proceedings of NATO*, 1994).

Western observers worried about other effects. Unlike the U.S., where the Internet was bringing together growing sectors of society in online exchanges and communities, in Russia, access to the network appeared to be escalating the divide between an increasingly elite business-research-academic core and the remainder of the population (Snyder, 1993). Many foundations recognized the dangers apparent in this gap and began work to broaden connectivity to civic organizations, local governments, and other social institutions, and to pursue wiring and other forms of connection for regions outside Russia's core cities.

The Russification of the Web, which supported use of Cyrillic fonts, also served as an aid in expanding access and use of the network, particularly in content development of Russian-specific pages. By 1997, Russian-language indexing and search engines were in operation, and some Russian web developers were saying they developed web pages only in Russian (Lakhman, 1997a)—a development that paralleled efforts in other countries to adapt the strongly Western-dominated conventions and structures of Internet technology for non-Western uses (Somogyi, 1996).

By 1996, Relcom had grown into a major commercial carrier with an estimated base of 300,000 customers and connections in more than 100

Russian cities (Voiskounsky, 1998). The Russian Non-Profit Center for Internet Technologies estimated 500,000 Russians had e-mail access in 1996 out of a total population of 150 million, with only 25,000 to 50,000 able to access a full range of Internet services (Fick, 1996). As of December 1998, the center listed 180,000 hosts in Russia with access by 1.5 million users, including 250,000 with home Internet access, 300 Internet service providers, and a count of 26,000 online information resources in Russian (Russian Non-Profit Center for Internet Technologies, 1998).

In Russia, the driving focus underlying the initial development of computer networking was academic rather than governmental, so the systems started with a strong emphasis on open access, at least among academic and business elites. On the other hand, the more limited telecommunication networks and the lower diffusion of computer technology placed an initially stronger content bias toward text and basic Web structures. This had the impact of initially restricting Internet diffusion and use. Still, the basic underlying structure of the Internet favors open access and reducing content bias, trends that can be seen in current developments.

CYBERNETIC DISCOURSE AS SOCIAL PRACTICE AND ONLINE COMMUNITY

Claude Shannon developed the mathematical theory of signal transmission while working at Bell Laboratories in the late 1940s. The cybernetic theory of communications that Shannon and Warren Weaver (1949) developed from that earlier theory characterizes the act of communication as a process consisting of source, receiver, and sent and received signals transmitted through channels affected by channel capacity: the element of bandwidth in computer networking and cognitive processing in humans. The digital communication technology that began spreading rapidly through the entire field of telecommunications in the 1980s was heavily influenced by information theory, affecting computers, telephones, transmission systems, television, and radio (Severin & Tankard, 1992). The transformation was more than a shift in technology, however. It also brought in a shift in mentality, in how people see, represent, and understand natural phenomena (Fantel, 1989).

To anyone with access to a computer network in the early days of the Internet, these dynamics were readily apparent. Suddenly, mere keystrokes could transport a user to a server in another state or hemisphere and, through the network's ability to flatten time and distance, conversation with strangers on the other side of the globe was as easy as that with a networked colleague in the next cubicle. Excitement and optimism about the potentials of online communication were pervasive and world-wide (Negroponte, 1995; Rheingold, 1993). Building upon long-standing streams of thought about the arrival of an information-based economy and global information society, many theorized that the overlay of an open communications system upon older communication channels historically constrained by geography, politics, and economics would lead to profound social restructuring and effects, including the emergence of online tribes and communities (Staple, 1997). On the networks, communication in Usenet newsgroups, freenets, experimental open-access community computing networks, and electronic bulletin board systems tested this idea, with online discourse serving as an opportunity to learn and explore network technologies and engage in social exchange.

For Russian and U.S. citizens, cybernetic discourse offered new models of open communications in the wake of the cold war and collapse of a centralized command economy that actively discouraged and controlled the flow of information. The barrier of the Iron Curtain stopped traffic in each direction. Now, through the Internet, the West had a communication channel to explore the viability of entering Russia's new markets. To the East, motives for communication included the need for partners, capital, and information to aid in restructuring. In each nation, interest in the Internet's developing abilities and support for global communication was high.

CREATING A FRAMEWORK FOR
U.S.–RUSSIAN CIVIC DISCOURSE

In 1993, as they sketched out their ideas for an online community, the developers of "Friends and Partners" (1994) faced fundamental decisions on the technologies and nature of exchange they were seeking to create between Russia and the U.S.

In Shannon and Weaver's cybernetic theory of information, structural aspects of channel capacity, signal flow, transmission, and noise all act as influences on the ability to exchange messages, as well as the types and forms of information that can be shared (see Severin & Tankard, 1992). Parallels in Internet civic discourse include both the choice of technologies available to participants for communication and the inherent cultural factors that exist among sets of users that influence the messages they exchange—the preference in Central Europe for structured, hierarchical communication, for instance, as compared to the U.S.'s tendency for free-wheeling egalitarian discourse (Gee, 1997).

Cole, in Tennessee, and Bulashova, at Pushchino State University near Moscow, considered these factors. Significantly, the two had never met in person, nor could they speak each other's language. Their communication occurred solely through e-mail and a primitive UNIX precursor to chat, and early on they realized how different Internet technologies favored, or encouraged, differing modes of communication (Bulashova & Cole, 1995). For the resource they were seeking to create, the two wanted an interactive communications system supportive of multimedia and yet sufficiently scaleable to work within the bandwidth constraints of the Russian Internet. Rather than using the menu-based text browsing system of gopher, which was increasingly popular at the time, Cole and Bulashova decided to gamble on the viability of the emerging World Wide Web and the Mosaic browser, which was able to integrate text and graphics using HTML and also allow access using a text only interface called Lynx to permit efficient access by Russians and others with slow or problematic connectivity. They also decided to provide guest accounts on the home server to allow those with only e-mail and Telnet access to reach, view, and take part in the initiative (Bulashova & Cole, 1995).

Similar decisions had to be made about the content to reside upon the site. Wanting to empower others to create information and community, Bulashova and Cole pursued the idea of creating a framework on which others might build (G. Cole, personal communication, April 9, 1999). The only areas in which active control was exerted were in decisions to ban nonrelevant commercial messages, communication about trade in Russian wives to Western men, and political discourse. Cole states:

> We've always actively discouraged the discussion of politics, partly because any time Natasha and I would discuss it between ourselves, we'd usually disagree, but we realized the way that the Internet communications mechanisms work, such as listservs and chatrooms, favors strong voices to the detriment of others, not soft voices, loud voices, and we felt like the medium was not appropriate for political discussion.

The developers decided on a two-fold model of development in which website content would be used to attract people who would then be encouraged to join a listserv, which Cole and Bulashova considered the heart of their operation. During three months of preparation before the January 1994 launch, they worked to seed the "Friends and Partners" website with a variety of material related to the U.S. and Russia, with content organized around a metaphor of a home featuring rooms that people were invited to move into and adapt to their liking. "We had no idea that people would do that. At that point we'd never seen anything like this, but it seemed like a good idea. And that is what we actually went to the Internet with on January 19th" (G. Cole, personal communication, April 9, 1999).

Announcement of the launch was posted to various Usenet newsgroups, including a central announcement site, comp.www.announce, and a number of Relcom sites in Russia. E-mail began flowing in immediately and, within 24 hours, approximately 7,000 accesses had occurred, a volume of traffic that threatened to overwhelm the University of Tennessee's network (G. Cole, personal communication, April 9, 1999).

CIVIC DISCOURSE AND DEVELOPMENT
OF "FRIENDS AND PARTNERS"

In the first e-mail message sent to the new list, the developers emphasized their commitment to cybernetic construction. "Natasha and I want to make so clear that our role in this effort is but to provide a 'home' for this information and to help facilitate work between people who wish to contribute" (Bulashova & Cole, 1994).

The listserv distribution also contained messages from eight new members: four from U.S. universities; one from a Russian computer consultant working in the U.S.; another from an Irish counterpart in Shannon, Ireland, offering to host a party for Russians in the area connected to Aeroflot operations; one from a foundation in London; and another from a career diplomat in the Netherlands. A similar cosmopolitan mixture was found among the client domains that accessed the "Friends and Partners" web server in its first week of operation. A total of 2,000 accesses occurred from 32 identifiable nations and included more than 400 Telnet sessions to the server's guest account (Bulashova & Cole, 1994).

By the second week of operation, listserv traffic had increased to the point that Bulashova and Cole devised a new format for the daily digests and began swapping editing duties back and forth on a weekly basis. At the suggestion of a listserv member, they also began to post a section of technical hints aimed to aid people in using the system. A message during the third week of operation by an American captured the spirit evident in early posts:

> I've been receiving the FRIENDS listserv for a couple of weeks now, and really look forward to each days [sic] postings.... I really believe we are at a very exciting point in human history here. We have an unprecedented opportunity to seriously, and aggressively wage peace. The hunger for

human connections across cultural, geographical, physical and political barriers is astoundingly evident in this project, and on the internet as a whole. (Daily Digest, 1994b)

Others turned to the service for more pressing needs. A user in Dresden posted the following:

> I am still missing direct communication from the x-ussr commu-nity...some hours ago I tried to contact colleague in Kiev by phone (fax & email NOT available) but the phone call was horrible...therefore, I would be very happy if it were possible to establish an email connection with the University of Kiev. Can someone help with this...? (Daily Digest, 1994a)

Patterns of users and messages were already becoming clear. U.S. educators sought advice on resources about Russia and potential keypals or partners for collaborative exchange. Westerners with former ties to Russia explored ways to renew them or obtain information on genealogy, history, and other matters. A couple with access through AOL solicited favorite recipes, and nongovernment organizations began using the listserv to communicate about needs, initiatives, and resources available for sharing. And, across categories, users asked technical questions about the listserv, website, and other aspects of the Internet. In this way, discourse explored the idea of common interests while supporting mastery of the still new channel of communication.

Messages from the East also appeared early on. A businessman in Kazakhstan asked for help in obtaining the e-mail address of large commercial companies, and a marine scientist in the Ukraine sought people who shared his interests in diurnal heating of the seas and, at a more personal level, repairing Ford Escort cars (Daily Digest, 1994c).

The aim of these messages and others like them to engage in personal off-list discourse represented steps toward realizing the goal of "Friends and Partners." To Cole and Bulashova, the topic that drew people together wasn't important; it was the act of communicating that mattered (G. Cole, personal communication, April 9, 1999).

As listserv activity increased, Web content also expanded. Individuals and groups volunteered to add content and launch subject-specific sites. The first partnerships that resulted in content included an agreement with Radio Free Europe/Radio Liberty to archive their daily postings, a gift from the University of Oregon of digitized music by the Irkutsk Philharmonic Society, the provision of a Web-based version of Glas-News newsletter, and contributions of software, fonts, and associated packages aimed at helping with the display and printing of Cyrillic text.

Some material was placed in FTP archives, and some in WAIS databases, which site visitors could search. Development accelerated, and soon the Ford Foundation, the Eurasia Foundation, IREX, and other NGOs with significant activity in Central and Eastern Europe joined as friends and began contributing information. Individuals also made contributions. A Dutch teenager, Dirk van Gulik, submitted a Perl script to create what Cole believes is the first chatroom in cyberspace, The Weaving Room, and "Friends and Partners" became home to the first Russian newspaper to go online, as well as to a popular magazine, *Russian Life*, which ultimately spun off as a self-supporting commercial entity. And a 121-member organization, the Alliance of Universities for Democracy, developed a site at the server.

In the years that have passed, the initiative has received grants and support from NATO, Sun Microsystems, the U.S. Department of State, the National and International Science foundations, the Russian Institute of Public Networks, and a number of other high-level organizations. Its list of awards and recognitions is equally long and features several significant honors, including an invitation by the Gore-Chernomyrdin Commission to provide a demonstration at the 1996 U.S.–Russian Commission on Economic and Technological Cooperation on how the Internet could be used to foster U.S.–Russian cooperation and exchanges.

Cole, Bulashova, and a growing team of associates, partners, and supporters have continued to reach out and support individuals and organizations interested in aiding U.S–Russian exchange, and the two cofounders created "Friends and Partners China" and "Friends and Partners Romania" operations, although neither has come close to the impacts and activity of the Russian initiative.

In 1998, four years after its inception, "Friends and Partners" shifted to a new level of activity. While continuing to support the initiative's many Web and listserv operations, Cole and Bulashova launched an ambitious Russian civic networking project, CIVNET-Russia, led by Bulashova, that aims to establish the first true civic networks in Russia. Aided by a $60,000 grant from the Ford Foundation, the program intends to strengthen civic and community networking initiatives in select cities and, through the process, expand online material, provide community outreach uses and training of the Internet, and improve regional network infrastructure. The two also led the development of MirNET, a joint U.S.–Russian project that is exploring collaborative uses of the vBNS next-generation Internet among U.S. and Russian scientists and aiding infrastructure development between the two nations. Indicative of the expectations attached to it, MirNET is supported by a $6.5 million five-year budget funded by the National Science Foundation and Ministry for Science and Technology of the Russian Federation. The scope and level of activity and supporting organizations involved in each of these initiatives signal a new phase of operations and impacts for "Friends and Partners."

CONCLUSION

In five years, "Friends and Partners" has aided the development of significant areas of online content about the U.S. and Russia. High-visibility projects that have come to be associated with the initiative—many originating with just one person and developing with "Friends and Partners" over time—include a "Moscow Life" journal by physicist Andrey Sebrant and his family; Mark Wade's Encyclopedia Astronautica, a space flight site endorsed by the Encyclopedia Britannica, and a Russian Legal Server. Organizations hosted on "Friends and Partners" servers include the American International Health Alliance, the Center for Civil Society International, and dozens of smaller programs and projects. Many have subsequently launched other initiatives, a second generation of development that Cole (personal communication, April 9, 1999) describes as "grandchildren."

Technical development of the website and associated Internet technologies has been an ongoing focus, and "Friends and Partners" has led in the development of freeware UNIX-based database systems for Web development, along with other tools intended to make maintenance and growth easier. These materials have been shared with other nonprofit organizations.

The initiative's aim to engage individuals in decentralized development and social construction of an Internet resource has been an unqualified success. Despite the fact that hundreds of people are able to post content to its web servers, bulletin boards, and chat rooms, few problems have occurred. Instead, a positive sense of community has prevailed in the many forms of communication and information tied to the initiative.

When Bulashova and Cole began "Friends and Partners," they sought to encourage conversation between individuals and, through that discourse, to build bonds of understanding and collaboration. As the initiative developed, the exchanges it supported have broadened into a lively and varied discourse involving schoolchildren through the elderly. Professionals, volunteers, students, and families all take part in the dialogue. "Friends and Partners" has created a community and it's one that increasingly exists off the Internet, as well as on it.

While grant-funded efforts such as MirNET and CIVNET can be pointed to as successes, the most important contribution of "Friends and

Partners" may lie in a fundamental deepening of understanding about what is meant by a community network. Early pioneers in social uses of the Internet spoke of electronic communities such as The Well as online entities that existed separate from everyday life and the physical world that surrounds us. The concept of cyberspace and notions of virtual reality, or virtuality, imply the same. "Friends and Partners" broke through that barrier. The initiative has shown that while technology may be a part of it, true community networking lies in fostering connections between people. And through people, these connections become networks and channels of communication powerful enough to take ideas and use them to transform the world around us. The Internet makes such connections more powerful and more visible. The rest is up to us.

REFERENCES

Bates, B. J. (1993, May). *The macrosocial impact of communication systems: Access, bias, control* [Online]. Paper presented at the 43rd International Communication Association annual conference, Washington D.C. Available: http:// excellent.com.utk.edu/~bates/papers/93ica3ab.html [1999, April 13].

Bulashova, N., & Cole, G. (1994). *Our story* [Online]. Available: http:// www.friends-partners.org/friends/ourstory/firstannounce.html [1999, April 4].

Bulashova, N., & Cole, G. (1995, October 5). *"Friends & Partners": Building global community on the Internet* [Online]. Paper presented at the Internet '95 Conference in Norfolk, VA. Available: http://www.friends-partners.org/friends/ ourstory/paper.html [1999, March 25].

Daily Digest for 94-02-07. (1994a, February). [Online]. Available: http:// www.friends-partners.org/newfriends/community/lists/newfriends/digest/ 1994/940207.html [1999, April 5].

Daily Digest for 94-02-10. (1994b, February). [Online]. Available: http:// www.friends-partners.org/newfriends/community/lists/newfriends/digest/ 1994/940210.html [1999, April 5].

Daily Digest for 94-02-16. (1994c, February). [Online]. Available: http:// www.friends-partners.org/newfriends/community/lists/newfriends/digest/ 1994/940216.html [1999, April 5].

Dyson, E. (1996, October 18). Toward a more mature Internet. *Transition, 2*(21), 6–10, 79.

Elshtain, J. B. (1990). *Power trips and other journeys: Essays in feminism as civic discourse.* Madison, WI: University of Wisconsin Press.

Fantel, H. (1989, December 31). The advance was digital, and it's just a beginning. *New York Times,* Section 2, p. 28.

Fick, B. (1996, October 18). The Internet lurches forward in Russia. *Transition* [Online serial], *2*(21), 12–16. Available: http://www.samovar.ru/lurch.html [1999, April 17].

Friends and Partners. (1994). *Initial announcement* [Online]. Available: http://www.friends-partners.org/friends/ourstory/firstannounce.html [1999, April 11].

Gee, J. (1997, April 21). Parlez-vous Internet? *Industry Week, 246*(8), 78–79.

Innis, H. (1964). *The bias of communication* (Rev. ed.). Toronto: University of Toronto Press.

Innis, H. (1972). *Empire and communications* (Rev. ed.). Toronto: University of Toronto Press.

Lakhman, M. (1997a, October 7). Mother Russia does a slow dance with the Net. *New York Times* [Online]. Available: http://www.nytimes.com/library/cyber/euro/100797euro.html [1999, April 9].

Lakhman, M. (1997b, October 14). Soros philanthropy nudges ancient Russia into future. *New York Times* [Online]. Available: http://www.nytimes.com/library/cyber/euro/101497euro.html [1999, April 9].

Lawton, G. (1993, September/October). The end of the party line. *Wired* [Online serial], *1*, 04. Available: http://www.wired.com/wired/archive/1.04/russnet_pr.html [1999, April 7].

Leslie, J. (1994, March). Mail bonding. *Wired* [Online serial], *2*, 03. Available: http://www.wired.com/wired/archive/2.03/e-mail.html [1999, April 14].

McCarty, P. J. (1995, October). Four days that changed the world (and other amazing Internet stories). *Educational Leadership, 53*(2), 48–50.

Negroponte, N. (1995). *Being digital.* New York: Knopf.

Platonov, A. (1994). "Relarn" project: Support of telecommunications in the interests of research and education. *Proceedings of NATO Advanced Networking Workshop* [Online]. Available: http://www.friends-partners.org/oldfriends/telecomm/nato/platonov.html [1999, April 12].

Pool, I. de S. (1983). *Technologies of freedom.* Cambridge, MA: Belknap Press.

Press, L. (1991). Wide-area collaboration. *Communications of the ACM, 34*(12), 21–24.

Press, L. (1992, June). *Proceedings of INET '92* [Online]. International Networking Conference, Kobe, Japan. Reston, VA: Internet Society. Available: http://som.csudh.edu/cis/lpress/articles/relcom.htm [1999, April 13].

Proceedings of NATO Advanced Networking Workshop [Online]. (1994). Available: http://www.friends-partners.org/oldfriends/telecomm/nato/ [1999, April 12].

Reynolds, J., & Postel, J. (1987, August). *RFC 1000* [Online]. Available: http://info.internet.isi.edu:80/in-notes/rfc/files/ [1999, April 11].

Rheingold, H. (1993). *The virtual community: Homesteading on the electronic frontier.* Reading, MA: Addison-Wesley.

Russian Non-Profit Center for Internet Technologies. (1998, December). *ROCIT statistical report about Russian Internet development* [Online]. Available: http://www.rocit.ru [1999, April 12].

Severin, W. J., & Tankard, Jr., J. W. (1992). *Communication theories: Origins, methods, and uses in the mass media* (3rd ed.). New York: Longman.

Shannon, C. & Weaver, W. (1949). *The mathematical theory of communication.* Urbana, IL: University of Illinois Press.

Snyder, J. M. (1993). *Technological reflections: The absorption of data communications in the Soviet Union* [Online]. Unpublished doctoral dissertation, University of Arizona, Tucson. Available: http://www.opus1.com/www/jms/diss.html

Snyder, J. M., Jarmoszko, T., & Goodman, S. E. (1991, March). International electronic mail gains significance in the Soviet Union and Eastern Europe. *Computer,* 81–84.

Somogyi, S. (1996, March 12). Nets without frontiers: Internet growth by language and culture rather than geography. *Digital Media* 5(10), 18.

Staple, G. C. (1997). Telegeography and the explosion of place: Why the network that is bringing the world together is pulling it apart. In E. M. Noam & A. J. Wolfson (Eds.), *Globalism and localism in telecommunications* (pp. 217–228). New York: Elsevier.

Stonier, T. (1983). The microelectronic revolution, Soviet political structure, and the future of East/West relations. *Political Quarterly,* 54(2), 137–151.

Voiskounsky, A. E. (1998). Investigation of Relcom network users. In F. Sudweeks, M. McLaughlin, & S. Rafaeli (Eds.), *Network & Netplay: Virtual groups on the Internet* (pp. 113–126). Menlo Park, CA: AAAI Press/MIT Press.

chapter 13

The Evolution of Cybernetic Civic Discourse in Post-Communist Poland

John Parrish-Sprowl
Indiana University Purdue University at Fort Wayne

Eric Paul Engel
University of Missouri

For the Polish nation, few moments, exceed the drama of the events surrounding the demise of Soviet influence and the subsequent rise of democratic government in support of a market economy. While such transformations provide a myriad of topics worthy of study, perhaps none is more interesting than the struggle to establish a civic discourse reflective of both the new Poland and its participation in the global market economy. Much has been written concerning these changes in Poland (see, for example, Blazyca, 1994; Golebiowski, 1993; Gucwa-Lesny, 1996; Kolarska-Bobinska, 1994; Sachs, 1994; Weclawowicz, 1996; Wyznikiewicz, Pinto, & Grabowski, 1993), although little has focused on the changing nature of discourse (Parrish-Sprowl, Carveth, & Desiderio, in press). The purpose of the present chapter is to focus on civic discourse in the emergent market economy and democracy in Poland.

It must be noted that no discussion of contemporary civic discourse is fully formed without the inclusion of newer communication technology in general and the Internet in particular (Lengel & Fedak, in press). Concomitant with the general political and economic transformation in Poland is the explosive growth of communication technology and the potential to participate in cybernetic discourse. As our field research will indicate, however, significant financial barriers still remain for much of the population. Still, a growing number of people are connected and the Internet should grow in importance in the civic discourse of post-Communist Poland.

In this chapter, we will first explore critical historical themes that help explain the traditions of Polish civic discourse and the rapid embrace of new communication technologies. These themes include democratic tendencies across centuries, the role of the Catholic Church, and changing geographic borders. Second, we will discuss issues of social structure, especially that of the central role of family and Polish cultural tradition as they relate to civic discourse. Third, we will examine the Communist legacy in current civic discourse. Of special concern here is the intentionally underdeveloped and poorly developed communication infrastructure. Then we will discuss current issues in civic discourse, including political climate and economic conditions, but especially the emerging developments in communication technology. Finally, we will discuss the implications of these strands as they intertwine to form current and future civic discourse in Poland, and the tensions between traditional Polish identity and an emerging cyber identity.

HISTORICAL BACKGROUND

Civic discourse in Poland has been shaped by a history influenced by democratic tendencies. For slightly over two centuries (1569–1795), Poland was united with Lithuania in the Polish-Lithuanian Republic. As Davies (1982) points out, "Its laws and practices were inspired by deeply rooted beliefs in individual freedom and civil liberty which, for the period, were exceptional" (p. 321). This is not to say that the Republic resembled contemporary democracies, but rights and privileges were much greater than those enjoyed by the rest of Europe. For example, the nobility was vested with the power to elect the king and at the same time enjoyed some immunity from the king's rule. Consequently, Poland enjoys a history of robust civic discourse, at least among the nobility. Of course it should be noted that about 60 percent of the population were peasants and the scope of their civil liberties was much narrower.

Still, this is the nation that produced a remarkable constitution filled with rights, one that actually predates the U.S. constitution by a brief period. Although it was never implemented due to the partitioning of

Poland by Russia, Prussia, and the Austro-Hungarians in 1795, it provides an indication of Polish thinking into the area of civic discourse. Davies (1982) sums up the significance of this document by stating:

> To later generations, this Constitution of the Third of May [1791] assumed a symbolic importance out of all proportion to its practical significance. It was the Bill of Rights of the Polish tradition, the embodiment of all that was enlightened and progressive in Poland's past, a monument to the nation's will to live in freedom, a permanent reproach to the tyranny of the partitioning powers. (p. 535)

This constitution, both in its development and subsequent lack of implementation, offers an important parallel to current civic discourse and illustrates the historical connection of a national discourse seemingly filled with discontinuity.

During the time of the Republic, Polish nobility focused much of its discussion on internal matters, dealing with the external only when necessity prompted. Unlike many of the other Catholic countries of Europe, Polish leaders felt little commitment to the crusades and tended to do battle mostly along their own borders. Indeed the nobility had no formal military obligation to the crown, thus the nation was left virtually unprotected from external threats. This facilitated a civic discourse concerned with internal issues, power struggles, commerce, and rivalries. Such conditions fostered great debates but little concern for defense, until it was too late. Thus, the Constitution of the Third of May reflected a civic discourse steeped in a vocal tradition, but with insufficient regard for any external exigent.

Throughout the late 18th and 19th centuries, Poland ceased to exist. Subjugation by neighboring governments from 1795 to 1918 forced a civic discourse that was more conceptual than practical. This is because, as Davies (1982) points out:

> During the five or six generations when it had no concrete existence, "Poland" as an abstraction, could only be remembered from the past, or aspired to for the future, but only imagined for the present. It had not merely been broken into three parts; it had been vaporized, transposed into thin air, fragmented into millions of invisible particles. (p. 7)

One consequence of the partition period was to engender a civic discourse that looked to the future in order to restore the past. One difficulty, of course, is that what constitutes the past depends on who is telling the story. Another is that geopolitical and economic circumstances continued to change, making "the past" inaccessible in a myriad of ways.

Dating from the 1790s, Polish civic discourse needed to fulfill three important functions. First, civil liberties, so much a part of the development of Polish public life, needed to be remembered. Second, a discourse that allowed Poles to cope with the uncertainties of external forces, which influenced and controlled their lives, needed to develop. Finally, perhaps most significantly, civic discourse needed to solidify and preserve a notion of Poland that would be both real and cherished by the Poles and recognized as important by external forces. Without the latter, Poland might never be reestablished as a sovereign nation. Because of Poland's history, some knowledge of the past is critical to understanding the present. It is these critical discursive traditions that help explain the unfolding of cybernetic civic discourse in present-day Poland. How this story unfolds requires some discussion of civic discourse and communication technology during the Communist period.

CIVIC DISCOURSE AFTER WORLD WAR II

With the close of World War II, Poland found itself both geographically reconfigured and under the thumb of the USSR. Deprived of long cherished civil liberties and faced with the reconstruction of the nation in the modern era, Poles carried forward the three themes of civic discourse outlined above. The Catholic Church, family, and communications technology played an important role in the civic discourse of the Communist period. The Church served as an oppositional institution, creating a place where public discord could be heard with some immunity (Weclawowicz, 1996). As a consequence, the Polish cultural identity deepened its connection with Catholicism during the communist period, providing an interesting irony, given the atheistic doctrine of the ruling ideology.

Family provided private space where a more open civic discourse might be practiced. This too has deep historical roots, in that the family was an important locus of cultural preservation during the partition period. Thus, family, for political as well as social reasons, plays a central role in the Polish social structure. Outside of the church and family, all other discourse that championed a Poland free of Soviet influence was facilitated by clandestine communication operations until the Solidarity movement in the 1980s. At this time, public demonstrations became important, but augmented rather than supplanted technology as a vehicle for civic discourse.

Underground radio, word processing applications, and photocopiers were all important in the civic discourse of those opposed to Communist rule and Soviet domination. These technological advances facilitated civic discourse during the time of martial law in the 1980s because they are portable, replaceable, and more difficult to find than a printing press. Furthermore, the very act of using these technologies often comprised an important part of civic discourse. For example, two informants shared with us the following story. In one Polish city, the Communists searched for an underground radio station but could not find one. A cemetery filled with Soviet soldiers slain in World War II has a vintage Soviet tank placed at the entrance serving as a memorial. The radio was being broadcast from inside the vintage tank. Because the location offered great visibility from all directions, the operators could shut down and vacate before the police arrived. The former opposition loves this story because of the irony that it offers, making a statement in and of itself.

CIVIC DISCOURSE IN THE NEW PARTICIPATIVE DEMOCRACY

One of the major reasons that the Communist government of Poland attempted to control availability and access to communication technology is because it facilitated civil disobedience. This, along with economic reasons, explains why Poland's telecommunications system was poorly developed and increasingly obsolete under the Communist government. Therefore, following the revolution of 1989, the country was left with an underdeveloped communication and information infrastructure, leaving Poland unprepared to participate in a global market economy. This will be discussed in greater detail below.

After Solidarity won the elections in 1989, the new leaders of the country decided to embark on a policy they labeled "shock therapy." The result was a full scale, rapid transformation to both a market-based economy and a fully participative democracy (Sachs, 1994). This transformation created circumstances that drew together historical themes and contemporary issues in Polish civic discourse. First, it allowed for the reestablishment of a tradition of civil liberties, albeit in a contemporary democratic system. Second, it established civic discourse concerned with external forces, although it redirected the concerns related to Soviet domination to participation in a global market economic system. Third, the newly opened communication and information environment placed renewed emphasis on the issues of Polish cultural identity. Finally, Poland needed to cope with the Communist legacy of a poorly developed internal and external communication infrastructure.

With centuries of foreign domination behind them, Polish leaders went about the process of creating a democratic government and the civil liberties associated with such a system. In many ways, this process represented picking up where they left off 200 years earlier with the 1791 Constitution and a substantial shift from the lack of civic discourse under the communist government. As a consequence, the number of newspapers, magazines, and radio and television stations grew rapidly (Miło, 1997), with the emergence of print media spreading much more quickly than electronic media due to economic reasons. In addition, satellite dishes, cable systems, telephone lines, and cellular communication systems also experienced rapid growth (Obuchowski, 1995). By the mid-1990s, Internet service providers covered much of the country and are continuing to expand. As citizens developed the right to engage in civic discourse, they developed the communicative means to do so.

Civic discourse emerged from the underground and became loud, boisterous, contentious, and multifaceted as Poles began to experience freedoms long denied. While not everyone participated, those who chose to do so became quite active (Blazyca, 1994). Political activity, including advertising in various media, grew substantially. During the 1993 elections, one could not travel anywhere in Poland without confronting advertising, public relations events, or campaigning candidates. The establishment of over 20 political parties is a testament to the growth of democratic civic discourse. In addition, new connections with the West further changed the civic discursive environment. Current news, commentary, political advertising, and other forms of civic discourse from Western Europe and the United States suddenly became readily available to Poles.

CONCERNS ABOUT PRESERVING CULTURAL IDENTITY

Connecting with the West in all areas of political and commercial life left many Poles concerned with the preservation of Polish cultural identity. This concern, with deep historical roots, changed its complexion after the 1989 revolution, such that the issue became one of integrating with the global market system rather than responding to external political pressures and influences. While this phenomenon is of global significance (Barber, 1995), it has particular importance in Poland. Some examples that illustrate the Polish obsession with preserving their culture include an article in *The Polish Sociological Bulletin* focused on what is unique about the discipline of Polish sociology (Podgorecki, 1993). In addition, *Chip* magazine, the largest selling Polish computer publication, focuses on what is new and unique in the Polish computer market. Wherever one looks in Poland, the struggle to maintain Polish cultural identity is evident. Cyberspace, by its very nature, simultaneously facilitates and undermines this effort.

Concern for civil liberties and the desire to facilitate a strong Polish identity created a compelling need for the development of a telecommunications and media infrastructure. First, new policies needed to be developed that would regulate these industries. Poland's 1991 laws regulating telecommunications are viewed as some of the most progressive in Europe (Obuchowski, 1995). Although the development has been quite rapid, it is still estimated that the Polish telephone and data line systems are one to two decades away from achieving parity with Western European countries. This projection is due in part to the cost of wiring the country and the time necessary to install lines when so little had been developed prior to 1990.

Broadcast media has been affected by the transition as well. Before television and radio could be developed, new regulations and regulatory structures were needed to replace the ones governing under the Communist regime. As a consequence, only in the mid-1990s has any significant development of private television taken place. Furthermore, cable television companies are installing lines as rapidly as possible to create a sufficient customer base to sustain the business. While audiences are growing, advertising revenues still lag substantially behind the West (Agencja Reklamy Polskiego Radia, 1998). These lower revenues contribute to the delay in developing a Western-equivalent communications infrastructure.

CURRENT ISSUES

Rapid economic growth, a relatively young population, and a culture steeped in the tradition of active civic discourse set the stage for a robust cybernetic civic discourse. But, as Blazcya (1994) points out, "Every change in the politico-economic order requires changes in the system of values, but the passage from the socialist formation to pluralism and a market economy must be based on a genuine revolution of values" (p. 53). Citizens' attitudes and actions around cyberspace is an excellent locus to judge whether or not a "revolution of values" is taking place. This is because the discursive environment in cyberspace, by its very nature, may be considered revolutionary even in an already democratic society, much less when moving from a totalitarian environment. To investigate the current nature of such discourse, we conducted field research in June 1998. This data gathering included interviews with the publishers of *Chip* magazine, the visitation of Polish websites, and focus groups conducted in two Polish cities, Szczecin and Warsaw. Six one-hour focus groups were conducted over a two-week period. Participants ranged in age from 16 to 63, totaling 37 in number. Three major themes emerged from these discussions. First, there is a generally positive attitude toward the Internet and the World Wide Web. Second, there are concerns about access to the Internet and, finally, there is a belief that cyberspace offered a mixed blessing to Poland.

Experience with computer-mediated communication (CMC) by the focus group members ranged from one exposure to daily use of e-mail. Not surprising is that age played a role in access. Those still in high school along with older participants had limited experience with computers, especially the Internet. Participants in the middle age range spent more time on computers in general and the Internet in particular due to work demands. Several of the participants routinely used e-mail, while only a few accessed the Web or CMC with any regularity. The only exception to this was the employees of *Chip* magazine, partly because of the content of *Chip* (computers) and because the magazine operates a very active website (Chip Online, 1999). All of the focus group participants had spent some time in chat rooms and playing games on the Web and most lamented their inability to explore cyberspace more frequently. This was especially true among the younger members of the focus groups.

Polish high school students serve as a particularly interesting group because they represent the future. They are the first generation of Poles to grow up with broad access to media, including international television channels such as MTV and the Cartoon Network. Most of them seemed to think of the Web as a natural extension of their electronic media experience. Given the opportunity, nearly every teen interviewed expressed the desire to become more familiar with the Web and wanted to utilize e-mail to connect with other people. Furthermore, some were able to envision commercial and political uses for both the Web and e-mail. This suggests that the future of cybernetic civic discourse in Poland is likely to be strong.

However, participants consistently cited cost as the major barrier to access. Internet time is considered to be quite expensive, especially to the home user. As a consequence, people spent much less time in cyberspace than they wanted, especially the high school students. This issue takes on a special importance, aside from the obvious problems any barrier creates due to the concerns tied to the transformation. Weclawowicz (1996) captures the problem when he states: "In terms of popular perception, the transformation seems to have been based on a transition from a poor society into a society of poor and rich; or from an egalitarian society, at least in theory, into an inegalitarian society with very evident divisions based on wealth" (p. 91). Since the primary barrier to accessing cyberspace is economic, the issue gets bound in the contemporary incarnation of a historic concern for equality. Thus, while people generally seem positive about the potential of computer-mediated communication, they are concerned about the potential for cost to create a two tiered societal structure where those who can afford access to communication forums will have greater civil liberties than those who cannot afford access.

THE FUTURE OF THE COMMUNICATION TECHNOLOGY IN POLAND

When asked about the Internet and the future, most felt that it offered a mixed set of blessings for Poland. On the positive side, the Web creates an opportunity for Polish citizens and companies to connect with people and markets they would otherwise not be able to interface for financial reasons. As a consequence, there is a growing presence on the Web of Polish government, academics, and business. For example, PolskaNet (PolskaNet, n.d.) lists business websites in Poland. Many organizations in Poland have websites, including most colleges and universities (compare DeMello, 1996), cities and provinces in Poland (compare Gaczorek, n.d.), and news and media outlets (compare Agencja KONTAKT, 1999; Gazeta Wyborcza, 1999; Presspublica Sp. z o.o., n.d.). The growing number of cites enables individuals with access to the Internet to discover Poland with much greater ease than ever before. Furthermore, it indicates that Poles recognize the Web as an important locus of discourse for all purposes.

The above passive sites, meaning websites that do not afford users any interaction, illustrate the post-Communist Polish commitment to the exercise of free speech, active international discourse, and global commerce. Perhaps more importantly, as Lengel (1998) points out, the opportunity for active Internet involvement is of even greater importance in the development of cybernetic civic discourse. Although none of the older participants in our research had participated in chat rooms, all of the younger folks had at least once. In addition, some of the middle-age range discussants belong to one or more newsgroups, as well as being regular users of e-mail. The most significant barrier to greater participation at the moment is an economic one, due to both the cost of infrastructure development as well as user fees.

On the negative side, many participants agreed with the notion that the Internet may complicate the Polish transformative discourse as much as it facilitates useful civic discussions. Some were concerned that such connections might undermine Polish cultural identity, especially among Polish youth. Several discussants noted that younger people already spend time and money on food, music, and other entertainment that is distinctly not Polish, with MTV and McDonald's the two most often mentioned culprits. As with media consumption in the West, the participants expressed concerns that time spent online is time not spent with the family. Given the critical role of the family in Polish society, this is an issue of special significance. Some participants noted that access to a global array of websites, newsgroups, and chat rooms can only add to the dissipation of Polish uniqueness, including the tightly knit fabric of family life.

Another concern expressed is that people might lose interest in local issues as they spend more and more time in online environments. Blazyca (1994) makes note of the low participation rates in "activities which could considerably speed-up this reconstruction" (p. 43). The apathy seems particularly pronounced among the young. Although this is not unusual in democratic countries, by the time Polish youth become older and more involved, they may be more international in focus rather than traditional Polish in their perspective. Given the civic history of the country, this might be both expected and a cause for concern among older citizens at the same time. In these concerns, we witness once again the recurring themes of Polish civic discourse, cultural identity, and a focus on local, internal issues. Global online systems may well fuel suspicion of external forces, albeit electronic and not military, in its contemporary incarnation.

POLISH CYBERNETIC CIVIC DISCOURSE IN THE THIRD MILLENNIUM

Cybernetic civic discourse has a solid beginning with a strong projected growth rate in Poland in the third millennium. This is due in part to historical cultural factors that are encouraging of the openness and contentiousness that the Internet facilitates. While many are concerned with long-practiced themes of retaining a uniquely Polish identity, most voices proclaim the move into cyberspace to be inevitable and positive. Thus, citizens are likely to move online as rapidly as economic circumstances will permit. However, if economic barriers to access are not mitigated rapidly in some way, attitudes toward cyberspace could turn decidedly negative among those who are denied. This in turn could temper the feelings of those who are connected. Because of the long-held sense of importance regarding egalitarianism in Polish culture, both the have's and the have not's will remain sensitive to this issue. One can hypothesize that the very fact that people generally do cherish equality in principle, it bodes well for a future solution to the problem.

Even as cyberspace changes the Polish communicative structures, Polish civic discourse is unlikely to let go of its cultural traditional in the third millennium. The international nature of computer-mediated communication may well heighten concerns related to cultural identity and external influence. On the other hand, perhaps the connection is merely coincidental. Had the Polish government retained sovereignty in 1791 and the Third of May Constitution been carried out, perhaps these issues would have been dealt with long ago. Certainly this issue was exacerbated by the 45 years of Soviet-led Communist domination, and as a consequence, cyberspace poses a contemporary dilemma. As Polish political and business leaders work diligently to attract foreign capital and contacts, they, along with other Poles, work equally hard at strengthening a sense of Polish identity both at home and abroad.

Cybernetic civic discourse presents the opportunity for meaningful discussion of contemporary democratic concerns. Life under the Soviet-dominated Communist structure afforded little opportunity to genuinely explore the nature of human relations in contemporary times. A growing number of Polish scholars, along with others interested in these issues in Poland, are online, and discussion of social, political, and economic issues is growing daily. One hopes cybernetic civic discourse will grow to include lively discussions of issues such as gender equity, ethnic differences, disability access, and STDs, to name a few. Right now these issues are the subjects of private e-mail among a small but growing contingent of Poles, but unfortunately, this is mostly limited to academics.

Poland is a nation conscious of the fact that it is undergoing a complete economic and political transformation (Golebiowski, 1993; Weclawowicz, 1996). Certainly the international movement to online environments can be considered globally revolutionary. In the Polish context, this move is simply part of a larger societal shift. Since the transformation in general is viewed by most as necessary, cybernetic space simply becomes part of the package. This presents the online environment in a positive light, but at the same time, citizens are vigilant for any signs that cyberspace might undermine traditional values. All of this being said, as long as cybernetic civic discourse is both shaped by and strengthens Polish values and identity, then it will be embraced as part of the democratic future of the country.

REFERENCES

Agencja KONTAKT. (1999, February 14). *Warsaw voice available on World Wide Web* [Online]. Available: <http://www.warsawvoice.com.pl/PL-dos/index.html> [1999, February 14].

Agencja Reklama Polskiego Radia. (1998). Ad rates for Polish TV1 & 2. Warsaw: Author.

Barber, B. R. (1995). *Jihad vs. mcworld: How globalism and tribalism are reshaping the world*. New York: Random House.

Blazyca, B. (1994). *The economic consequences of post-Communism in Poland*. Paisley, Scotland: Department of Economics and Management, University of Paisley.

Chip Online. (1999, February 12). *Chip Online Homepage* [Online]. Available: <http://www.chip.pl> [1999, February 13].

Davies, N. (1982). *God's playground: A history of Poland*. New York: Columbia University Press.

DeMello, C. (1996). *Colleges and universities—Poland* [Online]. Available: <http://www.mit.edu:8001/people/cdemello/pl.html> [1999, February 13].

Gaczorek, D. (n.d.). *Polish provinces on WWW* [Online]. Available: <http://www.cyfronet.krakow.pl/ack/cities>

Gazeta Wyborcza [Online]. (1999, February 13). Available: <http://www.gazeta.pl> [1999, February 13].

Golebiowski, J. W. (1993). *Transforming the Polish economy*. Warsaw, Poland: Warsaw University Faculty of Foreign Trade.

Gucwa-Lesny, E. (1996). Four years after velvet revolution: Who is better off? Who feels better? In *New socio-economic conditions*. Warsaw, Poland: Faculty of Economic Sciences, University of Warsaw.

Kolarska-Bobinska, L. (1994). *Aspirations, values and interests: Poland 1989–94*. Warsaw, Poland: IFIS.

Lengel, L. (1998, Summer). Access to the Internet in East Central and South-Eastern Europe: New technologies and new women's voices. *Convergence: Journal of Research into New Media Technologies, 4*(2), 38–55.

Lengel, L., & Fedak, D. (in press). The politicization of cybernetic discourse: Discourse conflict and the internet in North Africa. In M. Prosser (Ed.), *Civic discourse and discourse conflict in Africa*. Stamford, CT: Ablex.

Miło. (1997). *Media situation in Poland 1996*. Warsaw: Author.

Obuchowski, J. (1995). *Comparative models in telephony in central and eastern Europe: Mid-course in the transition from command to market economies*. Washington, DC: The Annenberg Washington Program.

Parrish-Sprowl, J., Carveth, R. A., and Desiderio, S. (in press). The post-Communist transformation: The challenge of creating a discourse of advertising in Poland. In W. Sitek (Ed.), *Kulture i Strukture II: Spoleczenstwo wobec wyzweu ryuku*. Wroclaw, Poland: Instytut of Socjoloii, Uniwersytet Wroclawski.

Podgorecki, A. (1993). The uniqueness of Polish sociology. *The Polish Sociological Bulletin, 102*(2), 149–160.

PolskaNet (n.d.). *Your best guide to business in Poland* [Online]. Available: <http://www.polska.net/> [1999, February 14].

Presspublica Sp. z o.o. (n.d.). *Rzeczpospolita* [Online]. Available: <http://www.rzeczpospolita.pl/PL-iso/index.html>[1999, February 13].

Sachs, J. (1994). *Poland's jump to the market economy*. Cambridge, MA: MIT Press.

Weclawowicz, G. (1996). *Contemporary Poland*. Boulder, CO: Westview Press.

Wyznikiewicz, B., Pinto, B., & Grabowski, M. (1993). *Coping with capitalism: The new Polish entrepreneurs.* Washington, DC: The World Bank.

chapter 14

Kultura/Technologie Mladych: Youth Culture and Technology in the Czech Republic

Zdenka Telnarová
University of Ostrava, Czech Republic

Eva Burianová
University of Ostrava, Czech Republic

Laura Lengel
Richmond American International University in London

S eventeen-year-old Jakub S. from Prague told his father, "I don't have to go to school. I'll just learn through the Internet" (S. Siňor, personal communication, December 18, 1998). Jakub is not alone. He and his counterparts in the New Europe have latched onto technology, particularly the Internet, with great passion. Like Jakub, some youth in the New Europe, whether they have access to the Internet or not, are more interested in surfing the Net than attending classes. It may be the case that youth learning materials on the World Wide Web and other Internet services are better equipped with current learning resources than the many schools and universities in the region, which have suffered financially since the fall of Communist rule.

Needless to say, after the fall of Communist rule, there have been significant changes, not only in education generally and educational resources specifically (see, for example, M. Černochová, personal communication, December 18, 1998; Hobzová & Hamhalterová, 1999; Mannova & Preston, 1999; see also Chapter 18, in this volume), but in most sociocultural and economic factors in the Czech Republic and elsewhere in the New Europe (see, for example, Lengel, 1998; see also Chapter 19, in this volume; Paletz, Jakubowicz, & Novosel, 1995). While most in the region have been burdened with economic difficulty, certain changes afforded moments of optimism for New Europeans: optimism for the success of the new democratic movements sweeping the region and for the opportunity to participate in the civic discourse once forbidden under Communist rule. Optimism has also emerged from the impact of information and communication technology, a topic that has been a key focus in the Czech Republic (M. Černochová, personal communication, December 18, 1998; Hlavenka, 1997; S. Siňor, personal communication, December 18, 1998).[1] This chapter analyzes one specific concern: the impact of technology on youth culture in the Czech Republic. It addresses both the challenges and successes of how Czech youth use technology to learn and dialogue about East Central European culture and to interact in ways not possible before accessing technology like the Internet. The research presented in this chapter builds on work in the area of global learning through technology (see, for example, Burianová & Telnarová, 1999; Gallego, 1994; Lengel & Murphy, in press; Preston, 1995) and emerges from the Czech authors' practical experience in higher and secondary education in the Czech Republic's Ostrava region. The primary research in this chapter presents the views of Czech youth who have access to technology and have made choices, like Jakub above, to delve deeply into "cyberspace," to participate in computer mediated civic discourse, and to feel connected to a world that is, for many in the New Europe, beyond reach through traditional means.

CHANGES AND OPPORTUNITIES FOR YOUTH IN THE CZECH REPUBLIC

Before the fall of Communist rule in 1989, Czech youth suffered from a lack of access to technology as well as a lack of creative, active learning opportunities, both within information and communication technology (ICT) disciplines and education generally. While nations such as Bulgaria did have excellent access to computers and other technologies under pre-1989 Soviet rule (see, for example, Bennahum, 1997; Lengel, 1998), others like Czechoslovakia suffered from a lack of technological resources. Only a few schools and universities in what was then Czechoslovakia were equipped with 8-bit microcomputers. At primary educational institutions, there were no computers at all. Computers at secondary schools were used only to study BASIC and PASCAL programming languages, a study opportunity open solely to select students in a special Information Science and Computational Technique program. Amazingly, in many universities and schools, Information Science and Computational Technique had been taught without access to any computers at all. Information and computer technology had not been used in other subjects due to inferior technical and software equipment, a lack of qualified instructors, and low instructor interest. Later, educational programs incorporating computers started to appear in schools in mathematics, physics, chemistry, biology, and other sciences; however, the quality of ICT application was weak and very restricted.

Since 1989, all universities and most secondary schools in the Czech Republic have been gradually equipped with contemporary information and communication technology. More recently, following the post-1989 technological access for higher and secondary education in the Czech Republic, the majority of primary schools are also beginning to be equipped with computer labs and learning centers.

Opportunities for Czech youth have also been impacted by the vast changes in the educational system since the fall of Communist rule. While Communist governance certainly valued education, it was an authoritarian-style of education that was imposed upon socialist nations, a style that marginalized youth's creativity, autonomy, and agency. Education was characterized by repression and/or distortion of "undesireable" information, a lack of liberal education, isolation from the world outside socialist nations, marginalization of local and national languages through the enforced Russian-only instruction, and admission restrictions based on political ideology.

After 1989, efforts have concentrated on eliminating the above problems and transforming the education system toward an open, pluralistic system that would place Czech youth at the heart of the learning process. Liquidation of the state monopoly resulted in new developments in educational initiatives, and civic and corporate partnerships that would benefit Czech youth. There appeared to be an expansion in numbers, structure, and the diversity of educational opportunities, particularly in the sector of secondary technical schools.

While these advances have been significant, there is still work to be done to provide Czech youth with the best opportunities possible. In contrast to the explicit problems discussed above, the more subtle elements that emerged during the 40 years of Communist ideology are perhaps most disturbing, as they have, in a number of cases, remained after the fall of Communist rule. The influence of Communist ideology is reflected in teacher and student passivity, carelessness, skepticism, reliance on a bureaucratic educational administration, a shunning of responsibility at the lower levels of this hierarchy and, most notably, an absence of a democratic approach.

Despite these subtle, lingering elements, technological access and advancements have brought new opportunities for Czech youth. Students can benefit from the use of computed aided design and presentation applications, access to databases and library services around the world, and computer simulations used in scientific experiments and engineering projects. Along with ICT generally, computer-mediated communication (CMC) has had a great influence on the academic and personal growth of Czech youth. The connection of Czech educational institutions to the Internet provides access to information on the global network and to the dissemination of institutional news and information, connecting the Czech Republic to the world in ways that were previously economically unfeasible. As a result of the increased access to technology through schools and universities, Czech youth have developed technological expertise and have mastered online communication and research both for academic work, personal correspondence, and cultural interests. Universities with special programs called "Dum deti a mladeze" ["A Home for Children and Youth"] regularly organize competitions for student-created computer programming projects. The technological expertise of Czech youth was recognized internationally when a team of students from The Charles University won the 22nd International Competition in Computer Programming Award in Atlanta, Georgia.

Further, in Czech schools, compared with those in other European countries, computers and software are increasingly used for creative work, such as graphic design, creation of websites, and computer game development, in addition to Internet-based information retrieval. Thus, and perhaps most interestingly, CMC is providing opportunities, before unknown, for young people to participate in post-socialist civic discourse in very creative ways.

RESEARCHING CZECH CULTURE AND TECHNOLOGY

To explore the creative ways youth use technology, we conducted primary research in the Czech Republic. The contemporary interest in the intersections of youth culture and technology elsewhere in Europe and in other regions such as Africa and Asia (see, for example, Amit-Talai & Wulff, 1995; CUYT, 1996; Liechty, 1995; Mestel, 1996; Milone, 1996; North, 1995; Sanger, 1997; Sherrell, 1997) grounded our research in the Czech Republic, where there is currently little to no research on youth culture and technology. Through a triangulated approach involving a number of research tools, the two authors of this chapter who teach at the University of Ostrava administered open-ended question-naires and indepth interviews, while all three authors conducted fol-low-up e-mail correspondence with the Czech youth involved in the research.

The respondents all live and study in Ostrava, an industrial region of the Czech Republic thath, prior to 1989, did not have any institutions of higher education. However, the quality of cultural activities, such as the-atrical and musical performances, is comparable to other regions, except perhaps for Prague, the cultural capital of the nation. The 150 respon-dents to the questionnaires and 16 indepth interviews included two main youth communities: first, students studying Information Systems at the University of Ostrava, and, second, students of Computational Tech-nique at Ostrava's Higher Professional School. It should be noted that the respondents, as students of information systems and computing, have far better access to technology than the average Czech citizen. At their universities and schools, they have daily access to the Internet and sophisticated software products. Eighty-five percent have their own PC and some of them have accounts with Czech Internet service providers in their homes.

The questions in the survey and in the interview protocol asked the respondents to think about the impact of information and communica-tion technology on Czech culture. After general demographic questions, the respondents were asked questions concerning how they used ICT for their academic, personal, and cultural interests. They were asked about their own access to technology. Further questions probed respondents' cultural interests and if and how they use technologies such as the Inter-net to access information about their interests. For purposes of this research, cultural interests are defined as "traditional" performing arts such as music, dance, and theater, but also range from "high" art (defined by cultural studies scholars as traditionally the domain of the bourgeoisie) to popular forms such as rock concerts. As mentioned above, youth is defined as those age 15 to 22. The youth's interest in how technology impacts Czech popular culture was a key component of the questionnaire and subsequent interview questions. Respondents not only were asked about the impact of technology on Czech popular cul-ture generally, but how technology can contribute to the preservation and promotion of Czech culture. Questions encouraged respondents to consider how various services of the Internet, such as websites, e-confer-ences, Internet Relay Chat (IRC), and other forms of computer-medi-ated communication impact Czech culture. Respondents were also asked what specific websites and CMC venues were of particular interest to them. Finally, questions concerned the representation of the Czech

Republic generally and Czech youth and Czech culture specifically on the Internet.

Respondents' comments and discussion were thematized within the qualitative research paradigm.[2] Themes emerging include the promotion of Czech culture, participating in Czech culture, connecting with others, and breaking down or creating cultural barriers. Examples of the respondents' commentary are included in the following analysis of these primary themes.

PROMOTING CZECH CULTURE AND EXPERIENCING "VIRTUAL" CULTURE

The most significant finding from the research is that nearly 90 percent of all respondents articulated that they use the Internet for culturally oriented information. In Ostrava, as in many industrial regions and cities around the world that often pale in comparison to cultural meccas like New York, London, and Paris, citizens take pride in the cultural and artistic events that take place in their city. The events and organizations that are lacking in Ostrava can be accessed through information and communication technology, particularly the Internet. For instance, Marek V., a 23-year-old amateur actor, director, and painter, and an Information Systems student at the University of Ostrava, can "attend" an art exhibition by logging onto the Internet. He understands that "computer displays can never replace the unforgettable atmosphere of a gallery or concert, but it provides an opportunity to visit an exhibition in a distant town or even in a distant state, which would be never possible in reality." Marek also notes that, while experiencing firsthand art at a gallery or music at a concert provides an "unforgettable atmosphere," he has seen excellent "virtual exhibition[s] on Web sites." These "virtual exhibitions" enable Czech art to be promoted internationally via the World Wide Web. Further, Vitasek, with his painting and technological expertise, might be encouraged to develop his own virtual exhibition, in order to share his work with others in the New Europe and elsewhere.

Czech schools and universities encourage cultural promotion and preservation through information and communication technology. Some university art programs use special graphical software. Music schools experiment with computer applications, which support composition and sound simulation. Schools and universities also encourage students to publicize their own cultural projects using ICT, giving students the possibility to meet other young people with similar interests and finding new possibilities to improve and enrich their own activities.

One such possibility is through the amateur youth theater *Tajfun* ["Typhoon"], founded in 1992 at the Maticni Gymnasium secondary school in Ostrava, and currently supported by the University of Ostrava. Members of this theater do not know of any other dramatic group with similar theatrical and cultural interests, in either the Ostrava region, or elsewhere in the Czech Republic. In the last six years, *Tajfun* have performed 75 original plays written by its members. *Tajfun* members also compose and record the musical scores that accompany the plays, as well as prepare the theatrical scenery, costumes, and choreography.

Tajfun contacted several youth theater groups in the New Europe to participate in a project called "Legends and Myths of Central Europe." Through both traditional communication channels and the Internet, *Tajfun* connected with other youth theater groups from Poland and Germany. *Tajfun* also developed an extensive website to promote the theater and its activities. While the University of Ostrava provides consultancy service and technical support to the *Tajfun*, the organization's website is created entirely by the members of the theater. The aim of the sites is to open a creative discussion on the Internet about amateur youth theaters, their function, and their current and future importance. They also aim to seek out opportunities to enter into future projects, particularly those involving international collaboration.

Jiri N., 19, a Computational Technique student at the Higher Professional School, writes "I think information and communication technology will greatly influence progress in our culture and it will [be] possible to pass it to the next generations. The Internet will play the main role in this process." Martin C. a 20-year-old Information Systems student at the University of Ostrava, says, "Many people in the Czech Republic are very interested in culture. Now many people have an access to the Internet" and they use it to research and dialogue about their cultural interests. Similarly, Michal B., age 21 and in the same program as Martin, notes "I think that the main role of the Internet is in advertising cultural events and in [providing] "virtual meetings" for people with the same interests." He has had such "virtual meetings" to share his musical interests with other Czech youth and appreciates the opportunity to listen to both Czech and other types of music on the Web. Marek, too, downloads Czech music from the Web and uses "the Internet to find [out about] when and where various concerts [are taking place], exhibitions, and online booking of the seats."

Richard B., age 21 and an Information Systems student at the University of Ostrava, writes, "on the Internet there are a lot of interesting websites about films, music, etc. You can watch demonstrations of films, listen to a piece of music. Then you can buy what you like." Richard's comment sounds rather simplistic until one remembers that, with the economic hardships that have burdened Czechs in the past few years, incidental purchases such as music CDs or cinema tickets are difficult, if not impossible for Czech youth. The ability to critically analyze a potential purchase through the Internet leads to the careful spending that is required in the Czech Republic.

Maria N., age 18, and a student in Computational Technique at Ostrava's Higher Professional School, commented on a website developed by Frantisek Fuka, a Prague-based computer expert and film connoisseur in his late 20s, who translates English-language films into the Czech language. His Web biography includes his experience with films: "After university, I noticed that I can understand English and that I don't like the way movies are translated into Czech. So I started translating for the film distributors (have a look at the Czech versions of *The Rock*, *Independence Day*, or *Star Trek: First Contact*), which led to my work for the *Cinema* magazine. Actually, I now have great part-time job: seeing almost all the recent movies (including those that are never released over here)" (CFWR, 1998). Despite his list of the above Hollywood action-thrillers, Fuka's biography does praise Czech films, rather than disregarding them in favor of the Hollywood norm. Fuka represents a number of Czechs in their teens and 20s who are active in promoting, preserving, and representing the Czech culture and language.

PARTICIPATING IN CZECH CULTURE

Not only are Czech youth interested in how technology can provide a forum to promote, preserve, and represent Czech culture and language, but many respondents participate in Czech culture through the Internet. While some respondents, like Marek, are painters or actors in amateur theaters, well over half of the respondents play, or are learning to play, a musical instrument. Considering the long-established tradition of Czechs being at one of the world centers for serious musical composition and performance, many respondents are continuing the tradition. A well-known Czech proverb comes to mind, "*Co Cech, to muzikant*," meaning "Every Czech is a musician." Most of the respondents, whether musicians or not, articulated that they used the Internet in connection with music.

Perhaps not each and every Czech is a musician, but many are going online to perform, collaborate in developing compositions and, generally, to share their musical work and ideas. Michal B., age 21 and a student at the University of Ostrava in Information Systems, says, "The Internet gives an opportunity to those people, who want to present their own work and who are not able to present their masterpiece in galleries and concert halls." One of these online musicians is a Computational Technique student at the Ostrava Higher Professional School, Daniel B., age 20. Music is his "great hobby" since he began "playing the classical guitar at common conservatory. Now I visit discipline [sic] of bass guitar. I am playing in a group. I can not imagine my life without music." Daniel appreciates the possibilities provided by the Internet, primarily the World Wide Web where he finds a vast array of musical lyrics and compositions by his favorite artists. He uses computers to create music, and is interested in learning to record music in digital studios. Daniel frequently visits the website www.musicshop.cz, where he engages in Internet Relay Chat. He writes, "There is great opportunity to discuss online with people interested in the same topic." Not all is well with Daniel's online connectivity with other musicians, however. He notes, "unfortunately...access to this channel is now limited," although he did not provide details as to the limitations.

Stanislav M., 18, another Computational Technique student at the Higher Professional School, has a similar background in music to Daniel:

> I am interested both in music and art. I have been playing the guitar for five years and I am a member of a dramatic and theatre group REGINA Breclav. I am interested in other culture too. I like listening to rock music. Thanks to the Internet I can get new texts and new music and it is very important for me as a musician. I can get information about various cultural events, concerts and theatre performances. I can read reviews and critics from the area, which interests me.

Stanislav argues that no one "can imagine the future without the Internet. I think it will be especially useful in the cultural area. For instance two musicians from different continents will be able to compose music. Or musical groups can make appointments in different towns [or] states via the Internet. I think it will be possible to use the Internet in many ways." Jiri B., age 20 and a student in the same program, has a similar experience with online music: "I am interested in modern music. I am informed about the news in this area and can watch concerts in real time.... I like listening to music and playing it.... The Internet helped me to find chords and music or texts, which would be very difficult to get it from anywhere else."

CHALLENGES AND SUCCESSES OF ACCESS TO TECHNOLOGY

The difficulty of obtaining information, be it musical, artistic, or general, is an important consideration in New European nations like the

Czech Republic, where libraries are inadequately stocked and international news and information can be prohibitively costly through traditional media. However, with information and communication technology, particularly the Internet, there is now vastly increased access to information for Czech users. While there are problems with information disseminated on the World Wide Web and other Internet services, with regard to reliability, organization, and quality, the information that Czech users can access through technology far outweighs that obtained through traditional sources.

Thus, despite the limitations of the Internet, it is increasingly an important tool for information and communication. While the respondents have far better than average access to ICT, quick, affordable access that many users in the "West" take for granted is still unknown to most Czech citizens. For example, Jiri B. states, "I think ICT will influence culture in the Czech Republic in the future but now this problem has not been very important because of the lack of technical sources. The access to the Internet has not been common yet. Perhaps there should be better opportunities in libraries, schools, and studies." Tereza B., a 20-year-old Computational Technique student at the Higher Professional School, would also appreciate easier and more affordable access to technology: "I hope that with the growing information technology it will be [the norm] to have the Internet access at home in the future."

Other respondents are more optimistic. Sarka V., 22, an Information Systems student at the University of Ostrava, writes, "Tools for the Internet access and publication via the Internet are improving all the time. The possibilities of the use of PCs networks for culture are enlarging." Sarka learns about other cultures through the Internet: "I can read some information about people living at the other end of the world and I can learn about its culture on a monitor of my PC thanks to the Internet." Perhaps Marek could introduce Sarka to virtual art galleries, because Sarka writes, "I am sure there will exist (perhaps somewhere already are) virtual galleries; now you can get matters of material life at the virtual shops, but soon the virtual shops with music or multimedia will be here."

Another respondent who has benefitted from access to technology is Michal N., 24, an Information Technology student at the University of Ostrava. He says, "I consider the Internet as a huge source of the latest information about anything. It is wonderful that I can [share] my opinion with other people at nearly any time." Michal also obtains books "accessible on the Net which I would hardly ever get anywhere else. And so I can for instance consult my experience from "K center" with *Mudr. Presl* (a television program devoted to the problems of the younger generation)....It is very valuable for me because I want to have as much information about culture...as possible."

Jiri B., however, is skeptical about wide access to information and communication technology: "I was thinking about the following problem: If all people had a computer at home connected to the Internet, how would it have changed the community? I think it would be very good and perhaps it will become reality in [the] future but I am not sure about its influence on people....I am afraid that common [face-to-face] communication between people will disappear."

CONNECTING WITH OTHERS BOTH WITHIN AND OUTSIDE THE CZECH REPUBLIC

Despite the fear of losing opportunities for face-to-face communication because of the Internet, other respondents are happy with the ability to connect with others both within and outside the Czech Republic. Marek V. writes, "I have [made a] few friends in the USA and I often exchange e-mails with them or I use Chats. We exchange our experiences in the area of application of computer graphics in art." While Pavlina P., 19, is new to ICT as a Computational Technique student at the Higher Professional School and has merely elementary experience of technology, she has "already been looking for information about further study (at University or Higher Professional School), sport, jokes, and other interesting things on the Internet. I was writing to people from the whole Czech Republic. I think the Internet will become the largest and the most useful base of information in advanced states in the world."

One significant example illustrates the usefulness of the Internet to enhance Czech culture, bringing people closer, and creating projects that would be difficult without ICT. In October 1998, the Antonin Dvorak Theatre performed the première of a ballet featuring Mozart's Requiem, choreographed by Canadian visiting choreographer Eddy Toussaint. The ballet received rave reviews, particularly due to Toussaint's cutting edge choreography. His approach also greatly influenced the Dvorak Theatre dancers in their future projects. The collaboration with Toussaint and the subsequent production may not have been possible without ICT. Igor Vesajda (personal communication, November 1998, artistic manager and prinicipal choreographer with the Antonin Dvorak Theatre, explains: "We have connected our computer to the Internet recently. When I was surfing on it I found some interesting information about Eddy Toussaint. His work captured my attention so I made a connection with him via the e-mail. I offered him cooperation."

Respondents commented on not only their own ability to connect globally, but how diverse members of their community could benefit from technology connectivity. Tomas P., 21, a Computational Technique student at the Higher Professional School, writes, "I think that one of the most important contributions of the Internet and the ICT is its utilization for disabled people. It is surely a great opportunity for them to be able to communicate with people all over the world via e-conferences. Some of those people cannot go for a walk, to meet other people so it is very important for them to have this opportunity for communication. For instance computers are very useful for deaf people."

BREAKING DOWN VERSUS CREATING CULTURAL BARRIERS

Along with linking disabled persons, many respondents articulated that the Internet provides a very important chance to break down cultural barriers by bringing different nations and national minorities together. More than half of the respondents mentioned it was one of the most important tools that should be used in solving national and international problems as well as reducing cultural bias, marginalization, and intolerance, both locally and globally. Michal B., for instance, argues that ICT "allows breaking barriers among nations and different races. The differences between people are [diminishing]. People are meeting together according to their common interests." Sarka explains, "The barriers and misunderstanding between people arises first of all due to information gaps. People tend to assume the unknown is bad, displeasing or primitive." The Internet, Sarka argues, is a "necessity" because it can make the "bad, displeasing or primitive" disappear through knowledge and understanding. "Today you can see websites with information about various states, nationalities, their history, personalities, culture and symbols." Nevertheless, Sarka notes, more appropriate representations of diverse global cultures are necessary on the Internet: "There is a lot of information but it still looks insufficient. There is not enough information about national minorities, disabled people or ill people, about their achievements."

Jakub J., a 21-year-old student at the University of Ostrava, comments on the impact of how "the Internet is faceless, anonymous." He notes that "this fact has many advantages and many disadvantages, but there is no doubt about one positive aspect. It gives everyone an opportunity to approach each other without prejudice. I can contact a person and I consider him [or her] equal to me. His [or her] appearance and his behavior do not influence me. I am interested in his [or her] attitude to common [cross-cultural] problems." Like Tomas and Sarka, Jakub is also concerned about how the Internet can benefit disabled persons: "Another advantage of the Internet [is that it] can help disabled people to communicate freely and nearly without any limitation."

Other respondents discussed the fact that it is not easy to "communicate freely" and "without limitation." Michal N. writes, "Unfortunately I have also some bad experience with the Internet. I am often frustrated with the fact that people can behave to[ward] each other so calm[ly] and impersonally on the Internet. I have my own experience that one is much more audacious 'online,' he is not afraid to write things which he would not dare [say face-to-face]." He emphasizes that he is not sure that such "audacious" discourse "is right or wrong. I have not responsibility to judge people." Perhaps Michal senses that some computer-mediated communicators do unnecessarily judge others. He says "the possibilities are great," but they are not always used for the most appropriate type of civic discourse.

Jiri N. also discusses how ICT can build, rather than break down, cultural barriers, by isolating those who participate too heavily in computer-mediated communication: "The Internet can build barriers between people instead of breaking them because a lot of things will be possible to solve via the Internet. We will not need the direct contact with other people. We will stay at home and we will communicate only via computer and so we will lose the ability of communication with each other. And this idea quite frightens me." Another fear of Czech youth is that with the predominance of the English language on the Internet, the Czech language may eventually be lost. Jakub notes that, as a speaker of English, he does appreciate the ability for "international contact (due to the English language)." However, he realizes that many of his counterparts speak only the Czech language. "Unfortunately the language barriers still exist and it is a great problem. To learn a foreign language and to be able to express one's feelings and thoughts is really very difficult."

CZECH YOUTH AND THE WORLD WIDE WEB

Fortunately, there are a number of interesting sites in the Czech language that allow Czech youth to obtain information about cultural and artistic events, as well as reviews of new books, films, and music. Czech youth are visiting websites that focus on Czech culture, music, film, and literature. Sites such as www.czech.cz and Culture.cz (Péder & Péder, 1998) focus broadly on Czech culture, with listings for fashion, art exhibitions, sports, and tourism. Culture.cz includes reviews of cultural events and interviews with leaders in the performing and creative arts. Also, respondents actively use sites like Seznam.cz ["List"], which provides news and cultural and political information, as well as acts as a search engine for different sites in the Czech Republic. Other sites are specific to one aspect of culture, such as music (Czech Musical Server, 1998; Kovar, 1998), film (AmatFilm.cz, 1999; Czech Movie Heaven Team, 1998; Filmnet.cz, n.d.); and literature (Kafka+, 1997; knihy.hyper.cz, n.d.). The Culture.cz site promotes and includes links to an intriguing site called Paranormal.cz (INFOSET, 1999), where international oddities such as Atlantis and the Loch Ness monster are matched with various "Czech Mysteries." Sites like Novinky.cz ["News"] are updated daily with arts and television programming and include pages for comics, sex and drug scandals, and other current issues like "skinheady" (Seznam, 1999).

As has been discussed in much research (compare Carter, 1997; Kroker, 1996; Lengel & Murphy, forthcoming; Peacock, Lengel, & Scott, 1999), most material on the World Wide Web emerges from technological superpowers, particularly the United States. Such sites tend to marginalize cultures and global regions outside the industrialized world. While Czech culture sites certainly promote Czech culture, they do at times succumb to "Western" norms and cultural ideals (or the lack thereof). One example is the shop.culture.cz site, which, in its video online shopping section, sells such titles as *Men in Black*, *Batman & Robin*, and *The Best of Pamela Anderson*. Similarly, the shop.culture.cz music section hails jazz, rock, pop, and country music, which emerge predominately from the U.S.

When some respondents commented on their musical preferences and the music they searched for on the Internet, there was a predominance of musicians and bands from the U.S. and the UK. For instance, Jiri B. writes, "I am interested in music from sixties to present. I love for instance The Beatles, Elvis Presley, Eric Clapton, but also Carulli Carcasi or modern music such as ACE of BASE, Sheryl Crow, Robert Miles, and others." Similarly, Tereza B., a 20-year-old student of the Computational Technique Higher Professional School, says, "I like the Rolling Stones, Aerosmith, Madonna—I prefer modern music. I like theatre, comedies, classical Shakespeare drama and musical plays. I love visiting castles and chateaus. I had an opportunity to see Web pages on these topics." While many respondents did mention specific Czech musicians and bands, one might be disappointed to see how the globalization and internationalization of the music scene has allowed "Western" stars to permeate the world. Similarly, the Czech Musical Service, "a daily news from the world of musicals," includes listings of productions scheduled in Prague, the majority of which originated in the U.S. or UK, such as

Les Miserables, *West Side Story*, *Pippin*, and *Hello Dolly*. Only one musical listed on the site is Czech: *Rusalka*, based on the opera by Czech composer Antonin Dvorak and featuring all Czech stars.

Despite such emphasis on "Western" cultural products, most Czech websites do promote the local and national cultures. Unlike the e-shopping site promoting "Western" goods and personalities such as Pamela Anderson, České filmové nebe (Czech Movie Heaven Team, 1998) is devoted solely to Czech films, actors, directors, producers, and cinematographers. Kulturní Stránka České Republiky (X-Media, 1998) includes detailed historical and contemporary aspects of the Czech Republic, a list of exhibitions taking place in the Czech republic, and links to other cultural and arts organizations such as the National Gallery. Most music sites, such as Czech Techno (Prvni Multimedialni/Czech Techno, 1998) and Rock.cz (Ed'asX, 1998), focus solely on Czech musicians and bands, promoting local cultures to users both within and outside the Czech Republic. These sites, the respondents argue, place the Czech Republic on the map, promoting Czech culture, which, they believe, goes unnoticed to the rest of the world.

While most of the Czech culture sites are user-passive, disseminating information with no opportunity for comment or contribution, a few, such as Culture.cz, Czech Techno (Prvni Multimedialni/Czech Techno, 1998) and Rock.cz (Ed'asX, 1998), include chat rooms and discussion groups to interact with other users about Czech culture and Czech techno and rock music, respectively. This opportunity is excellent for Czech youth who do not have the means to promote their creative endeavors through traditional media. Similarly, AmatFilm.cz (1999), a site for young Czech amateur filmmakers, provides listings of amateur film clubs throughout the nation, opportunities for filmmakers to discuss their own work and link with other filmmakers, and information about competitions. The České Filmové Nebe site (Czech Movie Heaven Team, 1998) allows users to review Czech films online. Even more interesting is the Musicsite.cz site (n.d.), which affords users with the opportunity to upload their own musical creations.

Also important for Czech youth are sites like Seznam (1999), which has a section on drug use, drug rehabilitation, and AIDS awareness. Sites like Seznam have been helpful to N. M., age 24 and an Information Technology student at the University of Ostrava, who found information on his addiction through the Internet: "[Struggling] with finding the meaning of life and with a lack of success I experimented [with drugs and had] serious drug problems." Though the Internet, "I have met 'Somebody' in the deepness, which lent me a hand and took me out.... Now I devote most of my free time to [helping] drug addicted people. I work with them in the street as a streetwalker of 'K center' in Prerov."

Out of all the Czech culture sites that were discussed by the respondents, the music sites seemed to be of greatest interest. Many respondents have a keen interest in both producing and consuming popular music. They believe the sites themselves, in their design, information, and navigational features, are more interesting to Czech youth than the other culture sites. For instance, Music.cz (n.d.), which features interviews solely on Czech bands, includes a header with an image of a "mosh-pit" and navigation guided by very "hip" java script "MouseOvers," buttons that change image as a user moves the mouse over them. Like Music.cz, the Sikkim.cz site features industrial bands and labels, and has gothic-style headers and images and black backgrounds. The navigational menu of Rock.cz is equally interesting, with a font that one could envision on a U.S. 1950s seaside cocktail bar called "Tiki Twirl." The Czech techno site (Prvni Multimedialni/Czech Techno, 1998) provides users with a stark black background, but stands out above all the sites with its unique logo, which moves around the screen manipulated by DHTML (Dynamic Hypertext Markup Language) and changes every time the user returns to the home page. Even more amusingly, the site includes "MouseOver" navigation buttons designed as pieces of fruit that change color as the user moves the mouse over each. The aesthetics of the sites remind one of the posters adorning walls of adolescents and university students; they make strong statements, boldly proclaiming independence, fun, and resistance to the aesthetic norms of adulthood.

NEW OPPORTUNITIES FOR CIVIC DISCOURSE

Bold proclamations of independence, fun, and resistance to the aesthetic norms of adulthood are part of youth culture in many areas of the world, not just the New Europe. However, such proclamations are perhaps more critical to youth in regions of intense change. Czech youth grasp on to music and its accompanying culture and imagery as significant illustrators of their own identity and their collective identity. Websites like Music.cz, Sikkim.cz, and Czech Techno provide a positive outlet for the frustrations and anxiety that often befall youth of any culture, let alone one that is in a constant state of uncertainty. Submersion in culture gives Czech youth a break from the fears that they experience in a nation where socioeconomic stability has not been enjoyed in a decade.

Despite the change and uncertainty, virtually all respondents believe that freedom of communication and of ideas is clearly improved, for both Czech youth and adults, since 1989. Information and communication technologies can play a powerful role in this new civic discourse. Marek argues, "Computer-mediated communication is giving us opportunities which were unknown before." Martin says, "Now many people have access to the Internet, and they use it" for the types of civic discourse that were impossible before 1989. Martin's brother, a student at the University in Brno, makes a magazine with political content. Martin says, "He succeeded to interview an American writer via e-mail. It would not be possible without the Internet" and unlikely during Communist rule.

NOTES

1. Information and communication technology has been a primary focus in news, educational, and business as well as day-to-day discourse in the New Europe. Numerous conferences and organizations are held in the Czech Republic that reflect this interest.
   Conferences include: The Second EU-CEEC Forum on the Information Society, Prague, July 14-16, 1997; Role of Universities in the Future Information Society (RUFIS), Prague, 1998, <http://web.cvut.cz/ascii/cc/icsc/NII/index.html>; MirandaNet conference on ICT teaching excellence, April 1998; POSKOLE conference on teaching and ICT, Sedmihorky, April 15-18, 1998; The Pedagogical Software conference, University of South Bohemia, Èeské Budejovice, <http://www.pf.jcu.cz>; The Computer at School annual conference, Ostrava, <http://www1.osu.cz/Inf/inf3.htm>; and "GYZA" conference on new educational programs offered by Czech companies, Gymnasium in Zabreh na Morave, <http://www.edunet.cz/rozc/konfnews.html>
   Organizations include: Centre for New Technologies in Education (CNT), housed at the University of South Bohemia, Èeské Budejovice, <http://home.pf.jcu.cz/~vanicek/cnte/index-cz.htm>; EDUNET, housed at the Department of Information Science, Novy Jicin, <http://www.edunet.cz>; MirandaNet, <http://www.mirandanet.com>; also, see EUNIS (European University Information Organisation, which includes many Czech members, <http://www.Imcp.jussieu.fr/eunis>.
2. For detailed discussions of the thematization process, see Kapoor (1998) and Lengel (1993).

REFERENCES

AmatFilm.cz [Online]. (1999, January 15). Available: <http://www.tradeweb.cz/amatfilm> [1999, April 17].

Amit-Talai, V., & Wulff, H. (Eds.). (1995). *Youth cultures: A cross-cultural perspective*. London: Routledge.

Bennahum, D. S. (1997, November). Heart of darkness. *Wired, 5*(11), 226–277.

Burianová, E. & Telnarová, Z. (1999, March). *The function of the University of Ostrava (Czech Republic) in the teachers' preparation in the ICT area*. Paper presented at the Computers and Learning (CAL99) conference, Institute of Education, University of London.

Carter, D. (1997). "Digital democracy" or "information aristocracy"? Economic regeneration and the information economy. In B. Loader (Ed.), *The governance of cyberspace: Politics, technology and global restructuring* (pp. 136-152). London: Routledge.

CFWR. (1998, September 12). *CFWR—Czech film web ring. Frantisek Fuka biography* [Online]. Available: <http://surf.to/fuxoft> [1999, January 24].

CUYT. (1996, August 26). *Center for Urban Youth and Technology* [Online]. Available: <http://www.albany.edu/cuyt> [1999, April 17].

Czech Movie Heaven Team. (1998) *Česke filmové nebe* [Online]. Available: <http://cfn.vsb.cz> [1999, April 17].

Czech Musical Server [Online]. (1998, December 13). Available: <http://www.musical.cz> [1999, April 17].

Ed.asX. (1998). *Rock.Cz* [Online]. Available: <http://www.lantanet.cz/jakubs/prehled/index2.phtml> [1999, April 17].

Filmnet.cz [Online]. (n.d.). Available: <http://www.filmnet.cz> [1999, November 23].

Gallego, M. A. (1994, Spring). A computer-oriented after-school activity: Children's learning in the fifth dimension and La Clase Magica. *New Directions for Child Development, 63*, 35–43.

Hobzová, L., & Hamhalterová, Z. (1999, March). *Czech experience of virtuality in education*. Paper presented at the Computers and Learning (CAL99) conference, Institute of Education, University of London.

Hlavenka, J. (1997, September). *Česky Internet—Odsouzen K Zaostalosti Nebo Ke Slave?* [The Czech Internet: Condemned to backwardness or to glory?] Paper presented at the "Role of Universities in the Future Information Society" (RUFIS'97) conference.

INFOSET. (1999, January 18). *Paranormal.cz home page* [Online]. Available: <http://www.paranormal.cz> [1999, January 23].

Kafka+. (1997, March 19). *Constructing Franz Kafka* [Online]. Available: <http://info.pitt.edu/~kafka/intro.html> [1999, January 24].

Kapoor, P. (1999). A chance of double lives: Phenomenological study of black female graduate experience. In T. McDonald & T. Ford-Ahmed (Eds.), *Nature of a sistuh: Black women's experiences in contemporary culture* (pp. 53-70). Durham, NC: Carolina Academic Press.

knihy.hyper.cz. (n.d.). *Czech literature site* [Online]. Available: <http://knihy.hyper.cz> [1999, September 2].

Kovar, K. (1998, November 19). *Music.cz* [Online]. Available: <http://www.music.cz> [1999, April 17].

Kroker, A. (1996). Virtual capitalism. In. S. Aronowitz, B. Martinsons, & M. Menser (Eds.), *Techno science and cyber culture* (pp. 167–180). London: Routledge.

Lengel, L. (1993, April). *Gender construction in graduate school: Cultural, academic, and social influences on graduate students.* Paper presented at the President's Panel of the Central States Communication Association Conference, Louisville, KY.

Lengel, L. (1998, Summer). Access to the Internet in East Central and South Eastern Europe. *Convergence: The Journal of Research into New Media Technologies, 4*(2), 38–55.

Lengel, L., & Murphy, P. (forthcoming). Cultural identity and cyberimperialism: Computer mediated explorations of ethnicity, nation and citizenship. In B. Ebo (Ed.), *Cyberimperialism: Global relations in the new electronic frontier.* Westport, CT: Greenwood.

Liechty, M. (1995). Media, markets and modernization: Youth identities and the experience of modernity in Kathmandu, Nepal. In V. Amit-Talai & H. Wulff (Eds.), *Youth cultures: A cross-cultural perspective* (pp. 166–201). London: Routledge.

Mestel, R. (1996). It's child's play. *New Scientist, 150*(2025), 24–35.

Milone, M. N. (1996). Kids as multimedia authors. *Technology & Learning, 16*(5), 22–28.

Musicsite.cz [Online]. (n.d.). Available: <http://www.musicsite.cz> [1999, April 16].

North, T. (1995). Tecno-culture on the final frontier. *Classroom, 15*(4), 12–15.

Paletz, D., Jakubowicz, K., & Novosel, P. (1995). *Glasnost and after: Media and change in Central and Eastern Europe.* Creeskill, NJ: Hampton.

Peacock, S., Lengel, L., & Scott, C. (1999, April 1). *The impact of student-centred on-line collaboration on future teaching and learning.* Paper presented at the "Writing and Computers 11" conference, University of Cambridge, England.

Péder, D., & Péder, V. (1998). *Culture.cz home page* [Online]. Available: <http://www.culture.cz> [1999, January 24].

Preston, C. (1995). *21st century literacy handbook, linking literacy with software: A handbook for education and training.* London: University of London, Institute of Education.

Preston, C., & Mannova, B. (1999, March). *Peach velvet: A revolution in collaborative lifelong learning for teacher educators across cultural boundaries.* Paper presented at the Computers and Learning (CAL99) conference, Institute of Education, University of London.

Prvni Multimedialni/Czech Techno. (1998). *Czech Techno* [Online]. Available: <http://www.techno.cz> [1999, January 23].

Sanger, J., Wilson, J., Davies, B., & Whittaker, R. (1997). *Young children, videos and computer games: Issues for teachers and parents.* Washington, DC: Falmer Press.

Seznam. (1999, January 23). *Jak jsem potkal skinheady. Lidé, vztahy, sex section of the Novinky.cz website* [Online]. Available: <http://www.novinky.cz/Index/Lide_vztahy_sex/1295.html?from=sekce> [1999, January 23].

Sherrell, R. (1998). Kids on the Internet. *Upscale, 9*(8), 46–54.

X-Media. (1998). *Kulturní Stránka České Republiky* [Online]. Available: <http://www.x-media.cz/culture/CZ_index_EE.html> [1999, April 17].

chapter 15

ZaMir Transnational Net: Computer-Mediated Communication and Resistance Music in Bosnia-Herzegovina, Croatia, and the Federal Republic of Yugoslavia

Amy Herron
DePaul University
College of Law

Eric Bachman
Balkan Peace Team, Germany

No communication link can stop a conflict or decrease tensions. No communication link can create peace. But if there is no possibility of communication, then there is no chance to work for peace. Open lines of communication are a prerequisite for conflict resolution
—Bachman (1996a)

The Yugoslav successor states, Slovenia, Croatia, Bosnia-Herzegovina, the Federal Republic of Yugoslavia, and Macedonia, have received much media attention in the last decade, largely due to the war. However, little, if any, attention has been given to the numerous peace efforts there—both local and international—or the positive influence these efforts have had. The ZaMir Transnational Net (ZTN), a digital electronic mail network that Eric Bachman helped found, has been one of the most valuable tools for the anti-war and human rights organizations in the former Yugoslav region. In Serbo-Croatian,[1] "Za Mir" means "for peace." Bachman and others created this network to improve communication between peace-oriented people and groups, humanitarian organizations, nongovernmental organizations (NGOs), independent media in the Yugoslav successor states, and refugees and their families. The technology of ZTN provided the possibility for civic discourse among peace-related people and organizations and the importance of this network has been widely discussed (compare Association for Progressive Communication, 1998a, 1998b; Bachman, 1996a; Iordanova, forthcoming). The ideology ZTN espoused can be best presented through its mission statement:

> The ZaMir Transnational Network aims to serve people working for the prevention of warfare; the elimination of militarism; protection of the environment; the advancement of human rights and the rights of people regardless of race, ethnic background, sex, religion, or political convictions; the achievement of social and economic justice; women's rights; the elimination of poverty; the promotion of sustainable and equitable development; more and better democratic structures in society, especially the advancement of participatory democracy; nonviolent conflict resolution; and to aid the communication between all people, especially for refugees. (Bachman, 1998)

In a situation where prejudice, hate, and fear between people of different ethnic backgrounds had been growing almost unchallenged, building communication links was of utmost importance during the war. These links helped people reach out to each other, begin new relationships, revive old friendships, and help organize the peace movement. Amy Herron, for example, used ZTN most of her 15 months of volunteer work in Croatia to correspond with many local and international NGOs as well as to seek out contacts for her music research, discussed later in this chapter. To better understand the significance of ZTN, it is important to understand some of the historical context that led to the development of the network.

HISTORICAL CONTEXTS OF THE YUGOSLAV SUCCESSOR STATES

Both historical events and current political activities contributed to the outbreak of war in Yugoslavia, which have been widely analyzed in current scholarship (compare Cohen, 1993; Kaplan, 1993; Lampe, 1996; Malcolm, 1998; Vulliamy, 1994; Williams, 1995). The death of Yugoslav President Josip Broz Tito in 1980 marked the beginning of a collective presidency rotating among the six republics and the two autonomous regions in Yugoslavia-Vojvodina and Kosovo. This collective presidency continued until the growth of nationalist interests in these republics tore Yugoslavia apart.

The Yugoslav Parliament's decision in 1988 and 1989 to abolish the autonomy of Vojvodina and Kosovo foreshadow the war beginning in 1991. This decision resulted from the rising nationalism in Serbia, which was encouraged by Slobodan Milošević. In 1990, the elections were marked by populist campaigns in each republic, which solidified the growth of nationalist forces and highlighted ethnic grievances.

On June 25, 1991, both Slovenia and Croatia declared independence from Yugoslavia. The Yugoslav National Army (JNA) tried to prevent Slovenian independence, but was met by strong resistance by the Slovene territorial defense forces. After 10 days of war, the international community helped negotiate a cease-fire and a three-month moratorium on the secession. By the end of the moratorium, the JNA had withdrawn from Slovenia. In Croatia, where a large minority of Serbs also lived (75 percent Croatian, 18 percent Serbs) (Hoffman, 1992), violent skirmishes escalated throughout that summer. In the face of Croatian moves toward independence, the Serbs in the Krajina[2] region of Croatia declared their own independence and backed up their claim with JNA support and arms (Weinberg & Wilsnack, 1997).

The JNA and local Serbs also took control of part of Croatia's Eastern Slavonia. As Croatia attempted to force the JNA to leave the country, fighting flared up around JNA bases in Croatia. As the fighting destroyed their homes in Eastern Slavonia and the Krajina, refugees fled to other countries and to other Yugoslav successor states. In December 1991, the European Community recognized Slovenia and Croatia as independent countries, but the war raged on. After many attempts, a successful cease-fire was finally brokered in January 1992.

Bosnia-Herzegovina's cultural diversity (44 percent Slavic Muslim, 31 percent Serb, and 17 percent Croat) (Malcolm, 1994) was both an asset and a source of tension. Faced with the secession of the two republics to the north and the inability to negotiate a peaceful settlement of the differences among the ethnic groups in the republic, political leaders of Bosnia-Herzegovina felt compelled to hold a referendum on independence. The Serb population tried to stop this referendum and eventually boycotted it. This put an end to negotiations and strengthened a strategic alliance between Bosnia's Muslims and Croats against the Bosnian Serbs.

The spring of 1992 marked the beginning of the war in Bosnia-Herzegovina and the siege of Sarajevo. Dr. Radovan Karadžić attempted to create a Serbian state within Bosnia-Herzegovina by fighting to link Serbia and the Serb-controlled parts of Croatia. By 1993, the Bosnian Muslim–Bosnian Croat alliance broke down. Serbs, Muslims, and Croats fought each other for control of parts of Bosnia-Herzegovina, which resulted in hundreds of thousands of refugees. As the war in Bosnia-Herzegovina continued, repeated attempts were made to negotiate a cease-fire. Various peace plans were developed and rejected.

The year 1995 was one of many changes. Croatian military took control of Eastern Slavonia (May 1995) and the Krajina (August 1995). Continued bombing of the besieged Sarajevo triggered the NATO intervention (August 1995) and the enforcement of a cease-fire in Bosnia-Herzegovina. Intensive negotiations brokered by the U.S. resulted in the Dayton Agreement, which was signed in December 1995. The NATO International Forces (IFOR) and later NATO Stabilization Forces (SFOR), together with the Organization for Security and Cooperation in Europe (OSCE) and the Office of the High Representative (OHR) to the UN, were given the task of implementing the Dayton Peace Accords in Bosnia-Herzegovina. The implementation of the Dayton Peace Accords established a Bosnian Muslim-Bosnian Croat Federation and the Bosnian Serb-controlled Republic of Serbia.

This cease-fire in Bosnia-Herzegovina has held. In many places, refugees are returning, and reconstruction is underway. The truce is still troubled by the difficulties encountered by returning refugees, and tensions still exist between the different parts of Bosnia-Herzegovina. SFOR continues to monitor the situation.

EVOLUTION OF ZAMIR: CONCEPTION OF THE NETWORK

Throughout the war, computer technology, such as e-mail and electronic conferences and later the World Wide Web, were spreading and became an integral component of the peace and human rights efforts. For many NGOs, it became a very important means of communication across the new borders and with international partners all over the world.

Beginning in the summer of 1991, anti-war and human rights groups in Yugoslavia increasingly began to organize themselves and coordinate activities; however, they encountered numerous communication difficulties. With the advent of war between Serbia and Croatia, normal avenues of communication were disrupted. Not only did travel by train or road between Croatia and Serbia[3] become impossible, but the destruction of many telephone connections further impeded communication. Telephone calls between Zagreb and Belgrade, for example, became almost impossible. The war increasingly was destroying the telephone lines. Further, the disruption of the postal system meant an almost total breakdown of communication, especially for those on opposing sides of the conflict.

One of the first attempts to improve communication between anti-war groups in this region came in October 1991. Several peace groups from other countries with good telephone connections to both Croatia and Serbia agreed to relay faxes between peace groups in Zagreb and Belgrade. However, this was not enough. Eric Bachman then helped the Antiwar Campaign Croatia, in Zagreb, and the Center for Antiwar Action, in Belgrade, begin plans to set up e-mail connections. The Internet was not yet readily available in the region, therefore a bulletin board system (BBS) using computers, modems, and telephone lines was used to allow Zagreb and Belgrade to connect directly to cities in other countries such as Austria, Germany, and Britain. Also, the BBS would connect to a gateway and enable the local users to exchange e-mail and news worldwide via the Internet.

Some of the existing BBSs in Slovenia, Croatia, and Serbia agreed to support the development of a larger network. The first phase for this development began in December 1991 and early 1992. Peace and anti-war groups in Ljubljana, Zagreb, Belgrade, and Sarajevo received donated modems and had regular connections installed between the preexisting BBSs in the AdiraNet in Slovenia and the GreenNet[4] in England.

Unfortunately, the BBSs in Zagreb and Belgrade did not connect regularly to the AdriaNet. This meant that the e-mail and news exchange usually did not work. Although several peace groups now had the means to communicate by e-mail, the local BBSs did not effectively enable people or groups in Bosnia, Croatia, Kosovo, Macedonia, Montenegro, Vojvodina, Serbia, and Slovenia to communicate with one another.

Wam Kat, an international volunteer experienced with e-mail, addressed the continuing problem of communication. In April 1992, Kat connected the Antiwar Campaign in Zagreb to the worldwide e-mail network by directly dialing the London-based GreenNet. This step provided excellent and speedy communication to and from the Zagreb Antiwar Campaign, but was also very expensive. Also, it was unable to help other anti-war and peace groups, especially those in Serbia. Therefore, the problem of connecting the warring regions remained to be solved.

CONCEPTION AND IMPLEMENTATION OF ZAMIR

The next attempt to set up e-mail connections came in 1992, when the Antiwar Campaign in Zagreb and the Center for Anti-War Action in Belgrade decided to set up their own BBS network. In July of that year, two new BBSs were installed, one in Zagreb (ZAMIR-ZG) and the other in Belgrade (ZAMIR-BG). Regular automatic connections via Austria allowed the new BBSs to route e-mail to each other and to and from the rest of the world. E-mail could be sent overnight from Zagreb to Belgrade and vice versa. Within 12 to 24 hours, letters could be sent and received to or from any system in the Association for Progressive Communications (APC) network and via a gateway to the worldwide Internet. This enabled users to send and receive messages to and from anyone with a valid Internet e-mail address and to read and write to electronic conferences[5] from all over the world.

All ZTN servers were "store and forward" computer systems, temporarily holding e-mail until it could pass the e-mail on to the recipient or to another forwarding system. The computers in this network used existing telephone lines and modems to connect with each other and exchange data. For instance, when Zagreb called Germany, Zagreb received not only its own messages, but also the messages for other sites that connected to Zagreb. When these sites called Zagreb, they received their messages as well as any messages for all other sites that might call them. This system enabled local BBSs to call the connecting BBS site closest to them, thereby reducing their long-distance costs. Also, using normal dial-up telephone connections was very flexible, since the routing structure could be easily changed whenever telephone lines were destroyed or became more accessible.

Another advantage of "store and forward" systems was that they did not tie up phone lines as long. Instead of working online, users read and wrote e-mail and news messages without being connected to the server. The users then made quick "netcalls" to send and receive mail and news. These were important features because phone lines were scarce. The opening of communication was a groundbreaking achievement in an area so ravaged by war.

TECHNICAL DIFFICULTIES WITH ZAMIR

Nevertheless, the ZaMir Network had its share of problems. The computer in Belgrade (an old, slow laptop with a small hard drive) was not adequate to handle a BBS. The limited hardware caused problems, and a single telephone line in the Center for Antiwar Action had to be shared between voice, fax, and computer communications. In Zagreb, the Antiwar Campaign had similar problems. It also needed a computer and telephone line dedicated solely to the BBS.

Another problem was the poor quality of the telephone lines in Belgrade. For example, some local telephone lines in Belgrade would not support any type of modem connection, regardless what setting was being used. Further, some international connections from Belgrade would not support more than 300 characters per second (cps), even though the modems were capable of supporting 1,500 cps. By using special modems and by switching to another, better-quality telephone number, they were able to achieve better and more reliable data exchanges.

In September 1992, the Center for Antiwar Action in Belgrade obtained a new computer that was dedicated solely to the ZAMIR-BG BBS. Together with a new modem and a dedicated telephone line at a new location, reliable communication was set up with the relay BBS in Vienna, LINK-ATU. The Brethren Volunteer Service (BVS) knew of ZTN's difficulties and sent volunteer Patrick Morgan to the center. Morgan's job was to support the communication project. After Morgan was trained to use the e-mail programs, he kept the e-mail system running and helped facilitate communication in general.

During December 1992, Zagreb was having additional computer-related problems. At that time, only a few volunteers were doing the technical maintenance. The hard disk crashed when no one was around who knew how to get the system running again. As a result, ZAMIR-ZG was offline for a month. In response to this problem, the Antiwar Campaign Croatia raised funds to buy new computers and another telephone line dedicated to Zagreb's BBS. Additionally, the Antiwar Campaign Croatia tried to organize funds to hire part-time paid system operators.

ZAMIR GROWS

By the summer of 1993, there were a total of 375 users in Belgrade (seven of which were groups) and 125 users in Zagreb (27 of which were groups). Other e-mail connections from Serbia to the outside world were still very difficult, if not impossible to use. This unavailability of access accounted for a large number of the individual users in the Belgrade BBS. The system operators in Zagreb, however, actively recruited as many groups as possible to join and use the system. Also, an increasing number of international humanitarian aid groups in Croatia made use of the system.

Each of the BBSs sent and received approximately 500 kilobytes a day, including public conferences and private messages. This cost approximately $120 (U.S.) a month per system. Users of the ZTN were not charged for the communication services. The local running costs (that is, telephone and electricity) were covered by the Center for Antiwar Action in Belgrade, the Antiwar Campaign in Zagreb, and Suncokret (a local humanitarian organization), also in Zagreb. Future plans called for raising more funds and spreading the costs among users.

ZTN continued to expand. The Zagreb and Belgrade systems set up electronic conferences in their own languages on ZTN and exchanged approximately 150 international electronic conferences (APC, USENET, and so on). More and more organizations began using the e-mail and news systems. The International Council of Voluntary Agencies (ICVA) set up its own BBS in Geneva (ICVAGE) and one in Zagreb (ICVAZG), both of which were connecting to and sharing conferences with ZTN. ICVA's system allowed it to have better contact with its member organizations working in Croatia and Bosnia.

ZTN was not home free yet. Emergency power systems, called uninterruptable power supplies (UPSs), were installed because of fluctuations in the electrical supply. New telephone lines were ordered for the Belgrade and Zagreb systems in order to give more users access to the systems. Unfortunately, these lines could not be obtained quickly. For example, the Zagreb system had to wait two years before a second line was installed and the installation costs were exorbitant—$1,000 (U.S.) for each line.

At the end of 1993, the ZTN systems that were linked via the server LINK-ATU in Vienna, Austria, changed to BIONIC, a nonprofit BBS in Bielefield, Germany. In 1994, three new BBSs were installed— ZAMIR-LJ in Ljubljana, Slovenia in February; ZAMIR-SA in Sarajevo, Bosnia-Herzegovina in March; and ZANA-PR[6] in Priština, Kosova,[7] in November.

The ongoing war made it very difficult to install the BBS in Sarajevo. It was almost a miracle to be able to get a telephone, electricity, and a computer working and installed in the same room within three weeks. The Sarajevo connection was being routed first through the ICVAGE system in Geneva because this was the only system able to call Sarajevo. The Sarajevo connection then went to BIONIC in Bielefield, Germany, and finally to the other ZTN systems. BIONIC became the central server in the ZTN connecting Belgrade, Zagreb, Ljubljana, and Sarajevo to each other and to the rest of the world via the Internet.

In October 1994, the Yugoslav successor states acquired separate international country codes, followed by a dramatic increase in international telephone costs. Calls from Ljubljana to and from Zagreb suddenly became international calls. Calls from Germany to Zagreb were less expensive than calls between Ljubljana and Zagreb, and calls from Germany to Zagreb were cheaper than calls from Zagreb to Germany. The "store and forward" systems then changed their routing so that Germany called Belgrade and Zagreb instead of vice versa.

The ZTN became a full member in the Association for Progressive Communication[8] (APC) network. The new domain that was implemented was "ZTN.APC.ORG." By the end of 1994, ZTN connected over 1,700 users on five different servers in five different cities.

ROUTING CHANGES AND PROBLEMS

At the end of 1994, the ICVAGE server in Geneva was taken off line because the ICVA was closing down its "Yugoslavian Task Group." This meant that Zagreb and Sarajevo now needed to directly contact each other which had previously not been possible. ZAMIR-SA did not have an international telephone line; consequently, Zagreb was responsible for calling Sarajevo. Reliable contact could only be made at night when the telephone system was less overloaded. The systems in Zagreb, Belgrade, and Sarajevo expanded in 1995.

Furthermore, a new server was established in Tuzla, Bosnia-Herzegovina. This was an expensive process. To get an international line in Bosnia-Herzegovina, a special application and a large deposit were needed. This new server made it possible for people in the Muslim controlled part of Bosnia-Herzegovina who had access to a working telephone and computer with a modem to use e-mail. Tuzla-ZG grew quickly and became the main server for Bosnia-Herzegovina outside of Sarajevo. The Tuzla server provided a backup when Sarajevo's server was down, and vice versa.

ZTN also provided connections for many humanitarian aid organizations. Other humanitarian aid organizations created their own servers. For instance, the ICVA in Zagreb and the offices of the Open Society Foundations (Soros Foundations) in Belgrade, Sarajevo, and Zagreb ran servers for their staff and member organizations and connected to the Internet at that time via the ZaMir network. In fact, the Open Society Foundations now provided a large portion of the funding for the network.

By the end of 1995, there were over 2,500 users of the public ZTN network. Five hundred of these were organizations. Additionally, 100 to 200 users were connected via the private servers (humanitarian aid organizations) in the ZTN.

PROBLEMS FACING ZAMIR

Zagreb finally had adequate phone lines to facilitate the large number of ZTN users. Three were for public use, one for intersystem data exchanges, and one for hotline voice support for the users. Belgrade was not as lucky. After three and a half years, the Belgrade system was still running on one phone line. Consequently, access was very difficult because of the large number of users. Sarajevo secured three additional lines after one year. If all lines were operating, access was quite good. However, the lines were still unreliable. At times, ZTN servers were supporting 300 active users for each available telephone line. This was possible by using offline e-mail and news programs that shared the limited telephone time more effectively.

Even though more telephone lines were becoming available to ZTN, their quality often remained poor. This caused the transferring of data to be extremely slow or made connecting difficult. For example, in Priština, the telephone system was extremely overloaded. Telephone users sometimes had to wait as long as 30 minutes for a dial tone. Once a dial tone came, there were only a few seconds to dial before the dial tone would disappear again. This problem was overcome by dialing into Priština to initiate the data exchange. By the end of 1996, there were seven servers in operation. ZTN was serving more than 5,000 individuals and organizations transferring 100 to 200 megabytes of personal mail each day, in addition to 800 electronic conferences from ZamirNet, APC, CL-Netz, Human Rights Net, ICVA Net, UseNet, and others.

CRISIS AND CHANGE

ZTN began in a time of war when the economy was falling apart. The new NGOs and activists had little funds. The NGOs who initiated the network offered its services at no cost. During the first years of the network, a number of international organizations donated funds to cover the hardware, software, maintenance, and running costs. The network's data transfer costs now ranged from $6,000 to $10,000 a month. The intention was to have outside funders subsidize the start-up costs of the network with the expectation that users would later pay a fee to cover the costs.

After five years of operation, the last of the outside donations covering the data transfer costs came to an end. Even though it was obvious that the systems would have to become financially self-sufficient, little was done to prepare for this situation. The local organizations responsible for the BBSs did begin to collect fees from the users, but they were not sufficient to cover the running costs.

The ZaMir network's data exchange often had to rely upon expensive dial-up international telephone connections. This was because in some cases there was no Internet access in the country, and in other cases, the Internet was available in the country, but ZTN could not get access to it. Also, ZTN needed to be flexible in the face of political difficulties.

In the summer of 1997, when ZTN had to begin to cover its entire cost, it became too much of a financial load for many of the local organizations. As Internet services became commercially available in Croatia, Slovenia, Bosnia-Herzegovina, and the Federal Republic of Yugoslavia, ZTN users who could afford the Internet left the ZTN BBSs and connected to the more expensive full Internet service providers in their respective countries. The ZTN systems had not moved quickly enough to become full Internet service providers (ISP) or to provide services needed by the NGO community.

By the end of 1997, both Zana-PR in Priština and Zamir-BG in Belgrade folded because they were unable to pay their share of the costs. Other systems in Tuzla, Sarajevo, Pakrac, and Rijeka were barely able to survive financially. The Antiwar Campaign Croatia was the only ZTN member organization able to set up a full Internet service provider with the help of two large donations.

There are several possible explanations why the ZTN systems were not been able to survive and grow. The people in the organizations managing the e-mail and news systems lacked business experience. The transition from a highly centralized market structure to free-market business methods involved significant changes and people were unprepared. Perhaps there was a lack of initiative and innovation, which would have helped keep the systems growing and enabled them to offer the new services needed by the NGO community and individual users.

Before the war, no strong tradition of NGO organization existed. People had to learn how to organize and administer such structures. The NGOs administering the ZTN systems encountered great difficulty developing the structures necessary to collect fees from users who for years were used to paying nothing for the service. It was also difficult to convince the users that they now would have to pay for the service. There were further difficulties with the national telephone companies that wanted to maintain monopolies on communications, including the new Internet. A combination of these problems led the ZTN member organizations to stumble. In spite of their early leadership in digital communications, most of the ZTN systems did not survive the changes in their countries and were not able to continue to support the NGO community there.

As of spring 1999, the only BBSs still in operation were Zamir-ZG in Zagreb and Zamir-SA in Sarajevo. Only the Antiwar Campaign Croatia has been able to develop a full Internet provider (zamir.net) for the NGO community.

ZAMIR IN ACTION: MEDIA, REFUGEES, HUMANITARIAN AID, RESEARCH, AND YOUTH GROUPS

The examples of how the ZaMir Transnational Net has been used are numerous. During the war, ZTN was a significant factor in the reconciliation and peace efforts in the region. In order to demonstrate ZTN's importance, examples of how ZTN has been used are given in the following areas: media, refugees, humanitarian aid, research, and youth groups.

Finding unbiased media about the war in Croatia and Bosnia proved difficult. ZTN was integral in making alternative media sources available to the public. During protests in Belgrade for democracy and against censorship, reports by people involved could be disseminated quickly through ZTN. These reports provided a different version of events from the "official" reports. Further, the Balkan Peace Team, an international organization dedicated to observing and reporting the activities of unstable countries, was able to use ZTN to communicate with each other and make human rights violations known to the world. Articles were solicited and sent over ZTN. ArkZin, the Antiwar Campaign's independent biweekly newspaper, used ZTN to keep in contact with many of its journalists living in other countries such as Austria, England, Switzerland, and the U.S.

NGOs, especially human rights and anti-war groups, used ZTN to make their reports and other information publicly accessible thoughout the war. People were able to read public reports and press releases from many groups, including the Antiwar Campaign (Zagreb); Autonomous Women's Center (Belgrade); Balkan Peace Team (Zagreb, Split, Belgrade, Priština); Center for Antiwar Action (Belgrade); Center for Peace, Nonviolence and Human Rights (Osijek); Helsinki Committee for Human Rights (Zagreb and Belgrade); International Volunteers Project (Pakrac); Suncokret (Zagreb); Women in Black (Belgrade); and Ženski Infoteka (Zagreb).

The diaries of Wam Kat provided an interesting form of public reporting via ZTN. Kat was a Dutch volunteer who worked in different humanitarian and anti-war projects. He began to write daily public diaries that he placed on the electronic conference APC.YUGO.ANTIWAR for all to read. His diary entries documented how the political processes reported on the evening news influenced day-to-day life. Via ZTN, the diaries arrived in people's cyberspace mailboxes around the world just minutes after Kat wrote them. These diaries now have been translated into a number of languages and have been reprinted in book form.

ZTN's "Letters" service was used to locate and maintain contact with refugees from Croatia and Bosnia. Refugees, relatives, and friends used this service to send e-mail messages to loved ones who remained in Sarajevo during the war. Volunteers at the Sarajevo site then delivered the messages to people and e-mailed their responses back to the original senders. Volunteers from around the world also made efforts to "snail mail" e-mail messages received from people still in the region to refugees in their countries. The "Letters" project was coordinated by a young refugee from Sarajevo who was then living in Belgrade, a U.S. volunteer working with the Institute for Global Communication (the U.S. branch of the Association for Progressive Communication), and the Forum of Tuzla Citizens, an NGO in Tuzla.

"Letters" was quite successful. During the war and siege of Sarajevo, ZTN system operators estimated that each of the more than 2,000 users of ZaMir-SA had forwarded messages for perhaps five or more friends or acquaintances. A person in Zenica, Bosnia-Herzegovina asked the "Letters" service in Belgrade to locate a friend. The only information known about this person other than his name was where he worked before the war. Three-and-a-half weeks later, he was located in Kenya. These friends were able to resume communication via ZaMir.

Another example is of a Muslim man in Sarajevo. He was separated from his retired parents who lived only three-tenths of a mile away in a part of the town occupied by Serbs. To communicate with them, he used ZTN to send an e-mail to a friend in Belgrade, who printed it out and used the normal mail system to send it from Belgrade to the Serb-controlled part of Sarajevo. The man's parents received the letter and replied in writing back to the friend in Belgrade, who then typed it into a computer and e-mailed it to the Muslim man in Sarajevo. Due to the slowness of the normal mail, the exchange took about three to four weeks each direction, but it enabled this family to communicate across the front lines.

A refugee support group in the Netherlands was actually too successful in finding missing family members via e-mail. In the Netherlands, family members of registered refugees had a right to come to the Netherlands as well. Due to the refugee support group's success, the Dutch authorities asked the group to take the computer out of the refugee center.

A number of humanitarian aid groups used the ZaMir Transnational Net to communicate among their offices in different cities in the region and with their main offices elsewhere in the world. ZTN worked closely with the International Council of Volunteer Agencies (ICVA), which used ZTN connections for data transfer to and from the Internet and with whom ZTN set up public and private conferences. This aided their member organizations in coordinating the distribution of food and shelter aid for the refugees and war victims in Croatia and Bosnia. Some 350 nongovernmental, nonprofit organizations, most of which were aid groups, used the ZTN for communication purposes.

ZTN was used to further research projects. For example, Agency Argument in Belgrade, a nongovernmental scientific institution, conducted applied political and sociological research with the aim of contributing to democratic tendencies in the Federal Republic of Yugoslavia. Agency Argument used ZTN extensively to communicate with the Institute of Ethnology and Folklore Research in Zagreb to conduct a study of media and the war. Through ZTN, they exchanged linguistic analyses of war reporting and analyses of the media imagery of political enemies.

Local volunteer and youth organizations also made extensive use of ZTN. The International Volunteer Project—Slavonia, Baranja (IVP) and three local youth groups—Youth Peace Group Danube (YPGD), Baranja Youth for Community Involvement (BYCI), and Action Youth Group (AYG)—were able to organize an international work camp through the help of ZaMir.

AYG was located in Osijek, Croatia, which consisted predominantly of Croats. BYCI and YPGD were located in the Baranja region and Vukovar city respectively, part of the former United Nations controlled region that consisted predominantly of Serbs.[9] These youth groups were an integral component to the peace process. Because of transportation problems and checkpoint barriers, IVP and the three youth groups remained in contact largely through ZTN.

Representatives from all four organizations met once a week for a series of months to prepare for an international work camp. Correspondence was maintained throughout the week via e-mail. The Osijek branch of IVP shared a computer with the Osijek youth group, the Vukovar branch with the Vukovar youth group, and the Baranja branch with the Baranja youth group. The organizations decided that the camp's projects would include repairing old and installing new playground equipment for Klasje, an orphanage in Osijek, and Radost, a kindergarten in Darda, a city in Baranja.

International volunteers were recruited by e-mailing different volunteer agencies that in turn posted the openings. Volunteers were recruited from Switzerland, England, France, Spain, The Netherlands, Slovenia, and the United States. Local volunteers and staff consisted of a mixture of youth group members, while the international staff consisted of IVP volunteers. During the camp, people made many new friends and maintained these friendships through e-mail.

WAR, PEACE, AND RESISTANCE MUSIC IN THE YUGOSLAV SUCCESSOR STATES

ZaMir has been a crucial link for other efforts in the Yugoslav successor states. One example is disseminating and researching war, peace, and resistance music, the focus of Amy Herron's 15-month research effort in Croatia. To clarify these different genres, war music is the music that advocates the war, promotes negative feelings toward a specific "side" in the war, and/or promotes a strong sense of nationalism. Peace music is music that advocates peace among people and countries and/or contains reconciliation messages. Resistance music is music that specifically advocates stopping the war without a particular side winning and is against war in general. All three of the genres evolved from Yugoslavia's unique history.

Music has developed as a means to express political attitudes and nationalistic ideals. For example, there have been cases where prisoners-of-war have been forced to sing their captor's nationalistic songs, which sometimes means no more than simply substituting "Serbian" for "Croatian" or vice versa (Burton, 1994). Over 95 percent of the music Herron found fell under the category of war music.

The majority of the resistance songs Herron found came from a record titled *Over the Walls of Nationalism and War*. She discovered this record by posting a summary of her research and a request for songs on zamir.youth.music.general, a ZTN conference. Through this conference, she began correspondence with Marko Vuković, who compiled *Over the Walls of Nationalism and War*. This record was distributed by D.I.Y.—an underground distributor. The recording label used was *Humanita Nova* (New Humanity), which is also underground. Marko and his partner, Vedran Meniga, created this label because they wanted to distance their work from the music industry. They also considered their work under this label as grassroots activism. The name *Over the Walls of Nationalism and War* was taken from an anarchist newsletter of the same name published in 1994.

The record consists of seven songs from seven punk bands: two from Croatia, two from the Federal Republic of Yugoslavia, two from Macedonia, and one from Slovenia.[10] The record jacket explains some of the reasons for creating *Over the Walls of Nationalism and War*. First, it was an effort to advance communication between people involved in the peace process (Humanita Nova, 1996). Further, the record demonstrates that despite the war, where "mutual intolerance rules," dialogue is both possible and necessary. The record conveys a strong anti-war message and was intended to speed up the peace process. Moreover, this record was a proactive initiative intended to transcend the mere philosophical stance against the war into one of activism and action. The participants in the record explicitly state that they cannot simply stand by and watch how deplorably those in power are governing people's lives (Humanita Nova, 1996).

Marko and Vedran used ZTN to help with international distribution, to communicate with foreign labels, and to arrange trades (records for records) (M. Vukovic, personal communication, October 17, 1998). Despite the nationalistic propaganda on all sides of the war, ZTN was able to provide an outlet for anti-war sentiment. Two examples are given in order to demonstrate the nature of this sentiment.

A Croatian resistance song from *Over the Walls of Nationalism and War* is "War Victims," by the group *Bijes zdravog razuma*. This song very bluntly states that this war arose because of a desire for supremacy and money. It further states that the people who really believe in nationalistic principles are naïve. Then with rage-filled voices, the song tells listeners to "refuse to listen (to the propaganda) if you really want something to change." The last line expresses the inherent worth that every (that is, all sides) person has. War costs—it costs lives, hearts, money, and pride.

> There are too many people with wounded hearts, broken souls, and heart-broken bodies.
> Death became a way of life, a present-day destruction.
> War victims are innocent people.
> Blinding hate, chased away through death.
> Are we common people guilty for all this shit?
> Do we have rights in our lives;
> Do we have to listen to the rulers?
> But I, I know that I am not a part of this, all this evil.
> Wake up! And you, refuse to listen if you really want something to change.
> I don't understand how everything came to this;
> I understand that this is a fight for supremacy, money, and power.
> And that the people who really believe in the ideology of nationalism
> throw out only naïve peons—
> Peons in powerful hands,
> Because I can only work from the beginning.
> What no one realizes is how much money it costs…

How much power and worth is inherent in every person's life.

The second example is a Serbian anti-war song entitled "Front Line," by *Totalni promasaj*. It depicts one possible experience that a soldier might have had on the front line of battle. This might have been the place where the soldier (using second person narrative) finally realized that everything "was a lie." The soldier questioned how he could do that (war) to his children. Now all he has are memories of better times. The narrator even contemplated thoughts of suicide, but did not go through with it because he recognized that suicide would not make any difference. Only after the narrator was shot does he realize that he was "just one more fool who [gave his] life for [his] country." The listener can hear the agony of the narrator with his final cries of "why?" The last line then sums up all of this suffering by declaring, "Now you don't care for the national pride."

When you saw yourself of the front line,
You saw how the brightness of your arms [was] fading.
Finally you understood that everything was a lie
And that your end is coming quickly.
The words said a few months ago
And all the promises fell into water.
How could you do that to your children?
Close by your head whistle firing bullets.
You can't understand why there were the bloody tracks behind you.
Now you would really like to kill yourself;
If only you knew it could change things.
With a tearful face you kneel in a swamp.
While through your head, pictures of your life pass by.
The memories of those better times.
You cannot reconcile the times lost forever.
You trusted so much,
But from everything came nothing.
You have no courage to kill yourself.
With a scream on your lips you run into nothing—
Let someone else do that for you.
While the bullets cut you and you slowly fall,
Everything is clear to you,
But now it's too late.
You were just one more fool who would give your life for your country.
And you ask yourself why?
And you ask yourself how?
And you remember how beautiful her hair was.
Now when everything is gone, it has come to its end.
And you ask yourself why?

And you ask yourself how?
Now you don't care for the national pride...

CONCLUSION

Had it not been for ZTN, many peace efforts through humanitarian, nongovernmental, local, and international organizations in the Yugoslav successor states would have been much more difficult, if not impossible. The development of communication technology, in particular the ZaMir Transnational Net, successfully enabled a diverse body of people to engage in civic discourse during a time when this discourse was difficult due to the ongoing war. ZTN challenged prejudice, hate, and fear by creating an avenue for dialogue, and dialogue is ultimately one of the most effective weapons against these destructive forces.

NOTES

1. Technically, "Serbo-Croatian" does not exist anymore. The language is now referred to as Croatian, Serbian, or Bosnian. The differences between these languages, however, are mainly dialectal.
2. Krajina means "military border" in Serbo-Croatian. It was created by the Austro-Hungarian Empire to further the conflicts already existing between Serbs and Croats. Serbs were recruited to live on the border of the Austro-Hungarian Empire specifically for the purpose of fighting off Ottoman invaders. Because of this role, the Serbs were given land, religious, and local governmental privileges not given to the Croats. This inequality also served to keep the ethnic tensions between Serbs and Croats high, therefore diffusing animosity toward the Austro-Hungarians (Dragnich, 1992).
3. Serbia is a republic of the Federal Republic of Yugoslavia.
4. GreenNet is a member of the Association for Progressive Communication (APC), to which ZTN also belongs.
5. In this chapter, "conferences," "electronic conferences," "newsgroups," and "bulletin boards" all refer to a public collection of messages, comments, and replies that are sent to an electronic conference or bulletin board for all to read. Each conference has a name describing the subject, for example, APC.YUGO.ANTIWAR. The contents of such a conference are copied from server to server throughout the Internet so that people all over the world have access to them.
    We will use the word *conference* to describe this Internet service for the duration of this chapter.
6. *ZANA* is the traditional name of the good fairy of the forest who helps people. The name was chosen by the people in Priština.

7. The spelling with an "a" at the end is preferred by ethnic Albanians, while the spelling with an "o" at the end is preferred by Serbians.
8. The APC is the worldwide network of communication service providers organized for and by the nonprofit organizations themselves.
9. The UN region consisted of Baranja, Western Sirmium, and part of Eastern Slavonia that included Vukovar. The United Nations controlled these sections from January 1996 (with the implementation of the Dayton Peace Accords) until January 1998. Osijek was in the non-UN-controlled section of Eastern Slavonia.
10. Bosnia was inaccessible due to the severity of the war still going on there while this record was being made.

REFERENCES

Association for Progressive Communication (1998a, December 17). *Programmes. Strategic uses: Real life strategic uses of APC networks* [Online]. Available: <http://www.apc.org/english/reallife.html> [1999, March 8].

Association for Progressive Communication (1998b, December 22). *Vínculos de Comunicación en Yugoslavia en Tiempos de Guerra. APC Programas de Trabio* [Online]. Available: <http://www.apc.org/espanol/reallife.html> [1999, March 8].

Bachman, E. (1996a, March 15). *COMMUNICATIONS AID in the post Yugoslavian countries: The origin and development of the ZAMIR TRANSNATIONAL NET (ZTN)* [Online]. Available: <http://aleph.ac.upc.es/intermed/slides/zamir.html> [1999, March 8].

Bachman, E. (1996b, June). *The Zamir Transnational Network*. Paper presented at the Internet Society INET '96 Conference, Montreal, Canada.

Bachman, E. (1998, April 6). *ZaMir Transnational Net, statement of purpose* [Online]. Available: <http://www.worldmedia.fr/sarajevo/archive/zamir.html> [1999, March 8].

Bijes zdravog razuma. (1996). Zrtve rata. On *Over the walls of nationalism and war* [Record]. Croatia: Humanita Nova.

Burton, K. (1994). Balkan beats: Music and nationalism in the former Yugoslavia. In K. Burton (Ed.), *World music: The rough guide* (pp. 83–94). London: Rough Guides.

Cohen, L. J. (1993). *Broken bonds: The disintegration of Yugoslavia*. Boulder, CO: Westview.

Dragnich, A. N. (1992). *Serbs and Croats: The struggle in Yugoslavia*. San Diego, CA: Harcourt Brace.

Hoffman, M. S. (Ed.). (1992). *The World Almanac and Book of Facts 1993*. New York: Pharos.

Humanita Nova. (1996). Liner notes for *Over the Walls of Nationalism and War* [Record]. Croatia: Humanita Nova.

Iordanova, D. (forthcoming). The Internet: Explosive expansion, curtailed access. In D. Paletz & K. Jakubowicz (Eds.), *Relapse into Communism? The media and socio-political consciousness in Central and Eastern Europe.* Hampton Press.

Kaplan, R. D. (1993). *Balkan ghosts: A journey through history.* New York: Vintage.

Lampe, J. R. (1996). *Yugoslavia as history.* Cambridge, England: Cambridge University Press.

Malcolm, N. (1994). *Bosnia: A short history.* New York: New York University Press.

Malcolm, N. (1998). *Kosovo: A short history.* New York: New York University Press.

Totalni promasaj. (1996). Prva borbena linija. On *Over the walls of nationalism and war* [Record]. Croatia: Humanita Nova.

Vulliamy, E. (1994). *Seasons in Hell: Understanding Bosnia's war.* New York: St. Martin's Press.

Weinberg, B., & Wilsnack, D. (1997). *War at the crossroads: An historical guide through the Balkan labyrinth.* New York: Balkan War Resource Group.

Williams, D. E. (1995). Probing cultural implications of war-related victimization in Bosnia-Hercegovnia, Croatia, and Serbia. In F. L. Casmir (Ed.), *Communication in Eastern Europe: The role of history, culture and media in contemporary conflicts* (pp. 277–311). Mahwah, NJ: Lawrence Elbaum.

Part IV

The New Europe in the New Millennium

chapter 16

The Future of Socialist Media in the Post-Soviet Era

Drew O. McDaniel
Ohio University

This chapter will place technological and cultural issues of the New Europe in a broader context by contrasting them with ones of socialist nations in Asia. During the 20th century, socialist ideology found its greatest acceptance in Asia and in Europe. However, the sudden 1991 disintegration of the USSR reverberated across the entire world, causing some type of political recalculation in practically every sphere. In the Western world, the most significant result was an abrupt end to the cold war. For the Soviet Union and its former close allies, political changes that would have been unimaginable just a few years earlier were set in motion. The Commonwealth of Independent States (CIS), a loose coalition of now-autonomous Soviet republics, entered into something of a confused state, especially the five republics of Central Asia. Meanwhile, the end of an era in Moscow meant a new era in Vietnam and Cambodia—and the beginning of experimentation with capitalist economic methods under the banner of Communism.

The technology and policy analysis presented in this chapter primarily deals with issues about mass communication. The aim is to highlight inherent problems of reforming and building democratic and open public discourse in socialist countries, particularly focusing on concerns peculiar to the Asian setting. This report is based upon field work conducted during the period from 1991 to 1998.

THE NEW EUROPE AND ASIA

As the political drama of 1989 through 1992 spun out, nations of the former Soviet bloc took many different trajectories. The varied political and social directions taken by European nations do not correspond to ones taken in Asia. This chapter presents a brief review of the Asian experience as a counterpoint to ones spelled out in other chapters. By seeing the unfolding events on a larger canvas, patterns may be placed in sharper focus. Countries of Eastern and Central Europe found the tug of history powerful—Germany reunited; Czechoslovakia disunited as Czech and Slovak republics; Poland unleashing an unexpectedly powerful economy; and so on. In spite of the half century of socialist government and the potent influence of Soviet relations, most European countries were able to summon up pre-World War II models for guidance in economic and social transformations. However, this call to history also had a dark side. Across the region, newly inflamed nationalism burst out in response to the political opening. An obvious case of the worst tendencies was Yugoslavia, but there have been other examples outside the Balkans, such as a growth in right-wing political movements in Germany. It became clear that the harmonious picture of Europe united in solidarity under the socialist banner presented by official media during the Soviet era had been wishfully optimistic.

Asian experience in the years after the Soviet dissolution has been both similar and dissimilar to that in Europe. Asian countries generally lacked pre-war experience as independent societies. Vietnam, Laos, and Cambodia ended colonialism only after 1950, and in Vietnam and Cambodia only after decades of bitter military struggle. Vietnam's joining of North and South in April 1975 ended partition invoked by the Geneva Conference of 1954, but the country continued to battle with economic and social problems occasioned by the reunification and by its military occupation of Cambodia. Cambodia's brief flirtation with the Khmer Rouge government of Democratic Kampuchea in 1975–1979 provoked Vietnam's military invasion and colonialization. Central Asia had a different set of problems. After 1991, economies of Asian socialist nations lost the security of trade agreements within the Soviet bloc, a situation that presented each country with a need to seek new markets. Across Central Asia, the capacity to develop economic resources varied widely, although the entire region was underdeveloped, compared with European republics of the former USSR. The most richly endowed was Kazakhstan, which had oil, natural gas, and mineral deposits, but it also had serious nuclear contamination in at least one large site, and the Aral Sea, whose shore had receded 150 miles from its original coastline, was considered one of the world's greatest environmental disasters. At the opposite extreme, Kyrgyzstan had few resources, and was dependent on a stagnant agricultural economy.

FORMER REPUBLICS OF THE SOVIET UNION

Central Asia consists of the five former republics of the Soviet Union located north of Pakistan, Afghanistan, and Iran: Kazakhstan, Kyrgyzstan (or Kyrgyz Republic), Uzbekistan, Turkmenistan, and Tajikistan. Although usually considered a single grouping sharing traits in common, they exhibit many contrasts. All are nominally Islamic, although the fervor of their religious practice does not begin to compare with nations to their south. Each republic has significant Russian communities that are culturally quite distinct from local populations, as well as settlements of other ethnic groups such as Germans and Iranians.

A brief glimpse of life in Kyrgyzstan is offered here to give the reader a sense of conditions in Central Asia and as a backdrop to the discussion of media and technology that follows. Khirgizia was a remote backwater of the Soviet Union, one that required more resources from the center than it could contribute. Kyrgyzstanis often compare their country with Switzerland—a small mountainous country with relatively few natural resources—and hope to copy that country's economic success. The vision of the Kyrgyz Republic exploiting banking and tourism to build a Swiss-style economy is appealing but implausible. Central Asia is far from potential tourists, and the infrastructure to support such an industry is totally lacking. Until 1996, there was not a single hotel of an international standard, and due to aviation fuel shortages, international flights to Kyrgyzstan are very few. Likewise, technical resources needed for modern banking such as electronic data and communication services are unavailable. So far, much of the effort directed at development, under prodding of the IMF and the World Bank, seems to be devoted to economic restructuring, that is, privatizing, state enterprises. This is unlikely to produce a rapid turnaround in conditions for local residents.

As a consequence of these factors, living standards have dropped precipitously. Even though the value of Kyrgyzstan's currency—the *som*—stabilized by the mid-1990s, much damage had already been done. The purchasing power of Kyrgyzstan residents' incomes were badly eroded by inflation and currency devaluation shortly after independence. Although there were signs of progress, deprivation became evident, especially among children and the elderly. According to reports of a study of 600 Kyrgyzstan women conducted by a U.S. sociologist under World Bank funding in 1994, 70 percent purchased neither clothing nor other nonfood household goods in the preceding year. Among these women, 20 percent had bought no butter and 14 percent no milk or milk products in the prior year ("Sad Statistics," 1994). Official statistics show that 69.6 percent of total family income was spent on food in 1994, as compared with 34.1 percent in 1990 ("The Empty," 1994). Conditions have continued to spiral downward. In February 1999, the International Red Cross issued appeals for contributions for Central Asia to forestall a health and nutrition calamity.

Housing seems to be a lesser concern, at least in cities, partly because a Russian out-migration has helped cut shortages. Although residential accommodations frequently appear to fall below international standards, this is a result of Soviet-era housing rather than current policies. Maintenance and quality of construction in the numberless apartment complexes that shelter residents along city perimeters seems to be a larger problem. Typical pension payments amount to about $25 (U.S.) monthly. This sum is insufficient to cover costs of an average comfortable apartment, roughly $30 (U.S.) per month. It is now possible for residents to buy and sell apartments, although only a small proportion can afford to own their flats.

Because the level of urbanization in the nation is relatively low, at 38 percent of Kyrgyzstan's 4.5 million residents, rural conditions are extremely important. A debate is underway on the merits of the collectivized agricultural system,which has been the mainstay of farm production across Central Asia. Increasingly, food produced on private plots are an important supplement to official supplies. Vegetables and fruits grown privately appear to be reasonably abundant, although they are not cheap. Also, the variety of foods is restricted and only available seasonally; mainly vegetables such as tomatoes, cucumbers, onions, and potatoes. Meat and milk products are usually available, but they are costly and not always of good quality.

Meanwhile, in Indochina, consequences of the Soviet Union's dissolution were muted because the USSR's withdrawal from Vietnam and Cambodia had largely been accomplished by the end of the 1980s. One decade after Vietnam's reunification, the economy was in terrible shape. Moreover, a baby boom at the end of the war had taxed the country's resources to the limit. The nation's population doubled in the two decades after 1976, causing population density to rise above 500 persons per square mile, and thereby making Vietnam the second most populous country in Southeast Asia. By 1995, 40 percent of the Vietnamese population of roughly 70 million persons were under 15 years of age.

For a period following the war, economic growth did not keep pace with population increases, hence living standards declined. A complicating factor was a large investment in military spending, approximately 20 percent of Vietnam's GDP, much of which was required to maintain forces in Cambodia. Despite efforts to develop agricultural exports, Vietnam had a negative balance of trade—about $800 million per year—by 1986. The government's general economic mismanagement led to hyperinflation of the *dong*. Once valued on a par with the U.S. dollar, it eventually fell to approximately 10,000 to the U.S. dollar by the middle of the 1990s. Finally, a major change in policy occurred at the Sixth Party Congress in 1986. Party officials recognized that the economy's difficulties had reached an acute stage and that drastic measures were required. The result was *doi moi*, or restructuring. Described as a "...restructuring [of] our thoughts, our perceptions, also our administrative machinery of economic management...," it amounted to a wide-ranging liberalization of the Vietnamese economy and a gradual introduction of certain market principles (Oanh, 1995, p. 9).

Cambodia, Vietnam's neighbor, is a comparatively small country with a population of approximately 10 million. Even though the nation is sometimes classified as a "failed nation-state," Cambodians have a strong sense of national identity and a relatively homogenous population. Government effectiveness and internal security are low, but the country is functioning in most capacities like modern states. Primarily an agricultural country, it is still trying to recover from the damage inflicted by the rule of the Khmer Rouge. In slightly more than three years, about 15 percent of the population vanished, victims of various inquisitions, starvation caused by incompetent government policies, or by fleeing the country—most by the former two. However, the problem is not merely the political fallout of the Khmer Rouge years, it is also a chronic lack of stable government. After independence, there have been five discontinuous governments: The first Sihanouk years, the Lon Nol regime, Democratic Kampuchea (Khmer Rouge), the State of Cambodia, and the present restored monarchy.

Unfortunately, purges by the Democratic Kampuchea government effectively eliminated an entire class of skilled and educated Cambodians. When the Royal University of Phnom Penh was reopened in the early 1990s, there were no faculty to staff it because fewer than 10 persons holding advanced degrees survived the Khmer Rouge years. Among the other categories exterminated by Khmer Rouge were journalists, writers, businesspersons, and intellectuals of all sorts. The Vietnamese military occupation of Cambodia did not quell the fighting with guerrilla forces, but instead made the whole country a battleground. Huge quantities of arms and armament were imported for the fighting, leaving Cambodia as one of the most heavily armed countries in the world—there are several times as many unexploded land mines in Cambodia as there are people, and they remain a leading cause of injury and death.

The elections of 1993 administered by the United Nations seemed to initiate a new political era, but the outcome proved less conclusive than expected. Prince Ranariddh, the new prime minister, was forced to concede partial authority to Hun Sen, whose political career started with the Khmer Rouge in the 1970s and with whom a large portion of the military was aligned. Consequently, from then until elections in 1998, there were two co-prime ministers and a constant tug of war over authority and legitimacy. Elections in 1998 settled this unsatisfactory state of affairs when it confirmed Hun Sen as the sole national leader.

The strength of ties between the Soviet Union and each of the nations mentioned here obviously differed enormously, and this is evident today in relationships with Russia. The Kyrgyz Republic is still very much linked economically, culturally, and politically to Russia. This is not true of the countries of Indochina; Vietnam is busy cultivating relationships elsewhere and Cambodia was more often aligned with China during its brief attempt to establish a Communist government.

SOVIET MEDIA POLICY

In order to understand mass communication in the former Soviet bloc it is necessary to examine the Soviet system of mass communication. This is because the USSR's system was presented as a model throughout its sphere of influence. The Soviet approach seems to have been exported uncritically because it was adopted in such unlikely countries as Vietnam and Cuba. Soviet ideology on mass communication had innate shortcomings that arose from the narrow perspective of those who evolved its guiding philosophical principles.

An oddity of Soviet ideology was that in some ways it became frozen by the untimely death of Lenin. Lenin led the new Communist state only six years, and by his death in 1924, the country was barely moving out of feudalism. Due to the general backwardness of the USSR, radio made little impact in the 1920s. This must have limited Lenin's vision when he wrote and spoke about media, which he conceived of as channels of communication to persuade and move Soviet masses to action. After his death, Lenin's words became part of the sacred text that defined Soviet media dogma for decades afterward. In spite of his limited exposure, Lenin was struck by the significance of radio, but saw it merely as an extension of print media, calling it a "newspaper without paper or wires." He noted, "It will be possible for Russia to hear a newspaper being read in Moscow" (qtd. in Paulu, 1974, p. 217). This inability of official policy to perceive electronic media as unique channels separate from print media persisted until near the end of the Soviet period. Even in the 1970s, the output of radio was officially specified not in hours of transmission, but in equivalent pages of newspaper text. Had Lenin lived to observe the full potential of radio, his perspective might have been different and official media policies might have given radio and television higher status.

The lack of emphasis on electronic media was manifest in numerous ways. For instance, even in the 1980s, the main television center of the Soviet Union depended on studio and recording equipment from the West and it appears there was little if any stress on technical innovation in electronic mass media, except in the area of communication satellites.[1] The failure to recognize television and radio as distinct and important media, coupled with officials' lack of interest in audience preferences, led to stupefyingly dull programming.

Even though possessing a confined ideological point of view, the popularity of broadcast media grew rapidly during the Khruschev and Brezhnev eras, due to the lack of other entertainment options. In the Soviet Union, there was practically no night life, and few diversions of any sort were available to ordinary citizens. Thus, inexpensive radio and television helped fill the void. According to Dingley (1989), public access to television grew from 5 percent in 1960 to 93 percent by 1986. Indeed, by the 1970s, technology began to become available in the Soviet Union, which allowed viewers and listeners to access not only local media, but Western channels as well. Audio tape recorders in particular, but also videotape recorders, allowed more and more of the Soviet public to tune out the frequently boring domestic programming in favor of rock and jazz music or foreign films. This trend also grew with cutbacks and eventual suspension of jamming of Western shortwave broadcasts.

Media in the post-Soviet period have been framed by the Gorbachev policy of glasnost. Mickiewicz (1988) characterized that strategy partly as a response to growing public cynicism and disinterest in official media in the late 1970s and early 1980s. During the Brezhnev period, public fascination with Western popular culture carried by shortwave broadcasts and by audio and video tape recordings reached new heights. Soviet commentator Mironenko (cited in Mickiewicz, 1988) argued that "We can no longer accept that young men and women often know more about events taking place on the other side of the globe than about what goes on in their own region..." (p. 34). Glasnost was meant to answer unexpected competition from the West by allowing official Soviet communication channels to carry alternative interpretations of events, albeit ones not challenging to official ideology.

The consequences of glasnost were quite different than ones antici-
pated by Soviet leaders. When media were allowed to report multiple
interpretations of events (shortages of certain products, minor corruption among workers, defects in consumer goods, or poor transportation
services, for instance), gradually the "correctness" of ideological interpretations began to be challenged also. The media actually became
important actors in questioning official accounts of historical events—for
example, the forcible incorporation of the Baltic states into the Soviet
Union. Consequently, according to Shane (1994), "When Gorbachev put
the brakes on reform in the autumn of 1990, one of his first and most
important targets was television" (p. 170). But reform in the media
proved to be irreversible. As events in the post-Soviet era played out,
radio and television have been at the frontiers of social, economic, and
political change. This is particularly true of independent media, which
began springing up in the form of pirate radio stations even before the
Soviet Union's dissolution. Some of these free-wheeling illegal stations
became legitimate private broadcasters once independence arrived.

Media professionalism, particularly in the field of journalism, has
struggled to gain credibility after the breakup of the Soviet Union. Neither print nor broadcast media have lived up to expectations. A number
of factors have contributed to media's failure to cultivate broad public
acceptance and confidence. Among these are an absence of a tradition
of free, open, balanced journalism; lack of properly qualified media
workers; political interference; and a lack of adequate financial
resources to sustain media.

MEDIA IN KYRGYZSTAN

The Kyrgyz Republic is home to an array of newspapers. Approximately
10 circulate in the capital of Bishkek alone. Small newspapers appear
from time to time, flourishing briefly then vanishing without a trace.
The large number of newspapers, as compared with radio and television
outlets, perpetuates the historical bias favoring print media promoted by
Soviet policy. Most newspapers are printed by the national publishing
house *Uchkun*, although a few employ small private printers. Publications are dependent on state printers for allocations of newsprint, and
supplies are often inadequate. Newspapers from Kazakhstan are available in Kyrgyzstan, but other foreign publications are seldom seen. Even
ones from Moscow are in short supply, a fact frequently bemoaned by
former readers, whose knowledge of international events has been
impaired by their disappearance.

Three official radio channels can be received in the capital: Kyrgyz Radio, Moscow Radio 1, and retransmissions from *Radiostantslya Yunost* or *Radiostantslya Mayak*. Each is available about 12 to 18 hours daily. Of the three, only Mayak uses a formatted program schedule; the others employ block programming. Kyrgyz Radio provides a wide range of program types embracing traditional, modern, and pop music, along with informational features and news. Several independent radio "stations" are on the air in Bishkek. The term "station" really means a program service utilizing a state-supplied radio transmitter. Stations must share a segment of each day's broadcast on a VHF FM transmitter. Government control over independent radio is assured by ownership of all transmitting facilities. By "leasing" portions of the day to private operators, officials retain ultimate control over broadcasts. This arrangement is not likely to change soon. Broadcasters report government opposition to stations setting up their own transmitters, and officials offer explanations, such as a shortage of frequencies, to justify their policy.

As elsewhere in the CIS, a highly developed, wired radio system relaying official broadcasts is available in urban areas. This system grew rapidly in the Soviet Union during the 1930s and 1940s because production of radio receivers could not keep pace with demand. Estimates placed the number of radio sets in the USSR at less than 2 million in 1950, with another 9.7 million wired speaker installations (Markham, 1967). The Soviet preference for large apartment block dwellings also favored the construction of wired radio systems, and the network in Bishkek delivers good quality audio signals of the main local radio service and of Moscow Radio 1.

Unaccustomed to competition, government broadcasting agencies were slow to respond to the challenge of private stations and found their audiences were greatly reduced by the mid-1990s. Now, state media officials pledge to rehabilitate their broadcasting operations, but complain about poorly trained staff and a lack of modern facilities. Despite these drawbacks, there are signs that government stations are battling back. For instance, at one point, a Kazakhstan independent station manager voiced "alarm" for the future of private broadcasting, noting that results of audience research conducted by the national polling organization showed that viewing of government television had risen sharply (although still at a low level), from 7 percent of the public a year earlier to 18 percent in 1994. A budget of $23 million provided by the government to Kazakh Gostelradio was supplemented by another $6 million from United States sources that year, allowing the government broadcaster to add a second national radio channel.

Private media are comparatively well developed in Kazakhstan, where a vigorous competitive media environment has sprung up, especially in the capital of Almaty. The Kazakh State Television and Radio Broadcasting Company is the national governmental service. Official broadcasts include two television channels on the air 18 hours daily, including one relayed from Moscow. Additional transmissions from Turkish television are also available. Official radio broadcasts are relayed on four channels, including two operated commercially (Hadlow, 1992). Commercial private radio and television enterprises have sprung up since 1991, mostly in Almaty, where the largest concentration of population is located. The most restricted broadcasting can be found in Uzbekistan, where radio and television services are exclusively government channels. Four radio services are transmitted from the capital of Tashkent, including two relayed from former states of the Soviet Union and two local channels. Each channel operates about 18 hours daily. Tajikistan has faced enormous difficulties in mounting credible media services. The civil war made journalists targets of assassination, and so conditions have not been conducive to development of enterprising mass media. Most broadcasting takes place within the official State Radio and Television Company, originating from the capital of Dushanbe, but there are some fledgling private broadcasters struggling to get a foothold. Turkmenistan, like Uzbekistan, has banned independent media. This country has the smallest population in Central Asia, and even though the country possesses natural resources such as gas and petroleum, its economy is performing poorly. The lack of development is evident in broadcasting, and facilities of the National Radio and Television Company are said to be outdated and not in good condition.

A TRADITION OF SOCIALIST JOURNALISM

Media in both Vietnam and Cambodia have been deeply affected by long military conflicts. For much of their post-colonial history, Cambodian and Vietnamese media operated within the tradition of socialist journalism. More than 60 newspapers have been authorized to publish in Cambodia, and while the majority of these are produced sporadically, their sheer number is extraordinary, given the small size of potential readership. This fact, along with the limited number of advertisers, ensures that few if any of the newspapers operate profitably. The lack of newspapers' earning power has been a factor in a host of professional abuses.

The broadcast media present a different picture. It is usually assumed that among mass media of Cambodia, radio is by far the most important because it has a truly national audience and reaches the 40 percent or so of the population that is illiterate. In addition, radio is cheap, does not need commercial power, and can be carried wherever people work, live, and travel. Both radio and television are dominated by the government; the main stations are operated by the Ministry of Information. A few private, low-power radio stations are on the air, but ones aligned with opposition political parties are subject to shut down.

International broadcasts are readily available. It appears that there is a large audience for Khmer broadcasts by the Voice of America and smaller audiences for Radio Australia, Radio Free Asia, and Radio France International, among others. In Phnom Penh, rebroadcasts of the BBC World Service on FM can be received 24 hours daily. Across the whole country, satellite transmissions of CNN and other international television channels are available, and satellite receiving setups are common in cities. Television is enormously popular in middle class homes. The government channel offers imported shows and a smattering of local productions, mostly news and current affairs. A small cable service is available in Phnom Penh, providing an assortment of international channels, especially ones from Hong Kong and Taiwan.

Vietnam's media development faced a wholly different set of issues. This country has a long press tradition; during French colonial times, hundreds of local newspapers were in print. The journalistic professional was respected and influential. Prominent figures worked in the media, such as Ho Chi Minh, who headed the weekly newspaper *La Paria*. Following reunification in 1976, there came a period during which new procedures and political philosophies were inculcated in the South. New government policies required all media to come under Ministry supervision based in Hanoi, even though offices established in Ho Chi Minh City acted as regional headquarters in the South. According to media workers, it was a difficult time of adjustment and this, together with serious economic problems throughout the country, meant little development occurred in the media. Under strict censorship, content of broadcasts and newspapers became increasingly dogmatic and tedious. However, after 1986, when *doi moi* institutionalized a liberalized economy, this tendency was reversed somewhat and a more tolerant official attitude was adopted toward the media. In a new market economy, newspapers suddenly were forced to compete for circulation and advertising revenues. To do this, they naturally had to become more sensitive to readers' tastes and preferences. In the first seven years after 1986, more than 200 new publications began distribution. The total number of newspapers, journals, and magazines reached 365 by 1993 (Martin, 1994). Five daily newspapers were in operation, supported by government subsidies and a small but growing amount of advertising.

A more open atmosphere for print media has not ended restrictions traditionally imposed on content. For instance, the historic role of the

Communist Party and its icons, such as Ho Chi Minh, and the preservation of a one-party state are not to be discredited in any way. On the other hand, government can be criticized, especially when stories focus on practices such as corruption or incompetence. Censorship and licensing of journalists are required, but enforcement is much more lenient than that before 1986.

Unlike print media, broadcasting enjoyed little revitalization under *doi moi*. Radio and television seem to have been caught up more completely in the bureaucratic tangle that has come to characterize state enterprises in the post-reunification period. In Vietnam too, the Marxist-Leninist ideological bias toward print media kept broadcasting from advancing quickly. Radio the Voice of Vietnam theoretically leads the list of government radio services. It covers the entire country through high-power transmitters based near its headquarters in Hanoi. In practice, however, it is not so popular in cities; many urban areas have competing metropolitan stations that present a more lively fare. As a result, the primary audience for Radio the Voice of Vietnam is found in the countryside, where its conservative contents and old-style block programming continue to be favored. There are, in fact, three different types of radio stations in Vietnam. In addition to the national broadcasts from Radio the Voice of Vietnam and the metropolitan or district stations, every one of the 44 provinces has its own station. This arrangement has produced a startling number of stations; totalling well than 320. Practically everywhere in the nation, listeners have a number of stations from which to choose. Vietnam, like the former Soviet Union, has many highly developed wired speaker installations, perhaps as many as 10,000 separate systems with combined service to one million units. These systems distribute not only over-the-air broadcasts, but occasional community programs produced at the local level.

The status of television in Vietnam is similar. Nationally, Vietnam Television is responsible for country-wide broadcasts, but there are also stations at the provincial and district levels, approximately 62 stations altogether. Satellite reception of internationally distributed services, such as STAR TV, has become popular in the cities, even though reception equipment remains prohibitively expensive. Video is also extremely popular. Kiosks selling or renting domestic and foreign videos can be found on the streets of every city. In spite of the costs of television ownership, it is acknowledged as the premier source of entertainment. Unofficially, estimates place Vietnam's regular television audience at about half of the population, although many viewers may have access to a set only at a shop or a relative's home. Demand was so great that Vietnam opened its own television assembly plant in the 1990s to manufacture inexpensive sets for local consumers (Marr, 1998).

The scale of the production and distribution system for electronic media is impressive; almost 20,000 persons are employed, not counting the tens of thousands who work for wired speaker systems. But the size of the broadcasting sector may be misleading. The system is badly underfunded, partially because the number of facilities spreads available funds so thinly. Much equipment in use is obsolete and in a poor state of maintenance. Quite a few facilities are not fully operational because equipment has failed and spare parts cannot be obtained or because technicians lack the knowledge to carry out repairs. Naturally, one can usually find the best equipped facilities in the main urban centers, but this is not universally true—since the district stations depend on the whim of local district officers, some districts have better facilities merely because local party councils place a high priority on broadcasting. I recall the story told to me by an officer of an international organization about a local district that needed an upgrade for its low-power station. A neighboring district owned an unused high-power FM transmitter, but no means of coordinating an exchange could be found. With no higher authority to impose a solution, the low-power transmitter continued to be used, while not far away the more powerful transmitter moldered away in a government warehouse.

SOCIALIST TECHNOLOGY EAST AND WEST

The economies of Central Asia and Indochina were placed squarely on the periphery prior to the unraveling of the Soviet Union. In the aftermath of the USSR's breakup, these countries generally were left behind by their former partners of Central and Eastern Europe. The absence of foreign cooperative assistance has been a major impediment to their technological development. In the 1990s, much was written and said about boom times along the Pacific Rim, but the acceleration of economic and technological development tended to be localized. While one country experienced rapid expansion, a neighboring country might find itself at a virtual standstill. In this way, Vietnam benefited greatly from the growth in regional prosperity, but Cambodia felt little effect.

Indeed, the Cambodian economy is in shambles, and the near future does not look bright. Most funding from abroad has been postponed until political stability can be achieved. This, in turn, has depended on the formation of a legitimate government in Phnom Penh. The 1998 elections may have set the stage for political stability, but a great deal of work will be required to revive the nation's economy. Full restoration of the agricultural sector depends on ridding the countryside of landmines, which may take decades. Also, education among Cambodians lags behind neighboring countries and will require a generation to improve. On the other hand, Vietnam's economic performance has been a marvel. Reform after 1986 produced a spurt of economic expansion. For a while, Vietnam's GDP growth made it a global leader, at close to 10 percent annual economic expansion. Later, as the Asian economic crisis spread, the country's growth rate dropped.

Legal barriers to the import of technology do not seem to be a problem in Cambodia; cellular telephones are popular, personal computers can be purchased at stores along city thoroughfares, and television and radio receivers can be found in city shops around the country. All these technologies are beyond the means of ordinary Cambodians, however, except for broadcasting, the popularity of which has reached remarkable heights. A nationwide survey of media habits found that 33 percent of capital-city residents reported that television was their most important source of information and another 31 percent identified radio as the most important information source (Women's Media Centre, 1997). Surprisingly, the pattern was not much different in rural areas, where 38 percent said television was the most important information source and another 30 percent chose radio for this purpose. These figures reveal the extent to which electronic media have permeated the entire social system of Cambodia, becoming part of residents' daily lives. The experience of Vietnam has been analogous. For instance, the spread of television reception via satellites grew so quickly that it caught authorities off guard. When the number of homes equipped with satellite-receiving gear reached into the tens of thousands, party officials became alarmed over the exposure to foreign programming. A directive issued in 1996 limited access to the technology, but enforcement was immediately placed on hold (Mares, 1998).

The gloomy economic picture of the Kyrgyz Republic presented earlier does not seem likely to change soon. The largest Kyrgyz development project was designed to open a gold mine in the vicinity of Lake Issyk-Kul, in the northern region of the country. After a protracted construction phase managed by the principal concession holder, a Canadian firm, the mine finally began to produce refined metal, but at precisely the moment when the value of gold had sunk to an international low. This situation, along with complaints about environmental pollution, has undermined confidence in the project. Even so, the availability of consumer goods has improved somewhat and the economy shows slight signs of improvement. Conditions elsewhere in Central Asia are not much different, although Kazakhstan and Uzbekistan seem to be showing more vigorous economic expansion. In particular, Tashkent, in Uzbekistan, has emerged as the de facto financial center for the region and is quickly expanding its industrial base.

One outcome of the unfortunate economic conditions has been a glacially slow spread of technology through most of Central Asia. For example, in the mid-1990s, I worked in a media resource center that UNESCO had built in the Kyrgyz Republic's National Library. One of the most popular features of the center was a satellite setup that allowed reception of CNN and BBC networks. At the time, this was one of the few such facilities in the country outside embassies. A steady stream of journalists passed through the center each day to catch up on Western international news reports. Meanwhile, outside the center, most homes still depended on ancient wired speaker radio systems for news and information. Television sets could be purchased, but mainly at state department stores, where Japanese- and Russian-manufactured sets sold at prices still too high to tempt most local residents.

The economies of Central and Eastern Europe have not been models of efficiency and growth, but they enjoy key advantages over the depressed conditions of socialist Central and Southeast Asia. There are several dimensions of Asian problems. First, there is a huge difference between Central Europe and Central Asia in their infrastructural development. Central Asia served the Soviet system as an agricultural region and a supplier of raw materials. Production of meat, cotton, and refined minerals were emphasized. Little industrial base had been constructed, so that after independence these states started from a much lower level than their European counterparts. The vast, flat, rolling steppes that characterize much of Central Asia's geography offer few advantages and present many obstacles for industrial and technological growth in the region, especially in transportation and access to global markets. Harsh winters in Kazakhstan and the craggy mountains of Kyrgyzstan are other examples of geographic barriers to technology development. Vietnam and Cambodia also have weak infrastructure in areas such as transport. Vietnam's major travel route is a single two-lane highway running north and south from Hanoi to Ho Chi Minh City and beyond. In certain portions of Cambodia, its highways are patrolled by armed bandits, gangs of whom await unwary travelers and those shipping goods.

Partly as a consequence of the infrastructure deficiencies, capital for technology development in socialist Asia has been scarce. Even in Vietnam, which has made substantial gains, the lack of U.S. involvement in the economy has hampered growth. Despite the normalization of relations, American aid and investment has failed to meet Vietnamese expectations. The economies of Central and Eastern Europe have seemed to demonstrate greater luster and thus have tended to draw a greater portion of foreign investment funds flowing out of North America. Western Europe, perhaps due to its proximity and a sense of cultural compatibility, may likewise find the former socialist economies of Europe less risky investments.

A particularly interesting example of technological adoption is the spread of the Internet in socialist Asia. Enthusiasm for accessing the Internet is surprisingly high across the entire region. In the socialist countries, evidence of a public eagerness to use the Internet has been observed for years, but barriers prevent most potential users from gaining access. In Central Asia, service providers offer at least some capabilities to users in major cities, even though a fully functioning network has yet to be built. Before independence, personal computers were practically nonexistent in the Soviet Union. Today, their numbers remain small, but are rapidly rising. Of course, a computer is not enough; dial-up access must be available. Throughout socialist Asia, telephone trunk interconnections and switches are generally of an inferior quality, a legacy of neglect during Soviet times. Problems in such facilities are now compounded by inadequate maintenance. Access to the Internet is limited not only by poor local telephone-line quality, but by international computer links that have restricted capacities. For instance, connection speeds usually available in Bishkek and Phnom Penh, although suitable for electronic mail, are too slow to support Web browsing.

DISCOURSE OF POLITICS AND CULTURE

Media policies in each of the countries covered in this report evolved from principles laid out in Marxist-Leninist ideology. While it is beyond the scope of this analysis to detail the complex implications of those political theories for media, a few points deserve discussion here because thinking about mass communication in socialist Asia is still defined in varying ways by Communism's core concepts. As previously noted, Leninist ideology tended to emphasize the primacy of print media and to conceptualize journalists as "propagandists." In this role, journalists were expected to engage actively in ideological argumentation and to urge the public toward goals set out by political leaders. The outcome of this policy was that journalists fell into habits of advocacy. As Mould and Schuster (1998) noted,

> The most obvious difference between Western and Soviet era/Central Asian journalism is the lack of distinction between opinion and fact. Many newspaper and broadcast media owners and reporters speak openly of "my mission," and take a polemical, "let's fix it" approach to social, political and other issues. (p. 3)

Stories that leave conclusions and interpretations to readers and listeners seem incomplete and indecisive to journalists trained in Soviet ideological principles.

Lenin served as editor and editorial board member of the historically important political newspaper *Iskra* (meaning *Spark*), which was published for a Russian readership in Germany. Objectives of the newspaper, which appeared in a December 1890 issue, illuminate Lenin's beliefs about the role of media:

> The journal should serve mainly for propaganda, the newspaper mainly for agitation...the light of theory must be brought to bear upon every separate fact; propaganda on questions of political and party organization must be carried on among the broad masses of the working class...the newspaper...must periodically record workers' complaints, workers' strikes and other forms of proletarian struggle...and draw definite conclusion from...these facts. (Tompkins, cited in Markham, 1967, p. 50)

Therefore, journalism in the Soviet Union assumed the responsibility of consciously shaping public opinion—toward pre-defined goals laid out by party ideologists. In other words, journalists became political workers. Politicization of mass communication in this way is at the heart of many problems faced by media in post-Soviet socialist countries. In justifying the conscious injection of political judgments in news, the editor-in-chief of the main Soviet television newscast *Bremya* once explained, "We don't believe there is such a thing as 'pure news'—news uncolored by bias, ideology, and opinions. All over the world, the way information is presented reflects a certain view of the world..." (Fanning, 1979).

It is easy to understand why political overtones endure in socialist media. Most Central Asia media professionals active in the 1990s got their training in Soviet institutions and were indoctrinated in Marxist-Leninist principles. The more fortunate of these earned university diplomas were in journalism departments, where studies dealt primarily with politics and ideology, not with reporting, editing, and writing. Their lifelong habits of political advocacy can be seen in the content of programs and in the style of news reporting across socialist countries of Asia. Among the few journalists in Cambodia who had university-level schooling, a large portion did their studies in the Soviet Union. One person I interviewed who had a journalism degree from Patrice Lamumba University in Moscow characterized his education as "useless."

The most politicized media probably can be found in Cambodia, which has fostered an uncompromisingly bitter, adversarial journalistic practice. Political patronage of newspapers is perhaps the most serious journalistic abuse, and it is widely recognized as an enormous problem. It appears that most, if not all, newspapers receive subsidies from politicians and/or political parties in order to meet expenses. Naturally, in exchange for such payments, politicians expect to influence the kind of stories that are printed. This is clearly an undesirable tendency, yet it is hard to imagine a completely nonpartisan journalism in the highly charged political conditions that prevail in Cambodia. But the purchasing of patronage has had a corrosive effect, undermining public trust in news media while contributing to antagonistic public discourse and to ever more polarized public opinion. There are a few exceptions to partisan journalism. The foreign language newspapers typically present a balanced diet of reportage and, in the case of *Phnom Penh Post*, solid investigative journalism. Although influential beyond their circulation size, these papers are read mainly by expatriates living in the capital city and a few elite Cambodian intellectuals. Only one or two Khmer language newspapers are viewed as providing minimally acceptable coverage.

Political reporting in Cambodian media reveals an appalling level of polemic and vitriol. The notion of source attribution or other techniques of report validation is little known. For instance, one story described a perceived lack of attention by the government officials in this way: "In taking a long look at the Ministry of Information, it seems that it hasn't fallen asleep yet, but it is acting as if in deep sleep; kicks delivered to the top of the head will not help!" ("Is it Time to Slash," 1997, p. 7). Another story described the king: "Preah Bat Norodom Sihanouk, the 74 year old King of Cambodia, who is currently staying in the old historic city of Siem Reap, and is illness ridden, full of hopelessness, and shame in his political life, wants to commit suicide" ("The King is Without," 1997, p. 6).

Political cynicism about the media has encouraged outright corruption. For example, brown envelope journalism—the payment for news coverage, so called because payments are reportedly delivered in plain, unmarked brown envelopes—is well entrenched in the country. Such payments are tantamount to bribes; they distort the news to suit interests of those who have money to pay for coverage. If bribery doesn't work, those who wish to sway news coverage can always rely on intimidation. Cambodian journalists often report threats as a result of their work. The ultimate threat comes at the end of a gun barrel, and more than a few journalists have met their deaths while pursuing their profession. A disturbing example was the March 30, 1997, grenade attack of a Khmer Nation Party demonstration in Phnom Penh. At least 15 were killed and dozens injured in this attack, which also took one journalist's life and seriously wounded several other news reporters.

Today, few Cambodians are familiar with news reporting that strives for the impartiality common elsewhere in Southeast Asia. Journalism remains mired in this politicized atmosphere in large measure because professional qualifications of few Cambodian journalists are suited to their level of responsibility. Few have had adequate training. Indeed, few have had adequate education; a 1995 survey showed that less than 10 percent of journalists had any university-level education and at least 15 percent had not completed secondary schooling (Palan & Sarayeth, 1995). Only after the Royal University of Phnom Penh established the Journalism and Computer Training Course in the mid-1990s was long-term training available. Previously, the preparation of journalists had been limited to on-the-job training at newspapers and broadcasting stations, supplemented occasionally by short courses offered under various auspices, notably the Cambodian Communication Institute (CCI) and the journalists' associations. Training may have been obtained abroad by a few persons, but there does not seem to have been any concerted effort to capitalize on such options.

FREEDOM OF COMMUNICATION IN KYRZGYSTAN

Unlike the general pattern of the region, Kyrgyzstan's national leadership has supported the development of what observers consider a generally free and open media. Press freedoms found in the Kyrgyz Republic were rejected by the Soviet system where the concept was disparaged as a tool for bourgeoisie as "a freedom it...exploited for its own selfish aims" (Prokhorov, 1976, p. 52). Such openness places the Kyrgyz Republic in the role of a pacesetter. This point is made repeatedly by media professionals in the country. Even so, they worry about the ability of government to sustain this policy in the depressed economic environment, especially if political opposition grows in strength. Yet in Kyrgyzstan, freedom of the press remains a constant preoccupation of media. The tenuousness of an open press policy was underscored early on when President Askar Akaev called for curbs on the press in a public speech in July 1994. Even though he noted that Kyrgyzstan had gotten favorable international attention for its media policy, he criticized what he considered "irresponsible" behavior of the press. Singling out the newspaper *Svobodnye Gory* as an offender, he suggested that courts halt its publication. This is just what a Bishkek regional court did later that year. The paper was charged with publishing "false information" and with "violating the norms of civil and national ethics" (Brown, 1994).

Among members of the CIS, attention of state media tends to be focused today not so much on ideology as on nationalism. The social and cultural traditions of the Kyrgyz people and their history and practice receive frequent broadcast coverage in the Kyrgyz Republic. Typical of early efforts was an ambitious "telemarathon," mounted in August 1994 to celebrate the unification of "80 nations and nationalities" in the republic. Titled "Kyrgyzstan is Our Common Home" (1994), the four-hour program highlighted cultural and folk traditions of different ethnic groups living within the country's borders. A year later, a, national commemoration of "a thousand years" of *Manas* (the epic story of the national hero and of the Kyrgyz people) was staged in 1995, occupying dozens of broadcast hours.

But nationalist themes evoke strong positive responses only from those whose ethnicity matches the national cultural norms they promote. In the Kyrgyz Republic, the Kyrgyz viewer may react with passion to the story of *Manas*, but the Russians, Tajiks, Uzbeks, and Germans cannot relate to it in the same way. The cultural pluralism of Central Asia is disguised by the labeling of each republic; in fact, the state boundaries are highly imperfect. Ethnic Kyrgyz are a bare majority in Kyrgyzstan, only 52 percent; Russians amount to about 22 percent and Uzbeks 13 percent. Cultural and language issues must be faced directly by the independent radio stations if they are to survive. Three of these that have operated since independence include Pyramida, MCN Radio, and Radio Almaz. Each has had widely divergent programming philosophies. Sharing a single transmitter, the three stations faced a recurrent turnover of audiences as the program on the FM channel swung from one format to another at different times of the day. Radio Pyramida (Pyramid Radio) featured call-in request shows during its time period of 6:00 am to noon. This naturally resulted in a mish-mash of music, reflecting the unpredictable tastes of listeners. Long sentimental Russian ballads popular in the 1950s were frequently requested, producing dreary down-tempo lulls during key morning hours. Beginning at noon and continuing until 6:00 pm, MCN's program slot followed, a service that its producers tightly formatted to attract young adult listeners, which included a generous serving of imported music. Radio Almaz (Diamond Radio) concluded each day with a six-hour programming block aimed at yet another group of listeners. Radio Pyramida and Radio Almaz were owned and managed by ethnic Kyrgyz, although their transmissions, like those of MCN, were in Russian. This factor alone tended to divide audiences along language lines—state broadcasting drawing more Kyrgyz and older listeners while independent radio appealed more to youth and Russian listeners. The staffs of both Radio Pyramida and Radio Almaz lacked a marketing orientation, that is, one responding to specific audience needs. The two attempted to reach general audiences with a mixture of music and informational programs. Their thinking about radio programming reflected the tradition of producer-oriented Soviet broadcasting, and was modeled along the lines of official program services available from Moscow. MCN pursued a contrasting strategy; it aimed to reach young adults 18 to 35 years of age, and selected its music accordingly. Pyramida also operated Pyramida TV, the lone private station in Bishkek, and it published a weekly newspaper called *Pyramida Plus*, containing radio and television listings along with a few feature stories. MCN was operated by a physician who owned a private clinic (MC in the name stands for "medical clinic"). MCN staff, unlike Pyramida and Almaz, were primarily ethnic Russians. Elsewhere in Kyrgyzstan, for example Osh and Dzhalal-Abad, independent radio transmissions can be heard, but the regularity and permanence of services seems less well established than in the capital city (Johnson, 1994). Distaste for private enterprise in the media is often expressed by citizens, many of whom still consider any form of capitalism exploitative. As socialist communication scholar Carlos Alzugaray of the University of Havana argued on this point, "In a capitalist society, actually, media are not in the hands of the people. There is no freedom because the capitalists control all the media.... It's better that they are in the hands of the government, because the government is neutral..." (qtd. in Jackman, 1999, p. 8).

As in Cambodia, there is a risk in being identified as a media worker in Central Asia. There are legitimate fears that government authorities, political activists, or members of the underworld could take revenge on journalists and broadcasters. Independent broadcasters were especially prone to threats. In interviews in August 1994, one independent broadcaster from Tajikistan referred to the nine journalists killed in his country in that year as proof of dangers faced by his colleagues. At the time, only one independent television station remained on the air in Tajikistan, due to the country's turbulent situation. The likelihood of physical harm to journalists and broadcasters does not seem so great in Kyrgyzstan, but the possibility of governmental action is real. According to Rosenberg (1994), this trend was widespread throughout the former socialist bloc, where official policies in the mid-1990s moved back toward greater control after a brief period of openness. Unlike newspapers, radio stations lack an overt political agenda, thus seldom encountering friction with political figures. Nevertheless, legal protections for private media do not exist in the present environment.

A constant source of complaint among media workers in all countries is the lack of responsiveness of government bodies. State agencies and their staffs frequently do not differ much in style or attitude from their Soviet predecessors. Bureaucratic inertia and distrust of private enterprise are part of the reason so few independent broadcasters have been authorized in Central Asia. In Uzbekistan and Turkmenistan, state-owned broadcasting operates basically unchanged from the Soviet pattern. The chief cause of resistance to media reform is a lack of turnover in government administrative personnel and political leadership after independence. Even though governments have undergone "democratization," the same personalities who earlier served in Party leadership roles frequently reemerged in key government positions. Throughout the region, government agencies associated with the media have undergone little reformation and their staffs largely consist of personnel trained and appointed under Soviet times. Often, their organizational cultures have hardly altered under new political regimes.

Vietnam's media organization faced a somewhat separate set of bureaucratic issues. During the decades of military conflict leading to independence and eventual reunification, guerrilla units operating in portions of the country also served political functions, extending Party influence and control into contested areas. When the war ended, these military units were transformed into full political entities as local Party councils. According to Party members interviewed years later, these local councils continued to function much as they did in wartime. The problem posed by this was that guerrilla military organization is of necessity highly diffuse, lacking much of the centralized command and control that characterizes conventional military structures. The autonomy and weak lines of control inherited from this tradition help explain the Byzantine complexity of media authority in Vietnam. The hundreds of radio stations at the district level are directly operated by Party councils, which, although they nominally report to the Ministry of Culture, Information, and Tourism for their media activities, enjoy wide latitude in decision making. In the end, the country's media system was built of three loosely coordinated levels: national, provincial, and district.

Vietnam also contends with lingering North–South cultural divisions. Officially, authorities dismiss these as insignificant, but economic, social, and cultural differences between the nation's two regions are obvious. Language variations certainly exist. I had to revise a questionnaire designed in Ho Chi Minh City when it was used in Hanoi in order to make the language compatible with accepted usage in the North. After reunification, economic management followed Soviet-style models that had become culturally ingrained in the agricultural-based North. This approach was imposed in the South, where a market oriented economy had been the norm. Resistance to centralized planning, especially from distant Hanoi, became a constant battle for officials in the South (Oanh, 1995).

LOOKING AHEAD

Economic conditions continue to limit media's potential in two ways. First, there are not many private enterprises to purchase advertising on independent stations and newspapers in socialist Asia; the level of retail activity simply is not high enough to support advertising for more than a few outlets. Those that do survive generally do not have managements that fully comprehend the role of advertising in the marketing process. This situation will change slowly in countries such as Cambodia and Kyrgyzstan because their economies are depressed. Media workers themselves have limited knowledge of marketing and effective advertising strategies. On the whole, media operators need to learn how to build audiences and readerships, and to identify their target markets for potential advertisers.

In spite of pessimistic notes sounded in this chapter, an aura of hope and enthusiasm surrounds the media in socialist countries of Asia. Residents of the Kyrgyz Republic speak with pride of the personal freedoms and opportunities promised by independence; again and again, people describe the republic as "an island of democracy." One senses this particularly in conversations with those working in broadcasting and the print media, but also in casual conversations with ordinary citizens. Telephone call-in talk shows open a channel of discourse for radio audiences, rap music in Russian offers listeners oppositional viewpoints, and, most importantly, traditional music and other artistic expressions long suppressed under the old Soviet system are freely transmitted on the independent stations of Central Asia.

Politicization of mass communication reinforces the public's instinctive distrust of the media practically everywhere in socialist Asia, and because it is so deeply rooted in journalistic traditions, it will not be easily eradicated. A strategy tried by a number of international organizations was to build stronger professionalism through journalists' associations. In Asia, these organizations date back to Soviet times, providing a range of benefits to members such as training, a network of professional contacts, and opportunities for social interaction. In Cambodia and Central Asia, journalists' associations provide legal assistance when members run afoul of authorities. This is important, because without the backing of an organized group, individuals have little power to influence disposition of their cases. The problem with the journalists' associations is that they themselves are prone to political divisions. In the Kyrgyz Republic, I observed that it was impossible to persuade some persons to join a journalists' group because of the perceived political orientation of the majority of members. Similarly, in Cambodia, there are two journalists' associations, each aligned with major parties and their coalitions. Both groups lack sufficient size to function adequately and consequently neither is able to have much impact on problems that arise.

An end to the divisiveness of cultural exclusivity does not appear to be close. If anything, pressures generated by ethnic diversity are likely to grow because up to now other issues have tended to deflect attention away from cultural conflicts. But as time goes on, and economic and internal political conditions stabilize, the forces of ethnic aspirations are likely to rise. Yugoslavia's example provides a chilling reminder of the capacity of ethnic issues to rip apart seemingly well-established states.

Technology could be an asset to ensure consolidation, but usually it has had the reverse effect, promoting rather than healing divisions within societies. In particular, the Internet poses a dilemma for policy-makers. It offers isolated nations a chance for their citizens to participate in a variety of global initiatives—commercial, intellectual, academic, and otherwise—yet it can serve as a medium of opposition and resistance too. Anti-government messages flow freely over Internet mail lists aimed at countries such as Vietnam, Cambodia, China, and many more. This can function as a kind of protective mechanism. As Cambodia opposition leader Sam Rainsy observed, "Sometimes [the Internet] can save lives. If someone is arrested, the world knows they have disappeared. If the world knows, there is hesitation from the authorities" (qtd. in Dupont & Pape, 1999). Typical of mail lists is "cam-net," a service that relays news and comment about Cambodia. Anyone can contribute to the daily digest of items that subscribers receive without charge. The collection relayed each day contains material culled from press service coverage and newspaper stories, as well as the reports or opinion pieces from anyone who cares to send their writings. Authorities' efforts to screen out offensive messages and websites have not been very successful, and such barriers probably cannot ever be effective, given the ungovernable nature of the Internet.

Concerns about political and social uses of the Internet have been inconsistent from country to country. In Central Asia and Cambodia, misuses of the network do not seem to be particularly high on the governments' lists of worries. Access to the Internet in Cambodia is made easy by an NGO, Open Forum of Cambodia. It provides user accounts to subscribers, who pay a modest fee, which for Cambodians amounts to $8 (U.S.) per month; foreigners pay $25 (U.S.). Services provided are strictly for e-mail, newsgroups, and a collection of public documents in electronic form; no facilities for Web browsing are available. The organization leases three lines from the Ministry of Post and Telecommunication's Cam Net system that provides international links to the Internet. By early 1998, Open Forum had 450 subscribers (it should be noted that this figure is not equivalent to the number of individuals who use the service). Across the region it is a familiar practice to spread the costs of subscriptions by sharing expenses of a user address among several persons. By this means, individual monthly fees can be greatly reduced—at the expense of privacy, however. Open Forum is the same organization, by the way, that also publishes a weekly summary in English of the Khmer language press for international distribution. In capital cities of Central Asia, similar Internet services are usually available, typically through the auspices of local entrepreneurs. Costs and limitations of services available are also equivalent to those in Cambodia.

In contrast to such *laissez-faire* policies, actions to monitor Internet uses in the People's Republic of China have been among the most aggressive anywhere in the world. One example is the conviction of Lin (Patrick) Hai, a Chinese software company owner, of "using the Internet to incite people to overthrow the state" ("Asia-Pacific," 1999). According to published accounts, Hai was accused of providing 30,000 Chinese e-mail addresses to *VIP Reference Magazine*, a journal published by a group in the United States opposed to the PRC's government. For this transgression, he was sentenced to a two-year jail term. Service providers in China must register all users with government agencies, and estimates place their total number at over one million. Although a small proportion of the Chinese population, the number represents a large segment of Asia's Internet clientele. Reportedly, the Chinese government has organized special task forces to monitor the Internet to cut down on the flow of unregulated communication and to block access to sites thought to be politically subversive or pornographic.

The Internet policy in Vietnam has been closer to that in China than in Cambodia. Experimentation with global networking began in the early 1990s. At that time, a project involving an Australian university made communication via e-mail possible. The popularity of e-mail soon grew at a remarkable rate; the volume of e-mail reportedly doubled every five months beginning in 1994 (Marr, 1998). Security concerns apparently gave government officials second thoughts, and requests for approval to expand Internet access and availability met with rejections. Only in 1997 was the public given more or less open access to the network, but fees were fixed at rates so high they were only affordable to a few private users. Additionally, government authorities have set up barriers to prevent users from gaining access to selected sites, particularly ones operated by expatriate Vietnamese living abroad. These restrictions have kept most citizens from using the Internet, and have limited access mainly to commercial firms, NGOs, government agencies, and the like. Only a handful of Vietnamese websites have been opened. These include a newspaper, *Nhan Dan*, and the Vietnam News Agency.

Another problem faced in Asia is the lack of support for scripts used by local languages. Although software is available for Khmer script, which is based upon Sanskrit, to adapt computers to its use requires a higher degree of skill and training than is needed for Roman scripts. Vietnamese script is based upon Roman script, but with variants, so it too needs adaptation in order to function properly on computers. At any rate, as has been noted, English is the principal language of the Internet and anyone who wants to gain full benefit from it needs to be proficient in English. An apparently inexhaustible demand for English instruction exists throughout socialist Asia, not just for purposes of Internet use but for the many other advantages conveyed by fluency in the language. Nevertheless, it will be a long time before language facility in English or any other international language has trickled down to the masses of ordinary residents in Asia.

A good question to end this chapter might be this: Will the spread of technology and refinement of media draw socialist Asia closer to its former partners in East and Central Europe? To this there seem to be two answers: yes and no. No doubt there will be more possibilities of global interaction, both for Europe and for Asia. Every new technical innovation seems to open more possibilities. Simultaneously, the steady progress of improvements in design and manufacture has shrunk costs, bringing technologies within the reach of battered economies in both regions. But the effect of spreading technology is equally likely to atomize cultures. The Internet excels in serving small dispersed interest groups, the effect of which is to separate and exaggerate psychological and social distances among communities represented on the network.

NOTE

1. Even this was forced on the Soviet Union by the enormity of its geography; the country spanned 12 time zones and was too wide an expanse to cover with a single geosynchronous satellite. The USSR built the world's only orbiting domestic communication satellite system to provide television relays and to link its major population centers in Europe and Asia with voice and data circuits.

REFERENCES

Asia-Pacific Prison for China Net dissident [Online]. (1999, January 20). BBC News Online Network. Available: <http://news.bb.co.uk/hi/english/world/asia%2Dpacific/newsid%5F258000/258805.stm [2000, February 8].

Brown, B. (1994, July 18). Akaev calls for press restrictions. Washington, DC: RFE/RL.

Dingley, J. (1989). Soviet television and glasnost. In J. Graffy & G. A. Hosking (Eds.), Culture and the media in the USSR today (pp. 6–25). New York: St. Martin's Press.

Dupont, K., & Pape, E. (1999). E-mail is a real revolution [Online]. NGO Forum. Available: <camnews.v001.n875.7> [1999, February 20].

The empty consumer basket. (1994, May 31). Kyrgyzstan Chronicle, p. 2.

Fanning, D. (Exec. Producer). (1979). Heroes, workers and the party line: Soviet TV. Washington, DC: Public Broadcasting System.

Hadlow, M. (1992). The situation of media in Central Asia. Paris: UNESCO.

Is it time to slash the throat of Khmer Rouge newspapers? (1997, November 2-8). The Mirror, p. 7.

Jackman, R. (1999). Revolution without change: Two perspectives on control of the mass media in Cuba. Unpublished paper, School of Telecommunications, Ohio University, Athens.

Johnson, E. (1994). Preliminary activity report. Washington, DC: Internews.

The King is without hope. He wants to commit suicide. (1997, October 12-18). The Mirror, p. 6.

Kyrgyzstan is our common home. (1994, August 23). Kyrgyzstan Chronicle, p. 1.

Markham, J. W. (1967). Voices of the red giants: Communications in Russia and China. Ames, IA: Iowa State University Press.

Mares, P. (1998). Reporting Vietnam: True confessions of a foreign correspondent. In D. Marr (Ed.), The mass media in Vietnam (pp. 146–163). Canberra, Australia: The Australian National University.

Marr, D. (1998). Introduction. In D. Marr (Ed.), The mass media in Vietnam (pp. 1–26). Canberra, Australia: The Australian National University.

Martin, P. B. (1994). Vietnamese media ride an economic boom. Unpublished paper, Institute of Current World Affairs, Hanover, NH.

Mickiewicz, E. (1988). Split signals: Television and politics in the Soviet Union. New York: Oxford University Press.

Mould, D., & Schuster, E. (1998). Central Asia. Unpublished paper, School of Telecommunications, Ohio University, Athens.

Oanh, N. X. (1995, April). Vietnam: Recent economic performance and development perspectives. Paper presented at the Fifth tun Abdul Razak Conference, Ohio University, Athens.

Palan, A., & Sarayeth, T. (1995). Women in the media in Cambodia. Phnom Penh, Cambodia: Women's Media Centre.

Paulu, B. (1974). Radio and television broadcasting in Eastern Europe. Minneapolis, MN: The University of Minnesota Press.

Prokhorov, Y. (1976). The Marxist press concept. In H. Fischer & J. C. Merrill (Eds.), International and intercultural communication (pp. 51–58). New York: Hastings House.

Rosenberg, T. (1994). Writers' bloc. The New Yorker, 70(32), 7–8.

Sad statistics. (1994, April 5). Kyrgyzstan Chronicle, p. 5.

Shane, S. (1994). Dismantling Utopia: How information ended the Soviet Union. New York: Oxford University Press.

Women's Media Centre. (1997, December). *Audience responses to Women's Media Centre of Cambodia television and radio productions and attitudes to media coverage of women and social issues.* Phnom Penh, Cambodia: Author.

chapter 17

Georgia's Media Future: Options and Opportunities for the Third Millennium*

Nicholas Johnson
University of Iowa

M edia and telecommunications policies are central to the functioning of any society. They affect—among other things—economic growth, the education of the young, levels of democratic
participation, the preservation of the culture, and the values of the people about everything from the role of women to the role of war—essentially every aspect of being human and living in a civilized community.
This chapter presents ideas on the future of media in Georgia, based on
my participation in the American Bar Association/Central and East
European Law Initiative (ABA/CEELI) Georgia Parliament effort (1998)
to review proposed legislative language, section by section, line by line—
most recently in 1998 in Tbilisi, Georgia.

*The ideas, discussion, and proposals in this chapter are not necessarily the
views of ABA/CEELI, the Federal Communications Commission, or other U.S.
government agencies; or the University of Iowa or other institutions with which I
am affiliated. In this case, much of this chapter is an expression of my views,
which are directly contrary to the views of those institutions—to the extent that
they have positions on these issues at all.

WORLD CLASS ELECTRONIC MEDIA FOR GEORGIA'S
FUTURE: SOME ALTERNATIVES

Many former Soviet Republics' policymakers assume they should attempt to construct a broadcasting system, using analog technology, similar to that in the U.S. in the 1960s and 1970s. It would include a public broadcasting system relatively independent of the government (to replace "State Television"), along with commercial television stations licensed and regulated by an independent body similar to the U.S. Federal Communications Commission. That is one option. There are, however, alternatives.

There are disadvantages to building a telecommunications and broadcasting system "from scratch." There may be a shortage of capital and experienced personnel. Or there may be an absence of audience expectation. In the case of Georgia, there is also the pre-existing state broadcasting system to overcome.

But there are also advantages. One of the advantages is the opportunity to "leapfrog" intermediate technologies. It is not necessary to create the analog broadcasting system of the 1960s in order to evolve toward the 21st century. One can start with a 21st-century digital system and simply skip the technologies of the 1960s, 1970s, 1980s, and 1990s.

There are also disadvantages to creating a 1960s television system. First, television stations are costly: studios, transmitters, antenna towers, cameras, and so forth. Second, the sum total of homeowners' total investment in receivers is an even greater expenditure, a multiple of the station owners' costs. Third, these costs do not produce much in the way of benefits. Unless an even more costly nationwide repeater (or "translator") system of transmitters and antennas is installed, vast areas of the country will be without any television reception. Fourth, the laws of physics (plus those of the State) restrict the number of conventional over-the-air television stations that can operate in any country at the same time and on the same, or even adjacent, channels. Thus, the 1960s technology creates an artificial limitation on the number and diversity of channels, with the resulting concentration of economic, political, and media power in the hands of a very few.

There is substantial research about various economic, social, and political issues in the Republic of Georgia (see, for example, Atal, 1998; Gachechiladze, 1996; Goodwin et al., 1999; Macfarlane, 1997; Russell, 1992; Suny, 1994). However, there are few, if any, regarding media and technology in the Republic. As a result, I do not know enough about either the Georgian economy, society, and technological capability, or the characteristics and costs of available technology, to make precise recommendations. But this part of the chapter is not about precise recommendations. It is about a "new paradigm," a new way of thinking about Georgia's telecommunications and media future.

Many of the ideas that follow are merely examples drawn from my previous work (Johnson, 1988, 1995, 1997, n.d.), designed to stimulate discussion and provide illustrations of the type of options that may be available to those who are planning and building Georgia's media future. Anyone Georgian who is open to new ways of thinking will almost certainly come up with approaches that are not mentioned here.

A "NEW PARADIGM" FOR GEORGIA'S TELECOMMUNICATIONS AND MEDIA FUTURE: SATELLITE BROADCASTING, CABLE TELEVISION, AND VIDEO DIALTONE

Small (50 cm) dishes for reception of satellite signals (with the accompanying receivers and other equipment) are now relatively cheap. Presumably, with the research and development and science and engineering capabilities in Georgia, they could be built in the country, thereby providing jobs and otherwise encouraging economic growth. The satellite uplink, and the satellite itself, are, of course, more expensive.[1]

Investigation may show that such a system would not be more expensive than the cost of providing country-wide coverage of Georgia using conventional, over-the-air broadcasting technology. Even if it were to be slightly more expensive, among the advantages of such a system are that: a) it provides full-country coverage throughout Georgia; b) 100 to 500 channels can provide outlets for substantially more "broadcasters" than an over-the-air system; c) it can also be used for Internet (data) communication (at least one-way, from the source to the user); d) unlike cable and "telephone" video delivery systems the incremental cost of adding an additional home viewer is virtually zero; e) it avoids the cost, aesthetic blight, and other difficulties associated with "wiring up" every home in Georgia for cable television; and f) of course, it also avoids the costs associated with transmitters, antenna towers, translators, and the other capital costs of establishing conventional over-the-air stations.

Cable television is only 10 or 20 years newer than over-the-air television technology. It is usually installed "over" (that is, after, in addition to) a broadcasting system, providing an alternative way of distributing programming from television stations (through a wire rather than through the air). Of course, it is also possible for a cable system to create its own programming, or contract with programming suppliers (who often use satellites to distribute their product). Although there is no theoretical limit to the number of channels a cable system can provide (by stringing additional cables or the use of fiber optic), some U.S. cable companies still offer only 50 channels or fewer. Unless required to do otherwise, the cable company, normally a monopoly, will seek to maximize profit by charging as much as possible for as little programming as possible—while maintaining a nonreviewable control, or censorship, over all channels.

Note that, rather than using a cable system as an *alternative* distribution network for over-the-air stations' signals, it could be created as the sole method for bringing audio and video programming into Georgians' homes. Presumably, such a system would need to be created as a "common carrier," that is, a system that would be forbidden to have any interest in the programming, and would be required to add such additional channels as are necessary to satisfy programmers' demands—at fair, regulated, equal prices for all.

An alternative to "cable television" would be to create a "telephone" system capable of handling voice, data, fax, and video (sometimes called "video dialtone"). Cable television typically has no capacity for switching—a basic necessity for conventional telephone systems. The video dial-tone option would be otherwise similar to that for cable television: a common carrier.

THE IMPACT OF THE INTERNET IN GEORGIA

The distribution of video signals is now in its infancy on the Internet. But, then, so were photographs and audio not that many years ago. Today, the video pictures are small, sometimes jerky, and the quality is not that good. But there are now plans to expand the capacity of the Internet by 100 times, or even 1,000 times.

Many radio stations now "broadcast" their signal over the Internet simultaneously, with conventional broadcast over the air. Presumably, the day will soon come when this will be true for television stations as well.

Thus, another possible option for Georgia would be to take the plunge with, say, a 10-year plan for conversion to Internet distribution of what is today thought of as "television" programming. Because "telephone" conversations and fax transmissions are now possible over the Internet, Georgia could find itself the world leader in this field.

WIRELESS INTERNET: SOLUTIONS TO CONNECTIVITY PROBLEMS IN GEORGIA

Of course, one of the drawbacks to Internet alternatives in Georgia today is that connection to the Internet is normally made with a "modem" through conventional telephone lines, which are both slow and not always reliable for this purpose. There is also the problem of electrical power outages, but presumably these would be resolved by the time the Internet conversion was in place.

There are a couple of solutions. First, if George ends up choosing the cable television alternative, it is possible to construct a system that can also provide Internet access to subscribers who use a "cable modem." Such a system, with its wider bandwidth, can potentially offer much faster interaction for users (that is, require less time for downloading large files). Second, the previous discussion of satellite distribution refers to "downloading" Internet material to a small dish. Such a system would still require uploading—today through the telephone (or cable) system.[2]

However, it is also possible to provide wireless connections between an Internet service provider (ISP) and a user. Not only does this avoid the problems (and costs) associated with telephone wire connections, it also substantially increases the possible speeds of transmission. While there have been efforts in the Republic, and elsewhere in the New Europe, to provide wireless telecommunications technology (compare Wolfe & Jaffe, 1994), there is still much work to be done to provide the communications access that Georgians require.

As explained at the beginning of this section, no single one of these ideas is being recommended—and certainly not all of them. All that is recommended is that they be used as a stimulus for "what-if" games, for thinking about (and then planning and building) possible future telecommunications and media systems.

CIVITAS GEORGICA: PROMOTING AWARENESS OF DEMOCRATIC PRINCIPLES THROUGH THE WORLD WIDE WEB

Georgia is now beginning to use the communications technologies that are now available and can better position the country to provide education for its children, jobs for its adults, and a better quality of life and more democratic society for all. For example, a not-for-profit organization called Civitas Georgica (1998a) was established in 1996, "to provide public information, to raise issues of a simple but fundamental nature and to promote awareness of democratic principles." The underlying principle of Civitas Georgia (1998a) is "that individuals and communities should know what is happening or is about to happen to them in order that they might be able to make informed choices about their own futures." The organization believes that "in the process of transition little attention is paid to: The relationship between state and society;

Actual data to enable us both to plan for our futures and to discover what is happening now; Positive criticism of decisions and decision-making process" (1998a). Civitas Georgia (1998a) intends to address these concerns by "Providing a vehicle for public discussion; Publishing materials to stimulate debate as well as to inform; Encourage and participate in individual and public development issues and practices; Assisting accurate data collecting process in the regions."

Through partnerships with both local and international organizations, such as the Open Society Georgia Foundation, Civitas Georgica (1998b) has developed a number of initiatives to meet the above goals. One recent effort is the "Local Elections In Georgia - Opportunity For Ethnic Minorities" project. The project was developed in reaction to the marginalization of ethnic minorities in the Republic. One outcome of the project is the publication and distribution of a booklet entitled "Citizens' Guide to Local Elections," which is in Armenian, Azerbaijanian, and Russian; all versions are currently viewable on their website. The guide addresses basic "what, why, and how" questions of local government, and the importance of and essential information about participating in elections. Particularly directed to the problems ethnic minorities have faced in the Republic, the guide will explain how minorities can defend their rights in the election process, "the functions of local election committees, how these committees should react on any violation occurred, and to whom should [minorities] appeal in cases when they consider that their legitimate rights are violated" (Civitas Georgica, 1998b). Unlike organizations outside of Georgia, such as the International Foundation for Elections (Scott, Edgeworth, & International Foundation for Elections, 1996), Civitas Georgica has a keen understanding of the concerns of those living in the Republic and assists marginalized communities by providing opportunities for raising awareness of democratic principles and discourse.

DEMOCRATIZING THE MEDIA: SOME ALTERNATIVES

In the U.S., it has been said, "Freedom of the press exists for the person who owns one." Of course, anyone can speak in the public park, or hand out leaflets on the public sidewalks. But the only citizens with meaningful First Amendment rights are those who have the capital, and the inclination, to acquire a major newspaper or broadcasting station. Needless to say, virtually all media owners support this view.

Less expected, perhaps, is that the Supreme Court of the United States does also. The Court says that the "freedom of speech" includes the freedom not to speak; or, more precisely, the right to keep others from speaking. The Court has ruled that media owners can censor the views of those who would like to engage in a community's democratic dialogue by using the pages of its newspapers or time on its radio and television stations. In short, not only do citizens not have the right to *free* newspaper space and broadcast time; they do not even have the right to *buy* space or time if the owner wishes to silence their viewpoint.

This would not be so serious in a media environment in which the "barriers to entry" (the costs, or other impediments to establishing a media outlet) were trivial. But in most U.S. cities, there is *no* meaningful competition for the dominant newspaper, only the cable system and a small handful of television stations.[3] So the implications for meaningful "free speech" by citizens are serious. The ease of web page creation, newsgroups, and e-mail via the Internet illustrates how a truly open system functions. However, its existence is by no means an adequate counterbalance to the power of dominant media to shape public opinion.

Given the U.S. Supreme Court's rulings, the position that follows is my own. It is not the view of most lawyers, judges, and law or journalism professors—nor is it the view of some of the professional journalists with whom I spoke in Georgia (though they are quite insistent that they should have free speech rights vis-à-vis their employer-owners).

DEMOCRATIC DISCOURSE IN THE NEW EUROPE

Democracy requires that all citizens have the potential right to participate in the democratic dialogue in a meaningful way, whether they choose to exercise that right or not. Under what circumstances should that requirement outweigh the rights of a media owner to publish or broadcast—or not—whatever he or she chooses?

A media owner should have the right to operate a newspaper or broadcast station with no advertising (for example, with support from subscribers, contributors, foundations, or from the owner's personal wealth). Such an owner (which might, in fact, be a trade union, church, or other organization with a particular point of view) should be free to edit, to "censor," however he or she may please.

But if an owner *does* choose to sell space or time, I believe he or she should not have the right to sell to some and not to others. This is especially true if there are a limited number of outlets reaching most of the community (as is true in all but the very largest of U.S. cities). Of course, I do not argue that *all* advocacy ads need be taken, only that the reasonable and rational selection process *not be based on content.*

Whatever one's position on this issue, there are other possible ways of democratising and diversifying the media that are far less controversial—and well within American law. Many of the options that follow did seem to be of interest, and potentially acceptable, to the Georgians with whom I spoke during a visit in early 1998. That is, there was a willingness to consider alternatives to top-down, hierarchical control of all content by a single media owner, whether state, public, or corporate.

The first option is producer power: Within the contemplated "public broadcasting" alternative to state broadcasting, there seemed to be support for the idea that the administrative budget and staff be kept lean, and that funding should go directly to producers, rather than through administrators. Indeed, some Georgians proposed a form of competition for these funds. Such an approach will encourage greater diversity as well as creativity.

Second, political and reply time: There seemed to be support for a number of proposals growing out of the U.S. Federal Communications Commission experience with its "equal opportunity"[4] and "personal attack"[5] doctrines.

There was a belief that at least public, and possibly commercial broadcasting as well, should make free time available to candidates.[6] The "fairness doctrine"[7] was only touched upon briefly, but there was little or no rejection of that idea.

Third, community access cable channels: In the U.S., cable companies are required to make some of their channels available, for free, to designated institutions (such as local governments or public schools) and also to individual citizens. Without detailing either the history or specific requirements, such programming is, for the most part, not subject to cable company censorship. Thus, any citizen with access to a video camera can present his or her views to the community. There seemed to be some openness to this concept in Georgia as well.

Fourth, access is fairness: Although never adopted by the FCC, when the fairness doctrine was under attack, there was a proposal that radio and television stations wishing to opt out of its requirements could do so by offering a fixed percentage of each segment of their broadcast day for the purpose of announcements by local community groups (which were usually brief). Of course, not all tendered announcements would have to be broadcast, but the system of selection would have to be other than content based.

Fifth, ownership limitations: All Georgians (to the best of my recollection) were agreed that there should be some limitations on the numbers of stations any one owner can control. There was no objection to the proposal that this limit be set at one station per licensee. Whatever the statutory limitation ends up being, obviously the more owners there are, the greater the potential diversity of programming and opinion.

Sixth, shared time stations: Giving every station licensee the right to broadcast 24 hours a day, seven days a week, creates an artificial limit on the number of "broadcasters" and the diversity of their programming. An obvious solution is "shared time." Under this approach, everyone who wants to broadcast can do so. For example, if there are 10 persons who wish to broadcast and only five stations, each can broadcast either a) a half-day, everyday, or b) a whole day, three or four days a week. As more wish to broadcast, there is less time per day for each; as some go out of business, there is more time to share. Administrative arrangements would be made to fairly share the costs of construction, and operation, of the stations.

Seventh, citizen's media reform organizations: There is at this point little Georgian experience with the voluntary associations so familiar in the U.S., from the time of Alexis de Toqueville to the present. Media reform organizations in particular have played a very significant role in the U.S. in encouraging greater FCC scrutiny of stations' performance, the creation of standards (and legislation) regarding children's programming, or the reduction in levels of violence in television programs.

Eighth, ombudspersons, letters, and news councils: How can the public participate in the process of mass media selection and distribution of news? Some U.S. newspapers have in-house "ombudspersons" (a Scandinavian concept and word), independent of management and journalists, to receive—and respond publicly, in the paper—to complaints from the public. Some papers—and even radio and television programs—receive, and broadcast the reading of, letters from the public critical of the programming. News councils are independent bodies of citizens—normally with no legal power—that hear and write opinions regarding public complaints about the media.

Finally, media literacy: television viewers in most countries, and especially those brought up on state television, accept TV programming as a given, something they are powerless (and disinclined) to affect. Television advertising is most effective with viewers who are relatively unsophisticated about the way commercials are created, and the techniques used to manipulate consumer choice. By including media literacy courses throughout the K-12 school system, it is possible to create a much more sophisticated television audience. Viewers can become more willing to make their own programs, to organize and present their views to stations and regulators, and to be more resistant to commercial appeals.

The point is that, just as there are options offered by new technology, so are there options with regard to the degree of direct citizen participation in the democratic dialogue. It is my impression that the Georgians are interested in including many of these in their broadcasting practices, policy, and law.

DIVERSITY AND DEMOCRATIZATION OF BROADCAST MEDIA

These thoughts are deliberately the last to be discussed because they will be considered by many to be among the most radical of those presented in this chapter. Even so, I believe it better to consider and reject them than to fail to consider them at all.

The advantages to a country of having a television system in place are well known. Clearly, television is very popular with viewers everywhere. For instance, the average American watches television four hours a day; the average set is turned on seven hours a day. The marketplace indicates that consumers everywhere are willing to make financial sacrifices and forego other purchases to have a television. In the U.S., where the multiple-channel offerings of cable are widely available, roughly 70 percent of all home dwellers are willing not only to buy a TV receiver, but to pay $15 to $50 a month for the cable service.

Television has proven itself to be one of the most powerful of all advertising media for the creation, and manipulation, of consumer demand. It can be a powerful engine driving a consumer economy—if that is something desired as a matter of national policy. When the whole nation turns to television—such as in times of national disaster or national joy—television can be both a useful means of communication and of unification.

Television can be used to divert and defuse what might otherwise be citizen protests, or government opposition. It is the "electronic circus" in the modern version of governing through "bread and circuses." Once in place, of course, it is politically somewhere between exceedingly difficult and impossible even radically to alter, let alone to do away with, television. Nonetheless, the disadvantages of television should be considered.

Many argue that it is harmful for children under the age of eight to be exposed to any television—regardless of content (Winn, 1985). The argument is that young children have a lot of learning to do; that many end up watching television for as many as 50 hours a week; and that the act of watching television—sitting motionless, "relating" to an electronic device—impedes their growth physically, emotionally, intellectually, socially, and spiritually.

As children grow older, there appears to be an inverse relationship between the amount of time spent watching television and their academic achievement; the more they watch, the lower their grades will be in school. There are now over 2,000 studies documenting the relationship between children's watching of televised violence and the amount of real-life violence in their behavior.[8]

There is an opportunity cost associated with adults' television watching; time spent watching television is time unavailable for other activities: physical exercise, interaction with one's children, adult education. Among the first activities to go are the evening meetings necessary to a civic society and its organizations, including democratic political activity.

To the extent the television is commercial TV, the consequences change radically. Commercial TV is not about programs, it is about delivering the audience ("the product") to the advertiser ("the consumer") at a cost per thousand viewers. Of all the objectionable "lowest common denominator" programming, it will be the "least objectionable program" (LOP; commercial broadcasting's expression, not mine) that will command the largest audience and, therefore, profit for the broadcaster.

Commercial broadcasting has an economic incentive to use cheap-to-produce programming that gets the audience's attention through violence, chase scenes, crime, and sexual themes. In doing so, it tends to drive out the teaching, and values, of parents, churches, schools, and the dominant culture. In their place, it substitutes the values of materialism, hedonism, consumerism, conspicuous consumption—the notion that "you will be known by the companies you keep," that your identity comes from the brands you use.

As a consequence of television's dominance in the economy, and the lives of the citizens, the station owners soon take on a disproportionate political influence as well. Already in Georgia, I was told—although I do not know if it is true—the Parliament was reluctant to impose as strict a prohibition on the TV advertising of tobacco and alcohol as it might have because of the political power of the broadcasters.

There are many reasons why a nation might wish to create, or expand, its television system. There are other reasons why, even if it does not wish to do so, it must do so anyway because of political pressure. But there are other reasons why it might wish to curtail the growth of television—or at least minimize its adverse consequences. One of the options would be an alternative medium: radio.

One of the central problems confronting Georgia in creating a broadcasting system is lack of resources. Until the economy substantially improves, there cannot be a lot of disposable income and demand for consumer goods. Without the existence of such a market, there is little reason to advertise. Without advertising, there is little income for commercial television. And without the prospect of commercial television income, there is little incentive for investors to make a capital investment in stations.

Nor are the economic prospects for "public television" much better. Viewers have little interest in, or experience with, special taxes for television. They believe they have a right to television programming for free. Needless to say, there is even less tradition of voluntary contributions, which U.S. public television relies upon for support. To the extent public that television sells commercials, and becomes dependent on corporate advertisers, it enters into the same ratings game as, and becomes almost indistinguishable from, commercial television. Finally, the more public television is dependent upon the state for financing, the more difficult it will be to project an image, and reality, of an independent public, as distinguished from the traditional state-controlled, television.

Given the economic realities confronting Georgia at this time, a two-phase plan might be worth consideration. The first phase would involve the development of a national public radio system. A two or three channel system, with nationwide coverage, could be developed for roughly one-tenth of what a national television system would cost.

Once this system was in place, the audience was used to "public broadcasting," the staff was assembled, the programming developed, and the financial support firm and adequate—all at a fraction of the cost of television—the second phase could begin. The second phase would be public television.

Radio has advantages over television, in addition to the cost savings in transmission. Georgia has (at least at the present time) an electric power system that involves power outages during significant periods of time. It is much more common (as well as cheaper) for the audience to have alternative power systems for radio receivers than for television: batteries, solar power, or internal power generators (a "dynamo").

There are significantly more channels (frequencies) available for radio broadcasting in the AM and FM bands than TV channels. Thus, radio offers the opportunity for a greater democratisation and diversity of the broadcast media than television. This distinction is multiplied by the fact that it is much cheaper for a potential broadcaster to go into the radio, rather than the television, business.

It is cheaper, both for the broadcaster and the audience, to provide nationwide radio coverage than television signals of similar reach. Radio signals can go farther, on less power, than television. At night, AM radio can cover enormous distances. And, for the reasons mentioned above, radio receivers (which cost less than TVs) can be used anywhere in the country—with or without electrical power facilities.

There are those who would argue that radio programming does less harm than television programming. It leaves more intellectual and artistic freedom to the audience member—who must make his or her own pictures inside the head.

The proposal that public radio be given priority attention is the one that received the least interest—primarily because of the inevitability of a television system once the people have become dependent upon it. It is, nonetheless, worthwhile passing along. Others may find it of greater appeal. Or there may be elements, or variations on the idea, that may prove practical.

CONCLUSION: GEORGIA'S FUTURE

These are exciting times for Georgia. A nation with a great cultural heritage, a nation that has survived centuries of challenge, is entering a new era. Dangers and challenges abound, but so do opportunities and options.

Central to Georgia's future will be the decisions regarding its public policy and laws affecting media and telecommunications. Those decisions will be made by Georgians; Georgians must make them.

That Georgia's leadership is open to new ideas, to alternatives to its past as it plans for its future, is one of the many strengths of this country and its people. This chapter represents but one U.S. citizen's effort to contribute to that process—with appreciation for the invitation to participate, and confidence in the ultimate result.

NOTES

1. Perhaps satellite transponders (channels) could be leased, rather than requiring Georgians to "own" the entire satellite. And perhaps foundations or other aid-granting institutions, or even corporations, could be interested in contributing funding.

2. "Uploading" is used to describe what happens when an Internet user sends out a message indicating the address of a web page he or she wishes to see. (E-mail or web pages *created* by the user might be other examples of "uploaded" material.) When the server on which the desired web page is located sends the page back to the user's computer screen, it has been "downloaded" by the user. Because, usually, far greater quantities of material are downloaded by a user than uploaded, the combination of satellite-distributed downloads (at relatively high speeds) and telephone modem uploads (at relatively slower speeds) makes for a workable system.

3. This pattern of concentration exists throughout other media as well. For example, there are currently six firms that control over 90 percent of all the world's music. There are a similar number of movie studios producing most

of the top-grossing films from Hollywood. In the book publishing industry, most of the competition has disappeared due to mergers.

4. "Equal opportunity" is found in Section 315 of the Communications Act. It requires that if a station puts on one candidate for public office, it is required to give an equal opportunity to all competitors.

5. The FCC's "personal attack doctrine" states that citizens may be verbally attacked by broadcast media owners, but, having done so, the attack then triggers a right of the person attacked to know what was said and to reply personally. (The distinction comes about because another requirement, since repealed by the FC., the "fairness doctrine," did *not* create a right in a given individual. It simply provided that a broadcast station must a) deal with controversial issues of public importance, and in doing so, must b) present a range of views on the issue.)

6. This idea was proposed in the U.S. in 1998 as a means of partial payback by broadcasters for the $70 billion worth of free frequencies recently given them by Congress and the FCC for high-definition television.

7. See note #5, above.

8. Some studies indicate the correlation is between the amount of time spent watching *any* television, not just violent television programs.

REFERENCES

American Bar Association and Central and East European Law Initiative (ABA/ CEELI). (1998). *CEELI's activities in Georgia (1996–98)* [Online]. Available: <http://www.abanet.org/ceeli/georgia.html> [1999, April 17].

Atal, Y. (1998). *Poverty in transition and transition in poverty: Studies of poverty in countries-in-transition: Hungary, Bulgaria, Romania, Georgia, Russia, and Mongolia.* New York: United Nations Educational.

Civitas Georgica. (1998a). *Civitas Georgica organization profile* [Online]. Available: <http://civitas.hypermart.net/public/civitas.html> [1999, March 7].

Civitas Georgica. (1998b). *Civitas Georgica projects and other activities* [Online]. Available: <http://civitas.hypermart.net/public/projects.html> [1999, March 7].

Gachechiladze, R. G. (1996). *The new Georgia: Space, society.* College Station, TX: Texas A&M University Press.

Goodwin, R., Nizharadze, G., Lan Anh Nguyen, L., Kosa, E., & Emelyanova, T. (1999). Glasnost and the art of conversation. *Journal of Cross-Cultural Psychology, 30*(1), 72–90.

Johnson, N. (1988, Fall). The semantics of computer communications. *ETC.: A Review of General Semantics 45*(3), 250–254.

Johnson, N. (1995, June). Save free speech in cyberspace. *Wired,* 131, 134.

Johnson, N. (1997, October). *The journalist in cyberspace.* Paper presented at the Warsaw Journalism Center International Conference, Palace of Culture, Warsaw, Poland.

Johnson, N. (n.d.). *Georgia (Formerly Republic of Georgia): Its evolving media law and policy* [Online]. Available: <http://soli.inav.net/~njohnson/njgeorgi.html> [1999, March 7].

Macfarlane, S. N. (1997). On the front lines in the near abroad: The CIS and the OSCE in Georgia's civil wars. *Third World Quarterly, 18*(3), 509–525.

Russell, M. (1992*). Please don't call it Soviet Georgia: A journey through a troubled paradise*. New York: Serpent's Tail.

Scott L., Edgeworth, L., & International Foundation for Elections (1996). *Republic of Georgia: Assessment and voter information campaign*. Washington, DC: International Foundation for Election Systems.

Suny, R. G. (1994). *The making of the Georgian nation*. Bloomington, IN: Indiana University Press.

Winn, M. (1985). *The plug-in drug* (Rev. ed.). New York: Penguin.

Wolfe, F., & Jaffe, T. (1994, November 7). Eastward ho! *Forbes, 154*(11), 18–22.

chapter 18

Collaboration through Technology Now and in the Future: Linking the New Europe with the World

Christina Preston
Institute of Education, University of London

Bozena Mannova
Czech Technical University, Prague

Laura Lengel
Richmond American International University in London

HARDSHIPS DURING AND AFTER COMMUNIST RULE

Zdena and Stanislav Novakova[1] have lived in seven different countries, although they have never left Prague. The impact of this kind of political instability and change is difficult for those outside post socialist nations to comprehend. Now in their 50s, Zdena and Stanislav had a difficult time during the Russian occupation. Their professional development was halted, because they were known for opposing the Russians, the last of several occupations of the Czech Republic. As opposition members, they were not allowed to teach or pursue their doctorates, and feared for the education and well-being of their children.

In 1968, Zdena stood on Russian military tanks in Prague's Wenceslas Square, verbally resisting the Russian soldiers occupying the city. In 1989, Zdena's son Jan followed her example. He was one of the students who organized the final uprising that ousted the Communists and spent considerable time talking in the factories to get the support of the workers. Unlike the efforts in 1968, this time the Czechs were freed from a stultifying regime. However, the aftermath of the regime has posed unexpected challenges for Czechs and others in the post-socialist nations of the New Europe; once the elation about the fall of the Berlin Wall settled, they were left with questions about the future and the stability of the region.

Despite their freedom from the Communist regime, many New Europeans, like Jan, are afraid and unhappy. Like many young people around the world, they are cynical about political processes. Currently, Jan is nervous and pale, studying for his final exams to be a physician. He has reason to worry; his professors are still following the authoritarian educational models set up by the Communist regime. They are often cruelly dismissive of their brilliant students, looking to trip them up rather than mentor and praise them. Despite seven years of conscientious and intense study, many medical students fail. Yesterday, one of Jan's major professors told all his students they were all stupid. Jan's self-esteem is low, despite his high grades. Worst of all, he fears that what he has so diligently learned by heart is likely to be out of date. Jan's partner, who managed to pass the exams, tries to provide both emotional and financial support, although she earns only $14 a month for working long hours in a local hospital. She is lucky to have a job. Jan fears he may never find appropriate employment in his home country and is already planning to go to the United States.

There are other stresses. Accommodation in New European urban centers like Prague is expensive; property costs are rising to the levels of London or San Francisco. However, salaries in the New Europe are about one-tenth of the norm in the "West" and dropping, with the exception of those provided by multinational companies (MNCs), including technology firms like Oracle, Microsoft, and Hewlett Packard. The spending power of professionals employed by these MNCs puts them in a new elite that have been building their own homes, buying expensive cars and clothes, and educating their children abroad. These are the ones who now travel without restrictions and often leave the region for further riches in the West. Professionals such as researchers and doctors, dependent on state salaries, are losing out in the economic stakes to the business executive and entrepreneur. Teachers are in a more dire situation; in nations like Russia, they have not been paid in months (Zuckerman, 1998).

Overall, life for most citizens in the New Europe is more problematic since democracy (see, for example, Bennahum, 1997; Boyle, 1995; Kober, 1993; Lengel, 1998), and there are signs of backtracking. Not only are students like Jan afraid for their future, but teachers, like those unpaid in Russia, are fearful as well (see, for example, Boyes, 1998; Preston & Mannova, 1999). They desire a dialogue with others, both within and outside the New Europe, who may begin to understand their conditions. They desire professional development and mentoring by others, particularly those in established democracies. Up until recently, however, this mentoring has only been available to those such as the new elite, who could afford to leave the country.

Now, however, those living in post-socialist nations like Jan, Zdena, and Stanislav do have a forum that connects them with others, in ways not possible before the growing use of information and communication technology. Through technology, organizations and communities in the New Europe are able to link with others both within and outside the region. One such community is MirandaNet, an international electronic community that spans the Czech Republic, Russia, Chile, Ireland, Japan, Mauritius, and Great Britain. In this chapter, we explore how members of this community, through both face-to-face and computer mediated peer mentoring and collaboration, engage in a dialogue that is building cultural and educational alliances across post-socialist nations and their Western European neighbors, as well as countries around the world. This chapter addresses specific cultural, generational, gender, and sociopolitical issues that have emerged in the development of such a broad-ranging electronic community. We reflect on globalization issues in the diverse educational and discursive cultures of the New Europe and the opportunity for civic discourse, which was previously forbidden under the Communist regime. We also explore the common professional culture that the community shares, regardless of national, cultural, economic, and political differences. These commonalities are prompted by an understanding across the MirandaNet community of the impact of globalization on research, mentoring, collaboration, and intercultural and international communication. Finally, we examine the impact of governmental and industrial sectors in developing online communities like MirandaNet and the future of culture and technology and online communities in the New Europe as it faces the third millennium.

DEVELOPMENT OF AN ONLINE COMMUNITY

The MirandaNet community was originally developed in Great Britain in 1992 as an information and communication technology-focused partnership linking government, industry, and education. This not-for-profit international fellowship of teachers, researchers, and industry representatives strives to enrich lifelong learning and communication using technology across social, vocational, cultural, and political divides. With a community spanning three continents, MirandaNet is engaged in the professional, cultural, social, and political challenges that confront global learning and discourse. For instance, teachers in the MirandaNet community in Brazil, Chile, and Ireland act as agents of civic discourse and social change in government-funded projects focusing on information and communication technology. Education is seen as the means of preserving democracy, where each citizen takes a role.

Global links are made when the founder, Christina Preston, consults with foreign governments and invites participation from educational professionals. Not only are government leaders consulted to gain support for the online community, but industry partnerships maintain and strengthen the technology needs of the community. Currently, Apple, BBC, Cabletron, Compaq, and Oracle are all involved in joint projects focusing on the impact of technology on the MirandaNet community. Valuable advice is also given by representatives from British organizations such as the National Association of Advisers for Computers in Education (NAACE, n.d.), the Office for Standards in Education (OFSTED, n.d.), the British Educational Research Association (BERA), the UK Department for Education and Employment (DfEE, 1999), and the British Educational Communications and Technology Agency (BECTA, 1999), and the Teacher Training Agency (TTA, n.d.). MirandaNet selects candidates in nations such as the Czech Republic for industry-funded scholarships on the basis of their commitment to using information and communication technology as a tool to manage change in learning, mentoring, and communicating. These scholarships were created as a way for educators to network with their professional colleagues on a variety of issues surrounding information and communication technology. Often, these professionals have had few opportunities or resources to develop the necessary skills for exploring the uses of computers (Preston & Cox, 2000). The online community participates in a discussion group and uploads research in the presentation space on the MirandaNet website (Dorner, 1998; Preston & Dorner, n.d.). This online dialogic space is where the online community can contribute to a new professional development culture and a new civic discourse.

What makes this online community unique is that it is not grouped according to discipline, national and ethnic origin, or geographical region. It is a community ranging from primary school teachers to university lecturers to company representatives who are interested in the impact of technology throughout both developed and developing nations. The community values the variety of perspectives that this mix brings to their understanding of the impact of culture and technology. The community and peer mentoring approach in technology-based collaboration has indicated the importance of long-term support, online mentoring, opportunities to present and publish findings from action research and, most importantly, close links with peer groups and a worldwide community.

"BREAKING OLD BOUNDARIES"/BUILDING NEW COMMUNITIES: COLLABORATION IN THE NEW EUROPE

The close links that develop within online communities often commence with face-to-face dialogue. As the MirandaNet community grew internationally after its start in the UK, technology experts in the Czech Republic were invited to participate as community members. The East–West collaboration began when Christina Preston gave a conference presentation at "Women, Work and Computerization: Breaking Old Boundaries—Building New Forms" in Manchester, England (Preston, 1994). Bozena Mannova, from the Czech Technical University in Prague, invited Preston to speak to the Czech Technical University's Electrical Engineering Faculty, where Bozena was the only woman on a faculty of nearly 70 members. During the conversation, Preston asked Mannova in which hotel she was staying in order to arrange a meeting to discuss the presentation. Mannova replied that she was staying in the Holiday Inn Manchester, but she would prefer to meet at Preston's hotel lounge. When the two women got to know each other better, Mannova confessed that she had been desperate to make contact with professionals outside of East Central Europe, and thought that attending the UK conference would be an excellent way to meet other professionals. Mannova could only afford the conference fees, so she had been sleeping each night on a bench at Manchester Airport. Later, she also admitted that she had declined a dinner invitation during the conference with Toshiba representatives because she was not sure if she was expected to pay and, clearly, she had no funds for anything other than the conference fees.

These examples relate to the socioeconomic difficulty that those in the Czech Republic and other nations have experienced since the fall of Communist rule. Desperate to connect with others outside her own community and her own country, Mannova resorted to half-truths to save face. Mannova, and many others, needed a global community in which to connect that avoids the insurmountable costs of international travel, accommodation, telephone calls, and other expenses. During Communist rule, only the politically favored had the advantage of travel. Thus, while Mannova had one opportunity to travel to the UK, Preston kept the connection with her new Czech colleague by funding her own trip from the UK to present to the Electrical Engineering Faculty at the Czech Technical University in Prague. Preston presented an approach to the use of computers in education that was new to the Czechs. Before the fall of Communism, the computing and electrical engineering curricula had not been developed for many years and still followed antiquated computer science precepts. Mannova was trying to introduce new ideas and a new pedagogical culture to the faculty. After being forbidden during Communist rule to do what she loved most, Mannova accepted two lecturing positions in computer science, one at the University and a second at the Arabska secondary school in Prague. Preston met many of Mannova's colleagues during her visit to the University and the Arabska school. Because of the enthusiasm to know more about new approaches to the teaching of information and communication technology in British schools, Preston awarded Mannova and her colleagues MirandaNet scholarships to collaborate in this growing global online community. Mannova's interest in participating in this community and developing a new professional and educational culture was intense, primarily since her career had been immobilized during communist rule because of her record of politicized opposition.

NEGOTIATING THE DIFFERING CULTURAL AND PROFESSIONAL ATTITUDES REMAINING AFTER COMMUNIST RULE

The consequences of politicized opposition were severe under Soviet rule. After decades of risking one's personal and professional stability by opposing Communist rule, the fear endures today for many in the New Europe. At the other end of the scale, widespread apathy was born of self-censorship and a desire simply to survive. What has been most debilitating for this region has been the cultural isolation and the sense of failure in securing civic discourse and intellectual freedom. In some nations in the New Europe, like the Czech Republic with its history of Austrian, German, and Russian rule since the 17th century, a professional and cultural context has developed, which is not confident in local or regional approaches and strategies, be they professional, educational, or political. Emerging from this past, the Czech government is still searching for stability. Several elections have shifted government leanings back toward the left.

Information and communication technology education is one area where local approaches and government support are just beginning to develop. Education generally is not a top priority at the governmental level in the New Europe, but the government of the Czech Republic is beginning to take a greater part in prioritizing and meeting teachers' funding needs and in redefining their role. Because technology initiatives in education are relatively new, Czech members of the Miranda-Net community have looked outside the region for guidance and established examples. For example, on their first contact outside the region, the Czech Miranda community was disposed to think that all democratic institutions were perfect. During their attendance at a London-based conference supported by the British Council and Toshiba, Czech members were surprised to find that the British teaching profession is also emerging from a negative past. They discovered that since Prime Minister Margaret Thatcher came to office, the teaching profession has been at war with Conservative government policymakers. Fundamental conflicts, due to a lack of consultation of educators by the government, have centered on the purpose of education, the content, the means of assessment, and the setting of standards. For example, Czech MirandaNet member Zdena Hamerahaltova (personal communication, April 1995), the head teacher of a secondary school in Prague, where the first MirandaNet computer lab in the Czech Republic is housed, was interested to learn of the automony of educators who have to develop their own pedagogical strategies in the UK. Conversely, she has been surprised by the level of governmental control over what is taught through the UK national curriculum from the earliest stages of education. She would have expected this level of control from autocratic governments rather than a democratic one.

Other expectations were also confronted in the community. For example, when Czech MirandaNet members interacted with those in the UK, the Czechs expected to encounter diversity between the professional stance on information and communication technology in each country as well as differences in access to technology. What they found instead is that Anglo and Czech professional differences have been subsumed in their joint endeavor to identify the governmental and industrial context in which teachers can operate best.

TECHNOLOGY INITIATIVES AND ACTION RESEARCH IN THE CZECH REPUBLIC

Czech MirandaNet members applied for and won a 30,000 ECU ($30,000 U.S.) Joint European Project (JEP) from Tempus, a European program that funds the development of educational initiatives in Central Europe. The JEP, coordinated by the Czech Technical University in Prague, has developed three more computer labs for training teachers in Prague and Ostrava, building on the one existing lab funded by Hewlett Packard and Microsoft at a secondary school in Prague. Czech MirandaNet members are using these labs to establish similar mentoring and professional development activities, as in the UK MirandaNet and other international MirandaNet centers. Through such projects, Czech MirandaNet members are encouraging collaborative, lifelong learning for teacher educators across cultural boundaries, distributing knowledge about ICT programs within the Czech Republic, and developing assessment and evaluation systems with experts from Helsinki University and the University of London's Institute of Education. Through Miranda-Net, three additional teacher education ICT training rooms were funded to offer Czech teachers the latest advances in computer-mediated communication (CMC), computer application development, multimedia, and video conferencing. The MirandaNet community also develops multimedia programs that are designed to stimulate learning among teachers and challenge the cultural stance of teachers in the New Europe and other global regions that house MirandaNet.

The Czech MirandaNet members were specifically encouraged to conduct action research, particularly in the area of teacher empowerment. Action research, defined as that which enacts or encourages local and global change for the achievement of a more equitable and sustainable society, is important in the New Europe. Despite the vast changes since the fall of Communist rule, change through education for a more equitable and sustainable New Europe is still a concern. Barber (1996) argues, "The trouble is that too little research actually results in real change. Part of the cause of this difficulty is that many teachers do not get to know what the research says or what its implications are" (p. 220). By encouraging the MirandaNet community to conduct its own action research and communicate its findings, such "real change" is possible.

Members of the Czech MirandaNet were funded to attend a conference entitled "An Action Research Approach to Classroom Projects in ICT" at the University of London's Institute of Education. The impetus of the conference was to convince teachers that they were able to conduct research projects in the classroom and discuss their findings with the MirandaNet community worldwide. Teachers were encouraged to be proactive and innovative about their own practice rather than waiting to be told what to do by an "expert." MirandaNet is not only concerned with proactive and innovative uses of ICT, but in the cultural and professional attitudes to technology. For example, Bridget Somekh (1994) presented a workshop on management of change issues. The Czechs began to realize that introducing new technologies is not only a matter of equipment, but a matter of changing attitudes, pedagogical development planning, and agreed implementation strategy. The Czechs were still at a stage that the UK had long since passed, when single, enthusiastic teachers in the classroom were leading innovation and experimentation. An emphasis on individual efforts does not ensure that processes are embedded within the overall school policy. The Czechs needed help in strategy and planning because during the 40 years of Communism, central directives had stunted the understanding and growth of these areas in Czech institutions. Thus, the new MirandaNet members were enthusiastic, yet hesitant about creating a new curriculum as well as a new professional and educational culture.

"EUROPEAN BRIDGES": CATALYSTS FOR CHANGE IN THE NEW EUROPE

Emerging from the "old" professional and educational cultures and totalitarian governments, MirandaNet members in the New Europe are concerned about being fixed in authoritarian educational and professional modes. However, through their interaction with the MirandaNet community, their international online exchanges, and face-to-face workshops and seminars, they facilitate both professional development and cultural exchange. For example, Czech member Lenka Zeranova was selected to attend MirandaNet workshops in London and Prague on the use of the Internet in teaching after designing a collaborative project with Melanie Maher, a MirandaNet member from Coombe Girls School in New Malden, near London. Zeranova and Maher, along with a Norwegian partner school found through the Internet, submitted the project for funding through the European Union program Socrates. The project, "European Bridges," had an overall aim of increasing collaboration in the European Union and to ultimately include professionals in other countries. Zeranova argues, "We feel that after a long period of political isolation, our Czech teachers can gain from seeing how other teachers work and sharing their concerns and interests. We are most interested in learning about collaborative and constructive learning which includes understanding democratic procedures and processes." She notes, "What is very new for us is the development of topic work and project learning. We have very little practice in this kind of independent learning." However, through the "European Bridges" project, Zeranova and her colleagues are using this international collaboration to develop educational projects that will give learners more autonomy, an autonomy impossible during Communist rule (L. Zeranova, personal communication, April 1998).

Mirka Černochova, a MirandaNet Fellow and member of the Faculty of Technology and Education at Charles University in Prague, has been focusing on the teaching of multimedia packages as a means of developing creative collaborative writing projects. She has been struck by the UK's emphasis on using software as a tool for creative learning rather than simply teaching students how to use software applications, with no particular focus in mind. Because of the enforced professional and educational culture during Communist rule, New European educators are excited about using information and communication technology for creative purposes. However, many feel a need for mentoring and guidance, and the continuous contact between professionals that is essential to the learning process. The British education scene is also rich with independent professional bodies for advisers, IT coordinators, and educational researchers, who contribute to MirandaNet activities. Understanding Czech national practice in the context of other international information and communication technology (ICT) strategies is enlightening. The Czech MirandaNet members are also members of the National Association for Advisers in Computer Education (NAACE), arguably the most influential professional body in the UK. They are also expanding their own ICT professional body, Poskole, which has held seven annual conferences. The international MirandaNet community sees these face-to-face interactions as a chance to learn about East Central European developments in software and classroom practice, which are equal to, or surpassing in, merit to developments outside the region (M. Černochova, personal communication, January 25, 1997).

PRESERVING CULTURAL IDENTITY AND LANGUAGE IN THE NEW EUROPE

During the years that Czech educational professionals have been members of the global MirandaNet online community, they have established a sister organization, Czech Miranda, which preserves their own identity, diversity, and language through information and communication technology. Preserving indigenous cultures and languages is a priority of all MirandaNet members throughout the world. Preserving local languages has been particularly successful, due to the efforts of the international MirandaNet community. Roger Wagner, in his book *Hyperstudio* (1994), argues that literacy involves the ability to communicate within the medium of one's culture. Often, the medium of one's culture strays from the traditional mode of reading and writing, which is why MirandaNet's

ICT initatives are important for finding other ways of communicating cultures.

Historically, many well-known geniuses found other ways to develop their knowledge, since their severe reading and writing handicaps hindered traditional learning approaches. Fortunately, they came from homes that could afford to expand their horizons outside the school culture and the confinement of written and spoken norms. Well known names like Einstein, Churchill, Edison, Farrady, and Yeats are cited by Thomas West (1991), who maintain that new developments in computer technology herald a significant shift toward the increased use of visual approaches to information analysis. The authors maintain that had Farrady been able to read and write better he would have been limited by other people's words. He was, instead, visualizing solutions to problems that had not yet been expressed in language.

Kress and Van Leeuwen (1996) discuss the shift in communication toward visual forms, which they see as a fundamental challenge to the hitherto unchallenged centrality of written language. For example, when images were used in UK secondary school science textbooks in the 1930s, they were illustrations of the text. Progressively, images have come to communicate in their own right, not dependent on written commentary and often adding another idea. Kress and Van Leeuwen's work on icons and symbols underline an increasing awareness amongst educational researchers about the limitations of communication through language alone in a heterogeneous and multicultural society. Mass media, which can draw on sound, picture, and animation, are more compelling for many pupils than their underresourced classrooms. Homes that can afford computers linked to the Internet have better access to current information in multimedia form than a school library.

Where traditional print sources can offer a certain level of communication and learning, multimedia can augment the role of written languages. An example is a MirandaNet project in Chile, in which Preston has been involved as an advisor for a national government agency called Enlaces. Enlaces is responsible for changing the learning culture in Chile through information and communication technology. It has developed a teaching and learning website called La Plaza, for use in all state schools. The Mapuche, the indigenous people of Chile, run their own government-funded schools, but students also attend regular state schools. Through multimedia technology, the Mapuche, who have no written language, have been using multimedia resources to visually and aurally communicate the essence of their culture to the outside world. Mapuche students, ranging in age from 4 to 15, are recording the sounds and narration and illustrating the audio with their own pictures. Mapuche teachers have been closely involved in this project. Miranda-

Net brings in the technology, instructs the teachers on using the hardware and multimedia software, then allows the Mapuche teachers to guide their students. As a result, an active learning approach has developed and students' self-esteem has risen. Interestingly, Mapuche children's performance in the regular state-run system has also improved, including their proficiency in Spanish, the language used in the national education system. The importance of this example is the value given to verbal, musical, storytelling, and other nonlingual forms of "knowing," which are not well covered in conventional educational systems.

Through their community network, MirandaNet Fellows know about the achievements of the Mapuche and have developed a similar project in Mauritius. The Mauritian system, which values only reading and writing in French and Hindi, currently have no place for multimedia-focused creative learning. Like the Chilean children, those in Mauritius have low self-esteem and frequently fail because all the emphasis in the classroom is on academic subjects that marginalize their indigenous language of Creole. With the new MirandaNet multimedia project in Mauritius, perhaps these students will find the enthusiasm to preserve their own cultural identity, as have the Mapuche.

Similarly, Czech students are being guided by the MirandaNet community to develop creative ways of articulating and preserving their culture(s) through information and communication technology (Kazdova, 1997). For example, Czech MirandaNet members at the University of Ostrava are guiding Czech youth in efforts such as the Tajfun theater project discussed in Chapter 14 of this book by Zdenka Telnarová, Eva Burianová, and Laura Lengel. The 15- to 17-year-old student members of the Tajfun theater group have connected with other youth theater groups in the New Europe to participate in a project called "Legends and Myths of Central Europe." Through computer-mediated communication, Tajfun is working with youth theater groups from Poland and Germany to preserve the cultures and languages of East Central Europe. Other MirandaNet members have guided students to coproduce theater, written and directed by Czech and Japanese students, and enacted through video conferencing, linking the two nations. The links made during these artistic practices have remained long after the performances.

These initiatives are important, because there is a tendency for such technology-based projects to develop, but as simply copies of "Western" cultures and approaches, rather than according to local and regional cultures in the New Europe. For example, lecturers at Charles University in Prague started learning about multimedia by studying 30 different CD-ROM titles, which were donated by Microsoft. The teachers planned to evaluate these products and use them as a basis for professional multimedia production. However, they abandoned this plan because of the emphasis on American content and language, which deflected them from concentrating on Czech and European approaches. In developing online services, European governments realize that if they choose Microsoft products, they risk locking schools into one commercial system. Supported by all European governments, the European SchoolNet, which aims to "raise awareness in the educational community of the value of the Internet as a teaching and learning resource" is against using Microsoft products as well because the culture of the company is perceived as didactic (EUN, 1999). Governments and organizations realize that Microsoft does not work in partnership with education, but presents a ready-made, U.S. corporate solution, which does not take account of the need for linguistic and cultural diversity in Europe. In 1995, when the Czech initiative to research CD-ROMs began, it was difficult to find CD-ROMs in the Czech language. European approaches were welcome, but there was insufficient finance in the European software industries to produce many CD-ROM titles for educational purposes. Because of insufficient finance, CD-ROMs are often pirated in the New Europe. With the pirating of CD-ROMs, Microsoft has again taken a stance against New European needs and initiatives, illustrated by the Bulgarian case discussed in the introductory chapter of this book.

MirandaNet initiatives, to bypass prepackaged products and to use teachers in software development, have uncovered important connections across very diverse communities. For instance, through their connection with the MirandaNet community, Chilean and Czech MirandaNet Fellows realized how similar their experiences were under authoritarian rule. For 40 years, while East Central Europe, South-Eastern Europe, and the former Soviet bloc was dominated by a left wing, aetheist dictatorship, Chile was under the thumb of the right wing. Under each authoritarian system, the MirandaNet members lost their right and responsibility to make decisions at the grassroots level, a process to weaken the spirit and lower self-esteem. The two women Fellows who opposed the dictatorships in Chile and the Czech Republic used the same metaphor in describing their own experience of the repressive regime they had endured. "After the coup, when I was an adolescent, *a lid came down on my head*. I lost my youth and my young adulthood in powerlessness. Now that the lid has been lifted I am peering into the light. But I do not know which way to turn" (I. Varlia, personal communication, May 1994). Similarly, close connections between the Czechs and the Irish are now developing as the peace process unfolds in 2000.

Through the MirandaNet community, these women, and many other community members, have decided which way to turn—to each other. Through the MirandaNet listserv, and the chat room on the MirandaNet website, community members share concerns, experiences, and ideas.

They realize that, while in the past they were alone and isolated, now they have a group that provides support and encouragement. Now that many members are no longer isolated but are struggling financially in ways not known during authoritarian rule, new concerns can be shared. For instance, one member wrote in the chat room about how, during Communist rule, the banning of meetings was easy to circumvent in Czechoslovakia. But, she wrote, authoritarian central control is insidious. Russian domination was the subject of covert protest meetings. Czechs were united against a common enemy and there was a heady companionship in those days, with time spent singing protest songs and telling anti-Russian jokes. She wrote, "In the days when the Russian puppets pretended to pay us and we pretended to work, we had time for each other. But not now. We have to make money. We have to make decisions. There is no humour and no uplift. We are all in the rat race like you."

Other concerns are shared by the community. In the MirandaNet chat space, Mirka Chenochova (personal communication, January 25, 1999) contributed her thought on gender and age marginalization through technology: "The gender issue raised here has an important aspect to it, since there are many women in science and technology education, and each are equally 'unfriendly to women.'" Another member (J. Cuthell, personal communication, January 28, 1999) responded, "If anything [computer-mediated communication] tends towards non-masculine discourse, rather than didacticism. But I may be wrong on that. Some of the threads I was involved in as part of a course on online teaching manifested all the things that are wrong with a male tekkie environment: the binaries of yes/no, right/wrong."

The online community also discusses their own views of MirandaNet and their role in the community. "MirandaNet is both a network and a community. The people share common interests, but what I find stimulating is the range of diversity, rather than simply interests in common" (J. Cuthell, personal communication, February 10, 1999). Another member comments that, through this online community, "there are no boundaries" (D. Butler, personal communication, February 12, 1999).

THE FUTURE OF CULTURE AND
TECHNOLOGY IN THE NEW EUROPE

At the third millennium, boundaries are not as strong as they have been in decades, or centuries past. Relationships between nation states, governments, multinational companies, and international organizations are shifting significantly on a global scale. The trend toward an expanding interventionist state, particularly in the New Europe, has been reversed and, as a consequence, concepts of citizenship are diversifying.

As evidenced by initiatives like MirandaNet in the Czech Republic and SuliNet in Hungary (ANSware/SuliNet, 1997), technology has become a resource for new alliances in a way that has not been possible before. The power of national governments in the New Europe and elsewhere around the world has been reduced. This reduction brings a new-found power to citizens and their ability to participate and engage in civic discourse. The impact of globalization and technology on citizens, governments, and business in the New Europe is immense. In the New Europe, where privatization is occurring at unprecedented rates, private and multinational companies are often financially healthier than national governments.

New European governments can still take a clear role as arbiter, encouraging businesses to share responsibilities in international affairs and the civic sector. In the *Empty Raincoat: Making Sense of the Future*, Charles Handy (1994) writes eloquently of the modern paradox in which rich capitalist nations transfer their attention from pursuing immediate profit to building up their intellectual assets: the civic returns on their research and development investments, education programs for employees, and spending on broad community concerns. Handy recommends that companies review their policies on the environment, including expenditure on the community.

Multinational technology firms in the New Europe, such as Intel, Oracle, Microsoft, Toshiba, and IBM, need to rethink their role in the community. For example, 48 corporate leaders in the "West" have formed the Business Council for Sustainable Development. Their stakeholders are becoming accustomed to annual results that build toward an improved future for the community. This alliance is powerful enough for national governments to take notice (Handy, 1994). The move toward privatization continues in post-socialist nations and, as corporate power is increased, more of such alliances can be formed in the New Europe. These future alliances can address the unique and ever-changing needs of New European communities.

The challenge to national governments and corporations inherent in technology access, development, and implementation is incorporating the technology in civic sectors and educational systems. MirandaNet is supported by technology corporations like Oracle, Apple, and Hewlett Packard. As an international industry/education partnership, MirandaNet creates links between industry, government, and citizenship. It is a exemplar for other alliances and partnerships between the New Europe and advanced capitalist nations.

As access to technology is always a concern in regions experiencing vast social, political, and economic changes (Lengel, 1998, forthcoming; Lengel & Murphy, in press), such alliances are crucial for civic discourse. In regions like the New Europe where citizens cannot afford the computers, telephone lines, Internet service providers, and even electricity that those in the "West" take for granted, technology alliances provide support to participate in both local and global dialogue, to build electronic communities that would otherwise be impossible. These electronic communities can be active agents for participatory dialogue and civic discourse, rather than passive media consumption (Heppell, 1993). Along with future alliances to provide more access and user opportunity to citizens in the New Europe in the third millennium, educational initiatives that creatively and critically use technology can be agents for change. As Beare and Slaughter (1994) argue in *Education for the Twenty-First Century*, "when the right relationship is established between people, culture and technology a new world of options emerges" (p. 166). The "right relationship" is crucial. As Casmir (1995) argues, "we do need to learn to use what technology and new ideas offer us in building our future" (p. 318). He does warn that building the future "must be done in a spirit of cooperative respect, which assumes that new foundations and value systems have to be found by all of us together, rather than by merely announcing new incentives so citizens will go along with old ideas" (p. 318).

This "spirit of cooperative respect" is the key to civic discourse. Advanced technologies and connectivity appear to have great potential to provide a forum for civic discourse, growth, and change. The opportunity to discover how to enact this growth and change is now available to citizens of the New Europe, citizens who were once forbidden to engage in developing their own future. The future is now in the hands of the citizens of the New Europe. As we continue to experience changes in the New Europe, or be concerned citizens in neighboring global regions, we will work to make the New Europe a desirable location for citizenship in the third millennium.

NOTE

1. Names have been changed to preserve the privacy of the individuals.

REFERENCES

ANSware/SuliNet. (1997). *SuliNet (School Net)* [Online]. Available: <http://www.distrib.sulinet.hu/distrib> [1999, January 20].

Barber, M. (1996). *The learning game: Arguments for an education revolution*. London: Victor Gollancz.

Beare, H., & Slaughter, R. (1994). *Education for the twenty-first century*. London: Routledge.

BECTA. (1999). New technologies in education special interest group [Online]. Available: <http://www.bera.ac.uk/sigs/newtech/index.html> [1999, February 13].

Bennahum, D. S. (1997, November). Heart of darkness. *Wired, 5*(11), 226–277.

Boyes, R. (1998, April 21). Havel's illness fuels Czech fear of future. *The London Times*, Overseas News Section, p. 14.

Boyle, M. (1995). The crisis of citizenship: The East German media, Nazis, and outsiderness. In F. L. Casmir (Ed.), *Communication in Eastern Europe: The role of history, culture and media in contemporary conflicts* (pp. 57–80). Mahwah, NJ: Lawrence Elbaum.

Casmir, F. L. (1995). Some summary thoughts. In F. L. Casmir (Ed.), *Communication in Eastern Europe: The role of history, culture and media in contemporary conflicts* (pp. 313–320). Mahwah, NJ: Lawrence Elbaum.

DfEE. (1999). *Welcome to the DfEE website* [Online]. Available: <http://www.dfee.gov.uk> [1999, April 10].

Dorner, J. (n.d.). *MirandaNet: Empowering lifelong learning* [Online]. Available: <http://www.mirandanet.com>

EUN. (1999). *European SchoolNet* [Online]. Available: <http://www.en.eun.org/front/actual>

Handy, C. (1994). *The empty raincoat: Making sense of the future*. London: Arrow Business Books.

Heppell, S. (1993). Teacher education, learning and the information generation: The progression and evolution of educational computing against a background of change. *Journal of Information Technology for Teacher Education, 2*(2), 229–239.

Kazdova, A. (1997). Telematika: Zmeni se Osnovy? [Telematics: Changes in curriculum]. *Ekonom, 21*, 48.

Kober, S. (1993). Revolutions gone bad. *Foreign Policy, 91*, 63–84.

Kress, G., & Van Leeuwen, T. (1996). *Reading images: The grammar of visual design*. London: Routledge.

Lengel, L. (1998, Summer). Access to the Internet in East Central and South-Eastern Europe: New technologies and new women's voices. *Convergence: Journal of Research into New Technologies, 4*(2), 38–55.

Lengel, L. (forthcoming). "Is the information superhighway passing us by?": Reactions to the Internet in developing nations. In M. Prosser & K. S. Sitaram (Eds.), *Communication, technology, and cultural values*. Stamford, CT: Ablex.

Lengel, L., & Murphy, P. (in press). Cultural identity and cyberimperialism: Computer mediated explorations of ethnicity, nation and citizenship. In B. Ebo (Ed.), *Cyberimperialism? Global relations in the new electronic frontier*. Westport, CT: Greenwood.

Mannova, B., & Preston, C. (1999, March). *Peach velvet: A revolution in collaborative lifelong learning for teacher educators across cultural boundaries*. Paper presented at the Computers and Learning 99 (CAL99) conference, The Institute of Education, University of London.

NAACE. (n.d.). *Advice, training, & support* [Online]. Available: <http://www.naace.org> [1999, February 13].

OFSTED. (n.d.). *About OFSTED* [Online]. Available: <http://www.ofsted.gov.uk/indexa.htm> [1999, April 10].

Preston, C. (1994). Creative telematics. In A. Adam et al. (Eds.), *Women, work and computerization: Breaking old boundaries—building new forms* (pp. 187–202). Amsterdam: Elsevier.

Preston, C., & Cox, H. (2000). *Teachers as innovators: An evaluation of the motivation of teachers to use ICT.* London: MirandaNet, Institute of Education, University of London.

Somekh, B. (1994, March). *Introducing ICT into the staffroom.* Workshop presented at the "An Action Research Approach to Classroom Projects in ICT," at The Institute of Education, University of London.

TTA. (n.d.). *Information and communications technology (ICT): New opportunities fund ICT training initiative* [Online]. Available: <http://www/teach-tta.gov.uk/ict/index.htm> [1999, September 1].

Wagner, R. (1994). *The Hyperstudio handbook.* New York: Hyperstudio.

Zuckerman, M. B. (1998, February). Proud Russia on its knees: Will the west come to its rescue? *US News and World Report,* 30–36.

chapter 19

Breaking Down the European Divide in the Third Millennium

Anna Lubecka
Jagiellonian University, Krakow, Poland

EAST–WEST: AN ETERNAL DIVIDE?

P resently, we live, as Vaclav Havel said, in one global civilization, but its universality is apparent and misleading. The global aspect of civilization constitutes merely a thin layer that hides a world bustling with all kinds of differences, be they culture-specific, historical, ethnic, religious, ethic, political, economic, or social (cited in Huntington, 1988).

So how does Havel's message apply to Europe, traditionally divided between the West and the East in the period of unrest, where we can observe both globalizing, and unifying tendencies, and equally strong and important trends of regionalization? Are there any premises to make us believe that the divide will continue in the third millennium or, perhaps, are we entitled to assume that after many centuries of the Western/Eastern dichotomy it will disappear? And if it does, what will be the costs paid by, first of all, East and Central Europeans for becoming members of the extended European Union? How will the necessity to accept West-European standards, particularly economic, affect their own identity? There is much fear and apprehension on both sides, but the process has been already started and there is no way to go back.

It seemed that with the fall of the Soviet Union and the Berlin Wall, which marked the end of the Communist regime, the East/West divide would automatically stop existing in Europe. However, the years that have elapsed since these historical events have shown that the process of unification, if at all possible, will take much time, effort, energy, and funds. Analyzing the present situation in Europe, we have to admit that despite the various trends aiming at globalization and neutralization of existing differences, there are still many more differences than similarities between the West and the East. At the same time, observing the mechanism of socioeconomic, political, and cultural changes, there appear many premises to believe that much will be done to erase or at least diminish some dissimilarities between the European East and West, while others will not only be preserved, but also strengthened.

TECHNOLOGY AND THE DIVIDE

Economy supported by communication technology constitutes an area of the most conspicuous differences and of the strongest and the most advanced attempts to diminish the gap between the two worlds. The necessary politicoeconomic transformations to modernize the post-Communist countries are inevitable, but the more or less acute forms of Westernization or even Americanization may entrap Eastern societies in the future. Observance of human rights, development of civic discourse, and education that aims at teaching citizens' virtues constitute other important issues with which new democracies are faced. Political and economic pluralism, inclusion of all kinds of minorities in the mainstream of society with all legal consequences of such an act, and democratization of all domains of life are difficult challenges for people whose experience of these issues is often very limited. Differences in the availability and use of the most recent communication technology add to the list of barriers, which, when overcome by the Easterners, will become a great chance of promoting their distinct identity all over the world, through the World Wide Web and other services of the Internet. As for culture and the culture-specific differences, two opposite tendencies delineate the direction of changes. On the one hand, this is culture that has become the strength of newly emerging states, as it allows them to get their own identity. On the other hand, however, this is the loss of cultural identity which is endangered by the worldwide phenomenon of globalization of culture, often manifested as "westtoxification" (Huntington, 1988, p. 140). The process of cultural Westernization/homogenization is sped up by modern technologies—the Internet, mass media, and telecommunication—not only accelerate the spread of information, knowledge, ideas, and fashions, but also reach thousands of people. Literally, the whole world has become accessible from one's own room, which is an unprecedented chance for the leaders in the race to technologization.

The fact that no form of isolation is possible and no country is self-sufficient has many consequences on developing new sensibility and new awareness of self and of other individual people and peoples on both sides of the eternal West–East divide. The important issues that have to be dealt with within the context of new relations between the West and the East are: what are the sources of that divide; what was meant in the past for both "worlds"; what differences are not only possible, but also want to be leveled by East Europeans; and finally, to what extent will the leveling according to Western standards meet expectations of governments and of people both from the East and the West?

SOURCES OF THE DIVIDE:
CIVILIZATION AND RELIGION

A historical perspective is necessary to understand the transformations that are operating in Europe at the moment. Let us get back to end of World War II and the division of Europe into two spheres of political domination, economic control and democratic liberties. During the years of the cold war that followed, the dividing line between the East and the West functioned as a delineation of two mutually hostile political structures and incompatible economic systems: the free world governed by the free market economy as opposed to the oppressive totalitarian Communism supported by a centrally controlled economy. Notice that even now the adjective *free* tends to be associated with the West rather than with the East. An example is the use of two terms, "the Western world/West" and "the free world" in such leading newspapers as the *New York Times* and the *Washington Post* in the years 1988 to 1993 (Huntington, 1988, p. 65), despite some slow changes in this respect. Although economy and politics were the major differentiating factors that gained prominence in the post-war period, the divide between the West and the East has always existed. It has been grounded in culture-specific differences between the two immense and powerful civilizations: the Western civilization and the Eastern civilization.

The West-European countries are heirs of the Greek and the Roman civilization and also of the Catholic Rome. Their legal systems, concepts of citizenship, social structure, tradition of democratic governments, and the idea of a nation representation in the Parliament stress the continuity between the ancient Greco-Roman prototype and modern Western democracies. Their common roots can be also noticed in their linguistic similarities. All the languages spoken in Western Europe belong to either Roman or Germanic language families, while Slavonic languages emphasize the unity of the European East (Hungarian, which belongs to the Ugro-Finnish languages, and Rumanian, which is classified as a Roman language, are exceptions). Linguistic differences are powerful carriers of culture-specific differences, whose role in shaping relationships on the international stage is immense.

Religious divide adds to the differences between the two Europes: the Catholic one and the Orthodox and Muslim one. Catholicism is the common traditional religion of the whole West. This is the Catholic religion that, as evidenced by history (for example, crusades, the Inquisition, and religious wars), had a very strong impact on the formation of the Western mind and identity. It has been an influential source of its politics, legal system, social order, and civic discourse, not to mention the whole sphere of culture and its various manifestations (for example, traditions, the calendar, and the arts).

The Eastern civilization *sensu largo* has more than one center, but, considering only its European boundaries, it is the Orthodox and also Muslim Russia that has been assigned the role of a political, economic, and cultural nucleus. Russia has always been a cleft country. It shares many features with the Roman culture, the source of Western civilization, but unlike the West, which was directly inspired by Rome, Russia became acquainted with the heritage of antiquity through Byzantium. The Byzantine roots of the Russian culture (especially conspicuous between the 12th and the 15th centuries) make it gravitate toward the East rather than the West. Also, the institutions and the values that define Western identity are alien to Russia (language, religion, democracy, social, economic and political pluralism, division between the church and the state, individualism, and so on).

Religion has always belonged to the most important identity markers of Russia and nowadays its differentiating function has even gained prominence. A progressing atheization of the West is in strong contrast with a religious revival in the East. For the Easterners, especially from the ex-Soviet Union, a return to the religion of their grandfathers is prompted by a strong need to recreate both their personal identity and the national identity of their newly formed countries. The Orthodox religion is a tangible link with the long history of these countries. It is its carrier and its "architect." After the fall of the Communist secular ideology, it was necessary to fill in the ideological void with religion in order to solve identity crises. Religious revival is also a manifestation of an attempt to recreate the civic discourse by new governments: suppressed and persecuted under Communism, the Orthodox church has emerged from the underground.

The main reason why religion got new status in all post-Communist countries is because of, first of all, political and economic instability of Central and Eastern European societies in transition. Their members have also become very open to various religious sects—for example, Satanism has gained popularity among teenagers, the group that, in a desperate search for identity, looks for confirmation of its own value through violence. Notice that unlike the Western version of the cult of Satan, human sacrifices are part of black masses in the East—Poland, Beloruss, Russia, and Ukraine (see, for example, "Dziennik Polski," 1999).

Strong and more stable than the East, the West has always been attractive to Central European countries "sandwiched" between the two powerful civilizations. The role of economic, political, artistic, cultural, and scientific leaders, which these countries assigned to the West in the past, has been continually reinforced since then by the policy of the West itself and by its ethnocentric attitude shown not only to the non-Western Europe, but also to the rest of the world. It is also since then that Western standards have set up pan-European standards of politics, economy, technical progress, democratization, and cultural development, to which all other countries must adjust if they want to become partners of West Europeans. Some non-Western European countries, especially the Central European Catholic countries, find this adjustment, particularly the shift of mental pardigms, much easier than the rest of the ex-Soviet bloc. This is so because despite the geographic position and then the geopolitical situation due to a new world order after World War II, they have pictured themselves as rather Western than Eastern.

Examples of their Western character are many, coming from history, literature, art, and politics. Westernization started with Christianization, which took place in Czechoslovakia, Poland, Lithuania, and Hungary between the years 1000 and 1300, and determined their future forever. Since then, they have gravitated toward the Christian West, with whom they have shared religion, sociopolitical structures, civic values, many moral standards, and cultural institutions.

The consequences of the religious and civilizational divide of Europe at the beginning of the second millennium continues to be felt. Despite a popular but simplified tendency of many Westerners to see all the ex-Soviet bloc countries as very similar, nearly identical because of their common recent past, they are not a monolith. There can be noticed an internal divide within them that is manifested on all levels of the life of a nation: political, in the degree of democratization; economic, in the Western-like industrialization; technologization; and cultural, in the degree of cultural affinity with either Western or Eastern civilization.

These are the cultural and religious similarities that may explain why the Catholic or Protestant East Central and South Eastern European countries and the ex-Soviet Republic, the so-called Baltic Republic, gravitate toward the West. The orthodox Moldovia, Ukraine, and Beloruss are pro-Russian and the Muslim Republics of Chechenia, Azerbaijan, and Tadjikistan are interested in developing economic and political cooperation with their Muslim neighbors (Turkey, Iran, Saudi Arabia) rather than with Russia.

The religious affiliation has a very strong impact on the development of political conflicts, from which domestic problems often confined to the territory of one country or one ethnic group switch to the international political stage as they impinge globally involving national and international groups. Chechenia is such an example. The conflict between Chechenians and Moscow has been transformed into an international conflict between the Eastern and the Western civilizations, between Western democracy and Eastern despotism, and also between Islamic and non-Islamic powers. Similarly, the crisis in Kosovo has crossed European borders and has become a truly international affair.

IDENTITY PROBLEMS IN THE NEW EUROPE

Identity is one of the most difficult dilemmas of the post-Communist countries, especially those that have always gravitated toward the West. The term "cleft countries" fits them, as these societies are torn between the legacy of the Western and of the Eastern civilizations, which determine not only their self-perception, but also their perception of other countries and relationships with them. For most Westerners, as I have already said, the identity of the Central and Eastern European countries has been once and for all defined by geography and by political factors, especially the October Revolution and the February 1945 Jalta Conference. The identity problem is extremely complex for the Central and Eastern Europeans themselves. It is so not only because of the external divide between the West and the East, but also because of the internal divide within the whole ex-Soviet bloc along the lines of geographic, cultural, and economic origin.

Following the research carried out in the early 1990s at the University of Warsaw (see, for example, Skotnicka-Illasiewicz, 1995), it is as if three different Europes appear in the social consciousness of Polish people, depending on the differentiating criteria they use for their definition. The Europe of the Center and of the Periphery is the result of using an economy-based criterion; the Europe - a besieged Fortress refers to the areas of concentration of political and military power; and the Europe -

a *Heinemat*,[1] for all the countries that are partners to each other, corresponds to a culture-bound divide.

The first two images assign an unquestionably superior position to the Western countries, while the general feeling of Easterners is that they have been given the role of humble petitioners who aspire to join their more powerful neighbors. It took 10 years for the three most advanced countries from the region—the Czech Republic, Hungary, and Poland—to join NATO, while others are still waiting for their turn. It must be admitted that even considering this political success, in terms of their economic and military potential, the countries of Central and Eastern Europe are placed on the periphery, as even the dominating role of the ex-Soviet Union as a world super power is rather a song of the past. This is the technical progress that touches upon all levels of life, and that is, on the one hand, a source of conspicuous differences between the West and the East, but on the other hand, a chance for the New Europe to erase the divide and to change the image of this underdeveloped world region. The newest computer technologies become more and more popular and available, which means that the flow of information is quicker, is often more personal, and involves many more people on both sides of the divide than ever before. One hopes that the chance to get to know better each other on a personal level will help to erase many negative national stereotypes and prejudices. It will also make the West look at the East from a less ethnocentric perspective.

It should be stressed that the division into core countries and the countries of the periphery, which amounts to passing a nearly automatic judgement that classifies the West to be better than the East, is often expressed by Easterners themselves in such common slogans as, for example: "We have to join Europe." Although it is immediately counterbalanced with the answer: "We have always been a part of Europe," the feeling of being "second-class Europeans" is strong. Integration seems a natural historical event and a *signum temporis*, but the economic costs of reforms that the average citizen pays turn out to be much higher for him or her than expected. It is very significant that at the beginning of the integration process, as many as 80 percent of the Polish population approved of it (Skotnicka-Illasiewicz, 1995). Despite some decline of that percentage observed at present—advantages are not as tangible as desired—Polish people will continue the transformation efforts. They have managed to rationalize their initial optimism, as the fear of marginalization is stronger than the fear of facing hardships that, in the long run, are believed to result in positive changes.

Being torn between feeling superior and at the same inferior seems to create an inherent component of Polish identity. This mutually incompatible duality has been called the "Polish complex" (see, for example,

Konwicki, 1975), as nowhere in Europe is the idea of national identity so polarized. Thus, Polish people feel superior or inferior, depending on the frame of reference against which they define their own identity: is it the Western or the Eastern civilization, is it the Europe of the Center and of the Periphery, is it the Europe - a besieged Fortress, or is it the Europe - a *Heinemat* for partner countries?

Polish people suffer from an inferiority complex in relation to Western Europe on two levels: economic and political. However, for the average citizen, the feeling of a political marginalization seems to be less acute than that of the economic one, despite a close correlation between politics and economy. Most everyday hardships are of economic origin: these are, first of all, economic factors, which are *sine non qua* conditions of participation of Eastern and Central Europeans in monetary, trade, and military unions and pacts. These are the economic policy and economic standards of the European Union, which delineate, to a great extent, the course of economic transformations in the Czech Republic, Hungary, and Poland—the countries that will be the first members of the European Union—and this is the degree of compliance with Western economic models, which determines further aid programs offered by the West.

As both economy and politics increase rather than decrease the differences between the East and the West, culture and also history seem to offer a chance to the Easterners to make them believe that they may act as equal contributors to the European cultural heritage and co-creators of its present state. Hence, the Polish people, for example, look for evidence of their links with the West both in the culture and in the history of Poland. Poland has always felt a much stronger affinity with the Western than with the Eastern civilization and Polish people consider their culture to be an heir of the cultural heritage of the Greek and Roman civilizations to the same extent as Western-European countries. They continue to revive the historical events that present Poland as a European power, for example, Poland as a "rampart" defending the Christian Europe against the Turks in the 18th century. The presence of Poland in the West is marked by the participation of Polish soldiers in the Napoleonian Wars, by creating Polish emigration centers in France and in England after the November and the January uprisings in the 19th century and by moving the Polish government in exile to London. Also, Polish cultural and civic centers have been housed by Western democracies. Maison Lafitte, for example, which publishes the periodical *Kultura*, a forum for civic discourse among the ex-Communist countries, is in Paris. At present, the myth of "Solidarity," a warranty of civic rights in the East and the only progressive power that was able to oppose the Communist regime, is a symbol of the existence of Western-type civic values in Poland. These are both history and culture, which act as facilitators prompting economic transformations and democratization of the political system in Poland and which also account for Poland portraying itself as a political, economic, and cultural avant garde of the East and of the Pan-Slavonic world.

The same arguments that are to make up for the inferiority complex felt in relation to the West are used as evidence of Poland's superiority in relation to other ex-Communist countries, for which it is additionally a Western country considering its geography.

WESTERNIZATION, MODERNIZATION, AND IDENTITY PROBLEMS IN THE NEW EUROPE

In general terms, Westernization tends to be synonymous with economic progress and associated with democratic political systems, which both promote and safeguard civic liberties. This accounts for Westernization being always attractive to Central and Eastern Europe, especially to the new countries that emerged after the fall of the Communist regime.

History shows many attempts to Westernize, that is to modernize and democratize the east of Europe a long time before the decisive events in the late 1980s and early 1990s took place. Tsarist Russia is an example of the reforms aiming at Westernization/modernization of the country. The ambition of Peter the Great, Catherine II, and Alexander II was to change Russia into a modern empire. However, their reforms were only partially successful, as Westernization was followed by growing despotism and tyranny of an Asian type. Peter the Great, for example, whose economic reforms were unmatched in his time (he built Petersburg and made it a new capital city, he modernized the army, industrialized the country, created a modern system of education, and even Europenized the fashions, to mention only the most spectacular of his reforms), became an autocratic ruler. He deprived Russian aristocracy of even the few democratic liberties they had. He is also responsible for eliminating any manifestation of political pluralism and civic discourse.

Peter the Great's policy to transform Russia into a Western nation gave rise to a conspicuous division between the pro-Western "occidentalist" and pro-Russia "traditionalists" still felt today. These groups are at war with each other as to the future of the country. The question they ask is if Russia should be modeled after the West or should it rather look for its strength in its past and in a religious revival of the Orthodox church, which serves as a link between the great Russia of the past and the Russia of today. The internal division of the post-Communist Russian society is evidenced in various polls. In 1992, for example, 40 percent of Russians from the European part of the country were "open to the West," 36 percent were "closed to the West," and 24 percent did not know which option to choose. In the elections in 1996, about 46 percent of the population voted on the pro-Western Jelcyn and other pro-Western politicians, while as many as 52 percent supported nationalists and Communists (Chugrov, 1992).

Despite a split into pro-Westerners and pro-Easterners in all the countries of the ex-Soviet bloc, the appeal of Westernization was especially strong just after the overthrowing of the Communist regime because Westernization offered to the East the longed-for values nonexistent under the Communist regime. Initially, the efforts aiming at modernization/ Westernization have been prompted both from above and from below. These were the new governments formed after the first democratic elections in New European countries, and those of the Western democracies, which pressed for the reforms from above and supported them with economic resources and various aid programs, focusing on such issues as ecology, privatization, and unemployment. An unprecedented political and economic activity of the citizens themselves, their enthusiasm and faith in success was the force from below that sped up the changes. Living under the Communist regime and cut off from the West, average people tended to idealize that world, especially its economic power and civic liberties. Freedom of press, freedom of association, freedom of religion, power delegated to voters in just and multiparty elections, political pluralism realized as civic discourse, depoliticized trade unions, observance of human rights, rehabilitation of the victims of the previous political system possible because of just, reliable, and an apolitical legal system, recognition of minorities and their rights, recreation of work ethos—these are only the major values that Easterners have always associated with Western democracies and that they hope to create or recreate in the process of political and economic Westernization.

The costs Easterners have to pay for the reforms that are to decrease the differences between the two Europes are not only economic. Westernization usually means deep transformation of social structures and also a need to reinterpret the sense of human existence of people who do not belong to Western civilization (Pfaff, 1978). *Individualism* and its subsequent values, for example, stressed as the most Western value, are not only alien to but also unappreciated by most cultures that do not belong to the circle of the Western civilization (see, for example, Lodge & Vogel, 1987; Triandis, 1990). This statement sounds true of all Eastern and Central European cultures upon which *individualism* has been somehow forced as a major condition of the Western-style modernization and its by-product.

What can be observed now is the slow process of indigenization, which consists in, first of all, a rebirth of non-western cultures. Dore (1984) applies the term "indigenization in the second generation" to the process of recognition of homemade values in Asian societies by the second generation of young business people, the so-called *scuppies* (saffron-clad yuppies) (pp. 420–421). In my opinion, the same sociocultural phenomenon can be observed in the most economically advanced ex-Communist societies, where it is a natural result of a country having achieved a certain level of economic growth, and consequently of political liberalization and democratization. Only in those societies, young, educated people full of entrepreneurial spirit may be offered many opportunities of making a career in their home countries. As also their sociocultural needs are answered by national cultures and economic growth lets them achieve high material standards of living, they are not interested in emigrating to the West. Economic status, intellectual capacities and access to modern technologies make this group of people attractive economic partners both to the West and to the East.

Indigenization illustrates an interesting thesis of Joseph Nye (1990, pp. 181–182) of a correlation between "strong" and "soft" power. "Strong power" is grounded in the economic and military potential of a given country, while "soft power" embraces culture and ideology. The spread of culture and of ideology depends on the degree of economic attractiveness and military power. Considering the nature of, first of all, economic relationships between the West and the East, it becomes clear why cultures of less economically prominent countries get so easily Westernized and why indigenization may start only at a certain level of development of economic structures.

Thus, a growing economic strength accounts not only for continuing modernization, but for changing its form as well: it is not equivalent with Westernization at all costs. It no longer consists in a direct transfer of Western economic, political, and social solutions, but in their conscious adaptation, which considers the impact of the transformations on the national character of each country. Changes in the attitudes of Polish consumers to the Polish and imported goods are a good example of indigenization of the consumption culture in Poland. After the initial period of the free-market economy, when all the goods from the West were uncritically judged as better than those ones made at home, consumers tend to be apprehensive and objective in their opinions. These are the quality and the price that make an article attractive, not its Western origin. The positive effect of globalization of the consumers' market by international corporations is manifold. The market becomes unified as the quality of national products gets higher to compete with foreign-made goods and the range of the West- and East-made goods becomes similar. Consequently, the standards of living are improved and similar to those offered by Western economies.

Mass and consumption cultures in the East are especially open to Westernization, as they themselves are products of the West. However, as the whole sociocultural background of the East significantly differs from the West, the effects of a "straight" import of mass culture institutions may be a kind of misfire. As a result, the divide within the target country increases. Consider, for example, the process of "McDonaldization" in the East. Although this kind of fast-food restaurant is efficient, time-saving, inexpensive, and available to the average consumer, none of these principles were met when McDonald's opened restaurants in the east of Europe. On the one hand, rather high prices limited the number of potential young customers; on the other hand, there were long queues to get to these restaurants, as they functioned as status symbols. The idea of an egalitarian ethos of mass culture was lost in its East and Central European version. Fast-food restaurants, malls, and cellular phones and other gadgets have become a new style of living that has divided Eastern societies into both elites and scum along economic factors.

THE NEW EUROPE IN THE NEW MILLENNIUM

The end not only of the 20th century but also of the second millennium makes us ask a lot of questions about our personal future and the future of whole civilizations. It seems that due to so many significant transformations of a social, economic, political, technological, and cultural nature, the East–West divide is likely to stop existing and the efforts to create one Europe will be finally realized. The objective of the societies to the East of the dividing line is to achieve the same or at least a comparable level of economic growth as of Western countries. The question if democratic changes will be introduced with the same tenacity as economic transformations is open to discussion. I will venture the opinion than they will be more difficult that in other fields.

As for culture, the impact of information and communication technologies, especially visible in the mass and consumption cultures, will continue the process of cultural homogenization and of cultural unification. These technologies—the Internet, mass media, and telecommunications—will both contribute to destroying and to strengthening the dividing line in European culture. As they offer nearly unlimited access to all aspects of Western and Eastern reality to thousands of people, they have the strongest impact on creating an identity of their users, mainly the young generation of educated people who will decide the future of

Europe. However, observing in the long term the processes of modernization and of Westernization in other parts of the world—in Asia, for example—it follows that these phenomena are not conversely proportional to each other after the country has achieved an economic success. The Asian world wants to become more modern but less Westernized, especially as far as cultural values are concerned (Huntington, 1998), and so does the New Europe. This is so because the cultural, social, and moral by-products of the Western-style modernization leave people on ideational crossroads. At the initial stage of modernization, Western values, although alien to national cultures, are attractive enough to fill up the value gap. A return to national culture is typical of these societies, which have achieved a certain stage of economic growth. Indigenization of culture, which is an answer to globalization, often "westtoxification," will assist cleft cultures in their search for identity.

There are many premises to make us believe that on the threshold of the third millennium Europe will be less divided in terms of economy and, hopefully, politics. Political stability should create favorable conditions for developing civic discourse even in the areas where democratic values are endangered at present, such as Yugoslavia and Kosovo. The cultural divide will continue and in order to define their cultural identity on interpersonal, local, international, and even intercivilizational levels, Europeans will have to face many more challenges than ever before.

NOTE

1. The German term "Heinemat" means "Fatherland." It is used here to describe the United Europe as a fatherland to all the nations and peoples living within its boundaries. It contextualizes Europe as a common home, bringing all the positive associations attributed to the idea of "home," such as comfort, safety, equality, and kindness.

REFERENCES

Chugrov, S. V. (1992). *Russia between East and West*. In S. Hirsch (Ed.), *MEMO3: In search of answers in the post-Soviet era* (pp. 124–165). Washington, DC: Bureau of National Affairs.

Dore, R. (1984). Unity and diversity in contemporary world culture. In H. Bull & A. Watson (Eds.), *Expansion of international society* (pp. 56–68). Oxford, England: Oxford University Press.

Dziennik Polski. (1999, March 5). Mord Rytualny [A ritual murder]. *54*(16 632), 1, 12.

Huntington, S. P. (1988). *Zderzenie cywilizacji* [The clash of civilizations and the remaking of the "World Order"]. Warsaw: Spectrum, Warszawskie Wydawnictwo Literackie "Muza."

Konwicki, T. (1975). *Kompleks polski*. Warsaw: Underground edition.

Lodge, G. C., & Vogel, E. F. (Eds.). (1987). *Ideology and national competitiveness: An analysis of nine countries*. Cambridge, MA: Harvard Business School Press.

Nye, Jr., J. S. (1990). The changing nature of world power. *Political Science Quarterly, 105*(2), 177–193.

Pfaff, W. (1978, December 25). Reflections: Economic development. *The New Yorker*, 140–149.

Skotnicka-Illasiewicz, E. (1995). Bariery adaptacyjne w drodze ku europejskiej integracji Polaków [Adaptation barriers in the process of the Poles' integration with Europe]. In A. Kapciak (Ed.), *Komunikacja miédzykulturowa. Zbliżenia i impresje* (pp. 101–113). Warszawa: Instytut Socjologii Uniwersytetu Warszawskiego.

Triandis, H. C. (1990). Cross-cultural studies of individualism and collectivism. In R. Dienstbier & R. A. Thompson (Eds.), *Socioemotional development: Nebraska Symposium on Motivation, 1988* (pp. 44–133). Lincoln, NE: University of Nebraska Press.

About the Editor

Laura Lengel began her research on culture and technology when she was a Fulbright Scholar and American Institute of Magreb Studies Fellow in North Africa. She is an international and intercultural communication researcher and lecturer with professional experience spanning Europe, Asia, North Africa, the Mediterranean Middle East, and the Americas. As a Central European American woman, Dr. Lengel's interests focus on women of the New Europe and their use of technology. Her publications, which have appeared in the *Journal of Communication Inquiry, Convergence: The Journal of Research into New Media Technologies*, and *Gender and History*, address technology, gender studies, and critical ethnographic field research. Dr. Lengel is currently an associate professor in communication at Richmond American International University in London.

Laura Lengel (far left) with students at St. Kliment Ohridski University, in Sofia, Bulgaria, where she was invited to research and present lectures on culture and technology.

About the Contributors

Eric Bachman has worked for the past 30 years with peace, anti-war, and environmental groups throughout Europe, such as the International Fellowship of Reconciliation and the German Federation for Social Defense, in nonviolent conflict resolution, action, and social defense. From 1991, he was invited by local anti-war and human rights groups in the Balkans to train groups in Croatia, Serbia, and Bosnia in nonviolence. He helped found and build the ZaMir Transnational Net (ZTN), an electronic mail and news network that connected NGOs in the region to the Internet. As coordinator of ZTN for six years, he also worked in the Internet program of the Soros Foundations/Open Society Fund. He is presently a coordinator for the Balkan Peace Team and a member on the executive boards of the German Fellowship of Reconciliation and the Association for Progressive Communication.

Benjamin J. Bates is an associate professor in the Department of Broadcasting at the University of Tennessee. His research efforts focus on the development of media systems, telecommunication economics and policy, and the economics and social impacts of information and information systems. He has published more than 30 articles and book chapters on these and related areas.

Eva Burianová is a lecturer in the Faculty of Science at the University of Ostrava in the Czech Republic. She is a systems engineer specializing in teacher training with new technologies. In collaboration with Zdenka Telnarová, she has published work with the Comenius and Tempus programs in the Czech Republic on the information and methodological center of new educational technologies and the implementation of telematics in education. She has also published work on forms of further teachers' education in the Czech Republic.

Margot Emery is a doctoral candidate in communications and information sciences at the University of Tennessee and a research associate of the university's Central and East European Center and Center for International Networking Initiatives. Her research interests are in social dynamics and political economics of information technologies and the role of information in open, closed, and transitioning societies.

Eric Paul Engel is currently a doctoral student in communication at the University of Missouri. He completed his MA in communication at Indiana University Purdue University Fort Wayne and his BA in communication at the University of Virginia. He has presented a paper and written a forthcoming book chapter focused on framing and web pages. Other work includes an ethnographic study in organizational change.

Elliot Glassman specializes in ethnic and minority studies in Budapest, Hungary, where he is completing a graduate degree in sociology at the Eötvös Loránd University's Institute of Sociology and Social Policy. He has also obtained Master's degrees at the International Studies Center of the Budapest University of Economics in Social and Political Studies and from the Central European University in History. His interest in the issue of prejudice, especially that found on the Internet, coincided with his brief stint as a journalist for *Internetto*, an Internet magazine in the Hungarian language.

Marina Grzinic lives and works in Ljubljana, Slovenia. She received her Ph.D. in Philosophy at the University of Ljubljana, on the topic of "Virtual Reality and Changed Aspects of Time and Space." She works as researcher at the Institute of Philosophy at the Scientific and Research Center of the Slovenian Academy of Science and Art, in Ljubljana. She spent a year in Tokyo on a post-doctoral fellowship for the promotion of science and technology from the Japanese government. Her publications address media art in East Central and South-Eastern Europe.

Amy Herron has conducted ethnographic field research on civic discourse and war, peace and resistance music in the Yugoslav states. She is a graduate in the honors program at Miami University (Ohio) and is currently studying international criminal and human rights law at DePaul University. She volunteered in Croatia for 15 months. While there, she worked for the Gasinci Refugee Center, the Karlovac Committee for Human Rights, and the International Volunteer Project—Slovania, Baranja.

John Horvath is a writer and former educator based in Hungary. He is a correspondent for *Teleopolis* in Germany and a regular contributor for *Toward Freedom* in the U.S. His main area of interest is in the process of political and social change in Central and Eastern Europe, as well as the sociopolitical challenges posed by computer-mediated communications.

Dina Iordanova teaches at the Centre for Mass Communication Research, University of Leicester, England. Dr. Iordanova received her Ph.D. in Philosophy at the University of Sofia, in Bulgaria. She is a lecturer with the M.A. program in mass communication by distance learning, which reaches students in the United Kingdom, Hong Kong, Singapore, Israel, and 30 other countries. Dr. Iordanova's books include the *British Film Institute's Companion to East European Cinema* (2000) and *Film, Mass Mediation, and the Balkan Conflict* (forthcoming). She has published numerous articles on East European-related issues in comparative cultural studies, women's studies, film, international communication, and technology in journals such as *Framework, Slavic Review, Film Criticism, Historical Journal of Film, Radio, and Television, Convergence*, and the *Journal of Film and Video*. She has taught graduate and undergraduate students in the areas of Eastern European studies, Soviet and post-Soviet media and film, images of women in film, Central-East European culture, Balkan culture, and women in Eastern Europe.

Nicholas Johnson is a former commissioner of the U.S. Federal Communications Commission and is currently teaching at the University of Iowa College of Law in Iowa City. He has participated in numerous initiatives in the country of Georgia, such as an American Bar Association/ Central and East European Law Initiative project on media law in Tbilisi in 1998. He has also written many internationally renown publications.

Priya Kapoor is an assistant professor of Communication at Portland State University, where she teaches international and intercultural communication, cultural studies, media criticism, all of which foregrounding issues of gender, race, class, and nationalism. Her dissertation, titled "Wisdom of Interplay: Dialogues on Development and Fertility Among Women in India," was awarded the Distinguished Scholarship Award by the International and Intercultural Division of the National Communication Association in 1996. Her most recent publications are in the following texts: *Nature of a Sista: Black Women's Lived Experience in Contemporary Culture* (1999) and *Whiteness: The Communicaton of Social Identity* (1999).

Geert Lovink, one of Europe's leading media theorists, lectures on media theory throughout the world. He is cofounder of the Digital City, Press Now, the Dutch campaign for independent media in the former Yugoslavia, and the Amsterdam-based providers desk-nl (culture/art) and contrast.org (politics). He edited the media art magazine *Mediamatic* from 1989 to 1994 and has authored various books, including *Data Dandy* (1994) and *Squatting the Movement* (1990). He also publishes in *Andere Sinema* (Antwerp), and is a member of the Editorial Board of *ARKzin* (Zagreb). He is a member of Adilkno, the Foundation for the Advancement of Illegal Knowledge, an independent alliance of media-related intellectuals. Lovink has been involved in organizing numerous media and technology conferences in Eastern and Western Europe and, together with Pit Schultz, he formed the international network Nettime, which propagates Net criticism. His work has been translated into five languages and published worldwide.

Anna Lubecka is an assistant professor in the Department of Public Affairs, Faculty of Management and Social Communications, at Jagiellonian University, in Krakow, Poland. Dr. Lubecka's pioneering research focuses on sociolinguistics and culture-specific features of interpersonal communication against business and nonbusiness settings. She was awarded a Research Support Scheme Grant from the Soros Foundation (1995–1997) for her forthcoming book on cross-cultural communication in Poland, titled *Polite Speech Acts in American English and Polish: A Cross-Cultural Approach*. She has authored another book and numerous articles. Dr. Lubecka has also been awarded a Tempus grant and a NAFSA Field Service Structured In-Service Training Grant to participate in the Institute for Intercultural Communication in Portland, Oregon. Lubecka spent a semester at the University of Connecticut (in Storrs) as a Visiting Research Scholar.

Bozena Mannova is an internationally renowned systems analyst who teaches information and computer technology at the Czech Technical Institute and various Czech Republic secondary schools in Prague. She is the director of MirandaNet Czech Republic, an online community of teachers and teacher educators in the Czech Republic, the UK, and Brazil. Bozena, together with Christina Preston (MirandaNet founder-director), were awarded the 1998 European Women of Achievement Award by the European Union of Women for their work in forming a unique alliance focused on improving the use of computers in education throughout Europe.

Noemi Marin holds an M.A. in English, University of Bucharest, and an M.A. in Speech Communication, California State University, Northridge. At present, she is a Ph.D. Candidate in Communication at the University of Maryland, College Park, writing on the rhetoric of exile and the discourse of public intellectuals from Eastern and Central Europe, and where she teaches on the fundamentals of gender and intercultural communication. Her academic experience is distinguished by numerous awards from Romania and the U.S., publications on Romanian culture and communication, and numerous papers presented at international conferences of the National Communication Association and Modern Language Association. She recently led a seminar on the impact of democracy, culture, and rhetoric 10 years after Communism at the National Communication Association Convention.

Bruce McClelland is currently finishing a doctoral dissertation on the Slavic vampire at the University of Virginia, where he has taught courses on folklore and anthropology. Prior to returning to academic life, he worked in the online information industry as a designer of system tools for full text information retrieval. Recently, his combined interests in Russian culture and information technology enabled him to serve as the director of the Internet Access and Training Program, supervising the establishment of Internet sites in seven countries of the former Soviet Union. Bruce is also a poet and writer, and has translated Russian poetry, including an online version of Osip Mandelstam's second book, *Tristia*, and has recently finished a novel in Russian. He holds an M.A. in Russian Literature and an M.F.A. in Creative Writing.

Drew O. McDaniel is Professor and Associate Director of the School of Telecommunications, Ohio University, where he was twice awarded the Ohio University Outstanding Graduate Faculty Member award. His teaching and research specialties are communication technologies and comparative media. In 1990, he was a Fulbright Southeast Asia Regional Research Fellow. Dr. McDaniel's recent work includes *Broadcasting in the Malay World* (1994) and *Fundamentals of Communication Electronics* (1995). He has authored numerous articles that have appeared in publications such as *Journalism Quarterly, Journal of Broadcasting and Electronic Media, Canadian Journal of Communication*, and *Journal of Management Development*. Dr. McDaniel serves as a United States representative to the Asia Pacific Institute for Broadcasting Development, a UN-chartered agency that provides research and training assistance to media organizations.

Jon Mided is a Ph.D. Candidate at the Graduate Research Centre in Culture and Communication at the University of Sussex, England. He has published work on lens media, culture and technology, and concepts of truth in digital media. Originally trained as a photographer, his photographic work has been extensively published in the international press, including *The New York Times, The Guardian, The Independent,* and *Time Out.* He is currently researching the shift from text-based to visual concepts of telepresence in virtual environments and teaches communication, media, technology, and lens media.

John Parrish-Sprowl is an associate professor of Communication and chair of the Communication Department at Indiana University Purdue University Fort Wayne. He is also a member of the faculty of the Indiana University Russian and Eastern European Institute. Since the beginning of the post-Communist transformation, he has conducted extensive research into the organizational, media, and cultural changes in Poland. His work in this area includes several public lectures, conference papers, book chapters, and a co-edited book published in Poland. Other works focus on organizational processes such as sales, development, and ethics.

Christina Preston, a senior research associate at the Institute of Education, University of London, is the founder-director of MirandaNet, an online community of teachers and teacher educators in the Czech Republic, the UK, and Brazil. She has long been an advocate for using advanced technologies as a catalyst for change in teaching and learning. As an independent consultant, Christina Preston advises on information and computer technology teacher-training issues with governments in Chile, Brazil, and the Czech Republic, highlighting the cultural impact of technology globalization on education. Widely recognized for her work, Christina and her MirandaNet colleague, Bozena Mannova, were awarded the 1998 European Women of Achievement Award by the European Union of Women.

Zdenka Telnarová is a lecturer in the Faculty of Science at the University of Ostrava, in the Czech Republic. Her areas of expertise are in database modeling, database technologies, didactics of information science, and the creation and utilization of educational software. She is interested in lifelong teacher training and distance learning through information technology. She has published work with Eva Burianová for the Comenius and Tempus programs in the Czech Republic on the information and methodological center of new educational technologies and the implementation of telematics in education.

Author Index

Subject Index